ACTIVITIES 1940–1946
The Collected Writings of John Maynard Keynes

Keynes at work, from a photograph in *Picture Post*, 10 November 1945.
(Radio Times Hulton Picture Library)

JOHN MAYNARD KEYNES

VOLUME XXVII

ACTIVITIES 1940-1946

SHAPING THE POST-WAR WORLD:
EMPLOYMENT AND COMMODITIES

EDITED BY
DONALD MOGGRIDGE

MACMILLAN
CAMBRIDGE UNIVERSITY PRESS
FOR THE
ROYAL ECONOMIC SOCIETY

Published for the Royal Economic Society

throughout the world, excluding the U.S.A. and Canada, by

THE MACMILLAN PRESS LTD

London and Basingstoke
Associated companies in Delhi Dublin Hong Kong Johannesburg Lagos
Melbourne New York Singapore Tokyo

and throughout the U.S.A. and Canada by

THE SYNDICS OF THE CAMBRIDGE UNIVERSITY PRESS
32 East 57th Street, New York, NY 10022, U.S.A.

Printed in Great Britain at the
University Press, Cambridge

British Library Cataloguing in Publication Data

Keynes, John Maynard, *Baron Keynes*
The collected writings of John Maynard Keynes.
Vol. 27: Activities 1940–1946, shaping the
post-war world employment and commodities
1. Economics
I. Moggridge, Donald Edward
II. Royal Economic Society
330.15′6   HB171

ISBN 0-333-24174-6
ISBN 0-521-23074-8 (the U.S.A. and Canada only)

CONTENTS

GENERAL INTRODUCTION

This new standard edition of *The Collected Writings of John Maynard Keynes* forms the memorial to him of the Royal Economic Society. He devoted a very large share of his busy life to the Society. In 1911, at the age of twenty-eight, he became editor of the *Economic Journal* in succession to Edgeworth; two years later he was made secretary as well. He held these offices without intermittence until almost the end of his life. Edgeworth, it is true, returned to help him with the editorship from 1919 to 1925; Macgregor took Edgeworth's place until 1934, when Austin Robinson succeeded him and continued to assist Keynes down to 1945. But through all these years Keynes himself carried the major responsibility and made the principal decisions about the articles that were to appear in the *Economic Journal*, without any break save for one or two issues when he was seriously ill in 1937. It was only a few months before his death at Easter 1946 that he was elected president and handed over his editorship to Roy Harrod and the secretaryship to Austin Robinson.

In his dual capacity of editor and secretary Keynes played a major part in framing the policies of the Royal Economic Society. It was very largely due to him that some of the major publishing activities of the Society—Sraffa's edition of Ricardo, Stark's edition of the economic writings of Bentham, and Guillebaud's edition of Marshall, as well as a number of earlier publications in the 1930s—were initiated.

When Keynes died in 1946 it was natural that the Royal Economic Society should wish to commemorate him. It was perhaps equally natural that the Society chose to commemorate him by producing an edition of his collected works. Keynes himself had always taken a joy in fine printing, and the Society, with the help of Messrs Macmillan as publishers and the Cambridge University Press as printers, has been anxious to give

Keynes's writings a permanent form that is wholly worthy of him.

The present edition will publish as much as is possible of his work in the field of economics. It will not include any private and personal correspondence or publish many letters in the possession of his family. The edition is concerned, that is to say, with Keynes as an economist.

Keynes's writings fall into five broad categories. First there are the books which he wrote and published as books. Second there are collections of articles and pamphlets which he himself made during his lifetime (*Essays in Persuasion* and *Essays in Biography*). Third, there is a very considerable volume of published but uncollected writings—articles written for newspapers, letters to newspapers, articles in journals that have not been included in his two volumes of collections, and various pamphlets. Fourth, there are a few hitherto unpublished writings. Fifth, there is correspondence with economists and concerned with economics or public affairs. It is the intention of this series to publish almost completely the whole of the first four catagories listed above. The only exceptions are a few syndicated articles where Keynes wrote almost the same material for publication in different newspapers or in different countries, with minor and unimportant variations. In these cases, this series will publish one only of the variations, choosing the most interesting.

The publication of Keynes's economic correspondence must inevitably be selective. In the day of the typewriter and the filing cabinet and particularly in the case of so active and busy a man, to publish every scrap of paper that he may have dictated about some unimportant or ephemeral matter is impossible. We are aiming to collect and publish as much as possible, however, of the correspondence in which Keynes developed his own ideas in argument with his fellow economists, as well as the more significant correspondence at times when Keynes was in the middle of public affairs.

Apart from his published books, the main sources available

to those preparing this series have been two. First, Keynes in his will made Richard Kahn his executor and responsible for his economic papers. They have been placed in the Marshall Library of the University of Cambridge and have been available for this edition. Until 1914 Keynes did not have a secretary and his earliest papers are in the main limited to drafts of important letters that he made in his own handwriting and retained. At that stage most of the correspondence that we possess is represented by what he received rather than by what he wrote. During the war years of 1914–18 and 1940–6 Keynes was serving in the Treasury. With the opening in 1968 of the records under the thirty-year rule, the papers that he wrote then and between the wars have become available. From 1919 onwards, throughout the rest of his life, Keynes had the help of a secretary—for many years Mrs Stephens. Thus for the last twenty-five years of his working life we have in most cases the carbon copies of his own letters as well as the originals of the letters that he received.

There were, of course, occasions during this period on which Keynes wrote himself in his own handwriting. In some of these cases, with the help of his correspondents, we have been able to collect the whole of both sides of some important interchanges and we have been anxious, in justice to both correspondents, to see that both sides of the correspondence are published in full.

The second main source of information has been a group of scrapbooks kept over a very long period of years by Keynes's mother, Florence Keynes, wife of Neville Keynes. From 1919 onwards these scrapbooks contain almost the whole of Maynard Keynes's more ephemeral writing, his letters to newspapers and a great deal of material which enables one to see not only what he wrote but the reaction of others to his writing. Without these very carefully kept scrapbooks the task of any editor or biographer of Keynes would have been immensely more difficult.

The plan of the edition, as at present intended, is this. It will

total thirty volumes. Of these the first eight are Keynes's published books from *Indian Currency and Finance*, in 1913, to the *General Theory* in 1936, with the addition of his *Treatise on Probability*. There next follow, as vols. IX and X, *Essays in Persuasion* and *Essays in Biography*, representing Keynes's own collections of articles. *Essays in Persuasion* differs from the original printing in two respects: it contains the full texts of the articles or pamphlets included in it and not (as in the original printing) abbreviated versions of these articles, and it also contains two later pamphlets which are of exactly the same character as those included by Keynes in his original collection. In *Essays in Biography* there have been added a number of biographical studies that Keynes wrote both before and after 1933.

There will follow two volumes, XI–XII, of economic articles and correspondence and a further two volumes, already published, XIII–XIV, covering the development of his thinking as he moved towards the *General Theory*. There are included in these volumes such part of Keynes's correspondence as is closely associated with the articles that are printed in them. A supplement to these volumes, XXIX, prints some further material relating to the same issues, which has since been discovered.

The remaining fourteen volumes deal with Keynes's *Activities* during the years from the beginning of his public life in 1905 until his death. In each of the periods into which we divide this material, the volume concerned publishes his more ephemeral writings, all of it hitherto uncollected, his correspondence relating to these activities, and such other material and correspondence as is necessary to the understanding of Keynes's activities. These volumes are edited by Elizabeth Johnson and Donald Moggridge, and it has been their task to trace and interpret Keynes's activities sufficiently to make the material fully intelligible to a later generation. Elizabeth Johnson has been responsible for vols. XV–XVIII, covering Keynes's earlier years and his activities down to the end of World War I reparations and reconstruction. Donald Moggridge is respon-

sible for all the remaining volumes recording Keynes's other activities from 1922 until his death in 1946.

The record of Keynes's activities during World War II is now complete with the publication of volumes XXV–XXVII. It now remains to fill the gap between 1923 and 1939, to print certain of his published articles and the correspondence relating to them which have not appeared elsewhere in this edition, and to publish a volume of his social, political and literary writings.

Those responsible for this edition have been: Lord Kahn, both as Lord Keynes's executor and as a long and intimate friend of Lord Keynes, able to help in the interpreting of much that would be otherwise misunderstood; the late Sir Roy Harrod as the author of his biography; Austin Robinson as Keynes's co-editor on the *Economic Journal* and successor as Secretary of the Royal Economic Society. Austin Robinson has acted throughout as Managing Editor; Donald Moggridge is now associated with him as Joint Managing Editor.

In the early stages of the work Elizabeth Johnson was assisted by Jane Thistlethwaite, and by Mrs McDonald, who was originally responsible for the systematic ordering of the files of the Keynes papers. Judith Masterman for many years worked with Mrs Johnson on the papers. More recently Susan Wilsher, Margaret Butler and Leonora Woollam have continued the secretarial work. Barbara Lowe has been responsible for the indexing. Susan Howson undertook much of the important final editorial work on the wartime volumes. Since 1977 Judith Allen has been responsible for seeing the volumes through the press.

EDITORIAL NOTE

This volume, the third of three concerned with Keynes's efforts to shape the post-war world, focuses on relief and rehabilitation, post-war commodity policy and employment policy.

The main sources for this volume are Keynes's surviving papers, materials available in the Public Record Office, and the papers of colleagues and friends. Where the material used has come from the Public Record Office, the call numbers for the relevant files appear in the List of Documents Reproduced following page 502.

In this and the other wartime volumes, to aid the reader in keeping track of the various personalities who pass through the pages that follow, we have included brief biographical notes on the first occasion on which they appear. These notes are designed to be cumulative over the whole run of wartime volumes.

In this, as in all the similar volumes, in general all of Keynes's own writings are printed in larger type. All introductory matter and all writings by other than Keynes are printed in small type. The only exception to this general rule is that occasional short quotations from a letter from Keynes to his parents or to a friend, used in introductory passages to clarify a situation, are treated as introductory matter and are printed in the smaller type. Throughout, Keynes's footnotes are indicated by symbols, while editorial footnotes are indicated by numbers.

Most of Keynes's letters included in this and other volumes are reprinted from the carbon copies that remain among his papers. In most cases he has added his initials to the carbon in the familiar fashion in which he signed to all his friends. We have no certain means of knowing whether the top copy, sent to the recipient of the letter, carried a more formal signature.

PART I
SURPLUS, RELIEF AND
COMMODITY POLICY

Chapter 1

SURPLUSES

Keynes's World War II involvement in the areas of relief and commodity policy, in addition to its links with the Article VII discussions and other proposals for post-war Europe, had its origins in British concerns about export surpluses.

These surpluses arose for two main reasons: the disruption of pre-war channels of trade by the war and ensuing blockade of enemy countries and the desire, for economic warfare reasons, to deny the enemy access to supplies of strategic materials. As a result of early attempts to buoy up primary exporters' positions and to deny the enemy supplies, Britain acquired titles to large stocks of primary commodities, Australian wool and Egyptian cotton to name only two, and faced the need to evolve a longer-term policy. On 19 July 1940 the Economic Policy Committee of the War Cabinet set up a Ministerial Sub-Committee on Export Surpluses 'to report what steps, such as restriction of production, purchase and storage, destruction, etc., should be taken to deal with surpluses in producing countries of commodities which should be denied to the enemy by our blockade'. The Sub-Committee's brief was further influenced by a statement by the Prime Minister in the Commons on 20 August which reiterated the arguments for continuing the blockade and committed Britain to a policy of building up stocks of food and raw materials for post-war relief purposes.

On 9 September the Ministerial Sub-Committee set up an official sub-committee to carry out its task. This sub-committee after surveying the situation recommended that Britain should purchase, with or without American help, £200 million in surplus commodities, linking the purchases with the goal of restricting or regulating future production. With the acceptance of this recommendation, Sir Frederick Leith-Ross was appointed on 9 November to co-ordinate and undertake the necessary negotiations. Keynes became the Treasury representative on the official committee set up at the same time to advise Leith-Ross.

Keynes had already been involved in some discussions on the surpluses issue the previous July, when he suggested that the authorities buy commodities above current requirements in countries willing to accept sterling under payments agreements and possibly re-sell the surplus in the dollar area to gain funds to cover current expenditures, thus gaining current dollars at the cost of future sterling liabilities which might subsequently be

3

exchanged for assets such as Argentine railways. When the Board of Trade, however, made such a proposal a month later, Keynes minuted.

To S. D. WALEY, *29 August 1940*

I should be surprised if this comes off. But there is just enough in it (e.g. in the case of Brazil) for there to be no need to discourage it.

But the main point to get into his [the Board of Trade official concerned] head seems to me to be that what we are likely to do anyhow within the sterling area may easily be more than a 50% share of the world requirements. Thus the right line of approach to U.S.A. (if and when it becomes prudent to approach them at all) is that *all purchases of surpluses throughout the world* should be shared with U.S.A. as the predominant partner (e.g. 75% to them, 25% to us). The possible gain to us of something on this basis is on an altogether greater scale than his suggested gadget.

J.M.K.

There matters remained until November, beyond attempts to keep South American countries sufficiently supplied with sterling through sales of commodities to meet their current obligations. However, after the presidential election in the United States, Whitehall returned to the consideration of a suggestion from the Ambassador in Washington that Britain approach the Americans on the global problem of surpluses. Through S. D. Waley, Keynes obtained a copy of the draft telegram giving Whitehall's views. When he saw it he minuted.

To S. D. WALEY, *25 November 1940*

I do not feel at all enthusiastic about this draft cable. It makes it all seem so boring. If we really want to get U.S.A. in, we ought to make it seem more interesting and of real significance to the world as a whole. As it is, we are simply appearing as suppliants pleading with them once more to give us financial assistance and to pull chestnuts out of the fire. On my view of the matter that

4

is not at all a correct view of the situation. If this is anything at all it is a world scheme of the greatest possible post-war significance, which the United States, if they understood it, would want to be very much in at the front row.

To achieve what I really want, the whole thing would have to be re-drafted and only after some general discussion. Meanwhile, paragraph 4 is particularly feeble, and I suggest for that the following redraft:

'With reference to paragraph 3 of your telegram, we recognise the political difficulties of the Administration in helping with international surpluses unless the scheme covers in some way or another their own surpluses. Obviously it is not within our power to incur any net dollar expenditure. But a general scheme in which the two Governments co-operate in all parts of the world will enable us to take our appropriate part in both the American continents without incurring any net dollar liability, our liabilities there being offset by United States Government's liabilities elsewhere. We believe that a suitable scheme of financial co-operation is feasible if the interest of the United States Administration can be secured for the principles underlying the scheme as a whole, but it would be premature to develop them in any detail at this stage.'

[copy initialled] J.M.K.

The telegram went off as amended by Keynes.

Just after Keynes saw the telegram, Sir Frederick Leith-Ross had sent him a draft outlining his ideas on the subject of surpluses as a preliminary to an approach to the Americans on the subject. Leith-Ross suggested that a surplus policy should have three objectives: the provision of supplies for post-war relief, the relief of producers whose markets had been disrupted by the war, and the regulation of production to avoid the recurrence of surpluses during the rest of the war and the creation of post-war imbalances. He then suggested Anglo-American co-operation to encourage, largely through financial assistance to the producers involved, the accumulation and storage of stocks for future sale to European relief agencies, while limiting

5

production. On reading the proposals, and after attempting to telephone Leith-Ross, Keynes wrote the following letter.

To SIR FREDERICK LEITH-ROSS, *23 November 1940*

My dear Leith-Ross,
Surpluses
I have not been able to get you on the telephone this afternoon, but have given a message to your secretary. However, perhaps I had better confirm what I said to her in a brief note.

I think your outline of policy quite excellent and have no criticisms whatever to make on the substance. I quite agree that the next step is to approach the U.S.A. I saw, a day or two ago, a draft cable which did not strike me as particularly happy—nothing like as good as your outline of policy. This draft cable had the faults, in my opinion, of being at the same time boring and producing the impression that we were suppliants of some kind trying to get something out of U.S.A. and make them pull out the chestnuts for us.

The chief thing, it seems to me, is to get the State Department and others concerned really *interested*. With this object, I suggest that perhaps the objectives of our policy as outlined on your first page might be amplified a bit. But that is my only suggestion.

Yours ever,
[copy initialled] J.M.K.

Keynes missed the first meeting of Leith-Ross's Committee on 6 December, which discussed a revision of the draft he had already commented on. However, he did comment by letter, giving rise to a further exchange.

To SIR FREDERICK LEITH-ROSS, *11 December 1940*

My dear Leith-Ross,
I was very disappointed not to get to the first Committee on Export Surpluses last Friday. But I was called down to the Board-room exactly at that hour.

6

I liked very much your introductory note dated December 4th. The only comment I should have made on it, if I had been there, is that you might perhaps have distinguished more sharply between the storable and the non-storable commodities. The former serve all three of the objectives of our policy; the latter only the second one, namely, the relief of the producing country. I would *never* buy non-storable commodities—and a grant in aid to pay for necessary imports is the only appropriate remedy.

The best way of helping India would probably be to give some guarantee as to the terms on which she could dispose of her surpluses subsequently. She obviously has no need of immediate financial assistance. But even the guarantee might be dangerous. For Heaven's sake don't touch jute on any terms. According to the latest information I have the present policy of the Government of India towards jute, very possibly dictated by political considerations, will leave some frightful mess for someone to clear up, and it will be far better for us not to have even the remotest connection with it. There have been wild fluctuations in the jute position before now, and I am sure that that is a problem from which we had better firmly dissociate ourselves from the outset. This is particularly easy, since there is no other country which produces jute.

Yours ever,
[copy initialled] J.M.K.

From SIR FREDERICK LEITH-ROSS, *13 December 1940*

Dear Keynes,

Many thanks for your letter of the 11th December.

There was quite a good discussion at the Surpluses Committee of my paper and the general lines were accepted, though a good many points of difficulty were raised. I have now circulated a revise, which I hope will soon go forward to Ministers.

I am not sure that I follow your point about never buying storable commodities. I dislike buying commodities, whether storable or not storable, if they cannot be shipped and have to be destroyed. Moreover, apart from fruits, there is no clear borderline between storable and non-storable

commodities. It certainly seems desirable to build up stocks of oilseeds, copra, etc. which cannot be stored very long but which can be stored for the best part of a year and turned over so that there would always be a supply available to meet a sudden increase of demand. As regards fruit, the only possibility is to increase juicing or drying; and a grant in aid may be the best way to keep the producers going.

I note what you say about jute. I have not followed what India has been up to, but I will ask for information.

Yours sincerely,

F. W. LEITH-ROSS

To SIR FREDERICK LEITH-ROSS, *17 December 1940*

Dear Leith-Ross,

My point about not buying non-storable commodities is really one which applies, in my mind, pretty generally. If we make outright purchases, the local authorities have little or no interest either in fixing a low price or in curtailing the next crop or in making satisfactory storage arrangements. We are carrying the baby lock, stock and barrel, if that is a good metaphor! There are many cases where this is of doubtful advisability, but particularly where they are non-storable. (I am assuming that we are not at cross purposes. I intended to write *non*-storable. In your comment you write storable. The above assumes that you mean non-storable, but perhaps it was I who made the misprint.) There is a further risk in the case of non-storable commodities that, for political reasons, we do not want to bear the responsibility where actual destruction becomes necessary. It is one thing to have to tell Parliament that we have been destroying valuable commodites overseas; quite a different thing to say that the local government have been forced to destruction in spite of the fact that we have been assisting them with a grant in aid.

Whilst, as you know, I am in major agreement with your latest document I feel that, if the Americans are to be brought in, we must first of all reach more definite conclusions amongst ourselves and have a more concrete scheme to put up to them.

8

I should like to occupy the next few weeks, not in premature and probably hopeless efforts to engage the Americans, but in preparing a thoroughly interesting and workmanlike scheme to put up to them a little later on. I have an increasing belief rather than otherwise in the ultimate importance and value of schemes for dealing with surpluses. But it is all hellishly difficult and I think we want to test general principles in particular cases, not in practice, but on paper, before we commit ourselves any further. Fortunately, there is no terrifically urgent hurry. This is a business which ought not to emerge from the thinking stage just yet.

> Yours ever,
>
> [copy initialled] J.M.K.

Later in the month, in response to a suggestion from the British Ambassador in Cairo as to the procedure for purchasing the 1941 Egyptian cotton crop, he wrote to Leith-Ross.[1]

To SIR FREDERICK LEITH-ROSS, *18 December 1940*

Dear Leith-Ross,
The Egyptian Cotton Crop
The general line of procedure recommended by Sir Miles Lampson[2] in his telegrams 1684 and 1685 seems to me very suitable, particularly the establishment of a commercial corporation which would raise part of its capital locally. But I suggest one modification. It would be very wise, I think, to press for the Egyptian Government taking a participation in this corporation. They are not short of sterling; indeed on the contrary. This is not a case where financial assistance in sterling for the purpose of spending it is necessary. There is, therefore,

---

[1] The problem was resolved through a joint Anglo-Egyptian Purchasing Commission which purchased at the same prices as the previous year a fixed amount of the crop, with an understanding that the next year's output would be restricted. The Egyptian authorities bore one-half of the cost.

[2] Sir Miles Lampson (1880–1964), 1st Baron 1943; British Ambassador to Egypt and High Commissioner for the Sudan, 1936–46.

9

every reason why they should share in the finance, and the creation of a corporation would provide a simple way of doing this. Indeed, there might be a great deal to be said in favour of the corporation taking over our existing holdings.

Another reason why I like the idea of a corporation in which different Governments could be partners is that this might facilitate the right arrangement hereafter between ourselves and U.S.A. If U.S.A. want us to participate in holding a part of their cotton surplus, we might pay for this share by giving them a participation in the Egyptian cotton surplus. The machinery of a corporation would greatly facilitate a transaction of this kind, since it would automatically provide for joint marketing in due course.

Is there any statement available of all the surpluses which we have bought up to date, or have committed ourselves to buy, with the prices and sums of money involved and any other relevant details? It would help me very much in getting a picture of the general position and thinking about a concrete scheme if I could have such a list.

In addition, I think it would be valuable to have a statement of the pre-war price of the commodity in the country in question and the range of price movement in the five years preceding the war. If there is any marked difference after allowing for freight etc. between the local price and the world price, that should be noted. In the large bible on export surpluses I do not find nearly enough material bearing on prices. There are a few figures here and there, but the information about price is remarkably defective compared with the information about quantities. Yet a sound price policy is perhaps more important than anything else, especially if the surplus scheme is to lead up to a system of stabilising commodity prices post-war.

Yours ever,

[copy initialled] J.M.K.

Keynes started regularly attending meetings of the Official Committee on Export Surpluses from January 1941. His first meeting saw him asked to take a hand with Leith-Ross in the drafting of a reply to American feelers on the general regulation of supplies. His second meeting, on 24 January, saw Keynes take up a position that he was to repeat frequently in the period that followed,

> In thinking of the finance of European relief, it was important never to lose sight of the change that had taken place in our own financial position. We should ourselves be in a position of great financial stringency... All the familiar creditor–debtor relations between ourselves and the Dominions, and in particular between ourselves and India, would be reversed. We should no longer be the financially powerful party in any transaction.

At the same meeting Keynes was delegated to raise with the Dutch the problem of their competitive buying of relief supplies with its unfortunate effect on prices and its tendency to waste still scarce dollars.

Keynes's December request for material on the prices of surpluses, coupled with a discussion of Argentine cereal prices in the course of December and January, led him to write to Leith-Ross on 7 February. A slightly revised version, which removed some infelicities of drafting, and a suggestion that sugar was a surplus commodity (which it was not), and added a reference to the fact that the telegram on Brazil was sent by the Ministry of Supply, had resulted from Keynes's persuasion at a meeting on 7 February, and went round to the Committee with J. W. F. Rowe's[3] table of prices[4] for its meeting on 19 February. This version, dated 11 February, appears below.

To SIR FREDERICK LEITH-ROSS, *11 February 1941*

Dear Leith-Ross,

I have been examining with much interest Rowe's table comparing the prices we are paying for surpluses with the average price ruling in various recent years. On the basis of Rowe's table we can scarcely claim, in most cases, to be paying what you might call safe prices on the basis of recent experience.

[3] John Wilkinson Foster Rowe (1897–1980), economist; University lecturer, Cambridge, 1932–62; attached to Ministry of Economic Warfare, 1941–3.
[4] Not printed (Ed.).

Some of them look all right, but others look very much the contrary.

I suggest for consideration that we might lay down a general rule, subject to the necessary exceptions, that where we are buying surplus commodities we should pay a price not higher than 10 per cent below the lowest average annual price of a recent year. This would not be a disastrous figure compared with what the producers in question had been used to quite recently. A higher level might be unsafe and might lead to awkward problems after the war, when we should be faced with the necessity either of maintaining prices or of suffering severe losses on our existing purchases. At this stage we should, I suggest, start with rock-bottom prices, though always prepared to make exceptions in special cases. But to establish as a general rule prices so satisfactory as those we are now paying will lead us into trouble.

The principal ground for exception should be the existence of a satisfactory measure of restriction. Where the quantity of the surplus is being kept down, there is, on every ground, a case for [a] more liberal price policy than is otherwise appropriate.

Let me take the commodities in Rowe's list individually. What we are paying for cotton, whether in Brazil or in Egypt, seems much too high. I have no doubt the explanation is to be found in the fact that these prices are in proper parity with the American prices. But then the American price is not a natural price but a result of the cotton policy of the American Administration. It is really unreasonable that we should be expected to meet the expense of a scheme as liberal as the American scheme for producers in other countries. Moreover, we have here a very direct selfish interest in acquiring our stocks at low prices from the point of view of Lancashire. You will see that the Egyptian price, according to Rowe, is 26 per cent above 1939 and 15 per cent above 1938. In fact it is as good a price as they have had for several years past. In the case of Brazil it is 10 per cent better than the 1938 price. At a recent discussion the Ministry of Supply agreed in the case of Brazil that they

should send an immediate telegram pointing out that, in the event of further purchases (and also in the case of current purchases if we are not already committed) we cannot be expected to pay so good a figure. When we were discussing Egypt, I was not aware of the relation of present prices to recent prices.

In the case of wool we have no doubt slipped into paying too good a price, partly because in the early days of the war we genuinely wanted it, and partly out of regard for the Empire wool growers. But in present circumstances prices should surely be 20 or even 25 per cent below the present figure.

Sisal looks too high, but I am aware of the argument that this is a case where we do not want restriction to be contracted unduly. But even so, a more moderate level looks appropriate. Perhaps the Dutch price has been dragging up the African price.

Sugar I believe is not at present a surplus purchase.

Ground nuts is on the liberal side. So is cocoa, which is a wildly fluctuating commodity. Cotton-seed is appreciably too high.

If we could back-pedal on our present price policy, it might not only save us many £millions, but put the whole business on a much sounder basis for more permanent developments. We have to remember that most of these commodities are not only in surplus now, but also likely, apart from the scramble immediately after the war, to be in surplus for some little time afterwards, since the stocks will be competing with the new current crops. I believe it in everyone's interest, the growers not less than ourselves, that we should take up a much stricter line.

I shall not be surprised if I am told by those particularly concerned that in each of these cases some special consideration, of which I am unaware, has played a part in determining the present price. I do not doubt it. One always finds that is so. But giving way to these special reasons in each individual case may lead nevertheless to an undesirable general position.

Yours,

[copy initialled] J.M.K.

After the meeting of the Committee on 19 February, Keynes reported to his Treasury colleagues.

To SIR HORACE WILSON *and others, 26 February 1941*

PRICE POLICY

At a recent meeting of Leith-Ross's Committee on Export Surpluses, I raised the general question whether we should not now reconsider the general basis of the prices which we pay for goods purchased in overseas markets in those cases where we are to a considerable extent in a position to decide the price.

In the first year of the war there was expectation of world inflation and no idea of important surpluses. For this reason we were very content when we were able to establish contracts on the basis of prices ruling immediately before the war. To-day the position has changed entirely. There is no prospect of a large rise in the prices of raw materials in the countries of origin. In more cases than not there are surpluses of which we are having to take possession whether we like or not. And in other cases our position as a monopoly purchaser enables us to influence the price to a very great extent provided we use our position in a moderate and reasonable manner.

I suggested to the Committee, therefore, that, subject to many necessary exceptions, we should start out with the idea that where we are buying surplus the price should be five, or even ten, per cent below the average annual price of a recent year, as a rule 1938, this same principle to be applied, but less stringently, where we are the main purchaser but not at present buying more than we can ship.

This policy would save us a great many millions of pounds. Since these millions of pounds would be paid to overseas producers, our overseas financial position would be that much better. In addition to this we might get a sufficient reduction in the prices of imports, particularly food, to offset some at least of the other factors tending to increase the cost of living. Here

14

is the one direction in which future changes might be on the right side of the account.

The general principle I was seeking to lay down met with considerable support. The representatives of the Ministry of Food and the Ministry of Supply and of the Board of Trade, all gave a general support.

On the other hand, it was realised that any change of policy would lead to a certain amount of difficulties with Dominions and Colonies, though I should have thought that a point must come, and perhaps has come already, when we must cease to be their milch cow to the same extent as at present. In particular Mr Caine[5] of the Colonial Office pointed out that the Treasury policy hitherto had been that there should be no direct subsidies to Colonies, and any support of their general economic stability should be given indirectly by purchasing surpluses etc. at prices good enough to meet the situation. Since it would not be possible to exclude such assistance in future, the suggested policy would require a differentiation between the commercial price and the subsidy hereafter, which would be a change.

Several members of the Committee thought that this would be a positive advantage. It would enable us to know just how much we were spending on subsidies, whereas at present it is difficult to disentangle the subsidy element from a favourable price. It was also pointed out by the representative of the Ministry of Food that a price fixed in one part of the world is apt to be used as a precedent for a more or less similar price elsewhere, with the result that what started out as a means of subsidising some small Crown Colony sets the figure which the Ministry of Food have to pay in other parts of the world where there is no need for subsidies at all.

It was felt that the matter was of so much importance that further discussion should be adjourned to a later meeting. But

[5] Sydney Caine (b. 1902), K.C.M.G. 1947; Colonial Office, 1926, Assistant Secretary, 1940; Financial Adviser to Secretary of State for Colonies, 1942; Assistant Under-Secretary of State for Colonies, 1944; Deputy Under-Secretary of State for Colonies, 1947–8; Director of London School of Economics, 1957–67.

it appeared that such further discussion would be facilitated if there could be a Treasury ruling that, subject to the necessary exceptions, the Treasury approved the proposed policy and would be prepared to modify previous rulings where necessary, including those which had aimed at excluding hitherto anything in the nature of direct subsidies or subventions as such.

P.S. Since I drafted the above I have the following comment from Mr Bewley:

Mr Keynes,

(1) I agree in theory with your view but I think it would be a pity to have it too *definitely* approved by the Treasury at the present stage. C.O. want a more elastic theory, and the India Office have something to say which no doubt you know. I think any directions given by H. J. W[ilson]'s Committee should be as elastic as possible.

There is also a critical letter from Mr Caine, giving the point of view of the Colonial Office. There is, I think, a good answer to several of his arguments, but his final formula, which is as follows, goes some way in the right direction.

It is suggested therefore that a precise general rule such as that suggested should not be adopted but that the following principles would be preferable in fixing prices.

(*a*) If cases occur in which purchases are made solely for the projected relief store they should be made at the lowest price possible; (in practice it is probable that where no element of assistance to a surplus arises it will be because the product is in short supply and the price will in fact be high).

(*b*) Where purchases are made partly or wholly for the relief of an industry or country the price should be fixed as low as will give the necessary minimum quantum of relief.

(*c*) Prices should be fixed in combination with other measures of control so as not to encourage excess production but so as to be sufficient to maintain in being the minimum productive capacity desirable in the light of probable post-war needs.

There is a warning that there will be an objection to a low price policy from the India Office. This country is liable to be

in a minority on an inter-departmental committee with the Dominions Office, the Colonial Office and the India Office always trying to get the highest possible terms for their clients!

I agree with Mr Bewley and also with Mr Caine that we do not want too rigid a policy. I suggest that the principle to aim at is that prices should be definitely lower than last year as a normal rule. The relationship to the lowest recent pre-war annual price is a useful mental standard against which to weigh the arguments in each particular case. Is it too much to say that the Treasury would like to see the overseas prices we pay 10 per cent below the first year of the war in all cases where we are in a position to dictate the terms?

The question how far subsidies should be disentangled from price policy is another issue. I should like to see them disentangled, since I believe the confusion of the question of subsidy with the question of correct price policy is a wasteful one.

Frankly, I am rather frightened by the atmosphere of comprehensive and open-hearted philanthropy which seems to prevail. It misinterprets our relative financial position both now and hereafter. It would be a bit of an exaggeration to say that the idea is for us to purchase everything the rest of the world wants to sell at a price thoroughly satisfactory to them whether we want it or not with the idea that we should eventually make a present to someone of the accumulations; but there is far too much inclination in that direction. I think that the Dominions Office, the Colonial Office and the India Office want pulling up very sharply, that they must not regard this country as a milch cow any longer, and that the merest hint that some one of the countries they are interested in might be slightly upset by what we are doing should not always be sufficient to cause us to desist.

[copy initialled] J.M.K.

The upshot of Keynes's paper was a Treasury Committee on the problem, as Keynes reported to the Surpluses Committee on 5 March.

Throughout the spring of 1941, Keynes continued to be concerned with

the arrangements for particular commodities. He also became involved in discussions surrounding Anglo-American negotiations on commodity agreements for wheat and cotton, then taking place.

To SIR FREDERICK LEITH-ROSS, *25 March 1941*

Dear Leith-Ross,

After reading Chalkley's letter of March 15th addressed to you, I feel that perhaps a warning note should be sounded at once about the United States' advocacy of quota arrangements for exports. This might work out, and is maybe intended, as a plan for securing U.S. exports irrespective of whether anyone has the dollars to pay for them or not. What happens if the quotas of the countries where we have money to buy are less than our requirements and the only exporter allowed to ship is a market financially out of our reach?

Since there is much to be said for quota arrangements on other grounds, it would be necessary to provide that, wherever there was such an arrangement, it would have to be taken to mean that the quota was available for purchase in terms of the currency of the purchasing country with no guarantee of transfer into the currency of the vendor country.

The U.S. Administration are squeezing us so hard that it becomes increasingly probable that we shall have no appreciable dollar purchasing power after the war for American cotton and will have to buy all we can from markets more easily financed. It would, therefore, be awkward if we had entered into an arrangement which would preclude us from approaching other markets on more than a limited scale and would give us the alternative between using dollars we could not afford and going without cotton altogether.

I can easily foresee the United States becoming increasingly keen on quota arrangements not guarded in the above manner as soon as they appreciate fully the probable post-war difficulties of their export trade.

Yours sincerely,
[copy initialled] J.M.K.

To SIR FREDERICK LEITH-ROSS, *1 April 1941*

Dear Leith-Ross,

Thanks for your letter of the 29th about possible demands from U.S.A. for quota arrangements. There is, of course, much else to be done, but nothing I can think of that can usefully be done by us.

This is indeed the outstanding economic problem of the post-war world,—how the U.S.A. is to redress her unbalanced creditor position. She is redressing it currently by lend/lease arrangements. She may continue to redress it in the immediate post-armistice period by making further presents to various European countries. Clearly this cannot go on for ever. What next? There are only three alternatives. Either that she becomes a reliable international lender, which is not very likely; or she imports more, which means a drastic revision of her tariff arrangements; or she seeks to export less, which means a drastic modification of her agricultural system. It is for her to choose. There is nothing we can do about it, except to try and safeguard ourselves against being ruined by entering into commitments we cannot meet before the period when the solution can be found.

Phillips is so busy putting strongly to Morgenthau our *present* lack of dollar purchasing power that I think, he would feel it confusing to enter the post-war lists at the same time.

On the question of agricultural products obtained under the Lease Lend Act, we have no definite answer. But you were probably right that it was in the nature of a try on. I understand that they are currently taking steps to provide us with certain agricultural products without any pledge on our part that we shall pay for them at once in raw materials. We have not been told as yet that they will be handled on the same lines as munitions, but they are content to make initial arrangements, leaving the question of if and how they are to be paid for, for later discussion.

Yours sincerely,
[copy initialled] J.M.K.

Keynes's next major involvement in the issues surrounding the problem of surpluses came during his 1941 visit to Washington. After discussions with Keynes in late January and early February, Leith-Ross had written to Mr Acheson on 14 February on the matter of a co-ordinated Anglo-American surpluses policy, suggesting a number of possible solutions to the problems involved. The letter received no reply, largely as a result of the passage of lend lease and the consequent need to sort out the details of Anglo-American financial relations. As a result, Keynes raised the matter directly with Mr Acheson on 27 May. The record of the meeting was by L. P. Thompson.

SURPLUS POLICY

On Tuesday, May 27th, Mr Keynes called on Mr Dean Acheson at the State Department to discuss with him the general problem of surpluses. With Mr Acheson were Mr Pasvolsky, Mr Hawkins and Mr Barker of the State Department. L. Thompson accompanied Mr Keynes.

Mr Keynes explained that he was a member of the London Committee on Surpluses and suggested that it might be useful if he were to set out his own ideas on the problem. He warned Mr Acheson that what he had to say should not be taken as reflecting in its entirety the agreed views of the London Committee. He wanted rather to set before them, off the record, his own idea of how the surplus problem might be handled to achieve worthwhile objects after the war; and then invite them to consider the general ideas. This might provide the best starting point for a mutual exploration of points of view.

Mr Keynes distinguished three possible approaches to the surplus problem. The first was that which the Americans had followed in their import-export bank loans. The loans had been made without conditions attached and the surplus country had been left entirely free to deal with its own surplus problem—the loans, of course, being a great help in releasing the country from immediate embarrassment. Secondly, there was the line which England had taken in dealing with the Australian wool surplus, by an outright purchase of the clip for the duration of the war and for one season thereafter. Here again no conditions had been attached, and no effort made to solve the problem as a problem. Thirdly, the assisting country might go into partnership with the assisted country in solving the problem. This had been done by England in her latest Egyptian cotton scheme.

Mr Keynes felt more and more convinced that the last method was the best. It enabled the assisting country to help the assisted not only with finance but with advice; and it left on the assisted country the onus of making adjustments in their output of the surplus commodity. Above all it brought

the two countries into partnership at the later and highly important stage of liquidation. Outright purchase or a loan against the surplus left the assisting country to compete with the assisted country in disposal of the surplus and the current crop after the war. That was manifestly an undesirable condition.

From the fact that the surplus problem had hitherto been dealt with by a series of measures to meet specific problems as they arose, it had naturally resulted that the U.S. had tended to concentrate on problems in the Western hemisphere, while the U.K. had concentrated on problems in the Empire and parts of Free France and the Belgian colonies. The Dutch, being financially strong, had been left to deal with their own problems, as had Canada. So far as concerned the finance required to carry the surplus, he considered this a reasonable and useful diversion of spheres. But for the later stages of the problem it was clear that international co-operation was highly desirable. Mr Keynes had in mind particularly (i) the problem of post-war relief and reconstruction in Europe and (ii) a permanent scheme of the 'ever-normal granary' type. For each of these, international, indeed world-wide, co-operation was required.

(i) *Post-war relief and reconstruction.* Mr Keynes stressed the impossibility of improvising a plan to deal with post-war relief on the morrow of the armistice. It was essential that plans should have been worked out in advance in as great detail as possible. To that end he considered that London and Washington should co-operate closely, both with each other and with the exiled governments of the overrun European countries. He suggested that the exiled governments should be invited to draw up statements of the products and commodities of which their country would stand in greatest need immediately the war was over. It would be explained to them that they should present their demands on a relief scale rather than a scale of comfortable living and that even when their demands had been presented they would be subject to adjustments to accord with the available supplies. When the demands had been collected and collated, a valuable picture would emerge of what commodities and what quantities should be accumulated and could be absorbed in the relief of Europe after the war. On the accumulation side he stressed that the problem should be approached primarily as one of present relief for the surplus countries rather than a mere commodity problem. The aim should be to keep the essential economy of the surplus countries in as healthy a condition as possible by extending to them well balanced relief. If the problem were treated purely as a commodity problem, the danger was that one country might receive too much relief and another too little.

Having thus obtained both sides of the picture, the Committees in London

and Washington would be in a position to adapt the surplus stocks to the post-war demand, in so far as that was possible. They could also see in advance what commodities were likely to be in such demand after the war that a certain surplus productive capacity should be maintained during the war even if that meant destroying the product in order to avoid building up an altogether excessive stock. Similarly there would be warning of commodities for which duplicate capacity had been created during the war and which would, therefore, present a continuing 'commodity problem' after the war, unless careful plans were laid to prevent a permanent surplus. (Wheat and sugar after the last war were examples of commodities which had suffered from duplicated wartime capacity leading to a permanent surplus.)

Mr Keynes suggested that, beside the necessity of planning ahead for the problems of post-war relief, there would also be the highest propaganda value (at a later stage of the war) in being able to inform the blockaded countries of Europe that we not only had plans for their relief but had physical stocks in existence, ear-marked for the precise requirements which the exiled governments of those countries had notified for the country concerned. He believed (and there was general agreement) that the demoralising effect of a reiterated statement on those lines could be very great when the pinch was beginning to be felt.

(ii) *Ever-normal granary.* Looking still further ahead, Mr Keynes believed that there might be found in this surplus scheme the beginnings of a comprehensive scheme for equalising the prices of the main commodities throughout the world. During the war we were compelled to deal with the accumulation problem, and after the peace we should be compelled to deal with the distribution problem. In both those processes we should be obtaining the most valuable experience on the very problems which an 'ever-normal granary' would present. It would be the greatest of pities if that experience were simply to be wasted. Mr Keynes was aware that a project of this kind was highly ambitious, but he felt that it was one which would appeal to the Vice-President and he considered that the fact that it was difficult and even grandiose should not exclude it from the long-range planning involved in dealing with the surplus problem.

The reaction of Mr Acheson to this was interested, but cautious. He gave the impression of not having thought along those lines before, and indeed at the end of the meeting he said that he felt his mind was much clearer now for giving thought to the problem as a whole. As the discussion developed he ventured further in asking questions and making suggestions in a way which suggested that his interest was growing.

Mr Pasvolsky was obviously interested and attracted from the outset. He was particularly concerned with the reverse adjustments which would be

necessary after the war in cutting down productive capacity which had been called into existence by the war but which would not be needed during the peace. He was also clearly taken with the idea of linking the problem of surplus accumulation with that of post-war distribution.

Mr Barker reverted to the point of continuing surplus problems. He said that duplicated production on the one hand and suddenly released consuming power on the other could lead to an undesirable boom in which a permanent excess capacity would be established or, at least, a vested interest created in a capacity which had been originally recognised as a merely transient wartime creation. Mr Keynes agreed in recognising this as a problem to be faced but felt that, if the relief and reconstruction programme were properly handled, demand for most, if not all, of 'surplus' commodities could be so appreciably increased that the problem of the continuing surplus would be greatly reduced.

On Mr Acheson's suggestion it was agreed that further consideration should be given in the next few days to the scheme outlined by Mr Keynes and, in particular, to the possibilities of co-operation between London and Washington. He would then arrange a further meeting with Mr Keynes before his return to England.

After the meeting, Keynes followed matters up with a letter.

To DEAN ACHESON, *4 June 1941*

Dear Mr Acheson,

It may perhaps be useful to both of us if I try to record what seems to me the main upshot of our conversation the other day about surpluses.

1. We agreed that the *de facto* situation was broadly speaking as follows:

(*a*) Where the financial conditions and other circumstances render outside help essential, Great Britain is looking after the problem in her own Dominions, apart from Canada, and in Africa. The Dutch, being financially strong, have been left to deal with their own problems, as has Canada. The United States has the primary responsibility towards her own surpluses and those of Central and South America.

23

(*b*) Where an important commodity overlaps more than one of these areas, preliminary steps are being taken for international conferences with a view to working out a more stable and more permanent policy. Particular examples of such cases are, up to date, wheat, cotton and cocoa.

2. We agreed that there was no particular reason to interfere with the above arrangements so far as the preliminary phase is concerned. But they are likely [to]—indeed it is advisable that they should—lead up to wider and more ambitious programmes. In particular, the surpluses which are being accumulated are well assorted for the purpose of furnishing first aid towards European relief and reconstruction after the war.

3. The international discussions relating to particular commodities, taken in conjunction with the arrangements for carrying and financing surpluses, might naturally lead on to a more ambitious policy for stabilising within reasonable limits the prices of the leading internationally traded raw materials and even for some kind of international holding cartel which would apply the idea of the ever normal granary to the international field.

4. Nevertheless it would be difficult to bring these more ambitious ideas to the practical level in present circumstances, partly owing to shipping difficulties, partly owing to half the world being at war and partly owing to the abnormal concentration of war demand in particular directions. For this reason the most practical measure might be something on a much more modest scale, limited in the first instance to those tasks which cannot be avoided. Those working together on a narrower field and discussing these problems in common might find themselves in a good position for widening their field of interest whenever circumstances might appear ripe for this.

5. I suggested that this more immediate limited field might cover the following ground: At whatever date the war ends and whatever particular form the political reorganisation of post-war Europe may take, the continent is certain to be denuded of the primary foodstuffs and raw materials. The governments of a

number of the occupied areas are represented in London or Washington. My suggestion was that we should invite the representatives of these countries with whom we are in contact to prepare a preliminary list of their probable post-war requirements in order of priority, covering e.g. the first six months after the armistice. These should then be studied by a joint Anglo-American Committee and criticised, since it would be contrary to human nature to suppose that they would not be on the ample side. The results would then be compared with the actual surpluses in hand and the prospective surpluses. In regard to prospective surpluses it would be useful to form some sort of estimate of the raw materials now required for defence and very far from being in surplus, which will suddenly become redundant when the war machine is stopped with little or no notice. It would then be possible to make provisional allocations, taking into account the probable acute shortage of shipping, matching the more urgent demands with what is most readily available. The next step would be to frame some sort of general idea of the appropriate means for financing such supplies.

I should repeat that I should not regard such discussions as the final end and aim. They would be of real practical significance and they might come to be of value and importance for propaganda purposes. Indeed they would be accomplishing a necessary job of work, which could not be avoided. But they would form habits of association and discussion between individuals of our two countries well qualified in these matters which might well be productive of further constructive developments on more ambitious lines. Meanwhile they would automatically link up our several activities in dealing with current surpluses and would also be of relevance in relation to the discussions of the international conferences treating of particular commodities.

I shall be in Washington next week, but I hope not much longer, and would welcome a further talk if your group can spare the time.

Yours sincerely,

J. M. KEYNES

P.S. There is one point I mentioned at our meeting, which is omitted above, but of which it is perhaps worth while to make a memorandum. I distinguished three possible approaches to the surplus problem in cases where financial assistance is necessary. The first was that which you have followed in your import-export bank loans, i.e. loans substantially without conditions attached, the surplus country being left free to deal with its own surplus problem with the financial aid thus accorded. Secondly, there was the line which Great Britain had taken in dealing with the Australian wool surplus, namely, an outright purchase of the clip during the war and for one season thereafter without any conditions relating to the Australian financial position as a whole. Thirdly, the assisting country might go into partnership with the assisted country in solving the problem, each providing a portion of the finance and sharing the ultimate profit or loss on winding up the scheme. This course has been adopted by Great Britain in her latest arrangement with the Egyptian Government for dealing with cotton. I expressed the opinion that the third method was the best and might lend itself to a tripartite partnership in appropriate cases. It did not relieve the assisted country of the onus of making adjustments in their output of the surplus commodity. Above all it brought the two countries into partnership at the later and highly important stage of liquidation when the surplus stocks would be in competition with the current output. Even with this method, however, there would remain the overriding importance of treating an assisted country's position as a whole and only giving such measure of assistance in the case of a particular commodity as might be justified, taking all the other elements in the situation into account.

When the State Department passed to Keynes a draft reply to Leith-Ross's letter to Acheson of 14 February, he wrote to his London colleagues.

To S. D. WALEY *and others, 5 July 1941*

It is, I think, advisable that I should send you a copy of the attached[6] immediately, although, as you will see, it is still in the drafting stage and may be modified; for the proposals of the State Department have implications of far-reaching importance for Anglo-American cooperation both now and after the war. They will be accepted, I think, by Leith-Ross with great enthusiasm.

I had hoped that I had made some progress in my conversations with the State Department, but that they should have accepted nearly the whole of what I was suggesting is a considerable surprise. In particular I had not expected them to agree to come into a joint scheme of surpluses throughout the world, and the suggestions for joint action in paragraph 9 are more extensive than I had anticipated.[7]

I am in close touch, of course, with Noel Hall.[8] Chalkley and Cairns[9] as well as with Phillips and Bewley. As a result of discussions with them, I doubt whether we shall be making any suggestions to Acheson to amend the draft except to make paragraph 9 about the proposed organisation a little bit clearer. I shall, however, ask him to confirm what is my impression, that his phrase 'though not necessarily equal', near the top of page 4, can be taken to mean that the United States would expect to bear a much larger financial share than U.K.

There are, however, several points which will need a great

---

[6] Not printed (Ed.).

[7] Paragraph 9 ran: 'Mr Keynes suggested and I agree, that the first job of such a body would be immediately to invite the Governments of occupied areas which are represented in London to prepare a preliminary list of their probable post-war requirements in order of priority, for, say, the first six months after an armistice. The Anglo-American Committee [suggested earlier in the letter] would then study and criticize these data, and compare the results with surpluses on hand and prospective.'

[8] Noel Frederick Hall (b. 1902), Kt. 1957; Professor of Political Economy, University College, London, 1935–8; Director, National Institute for Economic and Social Research, 1938–43; Joint Director, Ministry of Economic Warfare 1940; Minister in charge of War Trade Department, British Embassy, Washington, 1941–3; Principal, Brasenose College, Oxford, 1960–73.

[9] A. Cairns, Director of Statistics, Ministry of Food.

deal of thought before action can be taken, in particular the basis for financial sharing and the hint in paragraph 5 that something in the nature of blocked dollars will be employed. Please note in relation to Stirling's trade agreement discussions that in this paragraph the State Department have clearly been brought to contemplate the probability that we shall not be maintaining 'a substantially free commercial and monetary system' after the war. I should hope that on balance the arrangements adopted would be a means of saving us financially rather than otherwise and that they would also have the advantage of supplying other parts of the sterling area with some dollar resources for use after the war instead of their accumulating, as at present, unlimited sterling balances. At the same time, the major implications of all this are, of course, not in the realm of financial relief, but for the furthering of Anglo-American economic cooperation in the post-war world.

I suggest that this document should be for very limited circulation, if any circulation at all, at this stage, since only a short time is likely to elapse before Leith-Ross receives the authentic document in its final form. But there are so many possible implications in this (e.g. in connection with Australian wool) that I thought it better for you to have early news which way the wind is blowing.

I should not be surprised if Leith-Ross feels moved to pay his visit here soon after getting this. Whilst I (D.V.) will have returned by then, Bewley, Cairns and Caine, who have all been members of the Surplus Committee in London, will be on the spot.

[copy initialled] J.M.K.

Keynes also passed on to Acheson his comments on the draft.

To DEAN ACHESON, *8 July 1941*

Dear Mr Acheson,

It may save time tomorrow if I let you have in writing beforehand a copy of the only suggestion we have to make in your draft letter to Leith-Ross.

We think it might save a little time in setting up the organisation and be a little clearer if the middle part of your paragraph 10 from (*a*) to (*b*) was re-arranged as in the enclosed.

We have left out the word 'informal' before 'Joint Committee', but it will be quite understood that this body would not be one having at this stage any special executive powers. The other changes explain themselves, I think. We have added to the list of commodities those that seem ripe for immediate treatment. Indeed, wool, sugar and hides are all pressing. For the members of the Joint Committee to be in touch both with Washington and with London does seem to us rather important and, indeed, to give a good occasion for exchanges which might be valuable in other connections. But, with a permanent secretariat, it might not be necessary for such visits to be at all frequent. We have added (*d*) to cover such cases as that which is, I understand, arising in the Argentine. That Government wants to pick and choose in regard to the commodities about which it collaborates.

Perhaps you will let my secretary have a ring tomorrow what time would suit you for the discussion.

Yours sincerely,
[copy initialled] J.M.K.

Suggested re-draft of paragraph 10 of Mr Acheson's letter

To establish a Joint Committee to meet alternatively in Washington and in London charged with the following functions:

(*a*) The setting up of a joint secretariat of which the first task shall be a study of the immediate post-war needs of Europe,

particularly by collecting lists of requirements from the Governments of the European countries now resident at London, and of the potential supplies available to meet these needs.

(*b*) The study of ways and means of financing the holding of stocks, whether for European needs or for the handling of surpluses or for assisting international schemes of control for the principal raw materials.

(*c*) The preparation of concrete schemes for the handling of particular surpluses, such as wheat, cotton, wool, sugar, hides and cocoa, in conjunction with any international or other organisation charged with the negotiation of marketing agreements, and the initiation of studies with respect to any other commodities where such agreements appear to offer the possibility of successful action.

(*d*) To keep under consideration the inter-relationships between the schemes proposed for particular commodities and the conditions under which producing countries be admitted to the benefits of the stock carrying schemes.

When Keynes met Acheson on 9 July, the upshot was as follows:

Mr Acheson's draft letter to Sir F. Leith-Ross

I discussed with Mr Acheson yesterday the proposed re-draft of paragraph 10 of his letter. He is considering whether any of our suggested phrasing can be incorporated in the paper, but the opinion of himself and his group was that it would be better not to make any alterations of a substantial character at this stage for the reason given below. Bewley and I expressed agreement with this on the ground that the letter was much too good to spoil and it would be a pity to lose any further time in getting a move on.

Mr Acheson's reason for not wanting to make any substantial changes was that the draft in its present form had been carefully

considered and enthusiastically received by Mr Sumner Welles. Mr Hull has also, I understand, been given an opportunity to comment on it, but it is doubtful whether he has in fact given it any personal attention. But however this may be, any substantial change would have to be resubmitted. Moreover Mr Acheson thought that, if the committee was given too formal an appearance at this stage, he would have to consult the President. His present programme is that we should make some further progress on the present lines and that he should then put forward a more definite and concrete scheme to the President. He told us that he contemplated suggesting that the Vice-President, Mr Wallace, should act as chairman.

It certainly seemed, therefore, that it would be better to let matters take their present course without attempting to hasten them unduly, which might easily lead to the contrary result.

[copy initialled] J.M.K.

During his discussions with Mr Acheson on the draft reply to Leith-Ross, which finally went to London as drafted on 22 July, Keynes found himself in a difficult position. The Foreign Office in London proposed a meeting of Allied Governments in London for September in order to adopt a series of resolutions on post-war relief policy and its co-ordination, including the setting up in London of a bureau under Leith-Ross to help the Allies prepare estimates of their relief needs and to co-ordinate and collate the resulting estimates. Despite the fact that these proposals cut across Keynes's negotiations and that the Foreign Secretary discussed them with Mr Winant on 4 July, Keynes knew nothing of them until ten days later when N. F. Hall passed on a letter he had received from Leith-Ross. However, this lapse did not impair Keynes's relations with Mr Acheson, although it may have affected the reception of Keynes's drafting suggestions on 9 July, when Mr Acheson had already received a report of the proposals from the Ambassador in London.

On his return to London, Keynes reported his American discussions to the Surpluses Committee on 6 August.

Soon after the meeting, London received copies of a proposed International Wheat Agreement that had emerged from discussions in Washington on 3 August.[10] Keynes, resting at Tilton, turned to the proposed agreement in a memorandum circulated to the Surpluses Committee on 18 August.

WAR CABINET

OFFICIAL COMMITTEE ON EXPORT SURPLUSES

DRAFT INTERNATIONAL WHEAT AGREEMENT

Memorandum by Mr J. M. Keynes

As I am taking a week's holiday I should like to put in writing the *prima facie* points which seem to me to arise on the draft wheat agreement. I arrange my notes according to the various concessions which are asked of us. It is worth remarking that in return for these various concessions we are offered nothing whatever except the smiling faces of the exporting countries.

1. We are asked to undertake definite limitation of our wheat acreage at a low level even on the pre-war basis. No other country in the world is asked at this stage to agree to an acreage limitation. The exporting countries accept an export quota, but even this it is within their own power to change in various circumstances by granting supplementary export quotas. As regards their acreage, they also allow themselves a very wide latitude by the wide fluctuation in the quantity of stocks they are permitted to carry. The other importing countries will only be asked to limit themselves after the war. It seems fanciful to suppose that any of them will agree simultaneously to reduce the acreage which their farmers can plough and greatly reduce their tariffs so that the price their farmers get is much less than before. The importing countries are to cut their acreage, reduce their tariffs and pay a price for imported wheat more than double the average of the pre-war years. The only inducement offered them to do this is that we shall have set a good example.

[10] Keynes's papers from the Washington visit make it clear that he was kept informed of developments in these negotiations, as well as those on a cotton agreement, while he was there.

2. We are asked to police the agreement by agreeing not to take from the signatories more than their quotas. I believe that importance is attached to this because, on a previous occasion, when there was a similar scheme, the Argentines offered wheat in excess of their quota. Political reasons or political disturbances might lead to the same thing again. If this were to happen and the Argentines were to offer Greece or Italy wheat after their quota had been already filled, we should have to cut ourselves [off] altogether from further purchases of Argentine wheat. Nevertheless, this is a concession which I think we ought to be prepared to make, whilst at the same time asking recognition of the fact that it is a concession. The great gain achieved by the recent conference is an agreed system of proportionate quotas between the Big Four. That is a real achievement on their part. The quotas are reasonable in themselves reckoned as proportions. They are greatly in the interests of Canada, to whom the U.S.A. have made concessions. Thus we can reasonably be asked to help.

3. We are to promise to make it illegal to buy wheat below the price fixed by the Conference. This is not perfectly clear. But I think it is the consequence of Article IV(1) and Article V(5), Carlill's[11] summary of the agreement confirms this. That is to say, we are to cut ourselves off from buying any cheap wheat offered by Russia or by the Balkans or, as occasionally happens, by Poland or by France. We certainly ought to think twice before giving the Big Four this stranglehold over the price of wheat in the unforeseeable circumstances which will exist several years after the war. To agree to cut ourselves off from our traditional right to purchase wheat in the cheapest market raises political issues not to be overlooked. It is also worth calling attention to the fact that this article invites us to exercise discrimination in its extremest form against countries which do not bow to the will of the Big Four at a time when the United States

[11] Harold Flamank Carlill (1875–1959); Assistant Secretary, General Department, Board of Trade, 1928–40; delegate to Washington Wheat Meeting, 1941–2.

Administration in other contexts is asking us to commit ourselves to the principle that in no circumstances we shall ever do such a thing. No doubt the Big Four hope that, if we agree to this, they will be able to force Russia, the Balkans etc. to come into the agreement after the war. But the possibility of that remains to be seen.

4. We are not to be allowed to prefer a market where we have financial facilities. For example, if Australia owes us money so that the purchase of wheat there presents no financial problem, and if Argentine has invisible payments to make which she cannot easily remit, whereas we have neither United States nor Canadian dollars, nevertheless we should not be permitted to direct the bulk of our wheat purchases to Australia and the Argentine pending a more favourable financial situation with the two North American exporters. Mr Carlill has not followed his instructions to provide an escape clause against this contingency.

5. We agree to pay a minimum price for wheat fixed according to a formula. This formula is based on the average price of wheat over the seventeen years preceding the war, corrected by the current relationship of our Board of Trade wholesale index number to its average level over these same seventeen years. This has the effect of making no allowance for any economies in the cultivation of wheat relative to other things or to the acute surplus which appears to exist. But what is much more important than this, it has been deliberately arranged so as to bring in the years, now long ago, between 1922 and 1929 when wheat was selling at a very high price and there were three famine years. This was the state of affairs which provoked the intense cultivation of wheat and the fall of price after 1929. We are invited to govern our behaviour up to the year 1930 by reference to very abnormal temporary circumstances which existed some thirty years earlier.

The result of this chicanery is really fantastic. The price of wheat between 1922 and 1929 averaged nearly double what it

was between 1930 and 1939, so the effect of bringing these years into the calculation is easily appreciated. The effect of this is gravely accentuated by the fact that our Board of Trade wholesale index number, which is used to correct the price of wheat, was not correspondingly high in those years.

It is clear that if this formula is to be used, we should not allow the averaging period to be carried back earlier than 1930, which will still be nearly twenty years earlier than part of the period to which the agreement will probably relate. Even this would result in a price very much higher than ruled before the war, though this increase might be held justified by the increase in the general level of prices since that date.

The formula actually proposed would, according to my rough calculations, lead to a current price of about 53s a quarter, or approximately double the average price which ruled in the eight years preceding the war, namely 27s. My revised formula, which would carry both sets of averages back to 1930, but not beyond that, would, again according to a rough calculation of my own, not yet checked, lead to a price slightly in excess of 40s, which is already pretty high and surely the highest we should accept.

Recurring to the price formula proposed, which would lead to 53s at the present time, this is a minimum, not a maximum. The price has to rise at least 5 per cent above this, i.e. to 55s 6d before any quotas are released and there is no guarantee against still higher prices. Now at 55s 6d a very large part of the wheat now grown in this country could be grown at a profit, and certainly wheat would be a long way the cheapest agricultural product to subsidise. At this figure for imported wheat it would pay us to encourage the production of domestic wheat as compared with most other crops. Moreover, we shall have done very well if we can keep the post-war index number at the present level.

The effect on our balance of trade must not be overlooked. I fancy that we import something of the order of 30 million quarters of wheat a year. (This figure is out of my head. I have

35

no sources of reference by me.) If so, as compared with the average price of 27s we were paying before the war, this would worsen our balance of payments by about £40 million a year. How can we afford such a thing? Even a price of 40s, which we might reasonably be asked to agree to, would cost us an extra £20 million a year. But, after all, 20 is only half 40.

6. Finally, there is the relief proposal. This seems to me on sound lines, if the exporting countries will agree to it, and generous on their part. It is, of course, the only possible means open to them of lightening the vast surplus with which they will end the war. You will notice that the maximum stocks they are allowed to hold under the agreement *plus* the amount that they are thinking of giving away under the relief scheme, is of the same order of magnitude as their surplus carry-over will be at the end of this crop year, namely, an exportable surplus in those four countries alone equal to about three years' pre-war export takings of the world as a whole. Thus the relief programme is an essential condition of the rest of the agreement coming into operation at any foreseeable date.

We are asked to contribute to this. But Mr Carlill points out that the division of the 100 million bushels between ourselves and the United States has been left indeterminate. If we were responsible for (say) only a quarter of this, perhaps we might manage it.

7. As a footnote to (1) and (6) above, any undertaking we give as to our importing the minimum total amount should, of course relate to our total imports, not to our imports from the big four alone. If we agree to contribute to the relief programme under (6), perhaps this should be allowed to reckon towards our own guaranteed minimum imports so that we could in fact supply it out of our own agriculture and have that amount of margin, should we require it, for our own farmers.

(initialled) J.M.K.

N.B. All figures in the above are subject to checking. They are out of my head, not out of books of reference.

The memorandum was discussed at the Surpluses Committee's meetings of 20 and 29 August and 2 September. At the end of the discussions, Keynes reported.

To SIR RICHARD HOPKINS *and* H. WILSON SMITH, *3 September 1941*

THE WHEAT CONFERENCE

The Official Committee on Export Surpluses completed yesterday its report on the draft international Wheat Agreement for submission to the Lord President's Committee, which is, I understand, to consider it on Friday.

The Report is an agreed document, but, as Mr Waley and Mr Dunnett,[12] the Treasury representatives, were both absent on leave from the final meeting, the Chancellor may be glad to have from me notes on points of Treasury interest which may arise.

(1) The Chancellor instructed Mr Waley to agree to an offer on the part of this country to contribute 25 million bushels to the relief pool. Sir Frederick Leith-Ross and, according to his account, Mr Greenwood were strongly critical of this and thought it most inadequate. Sir F. Leith-Ross seems to strive in all these cases to secure that the financial burden falling on this country shall be as large as possible. When I challenged him why he held this view he replied that otherwise he did not feel confident that we should have a sufficient voice in the handling of the problem as a whole.

We pointed out to him, however, that the arrangement to which the Chancellor was prepared to assent meant a total contribution of 112 million bushels from the British Empire as compared with 102 million bushels from the United States and 36 million bushels from the Argentine. Surely, on any test, this should be sufficient. This is accepted in the Report, but the matter may be raised again at the Lord President's Committee.

---

[12] George Sinclair Dunnett (1906–64); Secretary, Imperial Economic Committee, 1933–9; Ministry of Food, 1939–46; Secretary, Commonwealth Economic Committee, 1946–64.

I should have thought that the Chancellor's proposed contribution is generous and that any further concession would represent, not a good, but a bad precedent. After all, we are not a wheat producing country. It remains to be seen whether the United States is going to help in the case of commodities which she does not produce herself. In order to make up for the inadequacy of the Chancellor's offer, Sir F. Leith-Ross proposed a clause that H.M. Government should undertake 'to provide a substantial proportion of the shipping required for the transport of the relief stock'. This might be a very heavy undertaking. Moreover, we pointed out that a considerable part of the world's shipping may be under the control of the United States at the end of the war and anyhow it would be no generosity on our part to say that we would be prepared to use lent-leased ships or charters for the purpose which otherwise we should have to return to U.S.A. So the above passage is left out, and the official reference to this subject much watered down. I mention it in case it is brought up again.

(2) We discovered one entirely fresh point which has come to light since this matter was last before the Chancellor. He will remember that we had been urged to restrict our own wheat acreage according to a formula, which admittedly was not very suitable for us, on the ground that this is the formula which would work out best in the case of Europe, and we must provide a good example for them.

Before accepting this we thought it well to investigate a question, which apparently the Wheat Conference had not thought worth investigating, namely, as to how this acreage formula would in fact work out in the case of the different European countries. We discovered, first of all, that it would involve them in an additional financial liability on the balance of trade, about equal to the size of the indemnity which Germany failed to pay after the last war. In the second place we found that this burden was very strangely distributed between countries. We had all of us begun by believing, and I

38

think this view was shared by the Wheat Conference, that the formula was mainly directed against France, which has in fact been the biggest sinner in raising the domestic price of wheat to an excessive level. On looking up the statistics, however, we found that France had not increased her acreage since the critical period and, therefore, would be entirely untouched by the formula.

What countries then would be affected? It turned out that those who would be most touched up would be the Baltic countries—Sweden, Denmark and the various Baltic States, all of which have increased their wheat acreage enormously since the critical date, with the result that they would have to come down to not much more than half their latest pre-war figures. Unfortunately these are precisely the countries which might enter into relations with Russia. We should have to think twice before forcing a violent agricultural revolution on these harmless countries. Those next affected are Greece, Switzerland and Portugal. Then come Czechoslovakia, Germany and Austria. Italy is not much touched, and France not at all.

The Wheat Conference have paid no attention whatever either to the future position of Russia or to possible regional arrangements by which, for example, Czechoslovakia would get together with Poland and Hungary.

You cannot touch the Wheat Conference draft at any point without finding that it is shoddy work.

(3) It was agreed by the Official Committee that a memorandum should be prepared setting out the background of our argument in full detail. It was also agreed that we should send out a further representative of the British Government, since Mr Carlill is acting rather as Chairman than as our representative and, in any case, has proved a broken reed. It was obvious that the memorandum could not be prepared or the new representative selected in time to be present at the renewed sessions of the Wheat Conference, if, as is at present proposed, they start up again on September 15th.

It was, therefore, the view of the Treasury representatives that the British Government should ask for a month's adjournment of the Conference until the middle of October in order to provide time for the preparation of material and also to allow further discussion with the three American representatives now in London and Mr McDougall, the Australian representative, also here. Sir F. Leith-Ross was strongly opposed to this, and the final draft was a compromise, the exact form of which I have forgotten.

Trying to rush this business seemed to us unfortunate from every point of view. If the highly critical draft telegrams go off without the background, we shall appear to the Americans to be wholly destructive. We shall have a much better chance of getting them to look at the whole thing again if we present a reasoned case to them.

There was, of course, no discussion in the Committee as to who the new British representative should be. Probably he should be drawn either from the Ministry of Food or from the Ministry of Agriculture. If the former department is to supply the representative, perhaps Mr Twentyman,[13] who is already in Washington, might act. The only disadvantage of this is that he has been absent from our discussions and that this is a new subject to him. If the representative is chosen from the Ministry of Agriculture, I believe Mr Enfield[14] would be the right man. He has taken part in the discussions, is very learned on the international side of all this and is mild and reasonable, but tenacious in debate.

J.M.K.

When the Ministerial Sub-Committee on Export Surpluses met to discuss the Official Sub-Committee's conclusions on 5 September, they agreed to

[13] E. Twentyman (d. 1945); Assistant Secretary, Treasury, 1939, Principal Assistant Secretary, 1941–3; U.K. representative on Interim Commission, 1943–5.

[14] Ralph Roscoe Enfield (1885–1973), Kt. 1947; entered Civil Service, 1913; Ministry of Agriculture and Fisheries, 1919–52; U.K. respresentative, International Institute of Agriculture, 1934–8; Principal Assistant Secretary, 1942; Chief Economic Adviser to Minster of Agriculture and Fisheries, 1945–52.

refer the wheat scheme back for further improvement, especially as regards acreage restrictions, the relief pool and the proposed procedure surrounding the proposals.

From this point onwards, work on relief and on commodities became more distinctly divided. As a result, future chapters will consider each strand separately.

Chapter 2

RELIEF

The meeting of Allied Governments-in-Exile, under discussion during the summer of 1941, took place at St James's Palace on 24 September with Mr Eden in the chair. The meeting established an Inter-Allied Committee on Post-War Requirements with a bureau, headed by Sir Frederick Leith-Ross, responsible to it.

A week before the meeting, Leith-Ross, anticipating its conclusions and in response to various requests he had received as to Britain's expected relief role, wrote to Keynes asking for the Treasury's views on the finance of relief and the use of surplus stocks already in the U.K. for relief purposes. On receiving the letter, Keynes minuted.

To S. D. WALEY *and others, 19 September 1941*

Sir Frederick Leith-Ross is, I think, pressing us to reach definite financial decisions at too early a stage. But he is entitled to have some rather more definite indications of the course of procedure which the Treasury would approve than he has at present. I suggest the following as a basis of discussion.

(1) The first question to be decided is whether our assistance is to be in the form of kind or whether we should prefer to contribute each to a joint fund administered by some relief and reconstruction body, which would then pay the fair price for supplies from whatever source. Sir Frederick Leith-Ross is assuming that our contribution will take the form of supplying those articles which we have immediately handy or which we have bought up in connection with surplus difficulties. I can see that from some points of view this is the convenient and natural arrangement.

Nevertheless, it might prove administratively difficult. Some of the countries concerned, e.g. Holland, can pay for everything in cash. Others can at least make some contribution in cash. I see much confusion in the distribution of a miscellaneous stock

of goods, some of which have been purchased and some of which have been provided free of charge, amongst recipients, some of whom will have to pay and some of whom will not, there being no relation between the goods that are received free of charge and the goods that are supplied free of charge.

Also, with Sir F. Leith-Ross's enthusiasm for giving so much stuff away as possible, we may be burdened with heavier charges if any article of which we happen to possess some is to be given free of charge than if we make a definite, considered contribution to a general pool.

I suggest, therefore, as an alternative a central relief and reconstruction fund of, say, £150 million (I put in this figure purely for purposes of illustration). These cash resources would be supplemented by receipts from those European countries which were in a position to pay for what they have received in whole or in part. We might contribute to this fund, say, £25 million. The relief body would then purchase all the goods distributed at a fair price from whomsoever held them. Thus we should not be tackled separately on wheat, edible oil, shipping services, etc. When we had agreed to contribute £25 million, that would be the end of the responsibility of the Treasury. If the goods which it was convenient for us to furnish were worth more than £25 million, we should receive the difference in cash; equally, if they were worth less, we should pay the difference in cash. This would not interfere with contributions in kind by countries which were only interested in some particular product. For example, the 150 million bushels of wheat which the four big exporters are prepared to contribute would be valued, and these countries would be credited with contributing to the general pool the equivalent of this value, receiving the identical sum in payment for their wheat.

Under this system the Treasury would know where it stood, and efficient and economical and equitable distribution might be facilitated. Of course, it assumes a definite agreement with

U.S.A. that they should be the major contributors. But that is surely a necessity of any scheme which pretends to be cut and dried or definite. The proportions I have in view are something like this (£m): the United States, 75, the U.K., 25, other countries including the Dominions, 50. The figures for other countries should not be too high at £50 million, since the wheat contribution contemplated by Australia, Argentine and Canada should be worth something more than £30 million.

(2) Whatever the decision on the above important point of principle, it would be premature as yet to fix the figures or to communicate them to the European countries. I suggest that the order of events should be as follows:

(i) We should await the collection and criticism of the requirements which the Allied Governments had been asked to put in to us. If it be true, as Sir Frederick Leith-Ross alleges, that the Allied representatives are constantly asking him what we are doing and what we are prepared to do, he should reply that this is an entirely premature question before we have even received from them a list of their requirements.

(ii) The returns of the Allied Governments must then be supplemented by estimates for other countries not included, in particular the enemy countries and France. Moreover, China must not be forgotten. The U.S. will certainly want them to be brought into the relief picture, and I hope we shall too.

(iii) These requirements would then be compared with the amount of stuff which looked like being physically available. We should thus arrive at some sort of idea of an order of magnitude. My estimate of £150 million for the amount needed to be furnished free of charge is a pure shot.

(iv) We must than assemble estimates of the financial resources of those concerned and what it would be fair to ask them to pay towards the relief expenses.

(v) We shall then be in a position to say about how large the relief fund ought to be, though that will really require a further decision, namely, whether we are trying to cover quite a brief

interim relief period of, say, six months or whether we are also contemplating the finance of a reconstruction period of from 3 to 5 years. Clearly the latter would require much large finance than the former. Possibly it might be wiser to stick to the former for the time being.

(vi) Having formed some idea of the appropriate size of the relief fund, we could then discuss with the United States and others concerned the right way of organising and administering it and the appropriate contributions from different contributors.

(3) The worst and most muddled and most expensive and most inefficient solution would be to allow ourselves to be tackled by each commodity and each Ally separately without any picture of the whole scene, with Sir Frederick Leith-Ross busy and insistent to give away as much as possible and to make sure that our contribution shall be as large and the contribution of others as small as he can manoeuvre to make them. Perhaps I do him an injustice, but frankly his recent attitude to these problems has seemed to me, and I think to others too, a real menace. Yet one must not allow oneself to be driven by his extravagance into too opposite a mood. We must play our part in this in no mean spirit. It looks as if we shall have to take the leadership in organisation and in initiation. We want the whole programme to be carried forward on grand lines and must not seek to be too small ourselves. Nevertheless, we shall have the gravest responsibility for our own reconstruction and for the maintenance of our own standard of life, and, as things look at present, I should have thought that anything much more generous than what I have suggested above (which Sir F. Leith-Ross would probably regard as derisory) would be imprudent and irresponsible, at least until we know much more of the attendant circumstances.

[copy initialled] J.M.K.

Keynes's suggestions of 18 September were subject to extensive Treasury discussion before he prepared the final version of a Treasury memorandum on 24 October. The same day he sent a copy to Leith-Ross.

45

TREASURY MEMORANDUM ON FINANCIAL FRAMEWORK
OF POST-WAR EUROPEAN RELIEF

1. The first question of principle is whether assistance by the different countries contributing to relief should be piecemeal in the form of kind or whether assistance either in cash or in kind should be contributed to a joint fund administered by some relief and reconstruction body, which would then credit the several contributors with the appropriate amount and adjust the result to the amount of each contributor's promise.

Preliminary discussions in the Surplus Committee have been on the assumption that our contribution would take the form of supplying those articles (whether food or raw materials required for the immediate post-war period) which we have immediately handy or which we have bought up in connection with surplus difficulties, and that other contributory countries should follow the same policy. From some points of view this is the convenient and natural arrangement. Nevertheless, it might prove administratively difficult and inconvenient. The appropriate distribution of the financial burden might not correspond to the ownership of available stocks, particularly of those immediately available. Some of the recipient countries can pay for everything in cash; others can make at least some contribution in cash; thus confusion might result in the distribution of a miscellaneous stock of goods, some of which will have been purchased and some provided free of charge, amongst recipients, some of whom will be expected to pay, some of whom will not, there being no determinate relation between the goods that are received free of charge and the goods that are supplied free of charge.

2. The Treasury would, therefore, prefer the establishment of a central relief and reconstruction fund. Contributions to this fund, whether in cash or kind, would be valued in cash at an appropriate price. For example, the 150 million bushels of wheat which the four big exporters are prepared to contribute would

be valued, and these countries would be credited with contributing this amount to the general pool. Any contributor in kind would be entitled to stipulate that no part of his contribution should be sold for cash to a Government requiring relief so as to ensure that all commercial purchases would be additional to his relief contribution. If, for reasons of convenience and expedition, any contributor were to furnish in kind an amount in excess of what was due from him to meet his promise of assistance, the excess would be either replaced in kind or repaid in cash.

It would be a great advantage of this system that the relief administration could then deal with the problems of wheat, edible oils, shipping services etc., without having to make separate and specific financial arrangements about each of them. If the principle of piece-meal contributions in kind were adopted, we should be faced with the same difficulties that arose in connection with wheat, namely, that it is not easy to fix the contribution in respect of a particular commodity without any knowledge of what this country would be expected to do or what other countries will do in the case of other commodities. If a central fund is set up as above, some preliminary contributions could be made to it, and the relief administration would then be in a position to go ahead with any commodity up to the amount thus made available, and when that was exhausted it could ask for more.

Under this system the Treasury would know where it stood, and efficient, economical and equitable distribution would be facilitated. Controversy as to how any particular supply is to be financed would be reduced to a minimum.

It is important in the case of staple supplies that, as far as possible, the relief administration should be responsible for supplies to those countries in a position to pay in whole or in part as well as in the cases where it is to be a free gift. In this event it might not be necessary for any country to make a contribution actually in the shape of cash. The cash receipts of

47

the relief administration could then be applied to make payments to those countries from whom it was convenient to take in kind more than the equivalent of their appropriate cash contribution after allowing for replacements in kind.

It would be essential to obtain the adherence of the United States to this form of organisation. But this would not necessarily involve any interference with the principle of the United States' assistance being furnished mainly in kind, on the analogy of lend lease. For assistance thus furnished could be used to replace an excess assistance in kind by another contributor. Nevertheless it would be very desirable to persuade them to give other assistance also. It would be for them to consider what was most convenient and appropriate in this respect. It should be emphasised that the proposals below and other provisions in this paper relate only to the relief period immediately after the end of the war, covering (say) six months to a year, and have no relation to the finance of a subsequent reconstruction period of from three to five years.

If this general principle is accepted, it will then be possible to proceed with preparations regarding particular commodities piece-meal. But if this principle is not accepted, then piece-meal handling will present almost insuperable financial difficulties.

3. On the assumption that the establishment of a relief fund as above is approved in principle, it would be premature as yet to fix definite figures for its aggregate amount or for the contributions of different participants. But this would not mean that the progress of organisation would be interfered with. The Treasury suggests that the order of events might be as follows:

(i) The list of requirements which the Allied Governments have been asked to hand in should be compiled, analysed and criticised.

(ii) The returns of the Allied Governments must then be supplemented by estimates for other countries not included, in particular the enemy countries and France. Moreover China must not be forgotten.

(iii) Simultaneously returns should be obtained of the amount of supplies which are likely to be physically available, and also the shipping necessary to convey them. The aggregate of these supplies would then be compared with the aggregate of the requirements. By this means some estimate can be made of the order of magnitude of the problem.

(iv) At the same time estimates should be assembled of the financial resources of those concerned with a view to considering in which cases it would be fair to ask for payment in whole or in part. The Dutch Government have already stated that they will relieve Holland 'under their own responsibility with their own means and with their own ships'; presumably this does not mean that they would not be prepared to collaborate with the relief organisation and to purchase supplies where convenient through them. The other Allies also in many cases have resources in gold and dollar securities, now safely frozen in the United States of America or Canada. In some cases also they have substantial and growing sums in sterling in London. The question of the amount of such sums allowed to be released would have a bearing on the contribution which this country could make.

The cash resources of some of these countries are very large. The seven occupied countries have £1,000 million assets frozen in the shape of gold and dollar securities, which is, of course, many times the total resources of this country. The resources of France in particular are very large. Russia is believed to have a very big gold reserve, the amount of which has not been made known to us. Certain other figures, of which we have recent information, are set out below [p. 50].

The claimants on the relief fund having least resources of their own are likely to be Germany, Italy, Poland, Hungary, certain Balkan States and China.

The Allies putting in their list of requirements should be asked to make a statement of their available resources.

(v) When all the above information has been assembled, we

£ million

Belgium	250	probably the
Holland	350	real figures are
Norway	30	higher
Czechoslovakia	1·6	
Poland	20	(assuming 16 recovered from France and 0·8 from Roumania)
Greece	40	
Jugoslavia	18	
Denmark	23	

shall be in a better position to say about how large the relief fund ought to be.

(vi) Having formed some idea of the appropriate size of the relief fund, we should then be in a position to discuss with the United States and others concerned the right way of organising and administering it and the appropriate contributions from different contributors.

4. Until the above information has been assembled it will be impracticable for the Treasury to attempt to estimate the appropriate contribution from this country. As at present advised they would not contemplate it as reasonable that this country should be expected to contribute the equivalent of more than one-third of the amount contributed by the United States; and this would only be possible if other attendant arrangements were favourable and helpful to us. They also think that countries other than the United States and the United Kingdom, that is to say, the Dominions, South America and Sweden, should be expected to contribute from a quarter to a third of the total fund. It would, however, be undesirable to make any communication of these figures or proportions to other countries until fuller information than is at present available had been assembled.

5. The Treasury have endeavoured to propose a general framework which will allow the main business to be got on with

with the least possible delay from financial considerations. For, inevitably, it will be difficult to reach firm proposals on the latter until many factors at present imperfectly known can be taken into account. The finance of the relief period will necessarily run into the finance of the reconstruction period. The amount of resources in the hands of the Treasury in the shape of gold or its equivalent at the end of the war is quite unknown. The question whether the United States will be prepared to continue lend lease arrangements to us or others beyond the armistice is highly relevant. The question of the scale on which overseas balances can be allowed to be withdrawn from London during the relief and reconstruction period has also to be considered. The method and scale of relief to the enemy countries is inevitably bound up with any provisions which may be enforced on them for restitution of stolen and requisitioned property. Thus it is important to establish a framework which does not make the initial preparatory arrangements unduly dependent on financial provisions, which cannot be determined with safety or prudence at the present time.

This memorandum resulted in further exchanges with Leith-Ross, both by letter and in meetings.

From SIR FREDERICK LEITH-ROSS, *27 October 1941*

My dear Keynes,

Many thanks for your letter of 24th October enclosing twenty copies of the Treasury memorandum on Financial Framework of Post-War European Relief. I am very glad indeed to have this as a basis of discussion. On the first reading, however, the proposals put forward seem to me to raise a good many questions. For example, the memorandum begins with the proposal that all contributions to the central relief and reconstruction fund should be valued in cash at an appropriate price. Surely this would be rather difficult to reconcile with the principle to which I have always understood the Treasury attach importance, that no specific accounts should be kept of lend lease supplies. I should have thought that the United States might well

51

use the lend lease machinery for relief supplies, and it would be rather difficult to make a clear distinction between lend lease supplies to us and for European relief. Again, at the top of page 2, the memorandum suggests that any contributor in kind to the relief fund would be entitled to stipulate that no part of his contribution should be sold for cash to a government requiring relief and I should have thought that such a stipulation would invariably be made. Later on in that page, however, it is suggested that the relief administration would be entitled to sell supplies to the countries which were in a position to pay in whole or in part. It may be that I have not fully understood what you have in mind, and I would like to have the memorandum examined by my people here and then to arrange a talk with you and anyone else at the Treasury who has been working on this.

Yours sincerely,

F. W. LEITH-ROSS

To SIR FREDERICK LEITH-ROSS, *28 October 1941*

My dear Leithers,

POST-WAR EUROPEAN RELIEF

My first reflections on the two points you raise in your letter of October 27 are the following:

(1) I do not think the principle of lend lease supplies to ourselves not being valued as against us need be an obstacle, for they would only be valued for accounting purposes as between the United States and the pool. You must remember that the United States already values its lend lease supplies precisely, since they have to be set against the appropriations. The principle to which you refer is that no accounting as between ourselves and U.S.A., only a list of the goods in quantity and quality, is furnished. Now the analogy to this is, I suggest, that the supplies are accounted for in money as between U.S. and the relief pool just as they are for the purposes of the appropriations. But there would not necessarily be similar accounting between the relief pool and the country in need of the relief, except where that country was actually paying for the supplies; that is to say, we should be supplying Poland with so many quarters of wheat and so many bales of cotton, so many

boots, etc. rather than a money value, though we should in fact know what the money value was and could produce this in any relevant context, just as the U.S. is prepared to produce, if it were relevant, the money value of the lend lease supplies to us. All this seems to me to be a matter of machinery, which could be worked out according to one formula or another as might be most convenient when we came down to the details. Moreover, it is only a hypothesis that the U.S. will be wanting to use the lend lease machinery, as it is now, for the relief supplies.

(2) Your second point results, I think, from our not making ourselves perfectly clear. The point in view is the following:-

The exporting countries contributing wheat to the relief pool are anxious, if I remember the scheme right, to make sure that the relief which is supplied would not deprive them of any normal commercial sales. They probably would not make so handsome a donation if they thought that these supplies would be used, e.g. for sales to Holland, which could perfectly well buy commercial wheat for cash. Therefore, one must provide that they have a right to make the stipulation that the relief wheat which they furnish only goes to the impecunious who are incapable of buying wheat out of their own resources. But we in general would have no motive for making a similar stipulation, particularly if the supplies which it was physically convenient to take from us for central administration were worth more than our proper financial contribution. Similarly, I see no reason why in general the United States would wish to make such a stipulation, though they might want to do so in particular cases. Clearly it would be a great advantage that some goods contributed gratuitously should be sold for cash and some goods distributed gratuitously should be bought for cash. Unless you have some system of accounting by which this is possible, I do not see how you are to get along at all. That is the essence of the proposal.

I take your last sentence to mean that you would like to have

a talk here after an interval for digestion before having a discussion with the official Surplus Committee. I agree that would be a good thing. If you will let me know when you are ready I will get a meeting arranged.

Yours sincerely,

J. M. KEYNES

From SIR FREDERICK LEITH-ROSS, *20 November 1941*

My dear Keynes,

I have been thinking further about the finance of relief supplies since our talk the other day, and I still feel that it would not be wise to settle beforehand the definite proportions in which the United Kingdom and the United States should contribute to a relief pool.

After the last war, relief financing was started by the United States putting up $100 million while we put up £12½ million; subsequently, we added only £ for £ to charitable donations but the United States extended large credits to the Allied countries. Finally, out of total Government credits in the immediate relief period of some £170 million, the United States found 88 per cent and we found 6½ per cent, the other allied Governments putting up the balance. I do not believe that we could have got off so cheaply if we had started by trying to fix proportionate contributions beforehand.

On the other hand, the framework of a relief organisation should be established as soon as possible and I do not think that we can wait for the results of the various investigations suggested in paragraph 3 of the Treasury memorandum before broaching this question with the United States. Any lists of requirements which we can get at present from the Allied Governments must inevitably be in the nature of guesswork. What is certain is that their full needs after the war are likely to exceed any possibilities of supply or shipment, at any rate during the first year. After the last war there was a relief organisation already working in Belgium. The Scandinavian countries, Holland, Switzerland and Spain were prosperous and able to help. There were large military stores and supplies of all kinds in France and Italy; and we continued to provide shipping and supplies for France and Italy after the Armistice, apart from the relief supplies to the rest of Europe. The official relief organisation dealt mainly with Belgium, Poland, Austria and Czechoslovakia, with some little assistance to Yugoslavia, Roumania and the Baltic States; yet some £170 million were spent in six or seven months and in many areas the supplies provided were admittedly far from adequate. After this war, the area of distress will be much greater and the resources

54

immediately available far smaller. Practically the whole of Europe will be denuded of stocks. There will be no relief organisation already working and neither we nor the United States will have supplies in any part of Europe which can be drawn upon quickly.

In these circumstances, I suggest that we should work on the following lines:

(1) The United States Government should be asked to join with us in establishing the nucleus of an international relief organisation to take charge of the whole problem. There would probably have to be a political council and an executive committee, with (say) an American Chairman and/or Director-General of Relief, and a British deputy; and with sub-divisions to be set up as and when required to deal with Programmes and Supplies, Finance, Shipping, etc. (a more detailed note on this is being prepared by the Department). Preliminary steps should be taken to earmark suitable personnel who should be ready to go out and take charge of the distribution of relief, in conjunction with the local authorities in the allied countries, as soon as the war ends. The American Red Cross and other such bodies might help in dealing with immediate destitution and medical services, and their operations should be linked with those of the official relief organisation.

(2) Some initial cash resources should be made available to this organi-sation, and I would suggest that we should be ready once again to put up £12½ million, available for expenditure in the sterling area, provided the United States will make available not less than $100 million. Similar credits for the relief pool should be obtained wherever possible from other allied or neutral countries.

(3) Moreover, stocks, at any rate of the main primary commodities, should be earmarked wherever possible and the different producing countries should be asked what contributions they are prepared to offer. I hope that the United States will be ready to provide large supplies from its stockpiles, and we should be prepared to make some contribution from our stocks of wheat, wool, etc. The donor countries might be asked whether they would agree to their gifts being sold, where possible, by the relief organisations, but I anticipate that they will want them earmarked as gifts for necessitous countries.

(4) I should have preferred these stock donations to be additional to any cash credits opened in favour of the relief organisation and I believe that this would be the best way of getting contributions from overseas producing countries. If the Treasury feel that any donations in kind which we can offer must be debited against our £12½ million, this could of course be done, though the U.S. Administration would then presumably follow the same line

55

and the original cash credits would soon be exhausted. I doubt whether it is advisable for us to press as a matter of principle for detailed accounts to be kept as between all the donor countries and the relief council. This seems to me a pure matter of accountancy.

(5) The extent to which each European country should get supplies as free gifts or on credit or against cash payment will have to be examined by some financial committee containing representatives of the Governments contributing to the relief pool, and the council, acting on the advice of the committee, will have to determine the conditions appropriate to each case. Their decisions will raise some very awkward political issues and I was very glad that you agreed that we should not insist on stripping the poorer European countries of such reserves as they may have. I am sure that this would be unwise both politically and economically, and I hope that the United States will be prepared to grant credits or extend lease-lend to our Allies, at any rate, pretty freely. Insofar as the importing countries can pay either out of their own resources or by drawing on credits granted to them, arrangements will have to be made to secure that their purchases are co-ordinated with the operations of the relief organisation, if they are not actually effected through its machinery.

(6) The treatment of the ex-enemy countries will be a problem for future settlement. It looks to me as if in the first instance they would have either to pay cash or to get credits, as it may be difficult to persuade the allies to allow them much in the way of relief gifts except through voluntary organisations. But the credits granted for this purpose will probably have to be written off later, and it will be desirable to treat Europe, so far as possible, as a whole in formulating shipping and supply programmes.

I should be glad to know if the Treasury would be willing to agree to the above programme.

I am sending a copy of this letter to Ronald.

Yours sincerely,

F. W. LEITH-ROSS

To SIR FREDERICK LEITH-ROSS, *2 December 1941*

Dear Leith-Ross,

EUROPEAN RELIEF

Your letter of November 20th. The fundamental conception underlying the Treasury Memorandum is that we should advocate that the relief organisation should, if possible, distribute all relief supplies and decide how much of the available tonnage

and commodities is to be allocated to each recipient and to what extent each recipient shall pay or receive gifts.

Under this conception we and the U.S.A. should make gifts to the relief organisation and the U.S.A., and not to individual countries.

The Treasury Memorandum proposes that, when the time comes, a maximum limit should be fixed to our gifts: the relief organisation would pay cash for supplies from the sterling areas over and above this limit, its cash being derived from the sales of goods to countries which can pay.

Admittedly this scheme may not prove acceptable, because countries which pay may prefer to buy for themselves, in co-ordination with the relief organisation. In that case the resources of the relief organisation would be limited to the gifts by the U.S.A. and the U.K. and other donating countries.

We agree that stock donations and shipping services may be the best way of getting contributions from overseas producing countries. Cash would then only be required for administrative expenses.

We fully agree with what you say in your first paragraph about not settling definite proportions of assistance between ourselves and the U.S.A. at too early a stage in the proceedings. I thought we had cleared away in our conversation any ambiguity about that in the Treasury Memorandum.

In regard to your concrete suggestions:-

(1) Sooner or later something of this kind is clearly advisable. Whether to ask the U.S.A. to set it up forthwith is a matter of timing. Would it not be better to get some agreement with them on general principles before proceeding to machinery? I should have supposed on our side much of the actual work would be done by officials who have been handling the same classes of commodities in the Ministry of Food and Ministry of Supply. At some appropriate date, the individuals to be charged with the new duties would have to be selected, but if we go ahead too fast the personnel will probably become mainly American

57

since they have so much more surplus manpower for these purposes than we have.

(2) seems premature. What would the cash resources be wanted for in the near future? It might seriously prejudice future arrangements to start on the basis of our putting up a third of the total, i.e. half the American contribution. We could undertake to pay the salaries of any British personnel allocated but, as I say, it is not obvious for what else it would be wanted.

(3) I do not see how at this stage of the war we can expect to go very far as regards earmarking stocks and asking the producing countries what contributions they can make.

This is possible in the case of wheat, and perhaps cotton and coffee, where surpluses are certain to exist at the end of the war. But as regards most other commodities surpluses no longer exist and it would certainly be wrong to earmark goods for post-war relief in such a way as to make them unavailable for essential war needs.

Apart from special cases such as wheat and perhaps cotton, we do not think that there is any obvious advantage in earmarking stocks before our own requirements are known and before the amount of stock is known. At any rate the question must surely be postponed until many other main matters of principle have been settled. It cannot arise for some months to come.

(5) What you propose here would seem to me to cut across the proposals for pooled finance. I can see advantages in the alternative you suggest but also very serious disadvantages.

Consider how your alternative would work in practice. We might have a situation in which France, Holland, and Belgium will pay for themselves; Poland and Czechoslovakia would get some grants from us and lease lend from the U.S.A.; Greece and Norway might be allowed to use their sterling credits from us and would obtain lease lend from the U.S.A.

This would mean that we should not be able to decide how much we could afford to contribute in the aggregate but would

have to have separate deals with each of the countries concerned. It would be difficult to secure the principle that anything extra to one of them was at the expense of another. We could not be sure that the order of merit for generosity from ourselves would be the same as from the U.S.A. Secondly, it would mean allocating contributions in kind such as the wheat contributions. The contribution from us would have to depend on how much the countries were getting from other sources. In fact it would be a highly confused sort of negotiations.

But I see a more fundamental objection than the above. The alternative just outlined might be possible in the case of our Allies but what about the ex-enemy countries? What you propose would involve us in making direct presents to Germany and the Americans to lease-lend to Germany and the like. Is this what you intend or think wisest? One of the great advantages of pooled finance to my mind is that resources are put up for relief as such and not for particular countries as such. I do not foresee that it would be much easier at the end of this war than it was at the end of the last war to vote direct grants of large sums of money to Germany, whereas it would be quite another matter to pool resources in the hands of a relief body for the assistance of distress everywhere.

Yours sincerely,
[copy initialled] J.M.K.

These exchanges proved rather inconclusive, for Leith-Ross continued to press Keynes and the Treasury on the financial issue. As a result, Keynes minuted.

To S. D. WALEY, *4 February 1942*

The truth is that the whole treatment of the finance of relief under consideration is really out of date. The Treasury Memorandum was based on the assumption that we should, after getting into contact with the Americans, have to agree to some

definite contribution, either absolutely or in proportion to what the Americans were doing. Nevertheless, I agree with you that to avoid a fixed contribution in any sense whatever would be much better. Can we persuade Leith-Ross to accept this except by starting the discussion all over again at the ministerial level? Leith-Ross purports to have a ministerial decision in favour of the general principle he is advocating. Thus he is entitled to stick to that until such a ministerial decision, if it really exists, is rescinded.

I suggest, therefore, that, without going into all the details of the organisation, the Chancellor might take up the whole matter again at Mr Greenwood's Committee. A good starting off point for this would be the new calculations about our prospective balance of trade, especially in the first two years after the war. This demonstrates so clearly our complete inability to make a contribution except at the expense of borrowing it from someone else, that it provides a good basis for a revision of our ideas, by which the Prime Minister's original pledge (which never in fact said anything about finance) is taken as a declaration of policy and organisation, not of free gifts on our behalf. The Chancellor might ask for a decision that, in view of the statistical forecast, it should be agreed amongst ministers that at the present stage we make no definite promises whatever beyond that which we have already provisionally made in connection with the Wheat Agreement.

Even if we were financially better off, this would still be a reasonable decision. The only matter which requires urgent attention is organisation. In practice Leith-Ross is holding this up by his preoccupation with the measure of financial assistance to be given by us in particular. It would be much better for him and his Department to start discussing organisation with the Americans and discover their ideas with explicit instructions that he has no authority to enter into financial obligations of any kind. So far from that impairing his position in discussing organisation, I believe it would strengthen it, since it would keep

the red herring of finance out of the picture at these early stages when, apart from our impecuniosity, we know far too little about the sums involved or about the means of relief to reach any sensible decision.

[copy initialled] J.M.K.

The upshot was the preparation of a letter from the Chancellor to the President of the Board of Trade to guide Leith-Ross in his discussions. A composite draft by S. D. Waley and H. D. Henderson went to Leith-Ross for comment. On the basis of these comments, a further period of drafting began spurred on by Keynes's plea to Sir Richard Hopkins of 21 April,

This is a major decision of policy. May I plead that it should not be fluffed for the sake of avoiding a personal difference of opinion, which is quite genuine on both sides but not for that reason avoidable.

The result was that, after Hopkins himself tried his hand at drafting, the final version that went to Mr Dalton under the Chancellor's signature was Keynes's.

To H. DALTON *from* SIR KINGSLEY WOOD, *1 May 1942*

My dear President,

1. I feel that the time has come to consider afresh the problem of post-war relief in the light of all that has happened during the last few months. These developments affect, as it seems to me, several aspects of the problem :-

(i) Recent investigations have made us vividly aware of the acuteness of our balance of payments problem, especially in the period immediately after the war, so that we shall be in a position of requiring assistance rather than of giving it.

(ii) Earlier discussions were based on the assumption of large surplus stocks of many commodities in the world at large. The prevailing tendency is now towards a growing scarcity of most commodities for immediate wartime purposes.

(iii) When the Prime Minister made the declaration which was the starting point of our study of post-war relief, the British Commonwealth was carrying on the war alone. We are now part

61

of a wide embracing alliance, of which the United States possesses resources available for post-war relief with which ours bear no comparison. Moreover, within the British Commonwealth it is probable that we alone will end the war with substantially reduced international resources, and that India and the Dominions will emerge with a position which is either substantially unchanged or greatly improved.

(iv) The relief and reconstruction problem no longer affects merely Europe and China, but covers areas in the Far East, to which no certain limit can yet be put. We may find ourselves with unescapable special liabilities in Malaya and Burma. It is impossible at this stage to say how far *collective* responsiblity will be considered to attach to these regions equally with Europe, and how far we shall be expected to assume a special responsibility.

2. Some of these aspects are further developed below, but there is one other overriding consideration. We are very much in the dark as to the form or scale of American assistance for these purposes. We have reason to believe that they are taking their responsibility most seriously and will, in due course, offer a scheme. Without further knowledge than we now have as to the nature of this scheme, it is most difficult for us to give a concrete form to our own assistance. Since it must, in any case, be insignificant compared with what they will be doing, it would be setting a wrong scale if we tried to put our entirely inadequate contribution in the forefront. Some progress can be made at once on several aspects of the relief problem. But is it not altogether premature to try to get down to details on the financial side until the Americans have opened up and communicated to us at least the general outline of what they have it in mind to propose? At present we have no means of knowing what form of collaboration on our part will be most useful.

3. For a period of, say, the first two post-war years, we ourselves shall be greatly in need of the continuance of lend lease assistance from the United States, and of similar assistance from

Canada. If we ourselves shall require external assistance upon a scale that is likely to be large, it is obvious that we are in no financial position to play more than a limited part in providing relief for others. For this reason it will be scarcely candid to allow discussions to proceed on the basis that the principal donors to post-war relief would be ourselves, in association with the British Commonwealth, and the United States.

4. None the less, until fairly recently, the idea that we should make a substantial contribution could be supported by powerful considerations of a different kind. Prominent among these was the expectation that the end of the war would probably find us possessed of large stocks of many essential foodstuffs and raw materials, and the fact that, in this event, our proximity to the European Continent would make us the most convenient source from which liberated European countries could be supplied promptly with goods that might be urgently needed to avert distress. If the countries from which relief supplies are actually obtained were expected to offer them as a free contribution, it might easily happen in those circumstances that a disproportionate share of the burden would fall upon ourselves. On the other hand, we could hardly insist on being paid in full for such contributions in kind by an international relief organisation, unless we were ready to contribute to its finances. It was with these considerations in mind that the Treasury suggested some time ago, with my approval, that we should propose to the United States Government the creation of a relief pool to which we should make a contribution fixed in terms of money. It was part of this idea that the relief pool would pay the supplying countries for the commodities which it obtained from them, that it would sell to those recipients which possessed sufficient financial means, and supply other countries free, or on easy credit terms.

5. I fear, however, that the course of events since this suggestion was made has gone far to destroy the assumption upon which it was based. Under the stress of war developments,

our stocks of essential commodities in the United Kingdom are likely from now onwards to undergo a serious depletion. It must be regarded as extremely doubtful whether we shall emerge from the war with reserves that can be made available for the relief of Europe, and I understand that the Ministry of Food and the Ministry of Supply take the view that we shall probably not have supplies to spare. It now seems more likely that our real contribution to post-war relief may have to be limited mainly to the provision of shipping facilities, and that it will fall to other countries to supply at any rate a large proportion of the foodstuffs and raw materials that will be needed; future discussions of the relief problem should, as it sems to me proceed on the basis of a clear recognition of this fact as well as of our post-war exchange difficulties.

6. This is the more important because we expect shortly to enter upon discussions with the Americans about the major questions of post-war financial and economic policy, in the course of which it will be essential for us to explain fully the difficulties by which we expect to be confronted in restoring equilibrium to our balance of payments. It would be unfortunate if we were to appear to cast doubt upon the reality of our apprehensions upon this matter by discussing the relief problem in terms which would only be appropriate to a country which had a large margin of financial strength.

7. I am now disposed to think that what we should aim at is that the United States should continue the lend-lease system to cover post-war supplies to those countries (which will probably include ourselves) which are unable to pay in gold and dollars, and that Canada and perhaps other producing countries should also agree to make their goods available on gift, or terms similar to those of lend lease, until the countries of Europe are in a position to resume their export trade on a scale sufficient to pay for their needs in cash. It seems reasonable to hope that the United States and Canada might agree to this, both for general political reasons and in order to maintain their exports of agricultural produce and other commodities. From several

points of view, this might be a more satisfactory arrangement than the earlier suggestion that the relief council should sell to those countries which could afford to pay and make gifts to those which could not. Under the latter plan we, in common with all other countries asking for assistance, would have to go before the council and give figures of our gold and foreign exchange resources in order to prove that we cannot pay cash for what we need; and I think we should try to avoid being placed in this position. For these various reasons I am clear that the functions of the relief council as previously put forward need to be revised. But I should agree that it would be premature to do this until we have a better idea of what type of arrangements is likely to commend itself to the United States.

8. What, then, can our financial role be? I have had an account of the discussions that have taken place on the official plane in regard to this matter and I am not unconscious of the difficulties. In the light of the above, you will appreciate how difficult, indeed impossible, it is to enter into definite commitments or even to make tentative proposals. I hope, nevertheless, that there is a *via media* on this question upon which agreement can be reached amongst us. It is clear that when the time comes we must be ready to do whatever lies in our power to assist. Nor is there any objection on my part to that being stated in plain terms to the Americans, but it seems to me essential that the probable difficulties involved in our balance of payments after the war should be made known to the American negotiators with equal emphasis at the same time. I see no difficulty in its being said that such stocks as we had available at the end of the war and were non-marketable over a reasonable period of time would be made available by us and that in the event it would be our object to make some small cash contribution for expenditure on the purchase of such stocks within the Empire. On the other hand, I do not think that we can rightly offer to America any commitment either that this will amount to any specific total or that we shall be in a position to decide how much we can contribute until we can foresee in what way our own external

difficulties can be met. If the discussions take place concurrently with discussions in London under Article VII of the Mutual Aid Agreement this will be easier.

9. In truth the problem seems to me to merge into the much larger question of general financial arrangements after the war for the rehabilitation of countries that are short of external resources, which will include both Russia and ourselves no less than the 'relief' countries. We shall do well to see it from the very outset in this larger perspective. For it can no longer be isolated and treated as a special problem in the way that might have seemed possible in the early days of the war.

10. The consideration of the issues I have raised may be a matter of some urgency, since I understand that the question of post-war relief is likely to be discussed with Winant upon his return to this country. I am therefore sending copies of this letter to the Lord President and to the Paymaster General.

Yours ever,
[copy initialled] K.W.

Mr Dalton replied to the Chancellor's letter on 13 May, saying that he was glad to see that the Chancellor agreed that when the time came Britain would do whatever lay in its power to assist relief. However, he took issue with the Chancellor's line on stocks, advocating a substantial contribution to a relief agency in that form plus a reasonable contribution in sterling for purchases in the sterling area. The Chancellor replied five days later, hoping that Britain might eventually be in a position to follow Mr Dalton's suggestions, but pointing out that the existing state of international thinking on relief did not require any specific commitments at that time. The discussion continued between Mr Dalton and the Chancellor, with one intervention by the Foreign Secretary, until 1 June, when looking over the proposals which Mr Dalton would put to the Ministerial Committee on Reconstruction Problems on 3 June[1] and his colleagues' reactions to them Keynes minuted.

[1] Put briefly, Mr Dalton's paper made seven points: Britain should pool post-war supplies with Allied Governments through an international organisation; supply arrangements should be co-ordinated; Britain should, subject to replacement, make non-essential stocks available temporarily to the relief organisation; Britain would maintain rationing until other countries

To S. D. WALEY, *1 June 1942*

POST-WAR RELIEF POLICY

I am not inclined to deal so sympathetically as the papers below with the memorandum of the President of the Board of Trade. Such general commitments as these, to apply in circumstances which cannot be clearly foreseen, are more dangerous than useful. The President of the Board of Trade may have become accustomed to a diet of his own words. But the Cabinet should be clear what words it is that they are likely to have to eat before endorsing this paper.

I hope very much that the Chancellor of the Exchequer will send the Committee a written paper calling attention to the following points:

(1) There is a confusion between what might reasonably be expected from us in the initial period of relieving acute want, say, three months, and what would be reasonable over a more prolonged period. There is no indication of time limits. The international organisation of relief is likely to last for a period measured by two or three years rather than months. Thus, generally speaking, our more extreme commitments, if given, should be limited to some such period as three months. This would not mean that we were prevented from extending them further if, when the time comes, we felt able to.

(2) This applies particularly to the commitments about rationing. It is reasonable that we should undertake to continue a system of rationing for a period, let us say, of not less than a year. (We may for our own reasons want to continue it beyond that but we should not commit ourselves.) We might also agree that our rations should not be increased above what they are at the end of the war in the first three months. But to undertake that for an indefinite period we should not increase our rations

were provided for; British post-war requirements should be subject to the same examination as those of other countries; Britain should do everything possible to re-provision Allied territories after their liberation and Britain should be willing to contribute to relief when the time came on the principle that she would do all that was possible in the way of assistance.

above what they are at the end of the war, which may, for all we know, be extremely severe, unless all the peoples of Europe have been fully provided for, seems to me a rashly altruistic undertaking. Certainly it should not be undertaken except after very careful thought. Moreover, the Prime Minister's announcement eighteen months ago related to the German people equally with the rest of Europe. I should have supposed that it would be rash politically to promise that we should not increase the rations in this country above the figure they stand at at the end of the war, however low, until the Germans had been fully provided for.

(3) It is not entirely clear what is meant by the 'pooling' of supplies. The proposed undertaking, however, would appear to commit us to placing in the hands of some outside body, the constitution of which is at present unknown to us, the whole question of what supplies should be allocated to this country. That is to say, we should no longer decide for ourselves what quantity of anything it was reasonable to import for the purposes of this country, but would have to accept whatever allocation is given us by a mixed international body. It does not clearly mean this, but it might mean it. Is it a sound and sensible proposition?

(4) Mr Waley has pointed out the obvious dangers of a commitment to reprovision allied territories as and when we re-occupy them prior to the conclusion of the war. It seems most unlikely that we could combine the shipping strain of active military operations with a relief scheme except on the most modest scale. Would it be honest to excite hopes which military considerations would almost certainly render unrealisable?

(5) It is proposed that 'so long as supplies are not adequate to meet the essential needs of Europe, we must maintain rationing in the U.K., subject perhaps to the reservation that the acceptance of this principle should not require the United Kingdom to reduce the rations existing at the time when relief operations come into force'. It is argued that readiness to accept

this policy would produce a good impression in the United States. It is not, however, linked in any way with the continuance of e.g. lend lease arrangements. Thus it would apply in a situation in which some parts of Europe at least were being supplied on lend lease terms, whilst we had to pay for ourselves. I doubt if it is realistic to make no distinction between those who are being cared for charitably and those who are looking after themselves. There is not even any condition that, e.g., Holland should enter into any corresponding commitments not to improve the feeding conditions of the Dutch out of their own resources until, e.g., the Poles can also be carried by charitable means to an equally high level. All this seems to imply general standards of altruism on the part of everyone except the United States which it may be unrealistic and impracticable to assume.

(6) In the main this paper relates to foodstuffs. The last paragraph of section 5, however, indicates that some at least of the provisions may be intended to apply to raw materials as well. This is exceedingly dangerous. For it would mean that we might be deprived of supplies necessary for exports just at the moment when the development of exports is essential to our national life. In the context in which it appears it seems that the question of the quantity of raw materials we should be allowed to import would not be decided by ourselves but by some inter-allied control. Here again there is no suggested time limit to the commitment. It is, I urge, of the utmost importance that it should be made clear that the whole of this paper relates solely to foodstuffs, and not to raw materials.

(7) What the Chancellor of the Exchequer has said about the possible financial assistance we can give is in danger of being twisted in a tendentious and jesuitical manner. The Chancellor should not agree to this limited quotation from his letter, unless there is a passage to make it clear that it is only in the event of the United States and others continuing help to us that we shall have any power to assist at all and, in no circumstances,

must we give the impression that our financial help is likely to be significant.

Are the Ministry of Food and the Ministry of Supply represented on the Committee to which this memorandum has been sent? Clearly they should be consulted. The association of this paper with the Board of Trade is liable to prevent the latter from performing its proper function of protecting our trade interests.

In several points the paper itself goes beyond the summary of conclusions, which is not an accurate summary of what has gone before. It is dangerous to approve a paper on the basis of an inaccurate summary, since it becomes ambiguous whether it is the detailed discussion of the body of the paper or the inaccurate summary which governs the situation.

If the author of this paper is entrusted with negotiations on this subject in the United States, should it not be made clear that he has no authority to enter into any commitment, but only to have conversations with a view to eliciting from the Americans the general line of action and organisation they favour? He should not be authorised to commit His Majesty's Government, in advance of specific approval of the actual form of words, on any point whatever.

[copy initialled] J.M.K.

S. D. Waley and Sir Hubert Henderson concurred with Keynes's approach to the President's memorandum. Keynes's minute went forward to Sir Richard Hopkins and formed the basis for the Chancellor's memorandum to the Reconstruction Problems Committee completed the next day by Keynes, Hopkins and the Chancellor.

After the meeting of Ministers on 3 June and several further meetings of officials and Ministers, Sir Frederick Leith-Ross received instructions for his forthcoming visit to Washington to discuss relief matters.[2]

---

2 Leith-Ross's instructions allowed him fairly wide latitude in matters of organisation subject to the provisos that there would be a London branch of the organisation for European relief and that the scheme would be under the direction of the Big Four powers. On supplies,

Leith-Ross reached Washington at the end of June. By the middle of July, his discussions with the Americans had reached a point where he could send a draft American proposal for an international relief organisation to London. Keynes's comments at this stage largely took the form of questions as to how the proposed organisation would actually work, in particular whether its Director-General should be the virtual ruler of Europe. Keynes's role during Leith-Ross's American visit is best exemplified in a note on the conversation with the Russian Ambassador following an evening with him on 6 July and a series of questions on the constitution of the proposed organisation.

From a letter to N. RONALD, *8 July 1942*

(4) I take this opportunity to report to you a conversation I had with Maisky a day or two ago bearing on the relief problem. (He was dining with me and we had a long and frank talk covering a very wide range of subjects.) He was, as you already know, very suspicious of the Leith-Ross Committee, chiefly on the ground that Leith-Ross had called together an Allied Committee and was then apparently treating it as something of a sham and a camouflage, conducting all the real business in a purely British Committee. I defended Leith-Ross on the ground that, until he had got into contact with the Americans, he really had nothing to tell the Allies and nothing significant was happening. When L-R returned from Washington it would be another matter. Maisky then went on to the question as to who would be responsible for dispensing relief in the different countries, but having, I thought, a fairly open mind about this, and saying that it might be the occupying Allies' army, the incoming Allied government or an international relief organisation, according to circumstances and opportunity. The main point he emphasised, however, was that the planning and policy body should be distinct from the operating executive body. He said that his government had had great experience of this sort of planning, that in the Gosplan days they had started by uniting the

he was only allowed to say that stocks and stores conveniently situated and not immediately required in the U.K. would be available. On finance, he was instructed to say that Britain's contribution would depend on future circumstances. On rationing he was to make no commitment before the complete scheme was available.

planning and policy with the operating body and had come to the conclusion that this was always a great mistake. I should say that there is a great deal of common sense in this standpoint. On the other hand, the kind of set-up indicated in Leith-Ross's last telegram, of a Director General of Relief, seems to presuppose something different. Maisky pointed out that one of the most difficult and important problems would be the allocation of supplies between the different applicants and that those settling that kind of issue would have to be quite different people, in possession of different contacts and information, than those concerned with the practical problems of organising purchase, transport and distribution. He, no doubt, has it in mind that the former task involves high politics. It does not much matter who is the engine-driver for the supplies, if their destination has been settled elsewhere. I did not pursue the discussion. But the point raised is fundamental and one, I had the feeling, about which the Russians are likely to take a strong line. You will see the inwardness of it without my having to say any more.

Keynes's minute on draft telegram to SIR FREDERICK LEITH-ROSS, *4 August 1942*

I should like to ask in addition a more general question than any of the above, namely 'How does Leith-Ross picture the set up as working in actual practice? A Russian Army is in occupation of Poland and Roumania; the Polish Gov^t is a camp-follower; the Roumanian Gov^t is interned; various kinds of food and materials are required for relief and also for the consumption of the Russian Army; relief is required for the Ukraine as well as for the Poles and Roumania; Jugoslavia and Greece are also applicants; for physical reasons only limited supplies can reach Dantzig, Constanza and Odessa. Does a Com^{ee} consisting of four British, Chinese, Russian and American representatives sitting in Washington settle these matters over the heads of the Russian Army and others concerned? Or what?'

'Does the Russian representative refer every major point to his Gov^t?' 'Does the Director-General refer every major point to his Comm^{ee}?' Again 'Does the Director-General deal *direct* with the military authorities and with refugee gov^{ts}?' And so on. In short what does it all mean in practical terms?

A revised proposal for a relief organisation became available on 18 August and serious discussions began in London on Leith-Ross's return in September. Keynes had meetings with Leith-Ross and the American Ambassador in late September and took part in the Treasury and inter-departmental discussions prior to the exploratory meetings with the Dominions on post-war matters, including relief, during October and early November. After those meetings, Leith-Ross prepared a long memorandum on the proposed relief administration. After a discussion of this draft with its author, Keynes commented.

To MR DUNNETT *and others, 18 November 1942*

SIR F. LEITH-ROSS'S NEW MEMORANDUM ON RELIEF ADMINISTRATION

This memorandum is valuable in that it brings to a head a number of important issues which have to be settled sooner or later. But many of these matters are not, I think, conveniently discussed at a very large inter-departmental gathering of 30 persons or more without prior ministerial instructions or, at least, indications as to the views of the Minister concerned or of the Government. This will be apparent, I think, if we take the issues one by one.

(1) Sir F. Leith-Ross again asks that H.M. Government should undertake to continue rationing in the U.K. so long as supplies (it is not clear whether in Europe or in the world at large) are not adequate for normal consumption. Personally I am in favour of a continuance of rationing. But it is a psychological and political question whether it is better to

announce this policy on the ground of shipping and exchange difficulties or whether it should be explained by the necessity of feeding Europe, including the enemy. It may be that the public after the war will welcome a continuance of hard times on the avowed ground that this is to feed (amongst others) the enemy. On the other hand, it may be better to put it on wider grounds.

(2) Sir F. Leith-Ross informs us that, as regards food, the Allied Governments have told him that 'they are prepared to accept an all-round rationing and have agreed to frame their estimates provisionally on the basis of U.K. rations suitably adjusted to known differences of standards of diet'. This general understanding is to be the basis of the proposal for continued rationing in this country. I feel that this presumes an all-round equality of treatment which is difficult to interpret and is likely to lead to serious political difficulties. If it means that because, e.g., Poland has always had a lower standard of life than U.K., their rations will be correspondingly reduced so as to be as much below their pre-war standard as ours is below our pre-war standard, the whole thing is rather meaningless. If, on the other hand, it refers to the kind of food eaten rather than the general standard of life, then it does presume a much greater degree of equality than used to prevail or is likely to prevail after the relief period is over. It not only raises the question whether the enemy is also to have the advantage of this equality, but also the question whether effective Allies, such as Greece and Norway, are to be no better treated than, e.g. Denmark, and, above all, perhaps the question whether those countries which are in a position to pay for their food are to have no more than those who are the recipients of charity. In short, it seems to go far ahead of any existing public opinion or of any discussions or decisions by Ministers and to be an example of an issue which it is not very helpful to begin discussing at a large inter-departmental gathering.

(3) Sir F. Leith-Ross enquires on behalf of the Allied Governments 'whether the needs of the Great Powers, including the

U.K., not only for food, but *also for raw materials*, are to be met out of a common pool, or whether these Powers intend to take what they require first'. The memorandum goes on to point out that, if a genuine pooling of supplies is intended, everybody's import programme must be submitted to an international authority making allocations on similar principles. If not, those who have money to pay must all be on the same basis. And (what seems to be a complete *non sequitur*), in this case, countries without resources 'will expect H.M.G. to insure supplies to them on a similar scale'. The implication of all this is that the best plan would be to have a genuine pooling of supplies.

This passage seems to me to indicate a truly fearful confusion of mind. The treatment of the complete import programme of all countries on similar principles, whether they have any resources to pay for them or not, reaches a degree of international communism which seems to go far beyond any known public opinion or any known or probable ministerial decisions. The suggestion seems to be that it should include us but not, so far as one can judge, the United States or the rest of the British Commonwealth.

I speak of a confusion of mind because it entirely ignores the special problems of a country like ourselves which, unless it is to go on living permanently on charity, must develop its exports. The principle suggested would mean that we could have no raw materials for export trade until, e.g., Poland has been put in an entirely similar position. It completely ignores the question of Russia, which no doubt would lap up all that was coming to it but whose degree of need or how the proceeds were used we should know nothing whatever about. Indeed it is a sheer piece of insanity, which is very alarming as coming from the British representative on the International Relief Organisation. I return below to the question of how best to distinguish between the 'relief' and the 'non-relief' countries. For the memorandum does do a service in calling attention to the acute issues involved.

Sir F. Leith-Ross asks to be put in a position to give an

assurance to the Allied Governments, in advance of any assurance whatever from the U.S. Government as to their contributions, that U.K. stocks and contracts in existence at the end of the war would be made available to the relief organisation. How far the safeguards introduced into the original version of this proposal (which are in effect such as to deprive it of any real value beyond eye-wash) are to be retained is not very clear. The main point is that for us to anticipate the United States with offers of relief must tend to create a false impression that we are in a position to take the leading part in all this.

(4) The next section deals with transport and shipping. This paragraph overlooks the probability that by far the greater part of the surplus shipping in the world at the relevant date will be within the control of the United States. No doubt, Sir F. Leith-Ross is right that plans on an inter-allied basis should be prepared. But the threats he holds out against us if we do not immediately proceed accordingly (and it is not by any means wholly on us that the decision rests) seem inappropriate. We are told that the Allies other than ourselves will then segregate their own tonnage for their own purposes and 'less fortunate Allies will then look to H.M.G. to provide them with shipping'. Not a word to the effect that the real surplus of shipping will be in the hands of the United States.

(5) On the question of finance, Sir F. Leith-Ross admits that further progress must await discussions in the United States, but adds that we ought to be thinking out which alternatives would be preferable from our point of view. This matter was in fact discussed in an earlier Treasury memorandum about as fully as is possible until we have some clue as to the lines on which the U.S. are likely to operate.

(6) Sir F. Leith-Ross calls attention to the difficulties likely to arise if Allied countries are required to pay for their food whilst the enemy receive food without payment. He suggests a provision requiring ultimate repayment by ex-enemy countries, which may be the only practicable solution of the dilemma. But

this runs into the question of reparations and the priority of various claims against the ex-enemy countries, including restitution and costs of occupation. It will not prevent the awkwardness that, for the time being, they are getting supplies without payment, whereas others are not. Possibly this may be partly met by the ex-enemy countries possessing some resources (surely Germany will end the war with some stock of gold), which could be applied in the first instance.

(7) Finally comes the question of the wider representation of Allies on the Anglo-American joint boards. No doubt something will have to be done in this direction. But here again Sir F. Leith-Ross handles the matter with what seem inappropriate threats. He suggests that the smaller Allies will be in a much stronger position to insist on whatever they want than can possibly be the case in practice. Probably it would be advisable to have some representation of the outstanding shipping powers, Norway, Holland and Greece on the shipping committee. But I should have thought that the other departments concerned were right in resisting a transformation of the existing boards into boards in any way effectively representing the United Nations as a whole. Those who are in fact providing the resources must retain the effective voice. All this seems to me to be a way of working up a fracas between the haves and the have-nots, rather than the opposite.

I turn to a general consideration. The chief lesson which this memorandum impresses on my mind is the importance of avoiding confusion between relief countries and non-relief countries. Since we have been looking forward to some possible continuance of lend lease after the war, and since we see little prospect of being self-supporting in the early period without some kind of loan, we are slipping into the position of being a relief country. Once that happens, one can see that, unless the United States strongly appreciates the unreasonableness of it, we, one of the victors in the war, shall slip into the position of

Poland, whilst Russia can be relied on to sail away quite safely, vouchsafing no information and obtaining the best of both worlds, victor and victim, have and have-not, relief and non-relief, simultaneously.

My first thought is that a line might perhaps be drawn between those countries which receive outright relief as such and those who have to obtain a loan in part to ease their situation, but are aiming, broadly speaking, at being self-supporting. Without prejudice to a tapering off of lend lease and to a continuance of it in some shape or form for a short period of (say) six months, it looks to me as though we must aim at being ourselves in the self-supporting class, and that any assistance we receive, apart from the tapering off of lend lease, must be on the basis of a repayable loan. Very probably Holland will want to take the same line, France and Belgium ought to. There may be one or two marginal cases. It is not quite easy to predict whether Russia would wish to be a relief or a non-relief country. But there are a number of those who will clearly fall within the relief category. Similarly in Asia. Australasia and India would clearly be non-relief countries, Burma and Malaya relief countries, China probably a relief country. We are then left with three categories: the non-relief countries; the relief Allies; and the ex-enemies. The first category would, of course, have to conform to such agreed poolings or controls as existed in regard to shipping or raw materials, this applying to the United States no less than to anyone else. But they would not be expected to conform to the same principles of allocation as the relief or the ex-enemy countries. The relief countries would receive supplies on as generous a scale as the resources at the disposal of the relief administration might permit, but there would be no implication of complete equality between them and the non-relief countries. Supplies to the ex-enemy countries would be worked out again on a third set of principles.

Sir F. Leith-Ross has produced so devastating a document because he in effect imposes on this poor country all the

burdens, obligations and limitations of being simultaneously a relief and a non-relief country. I repeat the question, whether such issues as those outlined above are suitably discussed at this stage by a vast inter-departmental gathering without ministerial direction?

KEYNES

The result of Keynes's minute was some delay in the work of the inter-departmental committee considering the relief proposals while the Treasury made up its mind. As the Treasury discussions progressed and the work of the inter-departmental committee resumed, Keynes turned away from relatively brief notes of criticism and back to the problem of relief finance. Stimulated initially by some proposals by S. D. Waley and following extensive discussions with Leith-Ross, Keynes prepared an extensive memorandum on the finance of post-war relief which went to both the Chancellor and Leith-Ross on 6 January 1943.

FINANCE OF POST-WAR RELIEF

1. It is to be expected that relief will have to be put into practice on a fairly extensive scale before the war comes to an end. This will necessarily occur if the reconquest of Europe is gradual and does not come about by a sudden collapse, or if the war in the Pacific outlasts the war in Europe. Thus, inevitably, at the outset relief arrangements will have to fit in to the war organisation and, if they have been running on these lines for a period, it is not likely that they will be reorganised in a hurry on different principles. On the assumption that a United Nations Relief and Rehabilitation Administration is set up in the near future, the general principles of the war arrangements will still have to be maintained for the time being; and even if a reorganisation is found necessary at a later stages, this is not our current problem or one which it is worth anticipating. Moreover, it is evident that the United States is starting on the lines of the existing war arrangements, and probably for them no other lines are

politically and constitutionally practicable without a great deal
of additional trouble and complication.

2. On the physical side this means that relief demands
become an additional set of demands to be considered by the
Combined Boards. The civilian requirements of all countries are
now to an increasing extent examined by the Combined Boards
and, whether or not they decide the relative priorities of relief,
the source of supply will naturally be settled by the same
procedure whilst the war lasts. This, of course, is without
prejudice to the question whether others of the United Nations
should be represented on the Combined Boards. However that
may be, it will be the task of the Combined Boards to co-ordinate
the relief demands with the civilian requirements of the rest of
the world (including U.S.A. and neutrals) and settle the best
sources of supply on shipping and other grounds. All our Supply
Departments support this procedure. No alternative is
practicable. Indeed, they would go further and would postpone
specific allocation to relief to the last possible moment so as to
avoid the danger of accumulating independent reserves for
different purposes in the same country or depot. Where for
reasons of urgency or of physical convenience the country
designated as the source of immediate supply requires subsequent replacement of the goods, it should be entitled to make
such replacement a condition of its compliance.

3. The allocation of sources of supply by the Combined
Boards would be solely concerned with 'efficiency' reasons on
the physical side, and the consequential financial considerations
would not fall within their sphere. This means that, when a
country is decided to be the appropriate source of supply, that
country would be responsible for making the appropriate
financial arrangements with the recipient country, and the
shipment of supplies, as recommended by the Combined
Boards, would or would not be conditional, as the case might
be, on arrangements for repayment (which are dealt with below).
In fact, the system would be a continuance for the time being

of the mixed cash-reimbursement and mutual aid arrangements adopted for war purposes.

4. On the financial side, that is to say, the arrangements would, as happens under the present lend lease regime, permit of payment being required in some cases while in other cases the supplies would be provided free. Some understanding would have to be reached with the U.S. about the criterion for deciding whether supplies should be paid for or provided as a gift. It would be reasonable for the United States to agree that a country should pay us if it has adequate sterling resources while getting supplies from the U.S. on lend lease terms if it has not adequate dollar resources. Generally speaking, we should expect payment from those countries which have sterling or gold resources available; but, where the United States or any other supplying country is also making a claim for cash reimbursement on the limited resources of a recipient country, it will be essential to get agreement on the policy to be followed. In particular, we must be prepared to agree that the sterling resources of a recipient country shall be available for payment to any member of the sterling area.

5. Subject to those financial arrangements, the donor government (be it the United States, Canada, Australia, the U.K. and Colonies, Portugal or Sweden) will find itself 'programmed' to supply various recipient governments and will recover the cost involved, where it has been agreed that it is a case for payment. When the Relief and Rehabilitation Administration has been set up, it would have to keep account of all supplies furnished, and it might have to be given some power of *virement* to meet emergency needs, especially where shipping services and supplies carried are furnished by different governments, or where there is a condition of replacement. But the general principles should be agreed beforehand so that the Administration will be able to distinguish between cases of payment and of non-payment.

6. These proposals are put forward on the ground that they

seem to be the only effective method immediately open to us of making relief supplies promptly available to meet urgent needs compatibly with the other demands on the limited resources. But they also have important advantages for their own sake. Under them the U.K. and Russia can continue to be regarded as entitled to receive civilian supplies under lend lease, and one may hope that the same system will continue, for a season at any rate, after the armistice. The system makes it possible to get to work without entering into premature obligations for large global amounts before any experience either of what is required or what can be supplied has been gained. For, under this conception there will be no central relief fund with a fixed limit any more than there is a central, fixed sum for lend lease and reciprocal aid. The U.S.A. would clearly have to play the major part as supplier; but we could play our part, in so far as our more limited resources permit, on the same general basis without, however, being involved in equal liabilities.

7. On the other hand, the arrangement would, undoubtedly, give large powers to the Combined Boards, and they might treat the United Kingdom as a source of supplies to the nations without resources to a greater extent than seems reasonable to us. Nevertheless, we are not signing a blank cheque since the Combined Boards are constitutionally no more than advisory bodies, recommending allocations to the governments concerned, but leaving the ultimate decision to the supplying government itself.

8. Again, if this system is accepted, it will not be easy for the U.K., as a recipient of food and raw materials, to get more than the Combined Boards allocate to it. No doubt we shall continue to occupy an influential position on the Combined Boards and can look to them to act reasonably. But this does not alter the fact that we ourselves would be largely subject to an outside system of allocation, which would be continued for what might prove an appreciable length of time *after* the war.

9. If this general arrangement is adopted, the precise extent of the U.K. contribution to relief would be a matter for settlement as and when it appears that we are the most suitable source of supplies. But when the time comes for the U.S. Administration to ask Congress to appropriate a large sum for the purchase of stocks of food for relief, we ought to be in a position to indicate our own intentions, showing our readiness to contribute so far as we can. On this, the following points arise:

(1) It will be necessary to raise the matter with the other members of the British Commonwealth. Clearly we cannot take on ourselves the relief responsibilities of the rest of the British Commonwealth. So far as food supplies are concerned, the Dominions will obviously be in a much better position to assist than we shall be. The preliminary soundings which have taken place give good reason to expect that Canada, at any rate, is prepared to make an important contribution.

(2) The U.K. itself will have certain emergency food stocks in this country which can be released as soon as the military authorities are satisfied that the contingencies for which they have been prepared are not likely to arise; and we may also be in a position to provide certain supplies from army stocks or from current production in the U.K. (e.g. seeds and possibly coal) as soon as the war is over. (Where we have originally obtained supplies under lend lease or as a gift from Canada, we should of course make no charge for such supplies when furnished to others as relief. The U.S.A. or Canada would obtain any payments due from the recipient.)

(3) The U.K. can do still more by allowing temporary withdrawals from other stocks in the U.K. against replacement. In such cases, it should be laid down that, where supplies have to be replaced from elsewhere, the Combined Boards should be responsible for securing replacement and arranging for the financial settlement to be passed on to the ultimate supplier. It

is very important to establish this principle, since it will facilitate the physical pooling of supplies and will make less necessary the segregation of separate supply stocks. If, therefore, the Combined Boards recommend that any stocks in the U.K. should be drawn upon, which we consider it necessary to replace, our representative on the Combined Board would only agree to the proposal provided effective arrangements are made by the Board to secure replacement from one or other of the producing countries.

(4) We should be prepared to accept responsibility as ultimate suppliers for such things, in addition to British produce, as army surplus stores, British shipping services and stocks of commodities of which we hold substantial surpluses, such as wool, Egyptian cotton and cocoa, though in certain cases, other powers, such as Australia or Egypt, may be partners with us and would have to agree, therefore, to the proposed arrangements.

(5) The best way of treating shipping services will need careful study. But presumably the question whether or not they are paid for should be governed by the same principles as would apply if we are furnishing goods. The U.K. have already agreed to furnish a certain quota of wheat or, alternatively, its equivalent in shipping services. If, as seems probable, sufficient wheat will be available from other sources, it will be desirable that the supply of shipping services to countries unable to pay for them should be the alternative adopted by the U.K.

(6) We shall need to cover in cash the expenditure of the relief administration in the U.K. and probably a share also of their expenditure on personnel and organisation abroad. This the Treasury have already agreed to in principle.

III

10. It may be useful to indicate how the financial arrangements suggested above might work out in certain particular cases. That relief shall leave no debts behind is the principle followed

throughout. Where a country has no immediate means of payment, no payment shall be expected.

(1) Poland, Czechoslovakia and Yugoslavia are outstanding examples of countries which have no important gold or sterling resources and would have to be supplied through relief gifts.

(2) Belgium and the Netherlands, on the other hand, both have substantial gold assets. In addition to this, at the end of September last the Netherlands had sterling balances of £m15·5 and the Belgian Congo of £m11·6. The indications are that both these countries would expect to pay in the ordinary way for relief supplies from United Kingdom and sterling area sources.

(3) France has very large amounts of gold, part of which is within our custody. Since her sterling balances proper are not very large in relation to her possible requirements (France £m18·8 and Free France £m6·2 on September 30th last), it would be necessary to raise the question of the use of gold at an early stage with whatever authority we consider to represent liberated France. This gold was frozen after the fall of France and has not, therefore, suffered depletion from war costs, except in so far as Germany has been able to purloin a small proportion (which, however, she will be expected to return). We should, therefore, explain in good time that we regard relief supplies as chargeable against the gold in our custody.

(4) At the end of September last Norway had no less than £m50 of sterling balances, which is likely considerably to exceed her requirements from British sources. As to the adequacy of her dollar resources we have no information.

(5) Greece at the same date had £m46·8. A substantial part of this is, from our point of view, a debt repayable by the Greek Government to us, and, from their point of view, the property of the National Bank as cover for the note issue. It would have to be for discussion with the Greeks whether one thing should be set off against the other, we remitting the debt if they agree to apply this strictly to relief. At any rate, there seems to be

enough to go on with, so far as we are concerned. Greece's dollar resources are not likely to be appreciable.

(6) Arrangements already exist for the finance of all supplies to Russia, and there is no reason for us to take the initiative in revising this. When the post-war period is reached, we could certainly expect to get a considerable off-set in the shape of exports (e.g. timber) from Russia.

(7) Relief to the enemy countries raises questions of principle not yet decided. Presumably an effort will be made to require payment from them in one shape or another.

Leith-Ross's reaction to Keynes's draft was not unfavourable 'allowing', as Keynes put it to Sir Wilfrid Eady on 11 January, 'for the fact that he is a maniac for the principle that everybody should supply everybody else free of charge on some sort of basis of international communism for a number of years to come'.[3] He tried to alter the drafting in a few places, but in the end contented himself with one small, inconsequential change. As revised, the memorandum, with the Chancellor's approval, became Treasury policy.

During this period Keynes remained, as usual, in close contact with Mr Penrose of the American Embassy. In early 1943, Penrose was preparing a report for the Inter-Allied Post-War Requirements Bureau on the likely food needs of the liberated areas in the 'emergency period' immediately after liberation.[4] He kept Keynes supplied with drafts of his report. On reading the drafts and discussing them with Penrose and L. J. Cadbury, a fellow director of the Bank of England, Keynes wrote to Leith-Ross.

To SIR FREDERICK LEITH-ROSS, *4 March 1943*

Dear Leith-Ross,

Dr Penrose has recently called my attention on several occasions to the extreme value for emergency relief purposes in Europe of the vitaminised chocolate which can now be produced.

[3] Keynes to Eady, 11 January 1943 (T160/1404/F18642/7).
[4] See Penrose, *Economic Planning for the Peace* (Princeton, 1953), pp. 133–9 for a discussion of the report.

He thinks that there is no more convenient or more helpful way of carrying to the children of Europe the essential vitamins and other chemicals they lack. Apparently chocolate can now be impregnated with these to any desirable extent. It keeps indefinitely. It is very nourishing. It is very substantially a substitute for the fats which are bound to be in short supply. It is also, if one wishes, a very convenient way of conveying milk, since almost any desired proportion of milk can be worked into chocolate.

After hearing this, it seemed to me that this might possibly be a very suitable form in which we could prepare a part of our contribution to immediate relief. I have not gone into the matter in any detail. But the following results of some brief preliminary enquiries look promising.

20,000 tons of chocolate held in reserve would be a very large amount and go a long way. It would cost about £2,000,000. We have, as you well know, a surplus supply of cocoa, not merely in West Africa, but actually, to some extent, in this country. The amount of sugar involved, namely about 9,000 tons, is small in relation to our stocks. I am told that there is redundant plant and no physical obstacle to manufacturing the stuff and holding it in reserve, except difficulties of labour. If a reserve of 20,000 tons were to be built up over a year, this would mean production at the rate of 400 tons a week. This would occupy the labour of 800 persons, 400 men and 400 women. Now, I notice in the latest return of unemployment that, though this is a small industry, and those concerned are few in number, nevertheless, relatively the figures would go some way to the above. In the cocoa, chocolate and sugar confectionery industry there are about 400 unemployed, 150 men and 300 women.

It seems to me that the amount of labour diversion which would be required to carry out this programme is very small in relation to the possible benefits. Moreover, it could probably be brought about without any diversion of labour whatever, merely by a reduction in the existing chocolate ration.

I believe that vitaminised chocolate is already being manufactured for the War Office and that they have some moderately large-scale experience in the matter. I suppose, however, that it would be the Ministry of Food which is chiefly concerned.

Anyway, I throw this out as a useful measure, for which we are perhaps particularly well qualified, for your consideration.

Yours ever,
[copy initialled] K.

Leith-Ross acknowledged the letter on 9 March but saved his reply until 19 April. The correspondence then continued.

From SIR FREDERICK LEITH-ROSS, *19 April 1943*

My dear Keynes,

With further reference to your letter of 4th March about vitaminised chocolate, I have been pressing the Food Ministry to get on with this, but Maud tells me that there are a good many difficulties. Experiments are still taking place as to the keeping qualities of the vitaminised product and there is an actual shortage of vitamin C. Finally the Food Ministry say (Ration X8323) that apart from any vitamin supply difficulties, it seems probable that our manufacturing capacity with concentrated industry would not exceed 5,000 tons in 1943.

I am asking Maud to pursue the question as rapidly as possible and I hope that you will give me your support in trying to secure the maximum production possible when the other difficulties have been cleared up.

Yours sincerely,
F. W. LEITH-ROSS

To SIR FREDERICK LEITH-ROSS, *25 April 1943*

Dear Leith-Ross,

VITAMINISED CHOCOLATE

I can, of course, say nothing about the keeping qualities of the product or the possibility of producing the necessary vitamin. I thought Penrose argued that it was a vitamin that lived well in fat, so that the keeping would be all right. On the

supply difficulties, however, I do think that one would be entitled to press those concerned considerably. For one thing, it would be thoroughly well justified to reduce the present chocolate ration to civilians in order to increase what could be put into store for relief. But, apart from this, as I mentioned, I think, in my previous letter, the amount of labour involved would be very small. In this connection Cadbury told me that when the chocolate industry was concentrated they closed down most of the efficient factories in England, because they happened to be in areas where labour was particularly scarce, and kept alive the less efficient manufacturers in Scotland. Today, however, the shortage of labour in the Scottish areas is just as serious as in the Midlands. He gave me some ratio—I forget what, but it was enormous—relating the efficiency of the closed down firms to those not closed down. The same manpower now employed, if working in the efficient factories, could, I formed the impression, provide the whole surplus you are looking for.

Yours,
[copy initialled] K.

During the rest of the negotiations that led to the founding of the United Nations Relief and Rehabilitation Administration (UNRRA), Keynes seems merely to have kept a watching brief. However, after one particularly trying inter-departmental committee on the exact functions of the organisation, he commented to Mr Dunnett, the official responsible.

To G. DUNNETT, *13 July 1943*

You have done your best, indeed all that is humanly possible! But whether I, therefore, know the answer to my question, I am not sure.

All this seems to me to be such frightful fundamental rubbish that one comment is as good as another. I cannot believe in chimaeras at my age.

I predict that the military will retain charge for a considerable time; that when we are in effective control of Europe we shall set up an Economic Council on the spot; and that those countries, such as Holland, which are paying for themselves will contract out of the Relief Section of the Economic Council.

Meanwhile we waste our words.

KEYNES

Keynes continued to describe UNRRA as a chimaera in the coming months as the Treasury continued to worry over its exact functions and the resulting financial implications. However, his major remaining contribution came during his autumn 1943 visit to Washington for the Article VII discussions. In the course of a discussion on UNRRA finance, H. D. White threw out the idea of using 1 per cent of a country's estimated national income as the basis of contributions. Keynes readily took up the suggestion, discussing it further with White before reporting.

To SIR RONALD CAMPBELL *and* R. LAW, *17 September 1943*

FINANCE OF EUROPEAN RELIEF

On my telling White that some of us were much attracted by his suggested formula for relief finance, he developed his ideas somewhat further as follows:

1. His idea of the mechanism would be that all supplies to Europe, whether gratuitous or reimbursible, should be invoiced in terms of money to the receiving parties and should indeed as soon as possible be handled on commercial lines. If the relief supplies were reimbursible, payment would be made by the recipient in the ordinary way. If they were non-reimbursible, then the supplying country would meet the invoices out of its quota of relief finance. There might have to be some general supervision for seeing that the prices were reasonable, this would be necessary anyhow. This invoicing in terms of money would apply equally to surplus stores, such as army cloth and boots, as it would to first-hand food or raw materials or machinery. This also seems a good idea and would ease the

transition, which one would wish to come about as soon as possible, into normal conditions.

2. He expressly added, what is of importance to us, that it would be convenient for transport services to be included in the price and he implied that the supplying country should be responsible for such transport charges. Financially this would be to our advantage. But I am not clear that it is right. It might be advisable in the case of non-reimbursible supplies shipped on British vessels that the costs of transport should be met out of our free credit.

3. It would be laid down strictly that the funds to be put up by a particular country would be only available for that country's own produce and for expenditure within its own boundaries. This would apply equally to the United States as to other countries supplying relief, but he would have it in mind if possible to introduce a joker into the appropriation to Congress to the effect that since it is important that relief supplies should interfere as little as possible with American domestic consumption, the Administration would be allowed a discretion to purchase from elsewhere with foreign exchange types of goods produced in America which it was not in fact convenient to supply from America because of local shortages. In this way he would in practice be able to use American funds to some extent, at least, to provide for cash purchases outside U.S.

4. He feels that if U.K. and Canada, and perhaps one or two other countries, with the hope of the rest of the world joining in later, were to agree to the flat 1 per cent this would strengthen the hands of the Administration in getting an initial percent relief allocation from Congress. At the same time he feels that this would be putting a too small burden on U.S. and if the rest do 1 per cent the U.S. ought to do more than 1 per cent. He suggested that possibly this might take the form of their offering to match with a higher percentage any other country offering a higher percentage (though I do not see quite how this would

work out in practice), or it might be if the 1 per cent fund proved inadequate that U.S. would supplement it whilst others would not be expected to ante up more than their original 1 percent.

5. On my asking what authority in Washington would have to take the initiative in getting a move on along these lines, he replied that it would be Governor Lehman.[5] He said that he is proposing to take an early opportunity of mentioning these ideas to Governor Lehman in detail. If later on we were sympathetic to them it would be a great help to him if our people could encourage the Governor along the same lines. I gathered that he may have already mentioned some sort of proposal of this kind in more general terms, but I do not think he has yet passed it on to others in the same detail.

KEYNES

Keynes himself took the matter up with Governor Lehman on 22 and 29 September. Lehman saw no snags in the idea and encouraged Keynes to push the idea forward, as he did in discussions with both London and the Americans. The proposal went to the first meeting of the UNRRA Council in Atlantic City and became the financial basis of the organisation.

Between October 1943 and the beginning of 1945 Keynes took even less part in discussions of UNRRA affairs beyond his then familiar warnings about future commitments and Britain's post-war economic position. However, by early 1945, the British were extremely conscious of the demands that would fall on them for future military, relief and reconstruction assistance throughout the world, as they were also of UNRRA's very limited activities in Greece, Yugoslavia and Italy, and were reconsidering the position. In this reconsideration, as expected, Keynes emerged as an even stronger critic of UNRRA as then organised and pursued his criticisms in a series of memoranda.

---

[5] Hon. Herbert H. Lehman (1878–1963); Director, U.S. Office of Foreign Relief, 1942–3; Director-General, UNRRA, 1943–6; U.S. Senator, 1949–57.

To SIR WILFRID EADY, *3 January 1945*

UNRRA AND BRITISH LIBERATED TERRITORIES
IN THE FAR EAST

I am very much of the opinion that Sir D. Waley is doing well to make a song and dance about this at the present moment. All the same, it will be very difficult to overcome the objection raised by Mr Dunnett. We might have started off differently, but we didn't. However much we may be sorry for this and dislike the consequences of the present position. I shall be rather surprised if it proves possible to overcome the state of existing commitment to which Mr Dunnett calls attention.

If so, this makes it all the more necessary to put into the common pool any further thoughts, constructive or otherwise, which one may have. The following are mine:

(1) I particularly dislike the idea of having to borrow from the U.S. Government for the purpose of rehabilitation in Burma and the Crown Colonies. Unless we are successful in merging this in our general requirements without making any specific request, there will be a considerable risk of this giving rise to the demand for a *quid pro quo* in the shape of what the President calls trusteeship. This is very near the surface of American policy and is especially dear to the President. This is a further reason, which may appeal to the Foreign Office and the Colonial Office, why, if any means can be found, we should bring UNRRA in. But, whilst it serves to fortify Sir D. Waley's position, it in no way helps us from the public point of view to overcome Mr Dunnett's difficulty.

(2) I should say that the amount of the assistance required is greatly overestimated. Mr Norman Young, in a paper below, argues that China's needs from UNRRA should be rationed to some such figure as 250 to 300 million dollars, though in fixing this figure he no doubt takes account of the fact that they already

have some additional dollar resources of their own, with which to supplement this. Even China's own maximum, admittedly fantastic, demand on UNRRA is no more than for 984 million dollars. Now we are told, apparently by our own authorities, that the requirements of Burma, Malaya and Hong Kong will be 1000 million dollars for relief alone, apart from a further 320 million dollars for rehabilitation. This estimate for relief exceeds China's own figure for herself and is three to four times Mr Young's figure. I should surmise that it is at least five times too high. I hope we shall get out of the habit of talking in these exaggerated terms as soon as possible.

(3) If we are unsuccessful in retracing our steps and bringing UNRRA in as regards these territories, at any rate we should regard their claims on us as dispensing with the necessity of any further contribution to UNRRA, even though there is a very proper claim for others to contribute more. If we decide that we cannot press for UNRRA assistance, we should at the same time decide that we should take any convenient opportunity of proclaiming the needs of our own territories as a reason why, in no circumstances, our contribution to UNRRA can be increased. It is also a reason why demands on us for relief during the military period should be kept to a minimum.

(4) Next, I would urge that this should be regarded, not as a United Kingdom, but as an Empire obligation. We ought to form an Empire pool, into which not only the Dominions, but as regards Burma, more particularly India, and as regards Malaya and Hong Kong the other Crown Colonies, should contribute. We cannot carry all these burdens unaided, and it will only lead in the end to humiliation if we try to. The balances of the Crown Colonies are so colossal that we ought to seek some contribution from them. Much the most seemly way of doing this would be to get them to make a fairly handsome contribution to the needs of their less fortunate brethren (or are they sisters?) amongst the other Crown Colonies.

(5) Finally, the really right thing to do is to liquidate

UNRRA and thus release our contribution to them, which in spite of its size, looks most unlikely to pull its weight. So far UNRRA is the world's greatest flop, and I see little likelihood of its recovering. It talks about having insufficient funds by way, I suppose, of providing an alibi, but, in practice, there is not a thing it does. The ideal course for us would be to carry on with the present military basis in the very small number of non-paying non-enemy countries and persuade the U.S.A. to revise the terms of this to the UNRRA proportions, which, if the UNRRA appropriation was to be released would be very easy for them. Through the disappointment with UNRRA we have been led along a path of nonsense. The sooner we take any opportunity to retrace our steps (which, of course, means a frank and fundamental discussion with Acheson) the better. I know we lack the genius (such as the Americans sometimes have) for drastic action; and that is the main cause of our undoing in many directions. But, if we accustom ourselves to the idea, we may come to see that here indeed is a case for drastic action.

Meanwhile, however, I agree with the line Sir D. Waley has been taking, namely, to leave the door open for our present policy to be reversed, though, as I have said, I have poor hopes of this ultimately happening.

KEYNES

From a memorandum to G. DUNNETT, *10 January 1945*

UNRRA

For a long time past it has been clear that an essential first step was to get rid of Lehman, who runs UNRRA as a branch of American politics, has his eye on Congress, is exceedingly timid and is physically incapable of racketing round the world, which the head of UNRRA must be prepared for, if he is to make a success of it, especially in the early days.

Instead of making a row and stirring things up, we appease, we turn a blind eye, we accept all the alibis produced, we pass

95

soporific resolutions of congratulation at international meetings and we provide the poor man with a staff no better than himself. That in practice is what 'everybody trying to make a success of UNRRA' seems to come to. Apologies! But it is because I am so much impressed with the vital importance, in all kinds of contexts, of adequate relief that I break out against accepting the existing situation.

I don't say that, if UNRRA is liquidated, nothing should succeed it. So, perhaps, I should amend my proposal to read, not a liquidation of UNRRA, but a radical reorganisation of its methods, its functions and its leadership.

From a memorandum to SIR WILFRID EADY, *21 February 1945*

I turn next to Mr Dunnett's memorandum on UNRRA. First of all, I should like to clear away a possible misunderstanding. I did not in my previous note on this subject intend that we should organise a unilateral breach with UNRRA. I entirely agree with Mr Dunnett that we must, certainly for the present, act in the closest possible collaboration with the Americans. If, however, he thinks that they are any more in love with the present set up of UNRRA than we are, I think he may be mistaken. If we handle the matter in the right way, I believe that we could get whole-hearted American support for a new and more comprehensive attack on the whole subject. Surely, it would be easy to persuade them that we must have an international body charged with the over-all problem of relief throughout the world, that UNRRA with its present constitution is lamentably failing to fill the bill and that we must, therefore, reconstitute UNRRA so that it can properly fulfil demands and requirements that can no longer be shirked or neglected.

I do not feel that Mr Dunnett takes sufficient account of the fact that UNRRA has not merely become constitutionally too limited in its functional outlook, which is partly its own fault and is partly not its own fault, but that even within its own limitations it is, under its present leadership, incapable of

efficient work. We shall be the accomplice in great misery and injustice if we deliberately shut our eyes to the fact that Lehman is not a leader capable of carrying the job. His staff, with some notable exceptions, is also dreadfully inadequate.

I advise, therefore, that what we should try to lead up to is a reorganisation of UNRRA in collaboration with the Americans. Nevertheless, as a first step and as a sort of compromise for immediate action, which might in the end lead to the right conclusion, I agree that there is much to be said for several of Mr Dunnett's recommendations.

Comply 1081, in which the State Department invite our opinion as to how essential Italian imports are to be financed after the cessation of the military period, brings us right up against one part of the problem, and gives us a peg on which to hang the first instalment of our observations. The later telegram, Comply 1169, commenting on this does not seem to me to help at all. In particular, the argument that UNRRA should not be brought in, because UNRRA is already arguing that it has not enough money, is the wrong approach. If UNRRA genuinely runs through all the money at present voted and can show that it has spent the money well and faithfully, there is no final obstacle to obtaining more on the UNRRA formula. Comply 1169 overlooks the essential fact that it is the preservation of the UNRRA formula which we have to do our best to maintain.

Let me begin by listing, perhaps incompletely, the problems which have to be faced.

(1) Relief in Germany.

(2) Relief in Austria.

(3) Relief in Italy after the end of the military period.

(4) Relief in Italy after the exhaustion of the present limit of amount for the military period.

(5) The paying Western Allies.

(6) The Balkans during the military period after the limit has been reached.

(7) The Balkans after the military period.

(8) Relief in Poland and other territories in Russian occupation.

(9) Relief in liberated British territories in the Far East.

(10) Relief in other Far Eastern territories.

(11) Refugees and displaced persons.

(12) Sanitation and health services.

Numbers (1), (2), (3), (4) and (6) are entirely unsolved. No provision of any sort has been made. In the case of (5) UNRRA has dropped out of the part one would have wished to see it play because it led the paying Allies to think at an early stage that its purpose would be to police rather than to help them. (11) I believe UNRRA is tackling to a certain extent, but is now backing out compared with what was originally intended. (12) I believe it undertakes in theory, though what scale of procurement has taken place I do not know. UNRRA has not been asked to undertake (9). (10) still lies in the future. (7) I believe UNRRA is committed to undertake. I believe that there are *pourparlers* about (8) and no doubt UNRRA will be expected to do something here in the long run.

When we first began to talk about UNRRA, we assumed that it would be a genuine international body covering the whole of the above, though, of course, not giving more to ex-enemies than was appropriate. I cannot see that there can be any other durable solution except reviving this plan. As appears from various telegrams, it would be most difficult to persuade the United States to take sole responsibility. We cannot afford to participate except on the UNRRA proportions and when the need arises to increase the UNRRA aggregate, we must aim to charge as deductable instalments against any new quota attributed to us what we have supplied during the military period and what we may have to supply to British territories in the Far East. That will preserve the principle that we contribute in the UNRRA proportion to the over-all relief problem.

I would urge, therefore, that we should take the earliest opportunity to secure the approval of Ministers to a major

démarche to the Americans on these lines. I would also urge that this is a matter in which the Chancellor ought to take the lead.

Meanwhile, as purely stop-gap arrangements, I think, as I have said above, there is something to be said for Mr Dunnett's suggestions, though, in the long run, they seem to me to lead us nowhere. For example, if we could get a breathing space by raising the military limit to $500 million, our proportion falling so that the burden on us remains the same, that would clearly be a useful step. But obviously that only gains us a very brief breathing space.

As regards Germany, I should try to protect UNRRA from excessive ultimate liability by the formula for making relief a first charge on reparations which I have suggested in a separate note.

The other interim measure I should favour would be to adopt an entirely *non possumus* attitude towards U.S. as regards future relief. Inform them that we cannot increase our present obligation on the present formulas, and they must not look to us for any further contribution in any part of the world. But, at the same time, I should say to them that we are in favour of getting back to a true conception of UNRRA. And, less officially, we should say in plain language what they already know perfectly well, that Governor Lehman must go, and probably a good many members of his staff, as an indispensable condition of bold and comprehensive management.

KEYNES

The upshot was that Britain and the Americans asked UNRRA to provide relief in full in Italy both during and after the military period. When this was agreed in London, Britain provided a second 1 per cent contribution, despite her financial straits, in August 1945.

In February 1946, at the end of the day, for UNRRA did not receive a third contribution, Keynes summed up the experience in a memorandum.

To SIR DAVID WALEY, *14 February 1946*

POST-UNRRA RELIEF

This file is an outstanding example of your thesis that Whitehall is stronger in heart than in the head. I find very little in this file which appeals to the head except the Treasury view that, in no circumstances, should we encourage the idea of the continuation of UNRRA; but the file certainly tends to improve as it reaches nearer the surface.

Unless the file is to go rather further back on its traces, I do not find much to complain of in your letter to Liesching. But it seems to me that, if we are not to be relied on for much further relief, the consequences go somewhat deeper.

In particular, the view that UNRRA should continue during the first half of this year and as long as possible thereafter on as handsome lines as possible implicitly assumes that UNRRA relief, or its equivalent, is not suddenly coming to an end. It is based on what I should have thought is the altogether mistaken idea that, if we fatten the chaps up for the next six months (and, of course, in practice we shall not be making them fat at all), that gives us the best chance of their standing on their own legs. My view would be that, if the total available for relief is on the inadequate side, it should be tapered off as gradually as possible. In fact these countries will never stand on their own legs so long as they can stand on someone else's. At some point the aids have to be removed. I should have thought it would be wiser to remove them gradually rather than suddenly. I should, therefore, have been in favour of spacing out UNRRA support so as to make it cover as long a period as possible. The difficulties of physical supply is another argument pointing in the same direction.

The next step in the argument would be to limit narrowly the list of countries which look likely to be fairly strong candidates for post-UNRRA relief. I think most of us agree that these are Italy, Austria and Greece. Poland is an agricultural

country, the requirements of which, after the initial period, are essentially reconstruction, and therefore, come under another heading. China is on a scale quite beyond our capacities and, anyhow, is a favourite candidate for unilateral American assistance; so here also we all agree, I think, that we can leave China out of our picture. All this reinforces, of course, the Treasury view that a continuation of UNRRA is not a good solution. If UNRRA continues, everyone will have to have its bit, very likely including Russia as well as Czechoslovakia, Jugoslavia and Poland. Indeed, it would be crazy to continue on purpose all the unnecessary headaches UNRRA has given us. Besides which, there is a recent message from Sir Wilfrid Eady, which you will have seen, to the effect that the chances of U.S.A. continuing to help UNRRA are nil. (Although they have so much more blood than we with which to sustain the heart, nevertheless the head is not so completely out of the picture.)

When one reaches the next stage of making any suggestion about the source of giving post-UNRRA help to Austria, Italy and Greece, I confess that the head begins to get rather perplexed. But I am inclined to think that the only hope is along very much the lines that you obviously have in mind, namely, that Italy and Austria should become American responsibilities, whilst we, if necessary, should take any responsibility we can manage for Greece. In my opinion the latter should take the form of allowing Greece to use her sterling balances. It is perfectly preposterous for us to give still further gratuitous relief to a country to whom at present we owe more than £50 million. The time for further assistance to Greece should not arise until their sterling balances are virtually nil, or, at any rate, have no excess over a minimum working figure.

I see no purpose in giving fancy figures for the aggregate post-UNRRA relief. Certainly not $750 million. Equally, I should have thought, not $500 million, which has no sound estimating behind it and looks to me still far too high.

I should, therefore, start the cable to Washington all over

again. I should begin by pointing out that, in view of the present policy of the Cabinet, they should be preparing on the assumption that there will be no further contribution from this country. They should approach their American colleagues with this news and ask them whether, in the light of it, they do not think it would be prudent to spread the existing UNRRA finance over as long a period as possible. Clearly a sudden cessation from liberal assistance to nil would be the worst possible arrangement. Unless the Americans are prepared to continue the work of UNRRA, perhaps with a little help from Canada, would not a tapering off be the right plan? If not, what do the Americans intend to happen when the UNRRA relief comes suddenly to an end?

The telegram might go on to say that, whilst we should like to see the UNRRA money last as long as possible, we certainly do not suggest that UNRRA itself should be given any further funds. We believe we are correct in thinking that that is also the attitude of the State Department. However that may be, the continuation of UNRRA would probably involve all the UNRRA countries getting a bit, whereas, in our judgment, there are no proper claims outside Italy, Austria and Greece.

There is one other private heresy of my own, which I should like to mention to you. Money loans and money reparations having worked out badly last time, we decided this time not to make the same mistake, and, therefore, have tried to turn everything into supplies and deliveries in kind. But experience shows that this has been a mistake of the opposite character and perhaps on the whole an even worse one. Perhaps it was inevitable in the early days before governments were established, but I believe it to be an utterly mistaken arrangement to-day. The remaining UNRRA funds should be divided in cash between the different recipients. UNRRA should provide procurement facilities to the best of its abilities to any country which desires to use them. Subject to this and to a clear understanding that the finance handed over was all they were

going to get, I should leave the recipient countries to spend the money to what they themselves think is the best advantage, leaving them to spread it over as long a period as possible and to take the consequences, if they do not so choose. In the case of scarce commodities, the allocations would, of course, have to be decided by the Combined Boards or other authority, possibly UNRRA itself. But, so far as possible, the countries themselves should have the spending of the money. They should also enjoy the proceeds, that is to say, they should be encouraged to sell the UNRRA supplies to their own public for as much cash as they could possibly get out of it and take in that cash in support of their public finances. It seems to me that the above would be an exhibition of head which did no injury to heart.

KEYNES

Chapter 3

COMMODITY POLICY

The discussions of surplus policy during 1940 and 1941 had touched on the problems of post-war commodity production and prices, as had the discussions of possible commodity agreements covering wheat and cotton. In his contributions to discussions, Keynes had touched on these problems and his early drafts of the Clearing Union carried some provision for international buffer stock arrangements. However, it was after the end of 1941 before he found an opportunity to devote himself to the details of such arrangements, even though he had received some encouragement earlier from R. F. Harrod and others to try his hand at such a scheme for inclusion with the Clearing Union in the Treasury's package of post-war proposals.

Early in 1942 work on a scheme began. On 6 January, Keynes reported to R. F. Harrod that he had dug out his 1938 article in the area[1] but had not gone further. By 20 January, however, he had completed a preliminary draft of a scheme which he circulated in the Treasury. He also sent copies to Leith-Ross, Harrod and Caine.

Unfortunately, this original draft, along with succeeding drafts of early February, late March and early April have not survived. This is doubly unfortunate because much of the correspondence on these drafts has survived. However, from the surviving correspondence, one can catch a glimpse of the issues raised by the early drafts and Keynes's attitudes to them. The outstanding issues raised in these discussions (as far as one can tell from the correspondence) and Keynes's reactions to or solutions for them were as follows.

(1) Should the scheme be Anglo-American or international in conception and in the early stages of its evolution? This point was naturally raised by R. F. Harrod, who at the time was the strongest Whitehall advocate of strictly Anglo-American arrangements for post-war planning. On this point, Keynes minuted.

---

[1] 'The Policy of Government Storage of Foodstuffs and Raw Materials', *Economic Journal*, September 1938 (*JMK*, Vol. XXI).

From a minute to SIR RICHARD HOPKINS, *23 February 1942*

On merits I agree with Harrod that there is a great deal to be said for Anglo-American control. If one is looking at it from the point of view of establishing sensible arrangements at a sufficiently early date and of the practical working of a difficult novelty, it is evident that the fewer those who have to be consulted, the easier it will all be.

On the other hand, I see great difficulties in getting such exclusiveness accepted. I do not agree with Harrod that such exclusiveness is likely to commend itself to the Americans. They will think we are trying to nobble them. Moreover we, on our side, will necessarily want to bring in the other members of the British Commonwealth. If so (and clearly we must bring them in), the Americans will want to balance this with Pan-Americanism and introduce the South American countries.

Then, as recognised by Harrod in his paragraph 5, it would scarcely be possible not to give a special position to Russia for certain and perhaps China also. By then it will be difficult to see how the Dutch can be excluded, and so on. By that time, evidently, one has to find some different criterion as to where to draw the line.

Apart from the above political difficulties, it seems to me awkward to exclude from the Commodity Control Scheme in particular any country which is largely interested in one of the commodities controlled; though this might be overcome by allowing in any particular scheme representation of all important producers and consumers, whilst not allowing them an equal position in the management of the control schemes in general.

I am inclined to think that the right compromise is to argue out the details of the plan in conjunction with the Americans without bringing in anyone else at that stage, but making it clear to one another that this is merely for the purpose of keeping order in the preliminary discussions. Nor would it follow at the next stage that *any* country could be allowed in merely for

the asking. We might begin with invitations to members of the British Commonwealth and of the Pan-American Union and to those Allies who are actually engaged in fighting, that is to say the Russians, the Chinese and the Dutch. In practice this means leaving for later consideration the occupied and enemy countries and certain minor powers, such as Sweden, Portugal and Spain, in whose case there is not much reason for participation in advance of the rest of Europe.

(2) What was the relationship between the price stabilisation aspects of the scheme and the problem of the trade cycle? In the first draft, Keynes only briefly mentioned this problem, while he concentrated more on the problems of particular producers and commodities. He admitted, however, to R. F. Harrod on 10 February that this issue 'was scandalously omitted in the first draft, due to haste in preparation and keeping too closely to my old E.J. article'. The second and later drafts attempted to treat the problem in more detail.

(3) How large should price fluctuations be in the scheme? Keynes's early drafts had proposed that the intervention prices be 10 per cent above and below the base price for each commodity. He also proposed that the base prices in the scheme could move by up to 5 per cent per annum. Some critics argued that 5 per cent was too large and that 2 per cent would be more appropriate, while others believed that 5 per cent was too rigid and that the control should be able to make larger short-term changes in exceptional circumstances so as to avoid disrupting the market. The Bank of England, using the analogy of exchange markets, suggested that the $\pm$ 10 per cent range was too narrow, as it would leave the situation open for speculators to make large profits. Keynes commented.

From a minute to SIR RICHARD HOPKINS, *15 April 1942*

(1) The Bank comparison with currency management is a false analogy. Currencies were not bought and sold at a difference of 20 per cent in the price. The buying and selling prices differed by a mere fraction. The whole nature of the control was wholly different from what is here proposed. Moreover, as Mr Waley has pointed out, the currency control was supplying foreign currency out of assets which were far from inexhaustible and

which speculators knew were far from inexhaustible. There is no sort of analogy here to the buffer stock controls.

(2) I should not myself expect that the outside speculator would find it worth while to operate when the possible fluctuations were within the limits proposed. His expenses would soon eat him up. This would not apply to professional merchants in the commodity in question. They endeavour to make their profits out of comparatively small turns, and it would greatly facilitate their tasks to be protected from extreme fluctuations and the risks attendant on them. But surely that is all to the good. I should claim this as one of the principal merits of the scheme. It would enable merchants to do their stuff within the prescribed limits of price range without having to run excessive risks. Except in cases where a surplus or deficiency was clearly in sight their operations might be expected to produce a still narrower range of fluctuation within the range set by the controls. Besides, they would relieve the control of an immense amount of day to day detail. I contemplate that in normal circumstances the bulk of the trade would go on exactly as at present through the professional merchants, who understand the business and satisfy with their services both producers and consumers. The fact that the business of the merchant is facilitated is a gain, not a loss.

(4) What was the relation of his buffer stock scheme to output restriction schemes which represented an alternative method of achieving stability in commodity markets? Were such schemes merely alternative means of covering all commodities? Or were different schemes appropriate for different commodities? These questions were raised in a minor way by the Colonial Office and in a more substantial way by the Ministry of Economic Warfare. J. W. F. Rowe of the Ministry argued that Keynes's buffer stock proposals were not applicable to commodities whose supply varied considerably with harvest yields due to weather, etc., as producers' unit costs varied widely. Minimum prices in these cases would lead to an expansion of output, particularly by high-cost producers, and the range of price fluctuations was too narrow to lead to output declines where necessary. As a result, output restriction would be necessary for such commodities as a supplement to the Keynes scheme. Keynes replied:

1. I do not agree that the scheme is not applicable to agricultural crops. He does not seem to me to allow enough for the fact that the price can fluctuate 20 per cent without any change in the basic price. Now it is quite true that the crop of an individual country can easily fluctuate in volume by more than 20 per cent. But in such case no conceivable international scheme can stabilise agricultural incomes in that individual country, since a different price would be required from the price anywhere else. If, on the other hand, you take the aggregate of all world producers, it would be abnormal for total world crops, e.g. of wheat or maize, to fluctuate by so much as 20 per cent. Thus, for the producers of the commodity as a whole there is a wide enough range of prices to allow reasonable stabilisation of income. Moreover, if the total world crop does fluctuate by 30 or 40 per cent, it is much better for all concerned that the buffer stocks should look after the excess fluctuation without allowing a corresponding price change. If, in such abnormal circumstances, the incomes of the producers do fluctuate by 10 or 20 per cent, that will be so excessively mild a phenomenon compared with what takes place at present that it is nothing to bother about.

Thus, so far from agreeing that the scheme is not applicable to agricultural commodities, I would claim that it is particularly applicable to them and would combine the interests of consumers and producers much more satisfactorily than any alternative I can think of.

2 (*a*) If a price 10 per cent below the basic price nevertheless induces an expansion of output by high cost producers, surely this would indicate that the price was too high. Under my plan the price would be reduced until it no longer had this stimulating effect. I should say that that, and not restriction, is the right remedy. Rowe may truly be right that the attraction of a guaranteed price will be very great. But, if so, we must get the benefit of this in the guaranteed price being appreciably lower

than the prices we have been used to in the past. If the effect of the guarantee, by diminishing risk, brings down effective costs all over the world by a significant amount, what higher praise could one give to the scheme? One would certainly not want to defeat this admirable consequence by trying to offset it by restriction.

2 (b) It seems to me that this only arises if restriction is a significant part of the plan, which is just what I want to avoid. In my scheme as drafted there will be no incentive to high cost producers to stay out of the scheme, since the scheme will be supplying world consumers at a moderate price. If the high cost producers want to stay out, let them. It will do them no good.

2 (c) Like some other critics, Rowe has, I think, overlooked the point that the small price decline of 5 per cent per annum is superimposed on the 20 per cent range round the basic price. A change of 5 per cent annum cumulative, together with this range, seems to me to be very large. Some critics have said it was too large. Others, like Rowe, have said that it was too small. I have mentioned this percentage as an indication and would not propose to bind the managers of the scheme not to make larger changes if required. But, as at present advised, it looks to me somewhere about right as a general rule.

As for the related Bank of England charge that the scheme was too *laissez-faire* and that no alternative to long-term planning existed, Keynes minuted:

From a minute to SIR RICHARD HOPKINS, *15 April 1942*

(3) One wonders whether the Governor really knows what his institution is advocating. I infer from the reference in (2) to 'a solution by way of international agreements on price and quantities' that the Bank consider the buffer stock proposals to be far too *laissez-faire*, in as much as they still allow a place for private trading. International agreements, by which prices were absolutely fixed and quotas rigidly determined for every pro-

ducer and perhaps for every consumer also, so as to freeze or stereotype world trade into a mould—what mould, calculated on what principles, I have no idea—seem to me terrifying, not least from our own special point of view.

(4) I suspect that this bias towards rigidly controlled state trading on Russian lines influences the general critical approach. The same bias seems to appear in (4) of the Deputy Governor's letter. In reply to his (4) I can only plead guilty of aiming at a plan which does take a middle course between unfettered competition under *laissez-faire* conditions and planned controls which try to freeze commerce into a fixed mould. At the same time, I admit that the draft sent to the Bank was open to criticism, or at any rate to misunderstanding, in the passage where the long-term economic price is discussed. I have endeavoured to remedy this in the text now in your hands.

(5) On what basis should prices be set under the scheme? Keynes in his earliest draft began by suggesting that a cost of production basis, ascertainable by ordinary accounting methods, might prove useful. However, under the influence of S. Caine of the Colonial Office he came to realise that with peasant producers the prices of competitive products might prove more useful.

(6) How would the scheme come into operation? The Ministry of Economic Warfare raised the problem of the acquisition of initial stocks by the Controls. If the post-war period proved to be one of excess demand, any attempts to build up stocks would lead to further inflation, output expansion and subsequent losses. In fact, the only useful role for the scheme would be in the face of an incipient depression. On this Keynes replied:

From a letter to SIR FREDERICK LEITH-ROSS, *25 February 1942*

3. I have tried to deal with this point, not by postponing the organisation of the control, but by providing that the clause requiring sales by the control at 10 per cent above the basic price should not come into operation until it had accumulated a sufficient initial stock. Has Rowe appreciated this point? Does it not sufficiently meet the problem of the transition? It is quite

true that it does not prevent prices from going too high in the initial period, if after the war there is great deficiency of a particular kind of stock. But that seems to me altogether outside the power of a buffer stock scheme and can only be prevented by some temporary arrangements for the rationing of consumers, such indeed as we must inevitably enforce in the period immediately after the war. Whether this can usefully be grafted on to the buffer stock scheme I am not sure. It seems to me to be rather part of the *ad interim* relief and reconstruction plans.

(7) What was the relationship between Keynes's scheme and national subsidy schemes? In his earlier drafts, Keynes was very permissive towards national subsidy schemes. However, Sir Frederick Phillips raised the consequent problems of producer and export subsidies for the working of the scheme in his comments on the second draft. Keynes accepted the point and attempted to meet some of the international repercussions of national subsidy schemes in re-drafting.

It was after these discussions that Keynes's fifth draft, dated 14 April 1942, was circulated to other Departments (as well as to the individuals consulted earlier) as an official Treasury memorandum that, after further discussion, would eventually go to the Official Committee on Post-war External Economic Problems.[2]

THE INTERNATIONAL CONTROL OF RAW MATERIALS

I. *The internationalisation of Vice-President Wallace's 'ever-normal granary', in preference to restriction, is the basis of these proposals*

1. This problem has two aspects—restriction and stabilisation. Producers are too easily interested in the former, perhaps because it carries with it the suggestion of higher prices. Restriction may be, sometimes, a necessary accompaniment of

---

[2] This same draft, mis-labelled the fourth draft, was published in the *Journal of International Economics* for August 1974 (pp. 299–315).

stabilisation. But chronic, as distinct from temporary, restriction can scarcely be in the general interest and must be the symptom of a malady, which should be cured rather than endured, either local in the shape of misdirected production, or general as a result of deflationary pressure and depressed demand. The proposals of this paper, whilst not rejecting the expedient of restriction where it seems unavoidable, are, therefore, primarily directed to *stabilisation*, both particular and general. They amount to an internationalisation of the 'ever-normal granary' proposals of Vice-President Wallace, which seem to go to the root of the matter and are likely to promote the *general* interest more completely than can be claimed for any projects which are primarily directed to restriction.

2. The extent of the evil to be remedied can scarcely be exaggerated, though it is not always appreciated. A study of the violence of individual price fluctuations and the inability of an unregulated competitive system to avoid them is given in an appendix. It is there shown that for the four commodities—rubber, cotton, wheat and lead—which are fairly representative of raw materials marketed in competitive conditions, the average *annual* price range over the decade before 1938 was 67 per cent. An orderly programme of output, either of the raw materials themselves or of their manufactured products, is not possible in such conditions.

3. The whole world is now conscious of the grave consequences of this defect in the international competitive system. Apart from the adverse effect on trade stability of the truly frightful *price* fluctuations which we have learnt to accept as normal, they also impose obstacles to the holding of an adequate *quantity* of stocks, the eventual effects of which are not less injurious. For although the difficulty of rapidly altering the scale of output, especially of agricultural crops, leads to what appear to be large stocks at the bottom of the market, nevertheless when the turn of the tide comes, stocks turn out to be insufficient for the reason that it is just as difficult rapidly to increase the scale

of delivered output as it had been to diminish it. Prices rush up, uneconomic and excessive output is stimulated and the seeds are sown of a subsequent collapse.

4. For many years the orthodoxy of *laissez-faire* has stood in the way of effective action to fill this outstanding gap in the organisation of production. Nevertheless there are to-day many signs that the world is ripe for a change. Assuredly nothing can be more inefficient than the present system by which the price is always too high or too low. Is not centralised international action capable of effecting a vast improvement of [the] system, at any rate in the case of the great staple raw materials, most of which can be readily stored without serious deterioration?

5. The details of any scheme must be governed by the special problems and requirements of the individual commodities. The extent to which each commodity is homogeneous and the facility with which it can be replaced by other commodities are factors which affect its treatment. The natural conditions of production of different commodities differ so widely, e.g. between annual crops, tree crops and mining undertakings, that no plan can claim to be applicable to all commodities. Moreover, the reaction of producers to price variations differs very greatly and the existence of a buffer stock scheme will itself create new conditions. For these reasons, as stated at the outset, schemes for the regulation of production—whether national or international—may be required if a buffer stock scheme is to work effectively. Any buffer stock plan must therefore be capable of adjustment to meet different requirements. Nevertheless certain general principles of operation can, it is suggested, be usefully prescribed and agreed.

6. The essence of the plan should be that prices are subject to gradual changes but are fixed within a reasonable range over short periods; those producers who find the ruling price attractive being allowed a gradual expansion at the expense of those who find it unattractive. Thus we should aim at combining a short-period stabilisation of prices with a long-period price

suggested in (xv) below, the Commod Control would be prepared at all times to buy commod, holding and storing it either in the consuming or (subject to the safeguards in (vi) below) in the producing centres as may be most convenient and advisable, at a price (say) 10 per cent below the fixed basic price; and it would sell commod at all times at a price (say) 10 per cent above the fixed basic price. It might be that this price range could be safely narrowed after experience of the working of the plan. It should not be the same for every commodity, and exceptional purchases or sales might sometimes be required by over-riding conditions. A study of the percentage deviations of crop yields from trend level in pre-war years, suggests that, even in the case of agricultural crops, a price range of 20 per cent will normally be sufficient to allow a fair measure of stabilization of producers' incomes for the world as a whole. It will not be sufficient to effect this purpose within each separate country. But to do so lies essentially outside the scope of an international scheme, since it cannot be brought about consistently with a uniform international price. There is, however, nothing to prevent individual governments from operating within the international scheme, if they wish to do so, with a view to a further stabilisation of the incomes of their own producers.

(iv) Within these reasonably wide limits free and competitive markets would handle the trade as they would in the absence of control. The safeguards against excessive price fluctuations provided by the Control should allow merchants to hold stocks and to operate with confidence within the determined range and thus relieve the Control of a multiplicity of detailed operations in day-to-day business. The operations of merchants within this range might effect, in practice, a still narrower range of normal short-term fluctuations except where an abnormal surplus or deficiency of current supply was clearly in prospect. But the Control would have to be prepared, if necessary, to carry a large part of normal, and well as abnormal, stocks. A consuming centre might be allowed to attract stocks by offering to bear part

of the cost of storage, provided it was not allowed, except by general agreement of all consumers, to bring within its jurisdiction an amount of total stocks out of proportion to its importance as a consumer. Generally speaking, the location of stocks should be as widely distributed amongst consuming and producing centres as climatic conditions for safe storage permit.*

(v) Apart from its contractual buying and selling obligations the Commod Control would itself deal in the market or arrange with merchants so as to keep its stocks in motion where they might otherwise deteriorate, replacing old stock by new stock, without, however, modifying its total stock except as the result of its contractual sales and purchases. It would be free to hold part of its stocks in the shape of futures, appropriately related in price to spot transactions, and to ease market difficulties by changing the position of its stocks.

(vi) Some provision would be necessary to prevent the Control from being saddled with responsibility for holding purely domestic stocks. Thus deliveries at producing centres should be accepted only at the Control's discretion; sales should not be made, unless the Control chooses, except on c.i.f. terms appropriate to some consuming centre; and the Control should not be under an obligation to accept sales from a producing country in any year exceeding its average annual export by more than (say) 25 per cent. These restrictions might be modified in the light of experience. But it would be prudent to limit the possible burden on the Control in the first instance.

(vii) At annual or, in the event of sudden changes in the situation, at shorter intervals the Commod Control would re-consider its stock position. If its stock was increasing beyond a stipulated figure, or at more than a stipulated rate, thus indicating that the price was unduly attractive to producers, or

---

* In the case of 'key' commodities the Commodity Controls might be required to take the instructions of the super-national policing authority for the preservation of world peace (if such a body is set up) as to the places of storage and the quantities to be held.

unduly discouraging to consumers, the basic price would be reduced. Similarly it would be raised if stocks were falling below a convenient level or at too fast a rate. A wider latitude would, of course, be necessary for commodities of which the yield was subject to the fluctuations of the seasons than in other cases. The Control would aim at making price changes small and gradual, and *downward* revisions should not normally exceed 5 per cent within a year. But it should be free to alter its basic price *at any time*, and in exceptional circumstances, by more than 5 per cent.

(viii) If, for unforeseen reasons, contraction of output became necessary at a faster rate than that to which the producers could reasonably be expected to adjust themselves, or if in fact production does not contract in response to the reduction of price, producers would be allotted export quotas proportionate to their average sales for export over the previous three years; and, if necessary, an international regulation scheme would have to be negotiated. But such schemes should contain provision ensuring

(1) that any reduction in the permitted scale of production was accompanied by an appropriate reduction in price;

(2) that the quotas assigned to countries subsidising their domestic production were gradually reduced in favour of countries which did not give such subsidies.

(ix) The Control would publish at frequent intervals full statistics of output, consumption and stocks and all other information valuable to producers and consumers.

(x) Subject to (viii) above, individual governments would be free to subsidise their own producers and to make any other arrangements for their benefit. But they would be expected to maintain a stable and consistent policy without frequent or violent changes and to act, so far as possible, with the full knowledge of the Control and in consultation with it.

(xi) The profits arising out of the difference between the Control's buying and selling prices might be sufficient to pay for the costs of storage and management. If, however, they were

inadequate for this purpose, a suitable levy should be imposed on all exports to meet the expense. This might not be necessary unless the Control were so successful that it was seldom called upon either to buy or sell at its contractual prices. Any net profits earned by the Control could be employed in the general interests of the industry, or to narrow the range of buying and selling prices, or to provide part of the fund for financing the stocks.

(xii) The finance of the storage and holding, for which large sums might be required if the system was extended to a number of commodities, would be provided through the International Clearing Union, with which the Controls would keep their accounts; or possibly, failing this, by an arrangement between central banks. It might be provided either by overdraft facilities; or, if the amount required altogether was greater than could be conveniently provided in this way, some part might be found from permanent or semi-permanent loans issued to the publics of the creditor countries, secured on the stock of the Control and guaranteed by the Clearing Union. For the purpose of such loans the requirements of a number of Commodity Controls might be amalgamated.

(xiii) Since the difficulty of accurately adjusting supply and demand may make it very convenient that the *potential* productive capacity should be in excess of normal requirements, it may be advisable to offer some inducement to maintain such extra capacity in existence. It would, therefore, be the duty of an efficient Commodity Control to find ways of conserving and suitably rewarding a prudent margin of excess potential capacity, charging the costs of this to the industry as a whole.

(xiv) A General Council for Commodity Controls* should be established, to which each particular scheme would be referred for examination before it was brought into operation, in order to ensure that its provisions were in conformity with the general principles formulated above. It would also be the function of

---

* If the Economic Committee, suggested in another connection, is set up, it would be natural for the General Council for Commodity Controls to be closely associated with it.

the General Council to review the condition of each of the Commodity Controls, and to issue annual reports upon their operation, and to make recommendations as to the policy which they should follow. Such recommendations would have as their object the protection of the general interest and especially the maintenance of a stable level of prices and the control of the trade cycle. The General Council should further be empowered to authorise, and possibly to require, modifications in the basic prices and the stipulated figure of stocks in particular control schemes. This would permit an adjustment of the prices of a particular commodity to a change in the general level of raw material prices or of other prices.

(xv) Special provisions would be required during the initial period when most materials are likely to be in short supply, which the Controls must not aggravate by endeavouring to build up working stocks. Moreover, it would be undesirable that they should fix basic prices under the influence of temporary conditions which might be considerably too high in normal circumstances. On the other hand, the transitional period after the war, when supplies of raw materials will inevitably remain under official control for the time being, will offer a specially good opportunity for getting the Controls organised. The conclusion is that during this initial period the Controls should do no more than underpin the market and give confidence to producers by fixing a reasonable basic price on the basis of which they would buy, whilst postponing their liability to sell on this basis until sufficient stocks had accumulated in the ordinary course of events. In any case, however, in which surplus export stocks already existed in the hands of governments, a Control should be prepared to take them over at an agreed price, thus solving the problem of how to prevent the liquidation of such stocks from interfering with normal current output.

III. *Commodity controls as a contributory measure to the
prevention of the trade cycle*

8. Superimposed on the meaningless short-period price swings
affecting particular commodities and particular groups of producers there is the fundamental malady of the trade cycle.
Fortunately the same technique of buffer stocks, which has to
be called into being to deal with the former, is also capable of
making a large contribution to the cure of the trade cycle itself.

9. At present a falling off in effective demand in the industrial
consuming centres causes a price collapse which means a
corresponding break in the level of incomes and of effective
demand in the raw material producing centres, with a further
adverse reaction, by repercussion, on effective demand in the
industrial centres; and so, in the familiar way, the slump
proceeds from bad to worse. And when the recovery comes, the
rebound to excessive demand through the stimulus of inflated
prices promotes, in the same evil manner, the excesses of the
boom.

10. But if the Commodity Controls are in a position to take
up at stable prices the slack caused by the initial falling off in
consuming demand and thus to preserve some measure of
stability of incomes in the producing centres, the vicious cycle
may be inhibited at the start; and, again, by releasing stocks
when consumption recovers, the Commodity Controls can
prevent the inflation of raw material prices which carries the
seeds of an incipient boom.

11. The very fact that in the aggregate large sums of money
may be involved in such storage schemes, though it aggravates
the technical and financial problems, is of positive assistance
when we come to the handling of the trade cycle. For we have
at our disposal a weapon capable of producing large effects by
rapid action, and of operating in the negative as well as in the
positive direction, so that it can function as a stabilising factor
both ways. By taking up or by releasing stocks, the complex of

Commodity Controls can operate in both directions on a scale and with an immediacy which is quite impossible for projects of public works. Organised public works, at home and abroad, may be the right cure for a chronic tendency to a deficiency of effective demand. But they are not capable of sufficiently rapid organisation (and above all they cannot be reversed or undone at a later date), to be the most serviceable instrument for the prevention of the trade cycle. Buffer stock controls to deal with the epidemic of intermittent effective demand are therefore the perfect complement of development organisations (or international T.V.A.) to offset a deficiency of effective demand which seems to be endemic.

IV. *Some difficulties reviewed*

12. The personnel and the powers of the Controls, and especially the initial negotiations laying down the general principles and regulations governing a particular Control, present obvious difficulties. What is the proper balance of authority between consumers and producers? How closely must each individual scheme conform to a general model? Is the practical management to be mainly commercial or official? How are dead-locks, arising from a conflict of interest, to be ultimately resolved?

These questions are not easily answered. But it is fair to point out that most of them apply equally to *any* schemes for introducing order into international trade. We may throw our hands in at the start on the ground that it is too difficult to improve this awkward world. But if we reject such defeatism—at any rate to begin with and before we are compelled to acknowledge defeat—then the questions to be asked at so early a stage of our work need only be whether this particular machinery for introducing international order is exposed to more difficulty on the above heads than alternative proposals directed to the same general purpose.

Now in certain respects the above proposals offer much less

practical difficulty than schemes which depend on organised restriction. They avoid the difficult and invidious task of fixing quotas which are fair and of providing means of subsequent adjustment which are acceptable. They require no policing. A minority of producers who prefer to stay outside the schemes present no special problem. They lose their rights to participate in the management of the scheme; they will not be helped in their local storage problems; and it is not obvious what they gain.

13. These proposals, whilst seeking to avoid the violence of short-term price fluctuations, essentially depend on persuading those concerned that the long-term *economic price*, meaning by this the avoidance of an artificially high price by means of a producers' monopoly and restriction of output, is the preferable and proper international policy, whatever domestic concessions by particular governments in favour of particular classes of their own producers may be desirable or inevitable. But this must not be taken to imply that basic prices should be fixed without regard to the requirements of a suitable standard of life for the majority of the producers concerned. A minority of producers with low standards of life must not be allowed to depress the international price of any staple commodity for all producers alike. A 'low' price is the 'economic' price in the above sense only if it reflects high efficiency, not if it merely reflects low standards. It is best defined as representing the long-period equilibrium costs of the most efficient producers on the assumption that the return to the latter is sufficient to provide them with proper nutritional and other standards in the conditions in which they live. It is in the interest of all producers alike that the price of a commodity should not be depressed below this level, and consumers are not entitled to expect that it should. The desire to maintain more adequate standards of living for primary producers has been the mainspring of the movement towards commodity regulation schemes in recent years, and this is a purpose which the buffer stock controls must be prepared to take over.

This raises the question of what is to be done if in fact producers with a depressed standard of life make use of the low costs resulting from this to obtain an undue share of output; so that the Control is faced with the dilemma of either accumulating excessive stocks or depressing the basic price below the figure which allows reasonable standards for producers generally. Restriction schemes should be regarded in such a case as a last resort, since we are faced with a persisting or quasi-permanent situation. The problem is, in fact, one aspect of the general problem how to deal with low-standard producers if there is to be complete freedom of trade and non-discrimination; and is a further reason for the conclusion that some 'protective' measures must be held in reserve as a proper defence of standards of life for other producers (this has an application to manufactured as well as primary products).

Whatever success may attend on efforts to raise nutritional and other standards to a decent level in all producing countries, there must necessarily remain, at least for a long time ahead, a wide difference between this 'decent' level and the level attainable in the wealthier countries. It is necessary, therefore, that buffer stock schemes should be framed on lines which leave each country free to give subsidies to their own producers, in order to maintain their standard of living at whatever level they consider suitable. None the less it must be recognised that a real difficulty arises if such subsidies are given on a substantial scale by the wealthier countries. For the effect of the subsidies is likely to be to maintain a larger volume of production in the countries giving them, and thus to check any tendency which might otherwise exist towards a redistribution of world production in favour of countries with more restricted economic opportunities. The resultant situation would thus be exposed in a considerable degree to one of the main objections to commodity restriction schemes, namely their tendency to stereotype the distribution of world output on the basis of past performance. In view of the probability that a considerable readjustment of the shares

of different countries in world production may be an essential condition of restoring equilibrium to the international balance of payments, this must be regarded as a serious objection. It would seem to be important, therefore, to try to secure a general understanding that subsidies given by particular governments to their own producers of commodities which are the subject of buffer stock schemes should be confined within moderate limits. It might furthermore be desirable as suggested above, to provide expressly that where buffer stock schemes are combined with commodity regulation schemes the quotas of countries giving subsidies should be reduced by a small percentage each year.

It should be added that the successful operation of buffer stock schemes on the lines here proposed must depend in the long run on the genuine acceptance of the principle that the long-term economic price (in the above sense) should be the aim of international policy. Serious dangers would arise if a plan were to be adopted which bore a general resemblance to the foregoing, but which did not contain provisions ensuring a progressive reduction of price if stocks continued to accumulate beyond a certain level. Upon this basis it might well happen that the attempt would be made to establish a world price at a level which could doubtless be defended as not excessive from the standpoint of the standard of living which it afforded to primary producers, but which might none the less result in the eventual discredit and breakdown of the plan through the excessive accumulation of stocks.

14. How comprehensive must the Controls be at the outset? Can progress be piecemeal?

There is no obvious objection, and indeed much advantage, in piecemeal handling by which we start off with those commodities which are most important or most in trouble if left unregulated or present least practical difficulties at the outset. Evidently some of the advantages claimed above would only materialise when the Controls had become somewhat compre-

hensive in their field of operation. But this does not mean that the system has to be born fully matured in a day if it is to come into effective operation.

15. Increasingly before the war governments were finding themselves forced to support their producers against the effect of other countries' restrictions on their markets, and the network of governmental controls established in this way and responsive to no economic stimulus was in some cases one of the main reasons for the accumulation of surpluses. The effectiveness of any buffer stock scheme must partly depend on the possibility of eliminating pre-war restrictions and securing general co-operation on the part of all governments in policies directed to the expansion of consumption.

16. Can the Controls function satisfactorily without degenerating more often than not into restriction schemes? Only experience can show. Restriction schemes, when they *are* unavoidable to supplement the buffer stock arrangements, should be regarded as a means of temporary relief – not a normal or a persisting expedient. For they tend to crystallise the price and the distribution of output between different countries as they exist at the date of the scheme's inception, or—worse still—as they existed over a period of years prior to its inception. In this way the signal advantages of free international competition, namely its adaptibility to changing conditions, both of demand and supply, and the proper advantage it gives to the cheapest producers, are needlessly thrown away. 'Stabilisation' must not rest on the absurd assumption that conditions of demand and of supply are fixed, or that the chief purpose is to protect the increasingly uneconomic producer from the natural effects of world competition. Our object should be to combine the long-period advantages of free competition with the short-period advantages of ensuring that the necessary changes in the scale and distribution of output should take place *steadily* and *slowly* in response to the steady and slow evolution of the underlying trends.

17. How are we to define what we mean by a commodity for this purpose, having regard to the variety of types and grades and to the possibilities of substitution between one article and another? Who is to decide the extent of diversity, as for example the range of price between highest and lowest, the size of maximum and minimum stocks, and the criteria for altering the basic price, to be allowed to one Commodity Control compared with others?

The first set of questions are practical and technical and cannot be either solved or dismissed in a general discussion.

These again, it may be pointed out, are difficulties common to *all* international schemes for introducing better order into the supply of raw materials. But both sets of questions point to the practical importance of the proposed General Council for Commodity Controls, which would have to undertake the initial task of organising particular Controls and approving their rules and regulations and of securing even-handed justice in all directions, as well as keeping a watchful eye on their subsequent operations. If the objection is made that the General Council will have large powers, the answer must be made that international economic controls, if they are to be effective, must have large powers. To object to such powers may be not much more than a polite way of objecting to the Controls themselves.

18. How much money will these schemes require? Will the amount be in reasonable relation to the means of supplying it?

It is difficult to frame an estimate before deciding how wide a range of the staple raw materials of international trade the schemes will endeavour to cover, or without entering in detail in each particular case into the number of months' stock it would be advisable to hold, or in advance of experience of the proportion of total stocks which the Controls would, in practice, be required to carry. One can only say that, potentially at least, the total amounts required, when all the possible controls are fully fledged, are large. An attempt has, however, been made to compile figures (highly approximate) so as to indicate the

order of the magnitude involved, for eight principal commodities—wheat, maize, sugar, coffee, cotton, wool, rubber and tin—which are given in Appendix II. These figures show that the total value of a year's international trade in these commodities, taking the average volume over the years 1935/38, was about £700 million at the prices of 1939 and £950 million at the prices of 1942. A year's stocks on this basis in the hands of the Control would be much too high; three months' would probably be too low—at any rate the Controls must be prepared to hold more than this; and some figure intermediate between these extremes might be appropriate. It must be pointed out that by no means the whole of the necessary finance is *additional* to what would be required otherwise. Normal stocks must be held and must sometimes accumulate to abnormal amounts, even in the absence of Controls, and the finance for carrying such stocks has to be found from somewhere. For example, it is estimated that the stocks of the above eight commodities (very unequally distributed between them) including the domestic surpluses, likely to be held at the end of 1942, outside Russia and the enemy and enemy-occupied countries, are likely to be worth about £900 million at present prices, and finance for which is being found already.

The existence of a Clearing Union, which could take the main responsibility for the provision of the finance, would so greatly facilitate a system of Commodity Controls which is essentially based on their having the financial capacity to carry an 'ever-normal granary,' that some might hold this project to be, in effect, conditional on the adoption of the former. This might, nevertheless, be an overstatement, if we remember that the scope of the proposed Commodity Controls could, if necessary, be limited to those cases where the governments and central banks of the countries chiefly concerned felt strong enough to arrange the necessary finance by agreement amongst themselves. The introduction of the Clearing Union into the picture means that the burden is pooled and is carried, in effect, by those banks,

namely those with credit balances, which happen at the moment
to be in a position to carry it without effort; whereas at present
the burden falls on the central bank of the producing country
precisely at the moment when it is least able to support it,
because the falling off of demand for its product is simultaneously
unbalancing its international position.

Closely associated with this advantage is another one of
scarcely less importance, namely that the raw material stocks of
a producing country are rendered by this means always liquid.
A producing country is always paid for its output at or above
a reasonable minimum price, whether or not the whole of this
output passes immediately into consumption, and paid for it *in
liquid cash* which it can employ on maintaining its normal
volume of imports and its normal standard of life, thus retaining
its own stability and being no longer the occasion, by repercussion, of instability in others. There can be no question that
the scheme proposed would be of the very greatest value to raw
material countries, especially to those which are financially
weak, with overseas debt and lacking in reserves or are highly
specialised in their produce.

It might well be, if the scheme came eventually to cover a
wide range of commodities, that there would be created an
excess liquidity of the world as a whole, if the finance were to
be provided entirely by Clearing Union credit. In this case an
appropriate part should be funded by a long-term international
loan issued under the auspices of the Clearing Union and
secured on the stocks of all the Controls, sufficient to cover an
appropriate proportion of the stable, as distinct from the
fluctuating, proportion of the pooled financial requirements of
the Commodity Controls as a whole.

19. In conclusion, it is worth mentioning that this scheme is
a means, and perhaps the only means, of implementing the
often-repeated undertaking of free and equal access for all
countries alike to the sources of supply of raw materials.

J.M.K.

Appendix I. The violence of the individual price fluctuations and the inability of an unregulated competitive system to avoid them

Wide fluctuations in the prices of raw materials between general boom and depression and between years of exceptional abundance and scarcity for particular commodities are well understood. But superimposed on those broad swings there are disturbing short-term fluctuations on a surprising scale, which are apt to be concealed from those who only watch the movements of index numbers and do not study individual commodities; since index numbers, partly by averaging and partly by including many commodities which are not marketed in fully competitive conditions, mask the short-period price fluctuations of the sensitive commodities.

The results of an enquiry made in 1938 into the price fluctuations of rubber, wheat, lead and cotton will provide an illustration. This enquiry examined by what percentage the highest price in each of the last ten years exceeded the lowest price *in that year*.

Rubber. There was only one year in the decade before 1938 in which the high price of the year exceeded the low by less than 70 per cent. The average excess of the year's high over the year's low was 96 per cent. In other words, there was on the average some date in every year in which the price of rubber was approximately double its price at some other date in that year.

Cotton. Since rubber may be regarded as a notoriously fluctuating commodity, in spite of its having been subject to an organised restriction scheme, let us consider cotton. Only twice in those ten years did the high price of the year exceed the low by less than 33 per cent, and the average excess of the year's high over the year's low was 42 per cent.

Wheat, however, was nearly as fluctuating in price as rubber, which may be a surprise. If we take the Liverpool contract as our standard, there was only one year in the decade when the highest price of the year exceeded the lowest by less than 47 per

cent; and the average excess of the year's high over the year's low was no less than 70 per cent.

Lead is mainly marketed by a small number of powerful producers acting with some measure of consultation. Yet, even so, the annual range of price fluctuations was on much the same scale as with the commodities already examined. Only twice in the ten years was the price range from lowest to highest less than 35 per cent, and the annual average was 61 per cent.

Thus for these four commodities—rubber, cotton, wheat and lead—which are fairly representative of raw materials marketed in competitive conditions, the average *annual* price range over the decade before 1938 was 67 per cent. An orderly programme of output, either of the raw materials themselves or of their manufactured products, is scarcely possible in such conditions.

There is a good theoretical explanation of this unfortunate state of affairs. It is an outstanding fault of the competitive system that there is no sufficient incentive to the individual enterprise to store surplus stocks of materials beyond the normal reserves required to maintain continuity of output. The competitive system abhors the existence of buffer stocks which might average periods of high and low demand, with as strong a reflex as nature abhors a vacuum, because such stocks yield a *negative* return in terms of themselves. It is ready without remorse to tear the structure of output to pieces rather than admit them, and in the effort to rid itself of them; which should be no matter for surprise because the competitive system is in its ideal form the perfect mechanism for ensuring the quickest, but at the same time the most ruthless, adjustment of supply or demand to any change in conditions, however transitory. It is inherently opposed to security and stability, though, for the same reason, it has the great virtue of being also opposed to stability in the sense of stagnation. If demand fluctuates, a divergence immediately ensues between the general interest in the holding of stocks and the course of action which is most advantageous for each competitive producer acting independently.

There are several reasons for this. The cost of storage and interest is fairly high, especially in the case of surplus stocks which strain the capacity of the normal accommodation. Reckoned *ad valorem* there is a wide range of storage costs between different types of commodities, from (say) 5 to 25 per cent per annum. In the case of many commodities, however, the charges are probably in the neighbourhood of 10 per cent per annum;* whilst the length of time for which holding will be necessary and the ultimate normal price are both matters of great uncertainty. The costs of centralised storage schemes, especially if interest charges can be kept at a minimum, should be very much lower.

There are, however, two other still more dominating factors. Experience teaches those who are able and willing to run the speculative risk that, when the market starts to move downward, it is safer and more profitable to await a further decline. The primary producer is, as a rule, unable or unwilling to hold, so that, if the speculative purchaser holds back, he will get the commodity still cheaper. Thus, even if it would pay him to buy at the existing price on long-period considerations, it will often pay him better to wait for a still lower price. The other factor arises out of the lack of incentive to the retailer or the manufacturing consumer to purchase in advance. By purchasing in excess of his immediate needs he may make a speculative profit or loss just like any outside speculator, but as a trader or a manufacturer his position will be competitively satisfactory when the time comes to use the materials, provided he is paying the *current* price. Thus a cautious user would rather pay the current price for his raw materials on which his own selling prices are based than run a speculative risk; and this attitude

---

* Mr Benjamin Graham in his book on *Storage and Stability* (p. 108) estimates the average commercial cost to dealers in the commodity exchanges of storing 23 standard raw materials at $13\frac{1}{2}$ per cent of their value per annum, exclusive of interest, whilst he considers that organised government storage could be provided at a quarter of this cost. His estimate of the commercial cost is considerably higher than the above, which is intended to include interest, but his average is considerably affected by the exceptionally high *ad valorem* cost of storing maize, oats and petroleum.

is reinforced by the fact that his interests are already bound up with activity in the demand for the commodity in question, so that he is multiplying unnecessarily the same kind of risk if he buys his material in advance of his needs. On the other hand, the long-term holding power of the outside speculator is limited—most participants in the market being more interested in a rapid turnover—and can only be called into action on a sufficient scale by a drastic fall in prices which will curtail current output substantially and appears to be a long way below any probable normal cost of future production. This adjustment of prices has to be all the more violent because, for a variety of technical and social reasons, both the consumption and the production of primary products have become increasingly insensitive to changes in their prices; and it is all the more disastrous because the tendency of international trade is to make many countries increasingly dependent on individual crops, for which they are specially suited, so that the social consequences of large movements in the prices of these specialised products are severe and the dangers of instability are enhanced.

Appendix II. World trade valued

Commodity	1935	1936	1937	1938	Average 1935/8	Price* per long ton in 1942 (f.o.b.)	Value of 1935/8 average at 1942 price (£m)	Price per long ton in August 1939 (f.o.b.)	Value of 1935/8 average at 1939 price (£m)
	World net exports† ('000 metric tons)								
Wheat	14,750	14,500	15,300	15,000	14,900	£8·2	120	£7·1	104
Maize	9,000	10,000	13,000	9,000	10,250	£3·2	32	£4·8	48
Sugar	9,650	10,000	10,500	10,500	10,200	£12·4	124	£9·5	95
Coffee	1,610	1,630	1,550	1,800	1,650	£70·3	114	£28·5	46
Cotton	2,650	2,900	3,000	2,540	2,770	$\{$ $\tfrac{3}{4}$ at £100, $\tfrac{1}{4}$ at £70 $\}$	252	£54	147
Wool	950	940	880	940	930	$\{$ $\tfrac{1}{2}$ at £168, $\tfrac{1}{2}$ at £130 $\}$	136	$\{$ $\tfrac{1}{2}$ at £168, $\tfrac{1}{2}$ at £130 $\}$	136
							778		576
	World absorption ('000 long tons)								
Rubber	936	1,038	1,095	934	1,000	(c.i.f.) £112	115	£79·3	79
	World consumption ('000 long tons)								
Tin	150	160	199	160	167	(c.i.f.) £275	46	£225	38
Totals of above values							939		693

* Ministry of Food and Ministry of Supply f.o.b. programme prices except rubber and tin for which approximate U.K. c.i.f. prices.
† Average of total net exports and total net imports as shown in *Yearbook of International Institute of Agriculture.*

The discussions with the Departments resulted in substantial changes in the sixth draft that eventually emerged. The major critics of the scheme were Sir Frederick Leith-Ross and the Ministry of Agriculture, both of whom took exception to what they regarded as an inadequate treatment of quota regulation proposals in the draft. In his attempt to meet his critics, Keynes went to considerable lengths, as he did to meet suggestions concerning the government of the scheme, the role and scope of price changes, the transition period after the war and long-term price policy. His re-draft, dated 28 May 1942, went to the Official Committee on Post-War External Economic Problems on 1 June. As this draft is relatively similar to the version that later emerged from the Committee in August 1942, we print the later version in full and note the changes from the earlier one as the Appendix (see p. 488).

Despite the relatively extensive discussion they had already received, when Keynes's revised proposals for primary product regulation reached the Official Committee the discussions and subsequent re-drafting occupied the months of June and July. However, the changes adopted, although they frequently went too far in the eyes of D. H. Robertson and R. F. Harrod, did not go far enough to satisfy the Minister of Agriculture and Leith-Ross. The former successfully pressed to submit a minute of dissent to the scheme as drafted; Leith-Ross's attempt to do the same failed.

THE INTERNATIONAL REGULATION OF PRIMARY PRODUCTS

I. *Preface*

Any international scheme to regulate primary products must be designed to promote the objects specified in the fourth and fifth points of the Atlantic Charter, which read:

'Fourth, they will endeavour, with due respect to their existing obligations, to further the enjoyment by all States, great and small, victor or vanquished, of access, on equal terms, to the trade and to the raw materials of the world which are needed for their economic prosperity.

'Fifth, they desire to bring about the fullest collaboration between all nations in the economic field, with the object of securing for all improved labour standards, economic advancement, and social security.'

2. Proposals which the United Kingdom and the United States of America may agree jointly to sponsor must be of a nature to commend themselves as reasonable and fair to third parties. It is essential to avoid any imputation that the two Governments in question are working together to further selfish ends or to perpetuate a questionable *status quo*. Commodity Controls must be recognised as being instituted not from some profit motive, but to ensure that the necessary changes in the scale and distribution of output should take place steadily and slowly in response to the steady and slow evolution of the underlying trends. It must be made clear that the object of the Controls is not profit but service. The world as a whole wishes to get away from the old ideas of monopoly and restrictive cartels. Opinion to-day favours a state of society in which necessary services are rewarded on a regular and equitable scale, without, however, cramping new developments, inventions and technical progress generally.

3. A scheme of international regulation of primary products must aim at striking a balance between promising a reasonable measure of security to the producer and making adequate provision for peaceful evolutionary change. The relative advantages as between one source of supply and another are constantly shifting, owing to changes in public taste, technological advances, improved transport facilities to places formerly inaccessible and adoption of substitutes, natural or artificial. It is not right to resist these natural currents. Governments should rather concert means for mitigating the shock to producers who, through circumstances which they cannot control, find themselves losing their markets.

4. A regulation scheme should have two distinct objectives: (*a*) the moderation of excessive fluctuations of prices about the long-term equilibrium price, and (*b*) the maintenance of long-term equilibrium between supply and demand at a price which provides to the majority of primary producers a standard of life in reasonable relation to the standards of the countries in which

they live. Buffer stocks are aimed at the first objective. They have the purpose of steadying prices and are intended, as their name implies, to absorb shocks. But to attain the second objective and to bring about long-period evolutionary changes, restriction or regulation of output may be necessary. A complete scheme must bring both these sets of arrangements into a consistent whole. To achieve the full object, however, something further may be necessary. A co-ordinating authority may be required to deal with difficulties arising between conflicting interests and to provide an adequate measure of conformity by the various Controls to a common pattern.

5. Stabilisation of short-term prices, subject to gradual changes in accordance with long-term trends, is wholly to the good. But lasting, as distinct from temporary, restriction of output can seldom be in the general interest of the world as a whole; and must be the symptom of a malady, which should be cured rather than endured, either local in the shape of misdirected production, or general as a result of deflationary pressure and depressed demand. It remains to be seen whether chronic restriction of output will be required in the post-war world over so wide a field as was becoming necessary in the decade before the war. We may reasonably hope that the adequate stimulation of demand and the raising of nutritional standards and the standard of life generally will have the effect of taking up the slack and absorbing potential production over a wide field. Certainly it will be a matter for great dissatisfaction if we should find it advisable deliberately to impoverish the world by forbidding a potential output of primary foodstuffs and other raw materials, whilst hundreds of millions of consumers go short of what they should have.

6. Nevertheless, the organisation of the world economic structure so that chronic gluts do not occur will present the gravest difficulties. We must be prepared for failures in particular directions and for progress in general which is only gradual. We do not disguise from ourselves that the constructive proposals

set forth in detail below are conceived in a spirit of hopefulness which may be disappointed. They assume a measure of international discipline and good-neighbourliness and, in general, a readiness of governments to accept proper standards of international behaviour, which did not exist before the war. They also depend on the effective substitution of an expansionist for a contractionist pressure on world demand, through the better management of the supply of international money. If the first assumption breaks down, trade in primary products may well relapse into its accustomed chaos. If the second fails, the scheme proposed may degenerate—or, as believers in full-blooded international planning might argue, regenerate—into organised regulation of the majority of products on a scale not hitherto attempted. On the other hand, a better ordering of our affairs may not be so difficult as it looks, if we tackle it boldly. The gluts which have disorganised production in the past have been small in relation to actual output and still smaller in relation to potential demand; and the disorder they have caused has been disproportionate to its origin. It is not true that the impulse of individuals to toil and to produce exceeds their readiness to enjoy and to consume; or that we have reached standards of life so high that our concern should be to hold back output and curb the bounty of nature. It is, rather, the task of this generation to devise, by taking thought, an organisation which can escape from an insane paradox by bringing production and consumption into a fruitful union.

II. *The internationalisation of Vice-President Wallace's 'ever-normal granary'*

7. One of the greatest evils in international trade before the war was the wide and rapid fluctuation in the world *prices* of primary products. The reason for this fluctuation was the frequent divergence between the supply of these commodities and the short-term apparent demand. The true demand for primary

products is not, of course, constant. But a progressive average with a base of, say, three or four years would, in the great majority of cases, show a steady level with long-term trends upwards in the case of some materials and perhaps downwards in the case of others; and with foodstuffs the demand (but not the supply) is often steady even over shorter periods. The apparent international demand as shown by purchases of new supplies in world markets fluctuates much more widely, since it is affected not only by fluctuations in true demand but also by the stocking and de-stocking operations both of users of raw materials and merchants whose business it is to deal in them and of speculators who enter and leave the market when they see an opportunity to make a profit. It must be the primary purpose of control to prevent these wide fluctuations and to allow trade to proceed in an orderly fashion—not, of course, by fixing prices for an indefinite period, but by providing that alterations shall be made gradually in accordance with the long trend variations in true demand and the response of supply to them.

8. The extent of the evil to be remedied can scarcely be exaggerated, though it is not always appreciated. A study of the violence of individual price fluctuations and the inability of an unregulated competitive system to avoid them (even when it is tempered, as it was in the case of rubber from 1934 onwards, by an international regulation scheme) is given in Appendix I. It is there shown that for the four commodities—rubber, cotton, wheat and lead—which are fairly representative of raw materials marketed in competitive conditions, the average *annual* price range over the decade before 1938 was 67 per cent. An orderly programme of output, either of the raw materials themselves or of their manufactured products, is not possible in such conditions.

9. We are now fully conscious of the grave consequences of this defect in the international competitive system. Apart from the adverse effect on trade stability of the violent *price* fluctuations which we have learnt to accept as normal, they also impose

139

obstacles to the holding of an adequate *quantity* of stocks, the eventual effects of which are not less injurious. For although the difficulty of rapidly altering the scale of output, especially of agricultural crops, leads to what appear to be large stocks at the bottom of the market, nevertheless when the turn of the tide comes, stocks turn out to be insufficient for the reason that it is just as difficult rapidly to increase the scale of delivered output as it had been to diminish it. Prices rush up, uneconomic and excessive output is stimulated and the seeds are sown of a subsequent collapse. The damage caused by such movements is not confined to producers; they are inimical also to the interests of consumers, if only because, as shown in Appendix I, the final prices of staple foods are susceptible to wide variation under the impact of violent fluctuations in the primary markets.

10. The details of any scheme must be governed by the special problems and requirements of the individual commodities. The extent to which each commodity is homogeneous and the facility with which it can be replaced by other commodities are factors which affect its treatment. The natural conditions of production of different commodities differ so widely, e.g., between annual crops, tree crops and mining undertakings, that no plan can claim to be applicable to all commodities. Moreover, the reaction of producers to price variations differs very greatly, and the existence of a buffer stock scheme will itself create new conditions. Any buffer stock scheme must therefore be capable of adjustment to meet different requirements. Nevertheless, certain general principles of operation can, it is suggested, be usefully prescribed and agreed.

11. The essence of the plan should be that prices are subject to gradual changes but are fixed within a reasonable range over short periods; those producers who find the ruling price attractive being allowed a gradual expansion at the expense of those who find it unattractive. Thus we should aim at combining a short-period stabilisation of prices with a long-period price policy which balances supply and demand and allows a steady rate of expansion to the cheaper-cost producers. Theoretically

there are two alternative methods of achieving this purpose. One may be described as *price stabilisation* by the creation and operation on an international basis of buffer stocks large enough to counteract short-term disparities between supply and demand, due either to a temporary divergence between apparent and true demand, or short-term excesses or deficiencies in supply (especially those arising from the seasonal fluctuations of agriculture), while leaving the field free for the long-term adjustment of supply to demand by long-term price variation. The other may be described as *output regulation* by fluctuating quotas, associated, generally speaking, with restriction. A quota system is sometimes a necessary accompaniment of stabilisation, but the experience of the last ten years has shown that quota regulation by itself, even when fully justified by the special circumstances of the case, is an imperfect instrument for steadying prices. The following proposals, whilst providing for the expedient of quota regulation where it seems unavoidable, are particularly directed to buffer stock stabilisation. They amount to an internationalisation of the 'ever-normal granary' proposals of Vice-President Wallace, which seem to go to the root of the matter and are likely to promote the *general* interest more completely than can be claimed for any projects which are primarily directed to restriction. Nevertheless, as we shall see, the treatment of the two aspects—price stabilisation and output regulation—must be closely associated in practice. For purposes of exposition in the concrete proposals which now follow, paragraph 12 is concerned with the first and paragraph 13 with the second; whilst in paragraph 14 an attempt is made to provide a connecting link between the two.

III. *The outline of a plan*

12. The broad outline of such a scheme is as follows. Let us call our typical primary product *commod*.

(i) An international body would be set up, called the Commod Control, with the objects of stabilising the price of

that part of the world output of commod which enters into international trade, and of maintaining stocks adequate to cover short-term fluctuations of supply and demand in the world market. It would not be directly concerned with the domestic price and production policy of commod produced and consumed within the same country. Further thought will be necessary to concert detailed provisions for the management of a Control. The members of the Control would primarily represent the chief exporting and importing countries, but the General Council referred to below should be represented on each individual Control and the appointment of independent members with expert qualifications deserves consideration. In some cases the number of members on a Control should be smaller than the number of importing and exporting countries, which might have to be grouped for the purpose of representation. The balance of voting powers also needs consideration. The exporting countries should perhaps be allowed a preponderant voice on questions of management and of detail not affecting the basic price.

(ii) An initial basic price c.i.f. at one or more of the principal centres of consumption (in terms of bancor if the International Clearing Union is in operation) would be fixed by the Commod Control at a reasonable level on the basis of current conditions, to be modified from time to time thereafter in the manner prescribed below by a process of trial and error based on the observed tendency of stocks to increase or to decrease. This does not mean a single price, but a complex of prices, according to varieties of quality, of dates in relation to the crop year in the case of agricultural commodities, and to position relatively to the cost of transport to the ultimate consumer. It should not be technically difficult to fix the complex of prices in proper relation to the basic price, provided a proper discretion is allowed to independent experts, for these margins are already established by trade practice.

(iii) Subject to special arrangements in the initial period

suggested in (xiii) below, the Commod Control would be prepared at all times to buy commod, holding and storing it either in the consuming or (subject to the safeguards in (vi) below) in the producing centres, as may be most convenient and advisable, at a price (say) 10 per cent below the fixed basic price; and it would sell commod at all times at a price (say) 10 per cent above the fixed basic price. It might be that this price range could be safely narrowed after experience of the working of the plan. It should not be the same for every commodity, and exceptional purchases or sales might sometimes be required by overriding conditions. A study of the percentage deviations of crop yields from trend level in pre-war years suggests that, even in the case of annual crops, a price range of 20 per cent will normally be sufficient to allow a fair measure of stabilisation of producers' incomes for the world as a whole. It will not always effect this purpose within each separate country. But to do so lies essentially outside the scope of an international scheme, since it cannot be brought about consistently with a uniform international price. There is, however, nothing to prevent individual governments from operating within the international scheme, if they wish to do so, with a view to a further stabilisation of the incomes of their own producers.

(iv) Within these reasonably wide limits, free and competitive international markets would handle the trade, as they would in the absence of control; and there would be no objection to state trading by any country which preferred that method. The safeguards against excessive price fluctuations provided by the Control should allow merchants or state trading corporations to hold stocks and to operate with confidence within the determined range, and thus relieve the Control of a multiplicity of detailed operations in day-to-day business. The operations of traders within this range might effect, in practice, a further narrowing of normal short-term fluctuations except where an abnormal surplus or deficiency of current supply was clearly in prospect. But the Control would have to be prepared, at times, to carry

a large part of normal, as well as abnormal, stocks. A consuming centre might be allowed to attract stocks by offering to bear part of the cost of storage, provided it was not allowed, except by agreement, to bring within its jurisdiction an amount of total stocks out of proportion to its importance as a consumer. Generally speaking, the location of stocks should be as widely distributed amongst consuming and producing centres as climatic conditions for safe storage permit. But, in the case of 'key' commodities, the Commodity Controls might be required to take the instructions of the supernational policing authority for the preservation of world peace (if such a body is set up) as to the places of storage and the quantities to be held in each.

(v) Apart from its contractual buying and selling obligations, the Commod Control would itself deal in the market or arrange with merchants so as to keep its stocks in motion where they might otherwise deteriorate, replacing old stock by new stock, without, however, modifying its total stock except as the result of its regular sales and purchases. It might be free to hold a modest proportion of its stocks in the shape of futures, appropriately related in price to spot transactions, and it should ease market difficulties by changing the position of its stocks.

(vi) Some provision might be necessary to limit the Control's liability to be saddled with responsibility for holding stocks destined for domestic consumption in the country of origin. Thus deliveries at the producing centres should be accepted only at the Control's discretion and re-sales should not be made, unless the Control chooses, except on c.i.f. terms appropriate to some consuming centre. It has to be remembered, however, that a fluctuating part of domestic production enters into international trade, for which the Control would have to allow and which it should facilitate.

(vii) The Control would publish at frequent intervals full statistics of output, consumption and total stocks, including those held privately, and all other information useful to producers and consumers.

(viii) At annual or, in the event of sudden changes in the situation, at shorter intervals of Commod Control would reconsider the whole commod position. In the course of the examination the Control would review the position not only of its own stocks, but also of total visible stocks throughout the world, and in appropriate cases crop prospects also. While the Control's power to stabilise prices is dependent on its own stock being adequate, it could not view with equanimity a situation in which outside stocks were accumulating rapidly even though its own were not. If, therefore, either its own stock or world stocks were increasing beyond a stipulated figure, or at more than a stipulated rate, thus indicating that the price was unduly attractive to producers, or unduly discouraging to consumers, the basic price would be reduced. Similarly it would be raised if stocks were falling below a convenient level or at too fast a rate. Both the appropriate quantity for the normal stock of an individual commodity and the appropriate maximum pace of increase or decrease in that stock depend on the special characteristics of that commodity. In the case of the annual crops the normal stock should be at least large enough to replace any temporary deficiency caused by exceptionally poor harvests. In the case of other products, such as tree crops and minerals, where new production follows some years behind the initiation of measures to increase it, the stock should be sufficient to bridge at least part of the possible gap where there is a pronounced upward long-term trend in demand. Where there are physical reasons why the response of supply to the stimulus of increased prices is necessarily slow, it is important that the potential capacity should be in excess of normal requirements, and it may be advisable, therefore, to offer some inducement to maintain such extra capacity in existence. It would be the duty of an efficient Control to find ways of conserving and suitably rewarding a prudent margin of excess potential capacity, charging the costs of this to consumers as a whole.

(ix) When a revision of prices, either upward or downward,

145

became necessary as the result of the survey under (viii) above, the Control would aim at making such changes as small and gradual as possible. It would not be wise to lay down a hard-and-fast rule as to the maximum rate of such changes in advance of experience. It must partly depend on the stability of world conditions in other respects. The immediately previous movement of prices within the range above or below the existing basic price would also be relevant. But it is to be hoped that *downward* revisions, at any rate, would not normally exceed 10 per cent within a year, and very gradual changes such as 2 per cent would be a mark of successful management. Nevertheless, the Control should be free to alter its basic price at any time and there should be no absolute limitations on its discretion in determining the amount of the change, save that during a world depression, defined by suitable indices approved by the General Council, it would not be permitted to reduce the basic price by more 5 per cent in one year.

(x) The profits arising out of the differences between the Control's buying and selling prices might be sufficient to pay for the costs of storage and management. If, however, they were inadequate for this purpose, a suitable levy should be added to the price of all exports to meet the expense. This might not be necessary unless the Control were so successful that it was seldom called upon either to buy or sell at its contractual prices. Any net profits earned by the Control could be employed in the general interests of the industry, or to narrow the range of buying and selling prices, or to provide part of the fund for financing the stocks.

(xi) The finance of the storage and holding, for which large sums might be required if the system was extended to a number of commodities, would be provided, if it comes into existence, through the International Clearing Union, with which the Controls would keep their accounts. It might be provided either by overdraft facilities; or, if the aggregate amount required was greater than could be conveniently supplied in this way, some

part might be found from permanent or semi-permanent loans issued to the publics of the creditor countries, secured on the stock of the Control and guaranteed by the Clearing Union. For the purpose of such loans the requirements of a number of Commodity Controls might be amalgamated. The question arises what could be done in the absence of a Clearing Union. It is possible that the finance could be provided by arrangements between central banks or by international loans as above. Thus it would be too much to say that the success of the scheme necessarily depends on the establishment of a Clearing Union. Nevertheless it is obvious that the difficulties of *ad hoc* financial arrangements would be considerable and that the Clearing Union would very greatly facilitate the buffer stock plan. Indeed the internationalisation of the 'ever-normal granary' might have been proposed before now if the facilities of a Clearing Union had existed. For the use of the Clearing Union makes it unnecessary to ask any individual Government to accept commitments of which the extent is difficult to foresee; and, when the time comes, it puts no burden on anyone since those credit balances are automatically brought into play which by hypothesis are not being used, without their potential liquidity to their owner being impaired. There is, moreover, no risk to the solvency or to the credit of the Clearing Union itself, since the fact that its balances are partly covered by stocks of a number of the most universally useful commodities must increase, and not diminish, their security. The underlying principle of the Clearing Union and the financing of staple primary products dovetail together in a perfect manner. Since, however, it might be necessary to limit the financial liability of the controls in the absence of a Clearing Union, a proposal with this object in view will be outlined in paragraph 14.

(xii) A General Council for Commodity Controls* should be established, to which each particular scheme would be referred

* If the Economic Committee, suggested in another connection, is set up, it would be natural for the General Council for Commodity Controls to be closely associated with it.

147

for examination before it was brought into operation, in order to ensure that its provisions were in conformity with the general principles formulated above. It would also be the function of the General Council to review the condition of each of the Commodity Controls, and issue annual reports upon their operation, and to make recommendations as to the policy which they should follow. Such recommendations would have as their object the protection of the general interest and especially the maintenance of a stable level of prices and the control of the trade cycle. The General Council should further be empowered to authorise, and possibly to require, modifications in the basic prices and the stipulated figure of stocks in particular control schemes. This would permit an adjustment of the prices of a particular commodity to a change in the general level of raw material prices or of other prices. It would also be given the powers outlined in paragraph 13 below in relation to restriction schemes.

(xiii) Special provisions would be required during the initial period when most materials are likely to be in short supply, which the Controls must not aggravate by endeavouring to build up working stocks. Moreover, it would be undesirable that they should fix basic prices under the influence of temporary conditions which might be considerably too high in normal circumstances. On the other hand, the transitional period after the war, when supplies of raw materials will inevitably remain under official control for the time being, will offer a specially good opportunity for getting the Controls organised. The conclusion is that the Controls should be organised as soon as possible after the conclusion of hostilities and before the period at which they might be expected to enter into active operation. In the initial stages they would be accumulating information and statistics; and they should during this period endeavour to establish a common doctrine between producers and consumers regarding reasonable basic prices for the commodities which they would control. The Council referred to in (xii) would have

a useful function to perform at this stage in correlating ideas about prices for all the commodities concerned. If these preliminary measures were carried through successfully, the individual Controls would be able to intervene on the downswing at points which would receive general approbation and so underpin the market and give confidence to producers, whilst postponing their liability to sell on this basis until sufficient stocks had accumulated in the ordinary course of events. In any case, however, in which surplus export stocks already existed in the hands of governments, a Control should be prepared to take them over at an agreed price, thus solving the problem of how to prevent the liquidation of such stocks from interfering with normal current output.

13. So far no provision has been made for quota regulation of exports or organised restriction. Such schemes were characteristic of the decade before the war, and covered, with varying degrees of effectiveness, a wide range of commodities. Opinions differ as to how far the necessity for these schemes was just one of many symptoms of the extreme economic malaise of that period and how far they are an inevitable accompaniment of the wide differences of labour costs and of the opportunity for diversification of output in different parts of the world. But there is likely to be general agreement that such schemes may prove to be necessary in the case of certain commodities even in the new circumstances, that any proposals for the international regulation of primary products must, therefore, provide for their possibility, and that careful precautions should be taken in handling an instrument which, if abused, is so liable to impoverish the world as a whole and waste its potential resources. In any event, there is one use of quota restriction which is in principle acceptable, namely, where it is avowedly temporary and for the purpose of effecting a smooth and gradual transfer from one source of supply to another.

Pre-war schemes differed greatly amongst themselves in the nature of their detailed provisions, and no attempt can be

usefully made here to provide a model or uniform scheme. It may be that there are certain intractable commodities presenting special difficulties which are better kept outside the general scheme and treated on separate lines. It may be that long-term planning, associated with quota regulation for exports, will be particularly required in the case of agricultural crops grown in widely differing conditions in many parts of the world, by importers of the crops as well as by exporters, the supply of which is, for several reasons, particularly insensitive to price changes. Opinions will differ as to how far these problems will persist unmitigated in the post-war world, assuming success in the policy of expanding and stabilising purchasing power and raising standards of consumption. It may be that we shall find ourselves more concerned to stimulate new sources of supply than to restrict those which exist. But the treatment of special problems, if someone knows a specific cure for them, is in no way prejudiced by this wider plan.

The following suggestions are mainly directed to the provision of suitable machinery within the general framework of international control, to decide when organised restriction is justifiable and the general lines it should follow with a view to keeping it within the narrowest practicable limits:

(i) If the exporting governments represented on a Commod Control are agreed amongst themselves that the basic price appropriate to the prospective long-term state of supply and demand would be below a reasonable international economic price, they shall be entitled to apply to the General Council for Commodity Controls for permission to enforce quota regulation of exports.

(ii) In making this application the exporters shall state—

(*a*) whether the importing governments represented on the Control support or oppose the application, and, in the latter event, the importing governments shall be entitled to explain the grounds of their objection;

(*b*) whether their proposal is due to causes which they

regard as likely to be continuing, or whether it is strictly temporary to allow a gradual transfer from high-cost to low-cost producers or from this particular output to an alternative product, and, in the latter event, the measures proposed for bringing the restriction gradually to an end within a stated period;

(*c*) if, on the other hand, the proposal is due to causes regarded as likely to be continuing, how far, in their judgment, the existence of over production is to be explained by—

(1) stimulation of exportable capacity by subsidies or their equivalent in some of the exporting countries,

(2) restriction of importing capacity by tariffs, subsidies or their equivalent in some of the importing countries,

(3) uneconomic competition by substitutable commodities,

(4) lack of opportunity on the part of some of the exporting countries to shift to alternative production,

(5) limitation of demand by the impoverished condition of potential consumers whose standards of living would greatly benefit by increased consumption of the commodity in question;

(*d*) what variations of economic cost exist between different producers and on different scales of total output.

(iii) On such an application being made, provisional export quotas, based on the actual share of the export trade in the previous three years, shall come into force immediately, pending the decision of the General Council on future policy (cf. the 'standard' quotas proposal in 14 (i) below).

(iv) Before approving a quota regulation proposal required for reasons regarded as likely to continue, the General Council shall endeavour to deal with the radical causes of the problem. If reasons (1) and (2) have been adduced, they shall invite countries subsidising exports to reduce or abolish such subsidies, and countries applying tariffs or other expedients which increase the cost to the domestic consumer (apart from recognised duties which are *bona fide* for revenue purposes and apply

to domestic produce equally) to abate them.* If reasons (3) and (4) apply, they shall consult with the Commod Controls concerned with suitable products or alternative production, with a view to diminishing any uneconomic competition (if its existence is proved) and to encouraging alternative production, providing, if necessary, financial and technical assistance to promote a shift in production. If the case for (5) is made out, they shall consider whether it is advisable and practicable to find some means of subsidising the consumption of the product in impoverished countries, in consultation with a Nutritional Council, if there is such a body.

(v) If the exporters have not reached agreement amongst themselves as to their proportionate quotas, these shall be fixed by the General Council, which shall pay attention, amongst other considerations, to the proportionate share of the export trade on the average of the previous three years. Whether the quotas are initially determined by agreement among the exporters or otherwise, the General Council shall diminish the share, progressively in each year in which restriction is in force, of any country which subsidises exports, which is a surplus country in the Clearing Union or which is a relatively high-cost producer; and increase the share of any country which is a deficit country in the Clearing Union or which is a relatively low-cost producer or which has special difficulties in producing alternative output.

(vi) The Commod Control shall fix annually a basic price at the lowest figure which corresponds to a reasonable international economic price for three-quarters of the exporting countries weighted according to their quotas. It shall also fix the aggregate, as distinct from the individual, quotas and shall only be liable to buy the excess of the aggregate quota over exports sold in the market. So long as restriction is in force, prices shall be

---

* In Appendix II illustrations are given, for wheat and sugar, to show how much scope there is for better international practice in these respects.

reduced by at least 2 per cent per annum unless the General Council agrees otherwise.

(vii) The duration of a restriction scheme shall not exceed 5 years in the first instance and, if it is renewed on the ground that there is still serious over-supply, the basic price for the next period of 5 years shall be significantly lower than that ruling during the first period, unless special reason can be shown by the Control to the satisfaction of the General Council, either on account of changes in other prices or because a major factor causing the need for a continuation of restriction is the high level of subsidy or protectionism in importing countries.

(viii) Other special features of a regulation scheme not covered by the above, including, for example, the sanctions necessary to enforce it, may be adopted by a Commod Control subject to the approval of the General Council.

14. It has been argued that there is a useful place for quota regulation, not as part of a restriction scheme designed to maintain an economic price, but as a normal aid and safeguard to buffer stock regulation in cases where the response of supply and demand to price changes is inadequate or tardy. Without such a support it is possible either that the Control would be taken by surprise or that no reasonable price changes would be effective, so that it would be deluged with offers which it could not refuse but which might seriously embarrass its subsequent activities. Moreover, the existence of such a machinery would facilitate the prompt introduction of a restriction scheme proper, whether temporary or quasi-permanent, where the case for this could be fully made out. Provisions with this purpose in view might be as follows:

(i) Each exporting country should have attributed to it a standard quota, to be fixed at the inception of a Control Scheme by agreement amongst exporters (or failing this by the General Council) and subsequently a moving average of its actual volume of net exports in the previous three years.

(ii) On the occasion of a reduction in price, designed to offset the tendency of stocks to accumulate in the hands of the Control, the Control should be authorised, at its discretion, to limit its takings from exporters to an amount (including their sales in the market) proportionate (i.e., in a proportion greater than, equal to, or less than the standard quota, but the same for all exporters) to their standard quotas; and in this case exporters should agree not to export to any destination in excess of their proportionate quota.

(iii) So long as such standard-quota limitation continues in force, the basic price should be progressively reduced—at a rate of not less than (say) 5 per cent per annum.

(iv) If the price thus reduced is approaching, or seems likely to approach, the minimum reasonable economic price, the Control would endeavour to secure action on the lines of § [paragraph] 13, inviting the General Council to approve a restriction scheme proper.

(v) Similarly on the occasion of an increase in price, designed to offset a tendency towards exhaustion of stocks in the hands of the Control, the Control should, if it thinks necessary, attempt to organise and assist an expansion of additional capacity in the exporting country most suitable for the purpose, either by reason of their being low-cost producers or because they are deficit countries (or tending that way) in the books of the Clearing Union.

Nevertheless (ii) above is open to great objection on the ground of the uncertainty it must produce in the minds of producers as to whether the buffer stocks scheme can be relied on to provide them with an outlet. If, therefore, adequate finance can be ensured through the Clearing Union, so that this safeguard is not necessary to the Controls, it would be better to omit this provision. It is only put forward subject to this qualification.

IV. *Buffer stocks as a measure contributory to the prevention of the trade cycle*

15. Superimposed on the meaningless short-period price swings affecting particular commodities and particular groups of producers there is the fundamental malady of the trade cycle. Fortunately the same technique of buffer stocks, which has to be called into being to deal with the former, is also capable of making a large contribution to the cure of the trade cycle itself.

16. At present a falling off in effective demand in the industrial consuming centres causes a price collapse, which means a corresponding break in the level of incomes and of effective demand in the raw material producing centres, with a further adverse reaction, by repercussion, on effective demand in the industrial centres; and so, in the familiar way, the slump proceeds from bad to worse. And when the recovery comes, the rebound to excessive demand, through the stimulus of inflated prices, promotes, in the same evil manner, the excesses of the boom. But if the Commodity Controls are in a position to take up at stable prices the slack caused by the initial falling off in consuming demand, and thus to preserve some measure of stability of incomes in the producing centres, the vicious cycle may be inhibited at the start; and, again, by releasing stocks when consumption recovers, the Commodity Controls can prevent the inflation of raw material prices which carries the seeds of an incipient boom.

17. The very fact that in the aggregate large sums of money may be involved in such storage schemes, though it aggravates the technical and financial problems, is of positive assistance when we come to the handling of the trade cycle. For we have at our disposal a weapon capable of producing large effects by rapid action, and of operating in the negative as well as in the positive direction, so that it can function as a stabilising factor both ways. By taking up or by releasing stocks, the complex of Commodity Controls can operate in both directions on a scale

and with an immediacy which is quite impossible for projects of public works. Organised public works, at home and abroad, may be the right cure for a chronic tendency to a deficiency of effective demand. But they are not capable of sufficiently rapid organisation (and, above all, they cannot be reversed or undone at a later date), to be the most serviceable instrument for the prevention of the trade cycle. Buffer stock controls to deal with the epidemic of intermittent effective demand are therefore the perfect complement of development organisations (or international T.V.A.) to offset a deficiency of effective demand which seems to be endemic.

V. *Some difficulties reviewed*

18. The personnel and the powers of the Controls, and especially the initial negotiations laying down the general principles and regulations governing a particular Control, present obvious difficulties. What is the proper balance of authority between consumers and producers? How closely must each individual scheme conform to a general model? Is the practical management to be mainly commercial or official? How are dead-locks, arising from a conflict of interest, to be ultimately resolved?

These questions are not easily answered. But it is fair to point out that most of them apply equally to *any* schemes for introducing order into international trade. We may throw our hands in at the start on the ground that it is too difficult to improve this awkward world. But if we reject such defeatism—at any rate to begin with and before we are compelled to acknowledge defeat—then the questions to be asked at so early a stage of our work need only be whether this particular machinery for introducing international order is exposed to more difficulty on the above heads than alternative proposals directed to the same general purpose.

19. Whatever success may attend on effort to raise nutritional and other standards to a decent level in all producing countries,

there must necessarily remain, at least for a long time ahead, a wide difference between this 'decent' level and the level attainable in the wealthier countries. It is necesary, therefore, that buffer stock schemes should be framed on lines which leave each country free to give subsidies to their own producers, in order to maintain their standard of living at whatever level they consider suitable. None the less, it must be recognised that a serious difficulty arises if such subsidies are given on a substantial scale by the wealthier countries. For the effect of the subsidies is likely to be to maintain a larger volume of production in the countries giving them, and thus to check any tendency which might otherwise exist towards a redistribution of world production in favour of countries with more restricted economic opportunities. The resultant situation would thus be exposed in a considerable degree to the objection that it would have a tendency to stereotype the distribution of world output on the basis of past performance. In view of the probability that a considerable readjustment of the shares of different countries in world production may be an essential condition of restoring equilibrium to the international balance of payments, this must be regarded as a serious objection. It would seem to be important, therefore, to try to secure a general understanding that subsidies (whether to promote exports or to exclude imports) given by particular governments to their own producers of commodities which are the subject of buffer stock schemes should be confined within moderate limits. It would furthermore be desirable, as suggested above, to provide expressly that where buffer stock schemes are combined with commodity regulation schemes the quotas of countries giving subsidies should be reduced by a small percentage each year.

20. The successful operation of buffer stock schemes on the lines here proposed must depend in the long run on the genuine acceptance of the principle that the long-term economic price (as defined in paragraph 4) should be the aim of international policy. Otherwise an attempt might be made to establish a world

price at a level which could doubtless be defended as not excessive from the standpoint of the standard of living which it afforded to primary producers, but which might none the less result in the eventual discredit and breakdown of the plan through the excessive accumulation of stocks.

21. How comprehensive must be the list of commodities subject to the proposed Controls? Can progress be made piecemeal?

There is no obvious objection, and indeed much advantage, in piecemeal handling, by which we start off with those commodities which are most important or most in trouble if left unregulated or present least practical difficulties at the outset. Evidently some of the advantages claimed above would only materialise when the Controls had become somewhat comprehensive in their field of operation. But this does not mean that the system has to be born fully matured in a day if it is to come into effective operation. It has already been suggested above that a commodity particularly intractable to this type of handling might be dealt with otherwise. Nor is it intended that special agreements, such as the recent Wheat Agreement, should be ruled out or forced into conformity with the general model if it is agreed by those concerned that there are good and continuing reasons for separate treatment. The object of the proposed Controls is to offer signal advantages to the producers of primary products. If the countries producing a particular commodity believe that they will be better off without a system of buffer stocks financed internationally, there can be no object in coercing them merely for the sake of uniformity. On the other hand, if they reach out after the advantages, they must also accept the discipline subject to any modifications which the General Council may approve.

22. Increasingly before the war governments were finding themselves forced to support their producers against the effect of other countries' restrictions on their markets, and the network of governmental controls established in this way and responsive

to no economic stimulus was in some cases one of the main reasons for the accumulation of surpluses. The effectiveness of any buffer stock scheme must partly depend on the possiblity of eliminating pre-war restrictions and securing general co-operation on the part of all governments in policies directed to the expansion of consumption.

23. How are we to define what we mean by a commodity for this purpose, having regard to the variety of types and grades and to the possibilities of substitution between one article and another? Who is to decide the extent of diversity, as, for example, the range of price between highest and lowest, the size of maximum and minimum stocks, and the criteria for altering the basic price, to be allowed to one Commodity Control compared with others?

The first set of questions is practical and technical and cannot be either solved or dismissed in a general discussion. They are difficulties common to *all* international schemes for introducing better order into the supply of raw materials. Both sets of questions point to the importance of the proposed General Council for Commodity Controls, which would have to under-take the initial task of organising particular Controls and approving their rules and regulations and of securing even-handed justice in all directions, as well as keeping a watchful eye on their subsequent operations. If the objection is made that the General Council will have large powers, the answer must be made that international economic controls, if they are to be effective, must have large powers. To object to such powers may not be much more than a polite way of objecting to the Controls themselves.

24. What commodities are sufficiently durable and capable of storage to be proper subjects for a buffer stocks control? It is not possible to draw a hard-and-fast line. For some com-modities the maximum number of months' stock might have to be kept below the usual figure because of the necessity to turn over the stock and replace it frequently. In other cases, for

example meat, the capacity and situation of refrigerated storage might be a limited factor; but canning or drying might come to the rescue. For some tropical or semi-tropical products storage is possible at some stages of processing but not at others. Among oil-seeds, for example, some can be more easily stored before decortication (as in the case of ground nuts) or after crushing, and in other cases, such as linseed, indefinite storage is practicable before crushing, whilst the degree of storability varies according as the product is to be applied to edible or non-edible uses. The whole notion of buffer stocks is complicated in this field by the high degree of interchangeability among the various components of the 'oils and fats' trade. There are some perishable commodities which are clearly unsuitable for storage; but in general each particular product requires its own appropriate handling. The technique and facilities for storage may well be expected to undergo continuing improvement, and the Controls could very properly finance development in this direction.

25. How much money will these schemes require? Will the amount be in reasonable relation to the means of supplying it?

It is difficult to frame an estimate before deciding how wide a range of the staple raw materials of international trade the schemes will endeavour to cover, or without entering in detail in each particular case into the number of months' stock it would be advisable to hold, or in advance of experience of the proportion of total stocks which the Controls would, in practice, be required to carry. The amounts required for 'normal' stocks are themselves large, and the amounts which would be required, if for one reason or another abnormal stocks had to be held for a time, are larger still. An attempt has, however, been made to compile figures (highly approximate), so as to indicate the order of the magnitude involved, for eight principal commodities— wheat, maize, sugar, coffee, cotton, wool, rubber and tin— which are given in Appendix II [I]. These figures show that the total value of a year's international trade in these commodities,

taking the average volume over the years 1935–8, was about
£700 million at the prices of 1939 and £950 million at the prices
of 1942. A year's stocks on this basis in the hands of the Control
would be much too high; three months' would probably be too
low—at any rate, the Controls must be prepared to hold more
than this; and some figure intermediate between these extremes
might be appropriate. It must be pointed out that by no means
the whole of the necessary finance is *additional* to what would
be required otherwise. Normal stocks must be held and must
sometimes accumulate to abnormal amounts, even in the
absence of Controls, and the finance for carrying such stocks has
to be found from somewhere. For example, it is estimated that
the stocks of the above eight commodities (very unequally
distributed between them), including the domestic surpluses,
likely to be held at the end of 1942, outside Russia and the enemy
and enemy-occupied countries, are likely to be worth about
£900 million at present prices, the finance for which is being
found already.

26. The existence of a Clearing Union, which could take the
main responsibility for the provision of the finance, would
greatly facilitate (as pointed out in § [paragraph] 12 (xi) above)
a system of Commodity Controls which is essentially based on
their having the financial capacity to carry an 'ever-normal
granary'. The introduction of the Clearing Union into the
picture means that the burden is pooled and is carried, in effect,
by those banks, namely, those with credit balances, which
happen at the moment to be in a position to carry it without
effort; whereas at present the burden falls on the central bank
of the producing country precisely at the moment when it is least
able to support it, because the falling off of demand for its
product is simultaneously unbalancing its international position.
Closely associated with this advantage is another one of scarcely
less importance, namely, that by this means the raw material
stocks of a producing country are rendered always liquid. A
producing country is always paid for its output at or above a

reasonable minimum price, whether or not the whole of this output passes immediately into consumption, and paid for it *in liquid cash*, which it can employ on maintaining its normal volume of imports and its normal standard of life, thus retaining its own stability and being no longer the occasion, by repercussion, of instability in others. There can be no question that the scheme proposed would be of the very greatest value to raw material countries, especially to those which are financially weak, with overseas debt and lacking in reserves or are highly specialised in their produce.

27. It may be claimed as an advantage of the scheme that it does not assume the maintenance of private enterprise in international trade and is compatible with the further development of state trading. For, after the war, whatever may be the trading mechanism of the United Kingdom or of the United States, there are certain to be some countries, particularly the U.S.S.R., where trade in some (or in all) commodities will be monopolised by the state. Such a system of trading gives rise to some awkward problems in international commercial relations, since it is difficult to define or to determine the degree of protective or of discriminatory action in the monopolistic purchases of a state institution. But some of these difficulties can be overcome if a single world price for a primary product can be set by the International Control. As in the case of the Clearing Union, we have here a plan for international co-operation which can be safely adoped in the common interest by every country alike irrespective of its national economic policy.

APPENDIX I

[Except for the following final paragraph Appendix I followed the fifth and sixth drafts. Therefore, it does not appear here.]

While the sufferings of primary producers resulting from this instability are by now generally appreciated, it is not so fully recognised that violent fluctuations on world markets are to an

important, though less, extent transmitted right through to the consumer. Statistical investigation of the degree to which this is true is practicable only on a limited scale since there are relatively few products having the required simplicity of raw-material content. Perhaps the best example for the purpose is bread; and it has been found that, over the decade to 1938, the retail price of the loaf in this country fluctuated almost as widely, though of course not so frequently, as the cost of the equivalent amount of wheat on the world market. Butter and cheese are more suitable than most things for similar investigation and here, too, the same conclusion holds good in only slightly less degree. Many of the more elementary foodstuffs, admittedly, are by reason of perishability non-susceptible to treatment by a scheme involving the maintenance of buffer stocks; but even these would acquire some secondary stability from greater steadiness in the cost of animal feeding-stuffs. So far as the plan helped, directly or indirectly, to keep the consumer cost of staple foods on an even course it would diminish the force of a powerful element in public unrest and simplify the processes of wage negotiation and social policy generally.

APPENDIX II

In the case of many agricultural commodities uneconomic production has been stimulated by government action, supported by subsidies and protection: the result of this is—

(i) to develop a chronic surplus capacity in the world as a whole;

(ii) to maintain high prices in many of the consuming markets and consequently to restrict consumption;

(iii) to restrict the volume of international trade and to depress the open market prices.

For example, as regards wheat, in 1934, the world market price c.i.f. Liverpool was about 5s per cwt; the import duties in force were: in France 10s 1d per cwt; in Italy 12s 4d; in Germany 18s 11d; even in countries like Czechoslovakia and Austria, the

duty was over 5s per cwt; and the internal price in France was 15s 6d per cwt, and in Italy and Germany about 14s, or about three times the world market price. The maintenance of this high internal price tended to restrict consumption, but stimulated production, until these countries were self-supporting and, in the case of France, developed an export trade in wheat. The world market was correspondingly contracted and the open market price fell to levels unremunerative to any producer.

The case of sugar is even more striking. The open market price c.i.f. United Kingdom, ex duty, averaged 4s 8d per cwt during the three years 1934–6. Java, Peru and other economic producers, dependent largely on the world market, could just afford to maintain production at this price, but their production had to be severely restricted and the markets open to them were constantly declining, till they supplied less than 20 per cent of the world consumption. Sugar was grown in other countries under every variety of protection and preference at all sorts of higher prices. The United States grew a quota of beet sugar at home and gave a protected market to the Philippines and a preferential market for a quota of Cuban sugar. The United Kingdom grew a quota of beet sugar at home and gave a preferential market to Empire sugar at much above the world price.* Australia sold her cane sugar production at home at 23s to 24s a cwt and exported a substantial quantity to the United Kingdom at the Empire price. But it was the subsidised production of beet sugar, above all, which disorganised the

---

* In 1937–8, the United Kingdom sugar supplies were obtained as follows:

	Tons	Price per Cwt	
		s	d
Foreign	509,000	5	5
Other empire	824,000	9	2
Colonial certified	357,000	10	2
Home-grown beet	418,000	18	10

(excluding assistance given to beet sugar industry which represented in 1936–7 5s 3d a cwt)

market. Out of a total world production of about 28 million tons, over 10 million tons represented the amount of beet sugar, produced in almost every case on the basis of a subsidised price much above the open market price. Moreover, the European beet sugar industries produced not only sufficient for home requirements, but also considerable quantities for export. The retail price in most European countries was determined, not by the open market price, but by the cost of subsidised production, on top of which was often added heavy taxation for revenue purposes; and total consumption in the different countries varied inversely with the retail price, e.g.:

	Consumption per head (in kilos per annum) 1935–6	Retail price (pence per kilo) 1935–6
Denmark	55·9	4·6
Sweden	48·8	4·5
Great Britain	47·8	5·0
Finland	29·7	6·9
Norway	31·9	7·0
France	25·1	7·6
Germany	23·4	15·0
Hungary	10·55	11·4
Italy	7·9	15·9

If subsidies and taxes were limited retail prices could be reduced and consumption would expand. Unless the reduction of subsidies was considerable this would not directly help the economic producers, as they would still be unable to compete with the subsidised home industry, but indirectly it would do so as the additional outlet on the home market would tend to decrease subsidised exports and thus increase outlets for economic production on the world market. Without some such increase of home consumption in the beet sugar countries or some reduction of their subsidised production, the outlet on the

world market for economic producers shrinks continually and the dumping of subsidised sugar depresses world prices to levels which are unprofitable, even to economic producers. None of the subsidising countries is likely to accept the simple abandonment of their subsidised production. The best that can be hoped for is that they will limit it to some agreed production quota on condition that total supplies are kept in reasonable relation to effective demand. The situation would be still further improved if general agreement could be reached that any subsidies given to domestic producers should be financed by the budget and not passed on to consumers by means of import tariffs or controls, as in that case the consumer would get the benefit of world prices and consumption would expand.

[Appendix III was identical to Appendix II of the fifth draft. Therefore, it does not appear here.]

The August draft, with a minute of dissent from the Ministry of Agriculture, served as the basis for the discussions with the Dominions on post-war international economic policy during October and November 1942. After these discussions, Keynes returned to his primary product scheme, re-drafting it in the light of the reactions he had encountered. By 27 November he had radically re-drafted the scheme, reducing and amalgamating sections i and ii of the August draft and re-writing Section iii completely. This draft after further alterations went back to the Committee on Post-War External Economic Problems in January 1943.

As the discussions resumed, Keynes to some extent, became more exasperated with his critics. The extent of his exasperation can be seen in a note to Sir Wilfrid Eady written in January.

From a minute to SIR WILFRID EADY, *January 1943*

THE PRIMARY PRODUCTS PAPER

1. I have made dozens of changes in response to my critics, and most of them, in my own judgement, improvements—some of them substantial. I have the advantage as a draftsman of

genuinely occupying, in my own mind, a middle position
between the critics of opposing schools, and I have tried to keep
the balance even. Must I produce another stencil? Or can I now
go again into print, which is much easier to read and judge? I
should like to produce a revised print at this stage to go round
to the whole Hurst Committee and (perhaps) the Dominions.
N.B. Clauson's promised detailed comments have not yet
arrived.

2. Taking the critics in order (more detailed comments
written on some of their letters which are attached below)...

Leith-Ross. I have made considerable use of these very
extensive comments and have adopted a large number of
them—but not all. Perhaps I should see him and run through
the outstanding cases of difference. The comments fall into two
very distinct groups—according to whether the glosses are by
an Elohistic commentator who is an extreme devotee of Free
Trade or a Jahvistic scribe who is an equally extreme devotee
of Restriction. I have more sympathy with the Elohistic
authority, but, if I meet him all along the line the paper would
receive a wrong emphasis and trench too much on the ground
of the Commercial Policy Paper. Also it does not seem prudent
tactics in a paper designed to protect the interests of primary
producers generally to make its principal purpose appear to be
the abolition of agriculture throughout the United States and
most of Europe. On a major proposal for rearrangement of the
text, I have tried to meet the substance of the complaint, but
have not adopted the actual suggestion made, which seems to
me to be open to grave objection and to make more difficulties
than it cures. I sympathise personally with Leith-Ross's comment (4) that there is too much detail about voting, etc. But I
introduced this as the result of discovering that this is the thing
in which the minor powers, as exemplified by the Dominions,
are most interested. Indeed Snelling presses me to be more
specific if I am to accept fully the conclusions of our Dominion
Talks....

Fergusson.[3] His contribution can only be described as barmy. One can try to meet, or compromise with, differences of opinion or criticisms of expression. But in this case every paragraph of his letter and several of his detailed comments show an almost lunatic misunderstanding of what the paper says or is driving at. It is a frightful nuisance. For it will be very difficult to clear up these sheer misunderstandings if they are produced at the Ministerial Committee. But Fergusson is such a good fellow and so all-but aware of the above that I should not despair of persuading him to certify himself.

At the beginning of February, the Official Committee on Post-War External Economic Problems had settled on a revised draft for circulation to the War Cabinet.

WAR CABINET
COMMITTEE ON RECONSTRUCTION PROBLEMS
THE INTERNATIONAL REGULATION OF PRIMARY
PRODUCTS

I. *Preface*

An international scheme to regulate primary products must be designed to promote the objects specified in the fourth and fifth points of the Atlantic Charter, which read:

'Fourth, they will endeavour, with due respect for their existing obligations, to further the enjoyment by all States, great and small, victor or vanquished, of access, on equal terms, to the trade and to the raw materials of the world, which are needed for their economic prosperity.

'Fifth, they desire to bring about the fullest collaboration between all nations in the economic field with the object of

---

[3] John Donald Fergusson (1891–1963), K.C.B. 1937; entered Treasury, 1919, Assistant Secretary, 1934; Private Secretary to successive Chancellors of the Exchequer, 1920–36; Permanent Secretary, Ministry of Agriculture and Fisheries, 1936–45; Permanent Secretary, Ministry of Fuel and Power, 1945–52.

securing for all improved labour standards, economic advancement and social security.'

2. Before the War, and especially in the 'thirties, primary producers suffered grievously from several causes:

(*a*) The prices of their products fluctuated violently within the same year, with the result that stock holding became too risky for merchants and stocks tended to accumulate in the hands of producers.

(*b*) They were subject to periodic slumps when prices fell below what could provide a reasonable standard of life.

(*c*) Their relative inability, compared with industrial producers, to curtail output exposed them, even more than the latter, to the effects of fluctuations in demand, and the prices of the products tended to fall in relation to the prices of the final products which they were buying.

(*d*) Their difficulties were aggravated in some important cases through excess capacity created by the subsidisation of high cost prodution, which was doubly injurious because, being accompanied (as a rule) by tariff or other restrictions against lower cost imports, it restricted consumption as well as increased supply.

(*e*) As a result of all this, the general depression of the decade before the War produced outstanding instances of chronic surpluses, actual and potential, where the world's economic system failed to discover means to enjoy the full abundance of the earth.

The measures of regulation which were improvised to deal with particular cases of difficulty had varying degrees of merit. But it cannot be claimed for most of them that they were sufficient or satisfactory or successful.

3. The remedies for these evils, which we may hope to apply after the war, must take various forms. But, apart from general measures to control the trade cycle and to remove impediments to trade, they should include a direct attack on the problems of primary producers. The outlines of proposals to this end are

discussed below. The details of any scheme must be governed by the special problems and requirements of the particular commodity in view. No plan can claim to be applicable to all commodities. Nevertheless, for a wide range of commodities certain general principles of operation can, it is suggested, be usefully prescribed and agreed.

4. Regulation schemes can have either or both of two distinct objectives: (a) the moderation of excessive short-term fluctuations of prices about the long-term equilibrium price, and (b) the maintenance of long-term equilibrium between supply and demand at a price level which provides to the majority of the producers a standard of life in reasonable relation to the standards of the countries in which they live.

5. The extent of the evil to be remedied under the first objective can scarcely be exaggerated, though it is not always appreciated. In the absence of regulation, a comparatively small excess of visible supplies, which has to be taken by an unwilling market, causes a disproportionate collapse of price, and an equally small deficiency of supplies causes prices to rocket upwards. A study of the violence of individual price fluctuations and the inability of an unregulated competitive system to avoid them (even when it is tempered, as it was in the case of rubber from 1934 onwards, by an international regulation scheme) is given in Appendix I. It is there shown that for the four commodities—rubber, cotton, wheat and lead—which are fairly representative of raw materials marketed in competitive conditions, the average *annual* price range over the decade before 1938 was 67 per cent. An orderly programme of output, either of raw materials themselves or of their manufactured products, is not possible in such conditions. If arrangements could be made by which temporary surpluses could be absorbed in a buffer stock and held firmly till they could be released to meet a subsequent increase of demand, the first objective would be met.

6. Buffer stocks have the purpose of steadying prices and are

intended, as their name implies, to absorb shocks. By this means prices should be confined, if possible, within a reasonable range over short periods; provided, however, that they remain subject to gradual changes, those producers who find the ruling price attractive being allowed a gradual expansion at the expense of those who find it unattractive. We should aim at combining a short-period stabilisation of prices with a long-period price policy which balances supply and demand and allows a steady rate of expansion to the cheaper cost producers. In this way we can hope to strike a balance between a reasonable measure of security to the producer and adequate provision for peaceful evolutionary change. The relative advantages between one source of supply and another are constantly shifting, owing to changes in public taste, technological advances, improved transport facilities to places formerly inaccessible and adoption of substitutes, natural or artificial. It may be advisable to retard these natural currents, but it would be a mistake, and probably futile, to resist them permanently.

7. If, however, there is a prospect of a persisting disequi-librium which fails to respond to reasonable changes in the world market price, other means may be necessary to attain the second objective above, namely, to regulate the pace and violence of lasting changes and to mitigate the shock to producers who, through circumstances which they cannot control, find them-selves losing their markets. Thus measures to stabilise prices may need on occasion to be supplemented by measures to smooth the transition to the new conditions and to regulate output meanwhile, so as to safeguard the standards of life of primary producers, as well as to ease the pains of change and progress. In the following plan carefully guarded proposals for restriction have, therefore, been added to the less questionable proposals for stabilising prices with which it begins. It is true that these run the risk of developing into chronic restriction of output. It remains to be seen, however, whether in the post-war world this will prove necessary over so wide a field as was thought

necessary in the decade before the war. We may reasonably hope that the adequate stimulation of demand and the raising of nutritional standards and the standard of life generally will have the effect of taking up the slack and absorbing potential production. Certainly it will be a matter for great dissatisfaction if we should find it advisable deliberately to impoverish the world by checking a potential output of primary foodstuffs and other raw materials, whilst hundreds of millions of consumers go short of what they should have.

8. A complete scheme must endeavour to bring these two sets of arrangements, when both are required, into a consistent whole. In adition, a co-ordinating authority will be required to deal with difficulties arising between conflicting interests and to provide an adequate measure of conformity to a common pattern.

9. Superimposed on the fortuitous short-period price swings affecting particular commodities and particular groups of producers there is the fundamental malady of the trade cycle. Fortunately, the same technique of buffer stocks which has to be called into being to deal with the former, is also capable of making a large contribution to the cure of the trade cycle itself. For the maintenance of good employment throughout the world, in industrial countries as well as in those producing primary commodities, this is of the first importance, sufficient by itself to justify the setting up of machinery for buffer stocks. This aspect of the argument is further developed in Appendix II.

II. *The outline of the plan*
10. *The General Council*

(i) A General Council for Commodity Controls shall be established, which each of the United Nations shall be invited to join as member states. Other states may be invited to join either at the outset or subsequently. A state may withdraw after adequate notice, say, two years.

(ii) Member states shall not be parties, and shall not allow

their nationals to be parties, to any scheme or cartel in respect of a primary product which provides for export quotas or price schedules, organised by or on behalf of the exporters of more than one country, or for an international holding pool, unless within two years of the establishment of the General Council it has been submitted to the Council's General Executive (see below) and has received its approval.

(iii) Member states shall agree to accept decisions in respect of their export quotas in the event of the establishment of regulation under §12 (vii) or §14 below.

(iv) Each participating state shall be entitled to nominate a member on the General Council, which shall meet annually to appoint (say) twelve members of a General Executive and to receive and discuss a report from this Executive. The voting power of each member state on the General Council might be proportional to its interest in international trade (and might be the same as in the case of the Clearing Union), and elections shall be made on the principles of proportional representation (so that a country or group of countries which possesses one-twelfth of the voting power will be able, in effect, to concentrate this voting power on one candidate and thus make sure of electing him).

(v) The General Executive shall appoint an independent Chairman, Vice-Chairman and General Secretary from outside their own number, who shall also act in these capacities at meetings of the General Council. All members of the Executive shall have the same voting power.

(vi) The General Executive shall be responsible for defining 'a primary product' for the purpose of the scheme, for delimiting the scope of the particular controls and for co-ordinating their policies. The definition of a 'commodity' and the range of produce to be handled by a single Control shall be determined by the Executive, having regard to the variety of types and grades and to the possibilities of substitution between one article and another.

11. *The Commod Controls*

(i) Any group of countries interested either as exporters or importers of any primary product or groups of allied primary products (which we may conveniently call *commod*) may submit proposals to the Executive to set up a Commod Control providing for any of the following: price control, buffer stocks, export quotas, the regulation of output, the encouragement of new sources of supply, the maintenance of reserve capacity. The Executive may invite any other countries, which appear to them to be substantially interested in Commod, to join in the discussion of the proposals.

(ii) An approved Commod Control would consist of such a number of members as is necessary to cover conveniently the countries principally interested, appointed, subject to the necessary exceptions, as follows: four-tenths by the exporting countries (electing by proportional representation on the basis of their exports in the five preceding years*), three-tenths by the importing countries (electing in the same manner on the basis of their imports) and three-tenths, being independent members, by the General Council. Decisions would be taken on the basis of a simple majority vote.

(iii) A Commod Control which provides for buffer stocks would be expected in general to conform to the principles laid down in §12 below.

(iv) A Commod Control which provided for a continuing regulation of output or of export by means of quotas or in any other way would be expected in general to conform to the principles laid down in §14 below.

(v) Nevertheless, variant schemes, departing in greater or less degree from these general principles, may be approved by the Executive on the recommendation of a Commod Control, if they are persuaded that special reasons make this advisable.

(vi) Where different commodities are capable of being sub-

* This may need some appropriate adjustment at the initial post-war elections.

stituted for one another, either by consumers or by producers, it shall be the duty of the General Executive to see that the particular Commod Controls concerned act in line with one another, and it may require from them joint or correlated action, especially in price policy—though the constitution of the Commod Controls and the representation of the Executive on them should be calculated to ensure this without express instructions from the General Executive.

(vii) More generally, it should be the function of the General Executive to receive periodic reports of their operations from each of the Commod Controls, to review their condition, and, if necessary, to make recommendations as to the policy which they should follow. Such recommendations would have as their object the protection of the general interest, and especially the maintenance of a stable level of general prices and the control of the trade cycle.

(viii) (a) A Commod Control would be concerned with that part of output which is available for export. It is not proposed that either individual Controls or the General Executive should have any authority over the prices paid to producers or charged to consumers in respect of domestic output consumed at home, although they may make representations to the governments concerned as provided in §14 (iv) below. Nor are they given any powers, beyond the right to make representations under §14 (iv), in respect of tariffs or subsidies which are part of the national policy of any member state. For whatever success may attend on efforts to raise nutritional and other standards, there must necessarily remain, at least for a long time ahead, a wide difference between the levels attainable in poorer and wealthier countries. It is necessary, therefore, that regulation schemes should be framed on lines which leave each country free to give subsidies, direct or indirect, to its own producers, in order to maintain their standard of living at the level which it considers proper.

(b) None the less, a serious difficulty arises if such subsidies

are given on a substantial scale, especially if they are allowed to operate as export subsidies. For the effect of the subsidies is to maintain a larger volume of production in the countries giving them, and also, if the method of tariffs is employed, to restrict consumption, thus checking the redistribution of world demand in favour of the most economic producers. The network of governmental controls established in this way and responsive to no economic stimulus was in some cases one of the main reasons for the accumulation of surpluses. The effectiveness of any buffer stock scheme must, therefore, partly depend on the possibility of eliminating pre-war restrictions and securing general co-operation on the part of all governments in policies directed to the expansion of consumption. Thus it is important to secure a general understanding that subsidies (direct or indirect) given by governments to their own producers of those commodities which are the subject of control schemes, should be confined within moderate limits and limited to produce which is consumed, as well as produced, at home.

(ix) Commod Controls would set their faces against any deliberate destruction of food which otherwise might take place locally whether or not incidentally to measures of regulation descibed below; and wherever appropriate they would make arrangements for unavoidable surpluses to be distributed for consumption in necessitous areas.

12. *Buffer stocks*

(i) A Commod Control may, with the approval of the General Executive, establish a buffer stock accompanied by provisions to stabilise prices within a certain range.

(ii) In this case the Control would establish an initial basic price on a uniform c.i.f. basis, and would offer to buy commod at a price (say) 10 per cent below the basic price and to sell it at a price (say) 10 per cent above the basic price. The buffer stock should be prepared, save as hereinafter provided in §12 (ix) and §14 (vii), to take any supplies offered to it at the lower

limit. The basic price would be modified by the Control from time to time thereafter by a process of trial and error with a view to keeping the size of the buffer stock within a defined range. If its own stock or world stocks were increasing beyond a stipulated figure, or at more than a stipulated rate, thus indicating that the price was unduly attractive to producers or unduly discouraging to consumers, the basic price would be reduced. Similarly, it would be raised if stocks were falling below a convenient level or at too fast a rate. For this purpose the Control would review the position, not only of its stocks, but also of total visible stocks throughout the world, and also the prospective supply. The Control could not view with equanimity a situation in which outside stocks were accumulating rapidly, even though its own were not. In other words, the object of the Control would be to discover by empirical methods a range of prices within which supply and demand would be in equilibrium when the influence of excessive short-period fluctuations on either side of the market had been smoothed away.

(iii) The basic price does not mean a single price, but a complex of prices, according to varieties of quality, of dates in relation to the crop year in the case of agricultural commodities, and to position relatively to the cost of transport of the ultimate consumer. It should not be technically difficult to fix the prices for the main categories of any commodity in proper relation to the basic price, provided discretion is allowed for variations in the differentials between grades; for such margins are already established by trade practice.

(iv) If the Commod Control cannot agree an initial basic price acceptable both to a majority of the exporters and to the majority of the importers, this price shall be fixed by the General Executive at the level which, in their judgement, is calculated gradually to bring about a proper relation between supply and demand without regulation of output, provided that this price is not below 'a reasonable international economic price' in the sense of §14 (vi) below.

(v) If, either initially or later, it appears that unrestricted

supply can only be absorbed at a price which falls below a 'reasonable economic price', the procedure of §14 shall be brought into operation, since the presumption will be that the price mechanism by itself is inadequate to establish a tolerable position.

(vi) The normal size of the buffer stock and its range of fluctuation would be fixed by the General Executive on the recommendation of the Commod Control on the following general principles:

(a) It should be larger for commodities subject to the fluctuations of the seasons or where experience shows that either supply or demand is particularly subject to sharp fluctuation or insensitive to price changes. Thus in the case of annual crops the normal stock should be at least large enough to replace any temporary deficiency caused by exceptionally poor harvests. In the case of other products, such as tree crops and minerals, where new production follows some years behind the initiation of measures to increase it, the stock should be reasonably sufficient against the possible gap where there is a pronounced upward long-term trend in demand.

(b) For some commodities the maximum number of months' stock might have to be kept below the usual figure because of the necessity to turn over the stock and replace it frequently. In other cases, for example meat, the capacity and situation of refrigerated storage might be a limiting factor, unless canning or drying come to the rescue. For some tropical or semi-tropical products storage is possible at some stages of processing but not at others. The technique and facilities for storage may be expected to undergo continuing improvement, and the Controls could very properly finance development in this direction.

(c) Where there are physical reasons why the response of supply to the stimulus of increased prices is necessarily slow, it is important that the potential capacity should be in excess of normal requirements, and it may be advisable, therefore, to offer some inducement to provide or maintain such extra

capacity. It would be the duty of an efficient Control to find ways of conserving and suitably rewarding a prudent margin of excess potential capacity, charging the cost of this to consumers as a whole.

(vii) The range between the Control's buying and selling prices, suggested above for purposes of illustration at 10 per cent on either side of the basic price, need not be the same for every commodity and could be varied from time to time (and perhaps narrowed) in the light of experience. It might be found advisable to allow a wider range for some agricultural prices than for commodities not subject to the seasons. A study of the percentage deviations of crop yields from trend level in pre-war years suggests, however, that, even in the case of annual crops, a price range of 20 per cent will normally be sufficient to allow a fair measure of stabilisation of producers' incomes for the world as a whole. It will not always effect this purpose within each separate country. But to do so lies essentially outside the scope of an international scheme, since it cannot be brought about consistently with a uniform international price. There is nothing to prevent individual governments from operating within the international scheme, if they wish to do so, with a view to a further stabilisation of the incomes of their own producers.

(viii) When a revision of prices, either upward or downward, becomes necessary, the Control would aim at making such changes as small and gradual as possible. It would not be wise to lay down a hard-and-fast rule as to the maximum rate of such changes in advance of experience. It must partly depend on the stability of world conditions in other respects. The immediately previous movement of prices within the range above or below the existing basic price would also be relevant. But it is to be hoped that *downward* revisions, at any rate, would not normally exceed 10 per cent within a year, and very gradual changes such as 2 per cent would be a mark of successful management. Nevertheless, the Control should be free to alter its basic price at any time, and there should be no absolute limitations

on its discretion in determining the amount of the change, save that during a world depression, defined by suitable indices approved by the General Executive, it would not be permitted to reduce the basic price by more than 5 per cent in one year.

(ix) Since it is of the essence of the scheme that price changes should be as moderate and as gradual as possible, it is necessary to provide the Control with some means to prevent the buffer stock from being quickly overwhelmed with offers if the effect of price changes works too slowly to give it the necessary protection. To facilitate this each exporting country shall have attributed to it a standard tonnage, to be fixed at the inception by agreement amongst exporters (or, failing this, by the General Executive) and subsequently equal to a moving average of its annual volume of net exports in the previous three or five years, subject to appeal to the General Executive by any exporter for revision on exceptional grounds. On the occasion of a reduction in price, designed to offset an excessive increase in the buffer stock, the Control shall be entitled at its discretion to fix a quota of the standard tonnages (the same proportion of its standard tonnage for each exporting country), in excess of which no country shall export to any destination; and to limit its takings from an exporter to an amount (including his sales in the market) not exceeding his quota. So long as such quotas continue in force, the basic price shall be progressively reduced at a rate of not less than (say) 5 per cent per annum—provided (as before) that this does not bring the price below 'a reasonable economic level', in which case the procedure of section 14 shall be invoked.

(x) On the occasion of an increase in price, designed to offset a persistent tendency towards exhaustion of stocks in the hands of the Control, the Control shall, if it thinks advisable and the General Executive approve, attempt to organise and assist an expansion of additional capacity in the exporting countries most suitable for the purpose, either by reason of their being actual or potential low cost producers, or because they are deficit

countries (or tending that way) in the books of the Clearing Union, or for reasons of a social and humanitarian character. The obligation of the Control to sell on the usual terms in relation to its basic price would, of course, cease with the exhaustion of its stocks. In time of scarcity, when such a situation was impending, some plan of allocating sales to importing countries might be required.

(xi) Some provision might be necessary to limit the Control's liability to be saddled with responsibility for holding stocks destined for domestic consumption in the country of origin. Thus deliveries at the producing centres should be accepted only at the Control's discretion and re-sales should not be made, unless the Control chooses, except on c.i.f. terms appropriate to some consuming centre. It has to be remembered, however, that a fluctuating part of domestic production enters into international trade, for which the Control would have to allow and which it should facilitate.

(xii) A buffer stock would not be applicable to highly perishable commodities and could only be undertaken in cases where the produce can be stored for a reasonable time. Even storable agricultural stocks would, however, require to be turned over from time to time, and, apart from its contractual buying and selling obligations, the Control would itself deal in the market or arrange with merchants so as to keep its stocks in motion where they might otherwise deteriorate, replacing old stock by new stock, without, however, modifying its total stock except as the result of its contracted sales and purchases. It might be free to hold a modest proportion of its stocks in the shape of futures, appropriately related in price to spot transactions, and it should ease market difficulties by changing the position of its stocks. A consuming centre might be allowed to attract stocks by offering to bear part of the cost of storage, provided it was not allowed, except by agreement, to bring within its jurisdiction an amount of total stocks out of proportion to its importance as a consumer. Generally speaking, the

location of stocks should be as widely distributed amongst consuming and producing centres as climatic conditions for safe storage permit. But, in the case of 'key' commodities, the Commodity Controls might be required to take into account arrangements made for the disarmament of the enemy powers.

(xiii) Members would be expected to furnish the Control with full statistics of output, consumption and total stocks, including those held privately, and other information useful to producers and consumers, which the Control would publish at suitable intervals.

(xiv) Within these reasonably wide limits, free and competitive international markets would handle the trade, as they would in the absence of control; and there would be no objection to state trading by any country which preferred that method subject to safeguards against its use for non-economic purposes. The protection against excessive price fluctuations provided by the Control should allow merchants or state trading corporations to hold stocks and to operate with confidence within the determined range, and thus relieve the Control of a multiplicity of detailed operations in day-to-day business. The operations of traders within this range might effect, in practice, a further narrowing of normal short-term fluctuations except where an abnormal surplus or deficiency of current supply was clearly in prospect.

(xv) The profits arising out of the difference between the Control's buying and selling prices might be sufficient to pay for the costs of storage and management. If however, they were inadequate for this purpose, a suitable levy should be added to the price of all exports to meet the expense. Any net profits earned by the Control should be employed to provide part of the fund for financing the stocks.

(xvi) Special provisions would be required during the initial period after the war when most products are likely to be in short supply, which the Controls must not aggravate by endeavouring to build up working stocks. Moreover, it would be undesirable

that they should fix basic prices under the influence of temporary conditions which might be considerably too high in normal circumstances. On the other hand, the transitional period after the war, when supplies of many primary products will inevitably remain under official control for the time being, will offer a specially good opportunity for getting the Controls organised. The conclusion is that the Controls should be organised as soon as possible and before the period at which they might be expected to enter into active operation. In the initial stages they would be accumulating information and statistics; and they should during this period endeavour to establish a common doctrine between producers and consumers regarding reasonable basic prices for the commodities which they would control. At the same time they could examine the probable scale of prospective demand and the best means of distributing and meeting it. The General Executive would have a useful function to perform at this stage in correlating ideas about the relative prices of the commodities concerned. If these preliminary measures were carried through successfully, the individual Controls would be able to intervene on the downswing at points which would receive general approbation, and so underpin the market and give confidence to producers, whilst postponing their liability to sell on this basis until sufficient stocks had accumulated in the ordinary course of events. In any case, however, in which surplus export stocks already existed in the hands of governments, a Control should be prepared to take them over at an agreed price, thus solving the problem of how to prevent the liquidation of such stocks from interfering with normal current output.

13. *The finance of buffer stocks*

We come next to the pivotal question of the finance of buffer stocks, for which large sums might be required if the system was extended to a number of commodities:

183

(i) It would be preferable that the whole of the finance required by the several Controls should be consolidated in the hands of the General Executive who would be responsible for finding it, and that individual Controls should rely on the Executive and be subject to such limitations of finance as the Executive may determine.

(ii) The necessary finance being thus consolidated, it might be obtained through an international commodity loan issued in blocks as required, secured on the buffer stocks valued at their basic prices, supplemented by a general levy (as in §12 (xv) above) on all the commodities covered by the schemes in the event of the aggregate value of the stocks as a whole falling below the net amount of the loans raised against them. Alternatively the capital of this international loan might be defined in terms of the value of the composite commodity made up of the various produce composing the stocks, so that its commodity value would be conserved irrespective of changes in the commodity value of money. In either case such a loan would be exceptionally well secured. It must be remembered that a large part of the finance required is not new, but is already provided from private or public sources. At the initiation, therefore, of any buffer stock scheme, countries already holding and financing either surplus or normal stocks of the commodity in question might be invited, especially if they are credit countries in the books of the Clearing Union, to subscribe the sums thus released, or a part of them, to the commodity loan.

(iii) There would be great advantages, on the other hand, if the fluctuating margin of the finance could be handled through the account of the General Executive with the Clearing Union —on the assumption that this or some similar institution is set up. In this case the General Executive would hold an increasing credit balance with the Clearing Union in times of general boom when the buffer stocks were running off, and an increasing debit balance in times of general slump when the buffer stocks were accumulating. By this means a stabilising factor of major

importance might be introduced into the world economic system. For purchasing power would be continuously withdrawn from the rest of the Clearing Union system during the development of boom conditions and would, on the other hand, be continuously augmented during the onset of a slump. The importance of buffer stocks as a measure contributory to the prevention of the trade cycle is developed in Appendix II below.

(iv) It should be a condition of assistance from the general pool of finance that a Commod Control, which was badly managed or failed to keep its financial obligations within the prescribed limits, could be taken over by the General Executive and, if necessary, wound up. Any resulting losses would be met, like less avoidable losses, as provided in (ii) above, that is to say, by a general levy on the turnover of all the commodities covered by buffer stock arrangements.

(v) No estimate can be framed of the total volume of the finance which would be required, before it is decided how wide a range of the staple raw materials of international trade the schemes will endeavour to cover, or without entering in detail in each particular case into the number of months' stocks it would be advisable to hold, or in advance of experience of the proportion of total stocks which the Controls would, in practice, be required to carry. An attempt has, however, been made to compile figures (highly approximate), so as to indicate the order of the magnitude involved, for eight principal commodities—wheat, maize, sugar, coffee, cotton, wool, rubber and tin—which are given in Appendix III. These figures show that the total value of a year's international trade in these commodities, taking the average volume over the years 1935–8, was about £700 million at the prices of 1939 and £950 million at the prices of 1942. A year's stock on this basis in the hands of the Control would be much too high; three months' would probably be too low—at any rate, the Controls must be prepared to hold more than this; and some figure intermediate between these extremes might be appropriate. A more comprehensive table taken from

The Network of World Trade (League of Nations), also given in Appendix III, indicates that stocks equal to six months exports of a wide range of primary products could be carried (at 1938 prices) with aggregate finance of (say) $m2,500. It must be repeated that by no means the whole of the necessary finance is *additional* to what would be required otherwise. Normal stocks must be held and must sometimes accumulate to abnormal amounts, even in the absence of Controls, and the finance for carrying such stocks has to be found from somewhere. For example, it is estimated that the stocks of the above eight commodities (very unequally distributed between them), including the domestic surpluses, likely to be held at the end of 1942, outside Russia and the enemy-occupied countries, are likely to be worth about £900 million at present prices, the finance for which is being found already.

14. *The quota regulation of exports*

A properly managed buffer stock scheme should prove effective in stabilising the position of the many commodities for which they are appropriate (see 12 (xii)), where there have been considerable price movements corresponding to changes of market trends, without any evidence of chronic maladjustment. In drawing up the general regulations for such schemes it has, however, been necessary to recognise that cases will arise where the use of the price mechanism, aided only by buffer stocks, will be inadequate, because, if pressed to its logical conclusion, it may result in bringing the price appropriate to the state of supply and demand below a level which the producers can be expected to tolerate. If it is merely that the price mechanism works too slowly, the provision of §12 (ix) above for the temporary quota regulation of exports may be sufficient. But for an obstinate disequilibrium between supply and demand at a price level reasonably tolerable to producers, including a disequilibrium arising on a commodity which cannot appro-

186

priately be covered by a buffer stock scheme at all, we may have to fall back on the organised restriction of production. The international regulation of exports may be the best means of ensuring this, but this would only be effective over a period, if it is supplemented by co-ordinated national schemes for the regulation of stocks and, where practicable, of production. Such schemes were characteristic of the decade before the war, and covered, with varying degrees of effectiveness, a wide range of commodities. Opinions differ as to how far the necessity for these schemes was just one of many symptoms of the extreme economic malaise of that period and how far they are an inevitable accompaniment of the wide differences of labour costs and of the opportunity for diversification of output in different parts of the world. But there is likely to be general agreement that such schemes may prove to be necessary in the case of certain commodities even in the new circumstances; that any proposals for the international regulation of primary products must, therefore, provide for their possibility; and that careful precautions should be taken in handling an instrument which, if abused, is so liable to impoverish the world as a whole and waste its potential resources. For restriction schemes are a natural and indeed, an inevitable, sequel to the buffer stock proposals, in the event of the basic price necessary to secure equilibrium between supply and demand being below 'a reasonable international economic price'. It is the interpretation of this last phase which is the crux of all such schemes. This is not a difficulty created by the present proposals. It is inherent in any form of restriction which aims at a just balance between the claims of producers and of consumers. Our plan cannot be expected to do more than provide an impartial and authoritative body for its estimation, failing agreement between those chiefly concerned on the two sides of the world market. For the problem involves too many factors incapable of precise measurement for its solution to be safely entrusted to a formula. A large element of common sense and of general judgment in the

light of all the known facts must be invoked in reaching a decision. The following is an attempt to combine effective regulation with adequate safeguards:

(i) If a majority of the exporting governments represented on a Commod Control are agreed among themselves that the basic price appropriate to the prospective long-term state of supply and demand would be below a reasonable international economic price, they shall be entitled to apply to the General Executive (see §11 (ii) above, where a scheme of regulation already exists), which shall also hear objections from consumers and minority producers, for permission to enforce quota regulation of exports, accompanied by control of stocks and, where practicable, by regulation of production.

(ii) In making this application the exporters shall state—

(*a*) whether the importing governments represented on the Control support or oppose the application and, in the latter event, the importing governments shall be entitled to explain the grounds of their objection;

(*b*) whether their proposal is due to causes which they regard as likely to be continuing or whether it is strictly temporary to allow a gradual transfer from high cost to low cost producers or from this particular product to an alternative product and, in the latter event, the measures proposed for bringing the restriction gradually to an end within a stated period;

(*c*) if, on the other hand, the proposal is due to causes regarded as likely to be continuing, how far, in their judgement, the existence of over-production is to be explained by—

(1) stimulation of exportable capability by subsidies or their equivalent in some of the exporting countries,

(2) restriction of importing capacity by subsidisation of domestic production or by excessive prices to consumers through high tariffs or their equivalent in some of the importing countries,

(3) uneconomic competition by substitutable commodities,

(4) lack of opportunity on the part of some of the exporting countries to shift to alternative production more required by the world economy,

(5) limitation of demand by the impoverished condition of potential consumers whose standards of living would benefit by increased consumption of the commodity,

(*d*) what variations of economic cost exist between different producers and on different scales of total output,

(*e*) the justification of the 'economic price' they propose.

(iii) On such an application being made, provisonal export quotas, based on the procedure of §12 (ix) above, shall come into force immediately, pending the decision of the General Executive on future policy.

(iv) Before approving a restriction scheme required for reasons regarded as likely to continue, the General Executive shall endeavour to deal with the radical causes of the problem. If reasons (1) and (2) have been adduced, they shall invite countries subsidising exports to reduce or abolish such subsidies, and countries applying tariffs or other expedients for fostering home production, to abate them.* If reasons (3) and (4) apply, they shall consult with the Commod Controls concerned with substitutable products or alternative production, with a view to diminishing any uneconomic competition (if its existence is proved) and to encouraging alternative production, providing, if necessary, financial and technical assistance to promote a shift in production. If the case for (5) is made out, they shall consider whether it is practicable to find some means of subsidising the consumption of the product in impoverished countries (in consultation as regards foodstuffs with a Nutritional Council, if there is such a body).

(v) If the exporters have not reached agreement amongst themselves as to their standard tonnages for the purpose of the scheme, these shall be fixed by the General Executive, which shall pay attention, amongst other considerations, to the pro-

---

* In Appendix IV illustrations are given, for wheat and sugar, to show how much scope there is for better international practice in these respects.

portionate share of the export trade on the average of the previous three (or five) import years. In any case, when restriction is in force, the General Executive shall be entitled to diminish the standard progressively of any country which subsidises exports, especially if this is not combined with control of production; and to increase the standard of any country which is a deficit country in the Clearing Union or which is a relatively low cost producer or which has special difficulties in producing alternative output.

(vi) If the Commod Control cannot agree a basic price under regulation acceptable both to a majority of the exporters and to a majority of the importers, this price shall be fixed by the General Executive at the level which, in their judgment, corresponds to 'a reasonable international economic price'. In fixing this price, the Executive shall have primary regard to the level which would provide the average (not marginal) producers of, say, two-thirds or three-quarters of the exporting countries, weighted according to their standard tonnages, with a standard of life in reasonable relation to the general standards of the country in which they live, and, where these standards have been low, shall err in the generous direction with a view to their gradual improvement. Subject to this, they shall aim at a level calculated gradually to bring supply into proper relation to demand without restriction; but, on the other hand, they shall also pay attention, especially in the case of wasting assets such as metals, to provisions which may be expected to conserve potential capacity and to maintain and, if necessary, increase output in succeeding years to correspond to prospective demand. They shall aim at levels which are not excessively out of line with the prices of possible substitutes or are likely, for any other reason, to react adversely on consumers' demand. In general, they shall be influenced by a regard for the best long-term interests of producers, provided no injustice or monopoly exaction is allowed against consumers.

(vii) When the basic price under restriction has been fixed, there is no reason why the operations of the buffer stock should

not continue as before—but with this important difference. With free output the price was the variable element by which the takings of the buffer stock were controlled. With restricted output the range of price becomes fixed, and the quota of restriction becomes the element which the buffer stock control must be free to vary. In this respect the plan would differ from most of those which have been operated hitherto, where quota restriction, whilst it has aimed at securing an economic price, has carried no guarantee of this price, so that, if demand falls below what was expected when the quota was fixed, the producer may suffer from restriction without the compensation of a tolerable price. If a minimum basic price has been fixed with the approval of the General Executive, the size of the quota can then be handled empirically by the buffer stock control, so as to keep the volume of stocks within an appropriate range, whilst keeping the price within the usual range of a fixed basic minimum.

(viii) The duration of a restriction scheme shall not exceed 5 years in the first instance and, if it is renewed on the ground that there is still serious over-supply, the basic price for the next period of 5 years shall be reduced by the General Executive unless special reason can be shown by the Control to the satisfaction of the General Executive, either on account of changes in other prices or because a major factor causing the need for a continuation of restriction is the high level of subsidy or protectionism in importing countries.

(ix) The details of a regulation scheme not covered by the above, particularly the sanctions necessary to enforce it, shall be subject to the approval of the General Executive.

III. *Conclusion*

15. We do not disguise from ourselves that the constructive proposals set forth above are conceived in a spirit of hopefulness which may be disappointed. They assume a measure of international discipline and good-neighbourliness, and, in general,

World exports of twenty-six products in 1938 ($000,000)*

Products	United States	Latin America†	Continental Europe	United Kingdom and Ireland	British Dominions and India	British Colonial Empire	French Oversea Territories	Netherlands Oversea Territories	Rest of World	Total
Cotton	224	78	17	—	88	37	2	—	154	600
Coal	56	—	242	183	10	2	4	1	32	530
Crude petroleum	112	293	5	—	7	7	—	8	23	448
Wheat	78	59	77	—	171	1	16	—	40	442
Wool	—	83	42	18	277	3	6	—	6	435
Petrol	122	12	40	4	—	53	—	115	48	394
Tobacco	156	17	121	—	12	11	2	20	20	359
Sugar	3	121	36	13	28	43	12	25	59	340
Copper	87	70	55	2	48	44	—	—	19	325
Butter	1	3	164	11	121	2	—	—	2	304
Gas and fuel oil	56	17	19	3	—	17	—	122	64	298
Rubber	—	5	—	—	1	176	18	74	13	287
Coffee	—	225	2	—	1	8	11	7	9	263
Beef, lamb, mutton	1	109	14	2	92	1	2	—	1	222
Maize	95	57	24	—	12	2	16	—	14	220
Pork	17	4	136	14	43	—	—	—	2	216
Tea	—	—	15	—	87	62	1	31	21	202
Rice	8	2	—	—	86	10	30	—	46	197
Iron ore	2	4	116	—	4	9	11	—	3	149
Silk	—	—	8	—	—	—	—	—	116	124
Wheat, flour	23	4	30	9	41	1	4	—	15	127
Tin (metal)	—	1	32	12	7	55	1	6	9	123
Citrus fruit	20	7	42	—	6	21	2	—	5	103
Total (23 products)	1,061	1,171	1,237	271	1,135	565	138	409	721	6,708
Exports of all goods	3,057	1,738	8,065	2,393	2,389	881	455	562	2,284	21,824

* As it did not prove possible to calculate 'frontier values' for exports of individual articles the figures in this table represent recorded values. The 'frontier values' of certain of the products of the United States and the group 'British Dominions and India' would be slightly higher than indicated.

† Excluding overseas territories of the United Kingdom, France and Netherlands.

a readiness of governments to accept proper standards of international behaviour which did not exist before the war. They also depend on the effective substitution of an expansionist for a contractionist pressure on world demand through the better management of the supply of international money. Yet a better ordering of our affairs may not be so difficult as it looks if we tackle it boldly. The gluts which have disorganised production in the past have been small in relation to actual output and still smaller in relation to potential demand, and the disorder they have caused has been disproportionate to its origin. It is not true that the impulse of individuals to toil and produce exceeds their readiness to enjoy and to consume, or that we have reached standards of life so high that our concern should be to hold back output and curb the bounty of nature. It is, rather, the task of this generation to devise, by taking thought, an organisation which allows escape from an insane paradox by bringing production and consumption into a fruitful union.

As the Appendices generally followed those of earlier drafts, they are not reprinted here. However, the additional trade statistics added to Appendix III appear opposite and below.

Distribution of trade in certain oilseeds and vegetable fatty oils in 1938

Product	World exports ($000,000)
Six oilseeds (fat content)*	318
Eight vegetable oils†	149
Total, six oilseeds (fat content) and eight vegetable oils	467

* The oilseeds considered are linseed, groundnuts, palm kernels, copra, soya beans, cottonseed. The fat content is calculated on the basis of the following percentages: groundnuts, 28 per cent; palm kernels, 45 per cent; copra, 63 per cent; soya beans, 14 per cent; cottonseed, 15 per cent; linseed, 33 per cent.

† Linseed oil, olive oil, groundnut oil, palm oil, palm kernel oil, coconut oil, soya bean oil and cottonseed oil.

Distribution of trade in certain fertilizers in 1938

Product	World exports ($000,000)
Nitrates of sodium, calcium and ammonia	57
Sulphate of ammonia	38
Natural phosphates	46
Basic slag	12
Superphosphate	11
Potash fertilizers	55

The Commodity Proposals were circulated to the War Cabinet on 5 March 1943. When the Cabinet discussed them on 8 April, it agreed that they should go to the Dominions. It also agreed that the proposals might be mentioned at the forthcoming United Nations Food Conference at Hot Springs but that they should be considered further beforehand by the Cabinet Committee on Post-War Commercial Policy.

On hearing of this last suggestion, Keynes minuted.

To SIR WILFRID EADY, *12 April 1943*

THE INTERNATIONAL REGULATION OF PRIMARY PRODUCTS

I see that the Cabinet have referred to a Committee, of which the Chancellor is to be Chairman, the question of reviewing the Primary Products scheme in its relation to other post-war schemes. It is not obvious from the Minutes what this relates to, unless it was some kind of act of appeasement to the Minister (presumably the Minister of Agriculture) who argued that the Report ought to make it clear that the creation of buffer stocks would not work effectively unless there were international regulation of primary products.

In case this is the right interpretation of the Minutes, perhaps it is well that I should put briefly the answer to this suggestion.

It is not, of course, a new one. It was made to the Official Committee by Sir Donald Fergusson on every occasion on

which they met and was also the subject of prolonged correspondence. Certain concessions and compromises—indeed too
many probably—were made to try to conciliate this point of
view. Such concessions and compromises had the result of
leaving Sir Donald Fergusson (he never had more than the
faintest support) in a minority of one, but they were not
successful in converting him. Nevertheless, the thought underlying the suggestion seems extraordinarily mistaken both from
the point of view of the interests of this country and of what
could be expected to work in practice.

Sir Donald Fergusson holds that every agricultural product
which is produced in the world ought to be planned internationally, every farmer being told some years beforehand what
he is to grow. Not only is the agriculture of every country of the
world to be planned by an international body, but a satisfactory
price is to be guaranteed all round, to be maintained by whatever
measure of restriction proves to be necessary.

Put down in black and white, this seems so balmy as not to
be easily credible as the representation of a policy seriously put
forward by a Government Department. But, if it does not mean
this, I do not know what it means, apart from what is already
provided for in the primary products scheme.

The political and other difficulties in the way of such a set up,
should it be desirable, are too obvious for it to be worth while
to develop them. But, apart from this, from the point of view
of the interests of this country, can one think of anything more
unwise than to instigate all the agricultural producers of raw
materials in the world to organise world-wide restriction schemes
with a view to putting up prices as high as possible against
consumers like ourselves? There may be cases in which measures
of restriction and unnecessarily high prices cannot be avoided.
But for us to take the lead in pressing such a thing on the world
surely should be out of the question.

The instruction of the Cabinet seems entirely vague. So one
may hope that it was merely intended as a method of polite

euthanasia for the suggestion incorporated higher up in the Minutes.

[copy initialled] K

Keynes was correct in his estimation, for the Committee on Post-War Commercial Policy approved the scheme as it stood on 30 April, recommending its use at the forthcoming Food Conference and its communication to the State Department in suitable circumstances. The War Cabinet accepted these recommendations on 4 May.

At the Food Conference, held at Hot Springs later in the month, the broad principles of primary product policy came up for discussion. The British representatives involved expounded the substance of the Commodity Paper at the Conference and handed a rough, unofficial, exposé of its contents to the State Department. However, they did not pass the actual document over.

Actual transmission of the document to the Americans did not take place until the Anglo-American post-war economic discussions of September and October 1943. Prior to these, under Keynes's influence, the British had prepared the ground by agreeing not to renew the restrictive pre-war Anglo-Dutch Rubber Agreement. The upshot of the resulting Anglo-American discussions, the main burden of which fell to Professor Robbins, who had been at Hot Springs, was an agreed set of objectives and the very broad outlines of an international organisation. The agreed document contained somewhat less emphasis on buffer stocks and probably greater safeguards against the improper use of quantitative restrictions than the original British plan. However, it also contained few restrictions on national sovereignty. The outstanding area of disagreement was on the role of subsidies to domestic producers in the scheme.

When it came to further British discussions and decisions on commodity policy after the Washington discussions, opposition to the proposed scheme came from the Minister of Agriculture in particular. He believed that the proposals made the long-term development of British agriculture impossible and he pushed for a policy on subsidies markedly different from that agreed previously. The same issue also affected the British attitude to the commercial policy proposals that had emerged from Washington. This disagreement on principles also strengthened a tendency amongst the Departments concerned to emphasise the need for a commodity-by-commodity approach to the problem rather than an agreement on the general principles of commodity schemes.

Throughout these discussions, Professors Robbins and Robertson carried most of the load. Owing to his concern with the Anglo-American monetary

proposals and his ill-health at the time, Keynes remained very much in the background. However, he did put forward a proposal for the finance of commodity schemes—an issue left open after the Washington talks and of some importance following the demise of the Clearing Union and the absence of provisions for financing such stocks in the proposed Stabilisation Fund.

THE FINANCE OF BUFFER STOCKS

The following general principles are suggested:

1. The Commodity Controls should get their finance from the General Commodity Council and should not each go into the market on their own. This would have the effect of increasing the control of the General Commodity Council, which could clearly refuse to finance buffer stocks on lines which it did not approve. It would also, by mixing the security, greatly increase its value as collateral for the purpose of raising loans, and would facilitate, as seen below, its further guaranteeing.

2. It would be preferable that the General Commodity Council should raise a long-term loan of not too large an amount as the foundation of its short-term finance. If the Reconstruction Bank comes into existence, this would be the most convenient channel through which to raise it with the guarantee of the Reconstruction Bank. If this falls through, then perhaps some special form of guaranteeing by the countries represented on the Commodity Council would have to be arranged. This loan should, as Professor Robertson insists, be floated in the countries which have the money and should take the form of free exchange. It does not seem to me necessary that it should be, in the first instance, a very large amount.

3. In the original proposals for buffer stocks provisions were contemplated by which each buffer stock would keep itself thoroughly solvent by means of levies. This feature should be retained. For this purpose the accounts of each buffer stock should be kept separately, each being debited by the Council with an appropriate proportion of the costs of the general finance. The individual buffer stock would be credited in the

197

first instance with the profit possibly arising from the difference between its buying and selling prices. If, after crediting this, the value of its stocks nevertheless fell below the market value by reason of a decline in price, the deficiency should be made good by a levy on future exports of the commodity.

4. The balance, and perhaps the major part, of the finance required by the Council should be financed by short-term, renewable bills. If the above provisions were fulfilled, these bills would be of the first order of quality. They would have behind them, first of all, the mixed collection of stocks owned by the various buffer pools; secondly, the duty of buffer pools to make levies to meet [any] deficiency; thirdly, the margin provided by the permanent finance raised by the Commodity Council through the Reconstruction Bank, or otherwise (the provision of this margin being in effect the main purpose of this permanent finance). The bills should, therefore, be attractive to any central bank which has surplus funds, and should be discountable at a very low rate of interest. The management would doubtless discount them with the lowest bidder. I suggest that the bills might be of the three months maturity, renewable, being in effect finance bills, but based on stocks of commodities constantly moving into consumption. The amount of such bills outstanding would, of course, fluctuate according to the volume of stocks which the buffer stocks were being required from time to time to hold.

5. The technique for drawing the bills might, I suggest, be as follows:

The producers of a commodity being purchased by a buffer stock would be paid by the central bank of the country to which they belonged drawing a bill on the General Commodity Council, secured as above. The central bank in question could then retain the bill, discount it with another central bank, or, alternatively, it should have the right to discount it with the Stabilisation Fund. The Stabilisation Fund could either hold it or offer it for discount to the central bank of any member which was in surplus with the Fund. When the bill fell due, the

Commodity Council would either pay it off, if they were in funds, or continue it with the existing holder, if the existing holder accepted what were considered the right terms; otherwise, by passing it on to the Stabilisation Fund.

If, as I hope, these bills, secured in the above manner on commodities and otherwise supported, were to be in circulation in large volume, they might play a most significant part in the general task of stabilisation. They would provide a means by which countries in surplus, but not wishing to lock up their money unduly, could hold external assets without too much reducing the Stabilisation Fund's stock of their currency. Furthermore, if, as one would anticipate, the buffer stocks would be buying predominantly when markets were bad and selling when markets were good, the fluctuations in the amount of such bills outstanding would be in exactly the right directions and again capable of exercising a stabilising influence on international finance as a whole.

KEYNES

16 March 1944

Although Keynes's proposal was discussed with the Dominions in March, while he was absent, it was not adopted owing to Bank of England opposition.

By the time that British officials were allowed to move forward again on the commodity and commercial policy fronts in late 1944, as a result of American proposals policy concerning commodities, trade and employments were merged into one omnibus organisation. The subsequent negotiations concerning this organisation lasted over a year before the series of Proposals for a Conference on Trade and Employment emerged from discussions in Washington in the autumn of 1945. The Proposals contained provisions for inter-governmental commodity agreements which were non-committal on the matter of buffer stocks, but generally anti-restrictionist in tone. The Proposals represented a series of guidelines for such agreements and lacked the detail of Keynes's earlier scheme. These were the subject of subsequent negotiations. Although the proposed International Trade Organisation was stillborn, provisions for commodity agreements remained in the General Agreement on Tariffs and Trade and the March 1947 guidelines of the Economic and Social Council of the United Nations for its Interim Committee for International Commodity Agreements.

PART II
INTERNAL POLICY

Chapter 4

THE BEVERIDGE REPORT

In June 1941, after pressure from the Trades Union Congress, Mr Greenwood, the Minister without Portfolio, announced in the House of Commons that he had arranged for a comprehensive survey of existing schemes for social insurance and allied services by an inter-departmental committee under the chairmanship of Sir William Beveridge. The survey of existing schemes was essentially complete by September, but owing to other commitments Beveridge did not then give his full attention to the problems raised by the survey. When he did so, he began to develop a comprehensive scheme going beyond the improvements in administrative detail that Ministers had expected. This put the officials on the committee in a difficult position, for being civil servants they could not sign a report, without consulting their Ministers and having them answer questions that would be asked of them later. If they did consult their Ministers and then signed a report, they would commit their Ministers individually and, given the number of departments involved, the Government, before the report was completely available. As a result, the Treasury successfully managed to reconstruct the committee so that the departmental officials became technical advisers and any eventual report became the sole responsibility of the chairman who would sign it alone.

As the reconstructed committee moved beyond its departmental enquiries, receiving evidence from outside bodies, Keynes became involved in several ways. Initially his contacts were with Beveridge himself, who sent him in March 1942 two memoranda outlining the heads of a possible scheme and the problems it would solve and his list of principal questions. After a formal acknowledgement that the subject was fascinating and a failure to keep a lunch engagement on 9 March, Keynes replied

To SIR WILLIAM BEVERIDGE, *17 March 1942*

My dear Beveridge,

I am very sorry to have to put off our lunch. But I had a minor infection, now got rid of, which led me to stay away from the office last week. This week I have been so busy that I have not cared to suggest a meeting. But could we meet next week. What

about lunching with me before the Council Meeting of the R.E.S. on Monday, the 23rd, say at 1 o'clock, at the United University Club? We must lunch early if we are to have a talk, since the Council is called for 2.30. Meanwhile, let me say that I have read your Memoranda, which leave me in a state of wild enthusiasm for your general scheme. I think it a vast constructive reform of real importance and am relieved to find that it is so financially possible. From rumours which had previously reached me, I feared that it was much more expensive.

My only comments, prior to our conversation, are on the following points of detail:-

(1) Unless I have misunderstood you, you are not making any adjustments for changes in the post-war value of money, though whether you are dealing in pre-war values or current values I am not quite sure. Obviously some appropriate adjustment will have to be made in all the figures, both of contributions and of benefits. But I suggest that this may give an opportunity for adjustments. It is much easier to leave a benefit where it is than to decrease it. Thus, in any case in which benefits are a little higher than the merits of the case require the adjustments might be less than in proportion to the change in values, thus leaving more money over for adjustments greater than the change of values in other cases. As a matter of drafting, the whole question of adjustments to the value of money needs perhaps to be made a little clearer. It is also important to make it clear, I think, that it is not intended in future to have frequent adjustments of this kind or put the benefits and the contributions on a cost of living sliding scale, but only to make such adjustments when there have been major disturbances as, for example between pre-war values and probable post-war values.

(2) If the scheme, one way or another, is so expensive as to be too severe a burden on the Budget, I do not think there will be anything wrong in principle in charging only current pensions on the year's outgoings and not setting aside accumulations to meet prospective pensions. It is a severe burden to

meet simultaneously pensions against which no funds have been accumulated and to accumulate funds for future pensions. The future can well be left to look after itself. It will have more resources for doing so than the immediate present. It might be interesting to have a calculation made as to how much money would be saved if the fund is charged only with pensions currently payable and is not called upon, at any rate in the early years, to accumulate against prospective liabilities. Otherwise, we put the maximum financial burden on ourselves when we can least support it, and at some later date, when the funds have been duly accumulated, the contributions will diminish.

(3) I am very keen on your proposed dimissal tax. But the details need a good deal of thinking about, especially the relationship to short-time. I should have thought the outright dismissal tax might be a good deal higher than you are suggesting. Where a man is temporarily laid off the employer might be asked to contribute say 5s, for any week in which he is laid off for two days or more. However, as I have said, the details of this need a good deal of thought,—more than I have given it so far.

(4) I feel you have been a little weak-kneed about voluntary industrial insurance. I should like to be much more drastic about this, thereby releasing substantial working-class funds. Indeed, I should like to see the new state fund take over employers' liability insurance by employers and industrial insurance by employed. I agree with you, on the other hand, in wanting to encourage Friendly Societies and similar organisations by which a man makes provision for more than his minimum relief in cases of sickness or disability.

Yours ever,
J. M. KEYNES

Keynes did have lunch with Beveridge on 23 March.

There matters rested for the time being. However, Keynes seems to have retained an interest, for, after looking at some of the papers circulated on the matter, Keynes also became involved in discussions with James Meade over the finance of the scheme.

To J. E. MEADE, *8 May 1942*

My dear James,

I should like to have a talk with you and Robbins about Beveridge's social insurance proposals. Will you ring up on Monday morning and fix a time? I do not look like being unduly occupied either on Monday or Tuesday—afternoons or early evenings.

Personally I am very much in favour of something on the lines of Beveridge's proposals, as I gather you are. My *prima facie* comments on one or two of the points you deal with in your paper are the following:

(1) I agree in theory that employees' and employers' contributions towards social insurance are inferior to a charge on general taxes. On the other hand, it seems to me essential to retain them, at any rate in the first stages of the new scheme, in order that the additional charges on the Budget may not look altogether too formidable. I think that Beveridge reached a very fair compromise in this respect by providing materially increased benefits whilst leaving the contributions broadly speaking at their present figure. I am sure it would be a mistake to aim at getting rid of the contributions, if one wants the thing to happen in the early post-war future. Proposals for abolishing or materially reducing them would only be in place after the post-war Budget problems had been satisfactorily solved and there is a margin of taxable capacity to dispose of.

(2) There are, I think, narrow limitations to the plan for stabilising consuming capacity in dealing with depressions, which are due to fluctuations in investment demand. One can prevent perhaps an aggravation of the falling off in effective

demand by stabilising consumption, but that is the best one can hope for.

(3) I am very much attracted by Beveridge's proposal for dismissal charges. In so far as the employers' contribution can be collected in this way, it would not run counter to the considerations I have mentioned under (1) above.

(4) I doubt if there is enough to be gained by fluctuating the rate of the contributions according to the state of trade. Quantitatively the effect would be hardly large enough to justify the complication. In your paragraph 15 you ought, I think, only to take credit for the employees' contributions in this context; I doubt if much would be gained by excusing the employers from their share. I do not dissent from the theoretical advantages claimed for the proposal, but I am a little doubtful about its quantitative efficacy.

(5) I agree with what you say about pensions and withdrawal from work. If, as is not unlikely, there is some sort of minimum wage provision, a good plan would be to diminish the amount of this minimum wage by a considerable proportion of pensions, thus allowing elderly people to be maintained in some form of usefulness at a rather cheaper cost,—corresponding to the lower rate of remuneration of juveniles.

I wonder if I could be put on the the circulation list for the E.C.S. papers. I often see them sooner or later, but they do not reach me by routine.

Yours,

J. M. KEYNES

Keynes met with Robbins and Meade on 12 May. The upshot was that the Economic Section went back to revise their proposals. When Keynes received the revised draft, he wrote to Meade.

To JAMES MEADE, *16 June 1942*

My dear James,

Over the weekend I read your revised draft on Social Security (E.C.S. (42) 14).

I am converted to your proposal in paragraph 30 for varying rates of contributions in good and bad times. If, under the Beveridge scheme, the amount involved is as much as £m230 a year, I agree there is something to play with. On the other hand, if 5 per cent is the minimum practicable rate of unemployment, this ought not, I should have thought, to be the dividing line. Something more like 8 per cent would be better as a standard with increasing contributions below that and fairly steeply declining rates above it.

I notice that *passim* in this document you have adopted the figures of £m6,500 for the national income, etc., appearing in the first draft by Stone and myself, copies of which were sent to you and Robbins. Please remember that this is only a draft and is at the moment a matter of high contention. Thus, this paper of yours should not perhaps receive wider circulation with these figures in it until the estimate of the Treasury document has been definitely agreed. I do not myself expect, when it all comes out in the wash, it will differ very materially from the present range.

Yours sincerely,

J. M. KEYNES

After the letter, the correspondence continued.

From J. E. MEADE, *17 June 1942*

My dear Maynard,

Many thanks for your letter of 16th June, 1942. I enclose a copy of the final version of our document on the economic aspects of the proposed reforms of social security. We are to give evidence to Beveridge's Committee on this subject on Wednesday, 24th June at 2.30 p.m.; and I do hope that the Treasury may be strongly represented at the Committee on this occasion.

The final version of our document was circulated to the members of the Committee yesterday before I received your letter. We are taking full responsibility for the figures of national income etc. in our document, and are putting the post-war estimates forward as our own guesses; and if the Treasury, at a later stage, submits that we have erred in our guess, I do not feel that this need cause any embarrassment. We have not suggested, and certainly shall not suggest, that the Treasury is responsible for our post-war figures. As a matter of fact, we have made it clear on page 3 (paragraph 9(c)) that we consider the figure of the post-war national income to be very uncertain. As the numerical example in that paragraph shows, the effect of a change in the estimate of the post-war national income is quite surprisingly small; and I do not think that any probable revision of this figure would greatly alter the line of our argument and conclusions.

I am glad to hear that you are in agreement with the proposal for varying rates of contributions in good and bad times. Our proposals in this connection are still very vague; and what I am hoping is that we may be asked by the Committee to formulate them a little more precisely. It seems to me personally that the rate of contributions should be capable of quarterly adjustments. The application of the scheme might take, I feel, either of two main forms. (i) Assuming 5 per cent to be the lowest practicable rate of unemployment, 'normal' rates of contribution for employers and employees would be fixed which (together with normal state contributions) balanced the fund at say, 8 per cent unemployment. Higher rates of contribution would be fixed on an increasing scale for unemployment between 8 and 5 per cent and on a scale decreasing to practically zero between 8 and, say, 12 per cent or more. In this case the idea would be that the fund would balance over an average of good and bad years. (ii) I, at present, favour a second alternative, which is to make the fund balance at the lowest practicable rate of unemployment of, say, 5 per cent. This is then considered to be the 'norm'. Rates of contribution are not raised above this level in any circumstances; and other measures must be used to prevent excessive booms. Employers' and employees' contributions are, however, levied on a scale declining to practically zero as unemployment rises to, say, 12 per cent. In order to maintain the balance of the fund, *special* state contributions are made to the fund from time to time to make up for the difference between the actual amount of employers' and employees' contributions and the amount which would have been so collected at 'normal' rates of contribution.

Yours sincerely,
[copy initialled] J.E.M.

To J. E. MEADE, *18 June 1942*

My dear James,

Thank you for the final version of your document on the Beveridge schemes.

In reference to your last paragraph, I much prefer (i) to (ii). It seems to me that it would be a great mistake to start the unemployment fund on the basis on which it was avowedly insolvent from the start, when the rest of the scheme would be already putting such heavy burdens on the Budget. I should have thought that this would greatly prejudice the prospects of the general idea you have in view.

Yours sincerely,
J. M. KEYNES

From J. E. MEADE, *19 June 1942*

My dear Maynard,

Many thanks for your letter of June 18th. I have been considering further this question of the variation of social insurance contributions with the state of trade activity; and I have come to the conclusion that I was confusing two problems in my letter of June 17th.

(1) Suppose that the total contribution per man employed required to balance the fund is 6s a week. This may be split into three equal contributions of 2s, payable by state, employer and employee. We may then apply the principle of variation of contribution according to the state of trade activity in either of two ways: (i) We may rule that the state contribution should stay constant at 2s and that the employers' and employees' contributions should rise above 2s when unemployment was less than, say, 8 per cent, and should fall below 2s when unemployment rose above 8 per cent. By a correct choice of sliding scale, we could hope to keep the fund in balance; but this would always be a matter of uncertainty which might upset those who thought it of great importance to keep the 'insurance' fund in balance in the long run. (ii) We would, however, rule that as employers' and employees' contributions rose (fell), so the state's contribution fell (rose) in such a way that the total contribution remained constant at 6s per man insured. In this way the introduction of the sliding scale could not at all affect the balance of the fund, and the uncertainty would all rest upon the amount of burden that, over an average of good and bad years, would fall on the state. I feel

that this type of arrangement might have certain advantages in so far as it was desirable to preserve the 'insurance' character of the schemes.

(2) I now see that the above choice is really quite independent of the choice as to the absolute level, on an average over good and bad years, of the state's contribution as opposed to the employers' and employees' contributions. If it is desired on an average of years to get the total contribution to fall in equal thirds on each of the three parties, under both 1 (i) and 1 (ii) it will be necessary to choose sliding scales designed for this purpose. The distinction is that if the choice is not correctly made, under 1 (i) the surplus or deficit will accrue to the insurance fund, while under 1 (ii) the state alone bears the risk of a miscalculation of the sliding scale. Either of the alternatives under 1 could be so devised that, over an average of years, the state bears any required percentage of the total cost of the benefits.

What I had in mind, I think, was that I would prefer 1 (ii) to 1 (i), if it is administratively practicable.

Yours sincerely,
[copy initialled] J.E.M.

After the Economic Section draft had gone to the Beveridge enquiry it was the subject of some discussion in the Treasury. After a meeting with Keynes on 25 June, Meade wrote to Keynes.

From J. E. MEADE, *25 June 1942*

My dear Maynard,

I am writing this letter (as a purely personal one which does not in the least commit Robbins or any other member of this section to any particular view), as a result of the conversation in the Treasury last Tuesday on our document on Beveridge's social security proposals. I wanted to take the opportunity of seeing what you would think of certain points which, on consideration, I should like to raise as a result of that discussion.

1. I agree that in certain ways, particularly in the drafting of the summary, our document probably gave an over-optimistic emphasis, although most of the points of substance are in fact introduced at one point or another in the text of the document. I agree that our document was at fault in failing to point out that the 'revenue' of 1941 included E.P.T. and N.D.C., income tax levied against deferred income-tax credits, and premiums and contributions for war risks insurance and war damage; and we should, I agree, have investigated how far the removal of these charges would have brought the revenue down to the necessary level (although I would deprecate any form

of words which suggested that the removal of such charges did not in fact represent a very considerable reduction of tax burdens!). We made these points very clearly and with great emphasis when we gave evidence to Beveridge; and I think that we must have removed any misapprehensions to which the drafting our our document may have given rise. We have promised to produce for him a revised version of that part of our document, and we shall consult the Treasury on this when we have had time to prepare a draft. We also made it very clear to Beveridge, in conversation, that as a result of uncertainty regarding the post-war world, we thought his proposals should be made in an order of priority, and not in a form which implied that they must all be accepted or all be applied at the same time.

I would, however, on this point, like to suggest that, for a number of reasons, the arguments presented to us at the Treasury last Tuesday were over-pessimistic.

(*a*) Has it not been forgotten (e.g. in the minute of Brittain to Gilbert which you gave to us) that if you remove E.P.T., N.D.C. and war risks insurance premiums (commodity and marine), just so much more income is liable to income tax and surtax? With income tax at 10*s* in the pound and with present rates of surtax, I should have thought that one was faced with a very much smaller net loss of revenue from these sources than was suggested to us.

(*b*) I have a feeling, if I may say so, that the Treasury was 'trying to have it both ways' on the subject of interest on the national debt in our conversations last Tuesday. A very large part (some £230 million) of the increase in total public expenditure for which we made allowance in our document between 1938 and the post-war period, was an increase in interest on the national debt. Surely at present rates of income tax, surtax and death duties, a very large proportion of this should represent an automatic increase in revenue. I don't think that Brittain's minute to Gilbert makes any allowance for this fact; and yet when one raised the question of relieving the position by a capital levy (of which more anon), one was met by the answer that it wasn't worth while as practically the whole of the gross savings would be taken up by a reduction of revenue.

(*c*) The transition from a war-time to a peace-time economy will be one in which personal consumption (sooner or later) represents an appreciably increased proportion of the total national expenditure. It must be remembered that indirect taxes on consumption will for this reason automatically increase at current tax rates and without any inflation of the national income. I have in mind particularly purchase tax, motor-vehicle duties, petrol duty, and certain import duties, although it may well be that more will also be spent on drink and tobacco. I do not think that Brittain's minute makes any allowance for this development.

(*d*) A small point. May not the Government end the war in ownership of quite considerable amounts of property of one form or another, from which it may be able to receive either an annual income or a lump sum with which debt can be diminished? I do not stress this, as I imagine that its numerical importance may not be great.

2. I would very much like to take up with you this question of a capital levy. I do not wish to dispute (e.g.) Hicks' arithmetic about a capital levy. But there are two points which I should like to add, and both of which seem to me to be of major importance.

(*a*) As I understand it, the reasons why the net saving from a levy is small is that both income taxation *and* the levy are extremely progressive. I very much favour the idea of very progressive income taxation and very much less progressive (or even proportionate) taxation on wealth. This seems to me to be in line with the views which you were putting forward on an annual tax on capital. In short, I feel that we ought to be prepared to consider the merits of a less progressive post-war capital levy.

(*b*) The reduction of debt which results from a progressive capital levy may considerably lessen the disadvantageous 'incentive' effects of a given level of rates of direct taxation, even though it does not result in any great net saving to the budget at the given level of rates of direct taxation. From the point of view of incentives, the important question is what are the average and, above all, the marginal rates of taxation which workers, 'enterprisers' and 'investors' have to pay on their earnings? The capital levy will give only a small net budgetary saving only in those cases in which *both* the levy *and* direct taxation of income are very progressive. But it is precisely in this case that the average and marginal rates of direct taxation on the rich will be reduced significantly (without any reduction in the existing schedule of taxation), because the levy will move the rich down from higher to lower tax brackets. I do not think that the utility of a capital levy of a given degree of progression can be judged solely from figures of the net saving to the budget. What is also wanted is a table of figures giving (at pre-levy rates of direct taxation) the distribution of taxable income before and after the levy among different levels of marginal rates of taxation. For example, we should find that, whereas before the levy x per cent of the taxable income of the community was subject to marginal rates of direct taxation of, say, more than y shillings in the pound, after the levy with the same schedule of taxes only $x-z$ per cent of total taxable income would be subject to such high marginal rates of taxation. Is it not worth while initiating such an investigation?

I would like to put my views on a capital levy rather more generally in this way. (I hasten to add that I do not put what follows forward as my ideas on a practical policy for the immediate post-war years.) Let us suppose that, owing to a high level of public expenditure which we consider for obvious

reasons to be very desirable, we reach a state of affairs which involves such high rates of taxation as to involve really serious 'incentive' effects on the community. Apart from abandoning the desired level of expenditure, there is only one form of relief that I can see,—namely the socialisation of property so that some part of the income from property can go 100 per cent to the state without involving high rates of taxation elsewhere. If one wants to do this without raising the question whether socialisation of property is desirable on other grounds, then one should go out for the socialisation of rentier property where income from property is mixed up as little as possible with income from work and enterprise. Clearly one would start with the national debt on these principles. I would, however, reveal that my personal El Dorado is one in which not only has the national debt disappeared; but the state also owns a considerable amount of other property (? railways, agricultural land, public utilities), from which—together with moderate but fairly progressive taxes—it raises revenue for a large volume of public expenditure.

3. Finally, I think, that we should investigate the possibility of finding other forms of taxation which have less adverse incentive effects than very high income taxes; and in this connection an annual tax assessed on capital seems to me to be one of importance. I felt, therefore, very much in sympathy with what you said on this subject. But does not this suggest that an enquiry into national capital (e.g. value, types of property, types of owners, etc.) almost as extensive as Dick Stone's present National Income Enquiry is wanted?

Yours sincerely,
[copy initialled] J.E.M.

Keynes replied on 30 June, at the same time sending a covering note on the exchanges of letters to Sir Richard Hopkins.

To J. E. MEADE, *30 June 1942*

Dear James,

Your letter of June 25th on the Beveridge proposals.

I agree with you that we have not yet got final or reliable estimates on either side of the balance sheet.

On the credit, i.e. revenue, side I agree that we have to take account of the points you raise in 1 (*a*) and (*c*). But I should have to look into it more deeply to know just how much adjustment

has to be made. As regards (*a*) there is danger of counting it twice, since in alleging that we can get through after the war without any significant subsidies to stabilise prices, we are already taking credit for the absence of the War Risks Insurance premiums as one of the reasons why there is a margin on the price front. (*c*) clearly takes one into the realm of guess work.

As regards your point in (*b*) no negligible part of the national debt takes the place of genuine assets which have been vested or sold and does not represent an increase of taxable income. The rest of the increase in taxable income ought to be taken account of in our figures of post-war national income. I think this has been done. But, whilst you are right that this part of the increase in taxable income is a good yielder of tax, some other parts are of the opposite character, and I should have doubted whether, on balance, there was much to take credit for.

I should like to put off discussing the capital levy issue at present. But there is one point perhaps worth making at once. One of the reasons in favour of a capital levy is that it might enable a level of taxation which was better from the point of view of incentive. But this is only the case if the proceeds of the capital levy are used to reduce other direct taxation. In so far as it is used to finance further social reforms, we are certainly no better off as regards incentives.

Turning back to the Beveridge proposals, we ought, I think, to be able to reach a rather closer balance sheet with a little more work.

Yours,

J. M. KEYNES

To SIR RICHARD HOPKINS, *30 June 1942*

Although Meade calls the letter of his below purely personal to me, I am sure he would not mind your seeing it. So I pass it on with my rejoinder.

As I have said in my last paragraph, I think we can get closer to this with a little more work. But my present impression is

that some of the figures in your note to the Chancellor go too far. I should feel much more inclined to stress the point of not counting too many chickens before they are hatched, whilst holding out reasonable hopes that, if all goes well, we could manage to do a great deal.

Take our recent discussion about the size of the post-war national income. Stone and I guessed it as £m6,500 ± £m200. Henderson thinks even the lower limit of £m6,300 too high. Since we are talking of 1946 or later, Stone and I would not be at all surprised at its reaching the higher figure of £m6,700, at any rate after a short time lag, and increasing thereafter by £m100 a year or more, measured in terms of prices 30 per cent above 1938. Now it will make all the difference in the world which of these forecasts turns out right. With a national income rapidly approaching £m7,000, we could afford all kinds of things which would be impracticable at £m6,500. For the purpose of progress it is the marginal £m500 which counts.

Now I think it would be the greatest mistake in the world to be too pesimistic about our approaching £m7,000 in a reasonably short time. But that does not prevent me from feeling that to commit ourselves here and now or in the near future to what we could only afford on the assumption of a national income comfortably in excess of £m6,500 would be very imprudent.

When considering how far the Beveridge scheme lends itself to several stages, I should be interested to know whether I should be right in supposing that it makes a great difference to give the higher pensions to those who have not paid for them in their contributions or to require that, at any rate, they should have contributed for (say) five or ten years before becoming eligible. Some provision of that kind might be very serviceable in giving us the necessary time lag. Thus contributions might be raised to a figure which takes account of a higher rate of benefit than is allowed forthwith to those who have not in fact parted with the higher contributions either at all or, at any rate, for a minimum number of years.

Look at it in this way:

	£m
Pre-war tax contribution raised to correspond to prices is	170
Family allowances, which is more or less inevitable anyhow	100
	270
Balance of cost of Beveridge Proposals (680−270)	=410
Contributions from employers and employed as proposed by him	=310
Deficit	100

If Beveridge economised £m100 on pensions, he would have a pretty plausible tale to tell. He asks nothing from the Budget proper except £m100 for family allowances. Employees contribution is balanced by benefits to be received. The increase in employers' contribution would not add above $1\frac{1}{2}$ per cent to costs.

[copy initialled] J.M.K.

On 30 June, Meade sent Keynes an even more detailed version of his Beveridge scheme for variations in the rate of social security contributions, as well as another memorandum on the post-war use of deferred income tax credits to stabilise demand, which he had drafted simply to try the idea on others. To these, Keynes replied

To J. E. MEADE, *1 July 1942*

My dear James,

Thanks for letting me see the more detailed version of your schemes for varying the rate of social security contributions. As I said before, I am converted to the general principle of this. It does not seem to me to present any particular difficulties in working out, and this is made obvious by your scheme, which

is quite a simple one. I can express no opinion on the question of administrative difficulties, but I should not have supposed that these could be insuperable, and are perhaps better left for the special experts on those matters to carry out in detail.

But the main point is that you are able to show fluctuations in income of an order of magnitude which is significant in the context. Indeed, I think you might have expressed your argument more strongly in the first section. So far as employees are concerned, reductions in contributions are more likely to lead to increased expenditure as compared with saving than a reduction in income tax would, and are free from the objection to a reduction of income tax that the wealthier classes would benefit disproportionately. At the same time, the reduction to employers, operating as a mitigation of the costs of production, will come in particularly helpfully in bad times.

Your second paper on the use of post-war income tax credits for the same purpose is interesting and might be useful. But I should keep it in reserve for the time being. It is not so good, I think, as your other proposal, which is quite big enough an experiment along these lines until we have more experience, both of what is needed and of what is practicable.

Yours ever,

J. M. KEYNES

By this time, as a result of the internal discussions hinted at in Keynes's covering note on his letter to Meade of 30 June,[1] it appears that the Treasury was worried by the financial implications of the Beveridge proposals. As a result, Meade was warned that his revised scheme for varying social insurance contributions had best be kept separate from Beveridge.

---

[1] See also below pp. 219–22.

To J. E. MEADE, *3 July 1942*

Dear James,

Thank you for sending me the final version of your paper on variations in the rate of social security contributions. I take it that, at the present stage, this is a document for purely domestic circulation. I note that in your covering paper you speak of it as part of the further draft for Beveridge. As you will probably have heard from Robbins, Hoppy had a word with him yesterday to the effect that this scheme will have a better chance if, for the time being, it is kept separate from the main Beveridge discussion.

Yours,
J. M. KEYNES

Given the developing Treasury worries over the Beveridge proposals, Keynes attempted to get a copy of the scheme from its author.

To SIR WILLIAM BEVERIDGE, *25 June 1942*

My dear Beveridge,

Can you spare me a copy of the authentic latest version of your proposals? Copies seem very scarce in this building. I have not had one in my possession long enough to know really what it is all about in the latest phase. On the other hand, I am receiving and having to deal with criticisms of it, which is awkward if one really does not know what is in the original.

From the criticisms made, I am rather alarmed lest it is being overweighted by the pensions part, for it seemed to me the least interesting and least essential of the whole.

Could you come to lunch with me again to talk it over? I suggest the Athenaeum on July 1st, at 1 o'clock.

Yours ever,
J. M. KEYNES

On 30 June, Sir Richard Hopkins wrote to Beveridge suggesting a discussion on the broader financial implications of the scheme in the context of reconstruction before he sent his proposals to the Departments for comment. Beveridge agreed readily to the suggestion. As a result he met Keynes on 6 July and had lunch with him the next day. After the second meeting Keynes minuted.

To SIR RICHARD HOPKINS, *7 July 1942*

NOTES ON CONVERSATION WITH SIR WILLIAM BEVERIDGE

(1) Sir William Beveridge wants to circulate his Part IV[2] with the rest of the documents. But he proposes to modify that part of it dealing with the security budget so as to emphasise the tentative character of this and to indicate the possibility of a pensions scheme at much lower rates.

(2) He would like to circulate this to the Ministry of Agriculture as well as to the members of his Committee, because there is an important proposal about agricultural insurance, of which they have not yet heard and which should not be kept from them any longer.

(3) He expressed himself as conscious of being in need of guidance and informed criticism over the wider financial aspects of the scheme, as distinct from the departmental details. It was obvious that, apart from any other discussions that go on, he would welcome an informal committee on what he calls the social security budget, with whom he could talk things over and discuss generally the methods of bringing the scheme as a whole within the financial possibilities, such committee to consist of representatives of the Treasury, the Economic Section and the Government Actuary with no-one else.

(4) He is by no means opposed to an economy by which

---

[2] Part IV of the draft Report under discussion, entitled 'Social Security and Social Policy', dealt with children's allowances, a comprehensive health service, maintenance of employment, a separate social security budget and post-war aims.

children's allowance is only paid, at any rate to start with, in respect of children in excess of one. Indeed, I understood him to say that he himself was personally actually in favour of that. This would be all the more necessary if the amount of the allowance is greater than 5s. He told me that he was being pushed hard by the nutritional experts to raise it to 6s 3d. This, however, would be on the assumption that the Board of Education was doing nothing for children's meals etc. Thus it might still be possible to keep to 5s, supplemented by an extension of the Board of Education's activities in the nutritional direction.

(5) He has by no means closed his mind to pensions on a much lower scale, such as 15s single and 25s double. Indeed, he said that he had started with that sort of figure in mind himself. The higher figure is to produce uniformity with the other social security weekly payments, and in order to reach the alleged subsistence level. This subsistence level is admittedly based on the payment of a rent of 10s, on the pensioner having no savings whatever, no assistance from members of his family and no capacity to earn anything. He admitted that it was a matter for argument whether it was right to assume this as the normal situation. Where all these conditions were satisfied, the pensioner would probably have to have a supplementary pension in any case, just as he does now. Thus, the difference between the low and high scale of pensions would only mean that the scope for supplementary pensions would be larger or smaller. I do not think it would be difficult to persuade him to come down to the lower figure, which would make a vast difference to the financial side, since the 15s would compare with 26s assuming a price level of 30 per cent above 1937. The higher rate is, however, associated in his mind with the retirement conditions, the arguments for or against which I am not well acquainted with, but by which he is much attracted.

(6) He declared himself as definitely in favour of the principle that pensions should not be paid to those who have paid no

contributions and do not need pensions. He agreed that, if his own transitional arrangements were not practicable, either other transitional arrangements must be substituted or the proposal to give pensions to those who have not contributed should be dropped. Here again he is quite open, I am sure, to argument and modifications.

(7) It is evident that the above suggestions, namely those relating to family allowances, to the normal pension scale and to pensions for those who have not contributed, are capable between them of reducing the total cost by a very large sum indeed. This is all the more necessary if there is to be any talk about raising children's allowances to 6s 3d and in view of the uncertain cost of the national health service. Sir William Beveridge says that he is in no position to give any kind of reliable estimate at present of the latter, but he is sure that £35 million is far too low. It might be nearer £m100. All this goes to show that it is very important to get clear on the social security budget before opinion becomes crystallised on the various items making it up.

(8) I explained that the proposal for a sliding scale of contributions according to the state of employment was closely bound up with other proposals for off-setting the trade cycle, and obviously ran into the question of alternating between a sinking fund and a deficit on the budget. For this reason Sir R. Hopkins deprecated any extensive discussion of what was essentially a separate subject. Sir W. Beveridge said he would be content with the brief reference to this possibility which is in his present draft without seeking to amplify it or enter into the details.

[copy initialled] J.M.K.

Following the meeting, Beveridge circulated his draft Report for departmental comment, after revising Part IV to reduce the number of illustrative figures for the social security budget and to leave 'large numbers of cracks suitable for the insertion of Treasury wedges'.[3]

[3] Beveridge to Hopkins, 9 July 1942.

During the subsequent Treasury discussions, Sir Richard Hopkins circulated a note raising the question of the wisdom of maintaining the fiction of the fund principle, which in the past had linked contributions and benefits closely, and suggesting that the Beveridge proposals be treated for what they were, a scheme for social benefits financed in part by contributions from the potential beneficiaries but primarily by general taxation. On receiving this, Keynes replied

To SIR RICHARD HOPKINS, *20 July 1942*

THE BEVERIDGE PROPOSALS

I

Contribution or Tax. Intellectually and on its merits what you write is unanswerable. The fixed weekly contribution is a poll tax on the employed and an employment tax on the employer —both very bad kinds of taxes as soon as the amount is high enough to be significant. But the formal conversion of the contribution into a tax should have, unless it was purely formal, far-reaching consequences, in particular a reform of the income tax. I make a preliminary excursion into the field of these consequences in III below.

I hope that we shall soon be ready to accept such consequences. But it may be that this is to move too far ahead of the political and even of the administrative climate. If so, then there is more to be said than you have admitted in favour of accepting the existing fictions for the time being. I call attention to the following arguments in favour of the 'fiction' of a contributory system:

(i) There is something to be said for regarding the cost of social security as a genuine ingredient in the costs of production and, therefore, properly paid for (in part at least) by the employer as such, though a poll tax on numbers employed may be a bad technical method. This is particularly arguable in the cases of seasonal and cyclical unemployment, accident and industrial sickness benefits, but also even of pensions. Should not the employer meet the total cost of providing him with a

healthy worker? If the unemployed were allowed to starve what would employers do when the demand for employment, seasonally or cyclically, increased again? Why should the general taxpayer pay for a pool of available dock labour? One can easily slip into a sophistry here—but there is *something* in it. The State does not meet the cost of repair, depreciation or care and maintenance of non-human machinery and other factors of production.

(ii) You imply that there is a deficit to be met by the State over and above a one-third contribution. Is this just to Beveridge? He excludes family allowances and health services from the fund. But contributions are to be such as to make the fund solvent on the basis of a 40 per cent State contribution when the scheme is fully operating and (presumably) a smaller State contribution meanwhile.

(iii) Here is a *de facto* source of revenue, accepted by the public as reasonable apart from the general corpus of taxation. Why merge it and risk losing its separate identity at a time when one needs every possible source of revenue?

(iv) It is politically impossible to release the employers from an *ad hoc* contribution and not the employed. Yet if both are transferred to general taxes, the employed will tend in the long run to escape their proper share.

II

The 'fund' also is, admittedly, to some extent a 'fiction'! Certainly it is not a fund in any actuarial sense. Nevertheless, it has, surely, most important advantages. We need to extend, rather than curtail, the theory and practice of extra-budgetary funds for state operated or supported functions. Whether it is the transport system, the Electricity Board, War Damage or Social Security. The more socialised we become, the more important it is to associate as closely as possible the cost of particular services with the sources out of which they are provided, even when a grant-in-aid is also required from general

taxes. This is the only way by which to preserve sound accounting, to measure efficiency, to maintain economy and to keep the public properly aware of what things cost.

The social security budget should be one section of the capital or long-term Budget. It is important that there should be a level charge on the ordinary Budget revised at longish intervals; and if Mr Meade's proposals are adopted, it will be doubly important to keep it out of the ordinary Budget. For the ordinary Budget should be balanced at all times. It is the capital Budget which should fluctuate with the demand for employment.

But there are secondary reasons why the fund is in present circumstances a valuable fiction—to put it at the lowest. Firstly, we can hope to start with good employment and relatively low pension charges in the first quinquennium and accumulate a surplus. Extra-budgetary funds accumulating surpluses are exactly what we shall pray for in the early period. Secondly, the existing Funds will end the war with a large surplus which can be appropriately transferred to the new fund, but not so easily paid into the Exchequer.

No, I am all for an extra-budgetary social security fund. The suggestion that to express the full consequences of the Beveridge proposals in terms of additional taxation as such is the best way of bringing their cost home to the public, involves sacrificing administration and long-term efficiency to what is essentially a political and short-term argument (which would, very likely, not prove sufficiently convincing).

I suggest below that the right solution is to make not a step back, but another step forward.

III

The objection to the contributory system and the Fund is not really, I suggest, to the *principle* of contribution to a Fund, but partly to the particular method of a poll tax and partly to the inevitable inadequacy of the contribution so long as it is a poll

tax. For everyone knows the objection to a poll tax of significant amount, which is unrelated either to profits or to earnings. But to have a better and more adequate contributory system leads us straight to a far-reaching reform of the income tax—which we all know is needed anyhow.

I venture a highly preliminary sketch below, without stopping to calculate whether or not the actual figures given (on a post-war basis) for the purpose of illustration, are anywhere near right. If we are not yet ready for something on these lines, then we had better keep to old-fashioned contributions on Beveridge lines, until we are.

In place of income tax, surtax and all existing or proposed social security contributions, substitute the following—

(1) *A Social Security Contribution* of (say) 2s 6d in the £ on all wages, salaries and Schedule D profits (before deduction of interest paid out), deductible at source, without any exceptions or any allowances.

(2) *A Corporation (or Profits) Tax* made up of (*a*) 2s in the £ on all interest paid out and profits divided or invested during the year outside the business, and (*b*) $\frac{1}{4}$ per cent annual capital tax on total capital invested in the business, beginning with an initial broad-brush valuation corrected annually by the addition of new gross investment in the business and the subtraction of depreciation and capital loss admitted by the Revenue. (Or if (*b*) is unacceptable or only practicable after a delay, substitute 3s for 2s under (*a*).)

(3) *A Property Tax* of 5s in the £ deductible at source from interest,* Schedule A income and income earned abroad (subject in the latter case to any agreements about double taxation).

(4) *A Personal Tax* on total taxed income from all sources (i.e. income after deduction of above taxes) with certain concessions to married men and bachelors with dependants, but

---

* Companies and other payers of Social Security Contribution and Corporation Tax out of gross Schedule D profits would retain the property tax on interest towards meeting the above.

with no other allowances whatever (deductible at source in the case of earnings) on (say) some such scale as the following on surtax principles, i.e. on the amounts of income between each of the following limits:

	Bachelor	Married
£	s	s
0–100	−2	−2
100–200	—	−2
200–500	+3	+2
500–1,000	3	3
1,000–1,500	4	3
1,500–2,000	4	4
2,000–2,500	5/-	
2,500–3,000	5/6	

Rising by 6d on each additional £500 of income up to a maximum of (say) 16s (i.e. a maximum of 17s for property tax and personal tax together).

No children's allowances necessary, since they are assumed to be paid separately. Earned income allowance and claims for expenses liberally (perhaps too liberally) met by the corporation tax and the difference between social security contribution and property tax. Insurance policies sufficiently subsidised by exemption of insurance companies from personal tax. Charges on personal income recoverable at property tax rate in the case of interest. Payments under covenant deductible only for calculation of personal tax. Charities exempt from property tax and personal tax, but not from corporation tax or social security contribution on Schedule B profits.

The social security contribution to be fixed for quinquenniel periods and paid into the social security fund. The state medical service, all social security allowances (except childrens's allowances), and all pensions (except war pensions) to be

charged on this fund. Contributions to be fixed so as to keep the fund self-supporting.

IV

I have now read Beveridge's proposals in full. It is impossible to express a valuable opinion on the financial aspect until some valid estimate of the cost is available. Much also turns on whether the experts accept the practicability of his transitional proposals. But to do Beveridge justice he does not *intend* to overwhelm the Budget and is fully alive to this side of the matter. His own transitional proposals (or some alternative to the same general effect) and his own proposal to limit children's allowances to children beyond the first, are both large-scale economies. He *intends* to fix the contributions when he knows the total cost, at a figure which will limit the state subsidy to 40 per cent on the maximum when the new pension scales are fully operative.

The chief further economy to press for is a reduction of the pension scale to 15s and 25s, i.e. about two-thirds of Beveridge's proposal.

KEYNES

On reading Keynes's note, Sir Richard Hopkins tartly remarked[4]
'I do not feel equal to settling between now and the 15th August Lord Keynes' suggestions for a complete remodelling of the system of direct taxation in this country and I think that for the present we must think of the Beveridge Scheme in the setting of present general principles which he at any rate does not suggest should be altered.'
He also suggested that the phrase 'social security budget' disappear, as it did from the finally published report.

After further Treasury discussions, Keynes, Professor Robbins and Sir George Epps[5] made up the small informal Committee, previously agreed with Beveridge,[6] to advise on the financial implications of the scheme. Before

4   T161/1129/S48497/2, 21 July 1942.
5   Sir George Selby Washington Epps (1885–1951); Deputy Government Actuary, 1926–36; Government Actuary, 1936–44.
6   See above p. 220.

the first meeting on 10 August, Keynes prepared a statement of the proposals to be made to Beveridge.

THE PLAN FOR SOCIAL SECURITY

(1) The estimated peace-time cost of the existing system is £315 million.

(2) The current cost of the full Beveridge proposals would be about £800 million, including universal general practitioner (but not institutional), dental and ophthalmic services and children's allowances (at 6s 3d per week for each child). This figure makes no allowance for a full national health service, for which no reliable estimate is yet available. Nor does it allow for the gradual increase of cost due to the growing proportion of the pensionable to the total population. On the other hand, the limitation of full increased pensions at the outset to retired persons who had paid contributions under the present contributory pension scheme, as suggested in the draft report, and the transitional arrangements for funeral benefit would save about £100 million a year temporarily, giving for the starting cost a round total of £700 million. Thus the full scheme, assuming that the transitional arrangements are judged to be practicable, can be put at £700 million, rising through a period of time to (say) £900 million.

(3) The object of this paper is, not to examine or criticise the full scheme on grounds of social policy or of administrative practicability, but to examine how far it can be divided into sections which would bring the initial stage within the range of financial practicability, pending the increase of the net national income to a figure which would allow a further margin for social services of one kind or another.

(4) If the draft scheme is adopted as it stands in all other respects, the following sums can be saved without severe disturbance, it would seem, of the main fabric of the proposals, by deferring certain parts of them or initiating certain other parts at a lower rate of benefit:

(i) If no immediate extension is made in the present scope of insurance of health, pensions and unemployment to persons not in the employee classes, and if there is no change in the position of civil servants and similar 'excepted' classes, taking, however, the opportunity to assimilate the special agricultural unemployment scheme to the main scheme, there would be a saving of £30 million.

(ii) To limit the immediate increase in the rates of benefit in health and unemployment for insured persons and adult dependents to the level of the pre-war unemployment benefit, increased by 30 per cent on account of the increase in the cost of living, and not to the full subsistence level (e.g. 22s for men over 21 in place of the full Beveridge rate of 25s), would save £28 millions.

(iii) To limit the immediate increase in the rates of pension for both contributory and means pensions to 15s a week for single persons and 25s a week for married couples, but without any change in the pension ages either for insured persons or for their wives and without any retirement condition, would save £90 million.

(iv) To grant children's allowances universally (i.e. not limiting them to the insured classes) at the rate of 5s a week for each child under age 15 (or, if over that age, at school), but excluding the first child in the family, and at the rate of 5s a week in place of 6s 3d would save £100 million (made up of £70 million due to exclusion of first child and a further £30 million owing to the reduction of the rate of allowance to 5s).

The above would give an aggregate saving of approximately £250 million in round figures, as compared with the initial cost of the full scheme, on the assumption of the proposed transitional arrangements being put into force; and a saving of £350 million, as compared with the current cost of the full proposals apart from the transitional savings.

(5) The full annual expenditure in the first year (say 1944) on social insurance benefits as thus enlarged would be approximately as follows:—

	£m
Pensions (contributory and means)	160
Unemployment insurance	77
Sickness benefits (including dependents' allowances)	46
Industrial disability benefits	4
Maternity benefit	3
Funeral benefit	4
Medical treatment for insured persons and their dependents	29
Dental and Ophthalmic treatment for insured persons	11
Administrative expenses	15
	349
Supplementary pensions (say)	20
Unemployment assistance	22
Universal children's allowances (excluding 1st child)	58
Total expenditure	449

(6) The above makes the same assumptions as does the estimate given above of the full plan as regards the immediate provision of medical benefit. That is to say, it assumes medical benefit free of cost to the dependents, both adult and juvenile, of insured persons instead of, as at present, to insured persons only, and the extension of this benefit to the wives and widows of insured men who have passed age 65 and to the widows of insured men; and also dental and ophthalmic treatment free of cost as a statutory benefit to insured persons.

(7) If we assume that the industrial disability benefits are paid for by special contributions from employers, and if supplementary pensions, unemployment assistance and children's allowances be regarded as non-contributory services, the cost of the contributory services included in the proposed first stage would be £345 million. From this there falls to be deducted an annual income of about £11 million, being the

Comparative weekly rates of benefit

	Pre-war			Now		
	Health		Un-employment	Health		Un-employment
	Sickness*	Disablement*		Sickness*	Disablement*	
	s	s d	s	s	s d	s
Men (over 21)	15	7 6	17	18	10 6	20
Women (over 21)						
Spinsters and widows	12	6 }	15	15 }	9 }	18
Married women	10	5 }		13 }	8 }	
Dependents						
Adult	—	—	10	—	—	10
Juvenile						
First child	—	— }	3	{	{	4
Second child	—	— }		{	{	4
Others	—	—				3

232

Comparative weekly rates of benefit (cont.)

	Proposed			Pensions		Beveridge rates for all benefits
	Health		Un-employment	Pre-war and now	Proposed	
	Sickness	Disablement				
	s	s	s	s	s	s d
Men (over 21)	22	15	22	10	15	25
Women (over 21)						
Spinsters and widows	20	13	20	10	15	{ 25 / 20†"
Married women	13	13	13	10	10	15
Dependents						
Adult	13	13	13	10	10	15
Juvenile						
First child	5	5	5	5	5 }	5 }
Second child	5‡	5‡	5‡	3	5‡ }	6 3§
Others						

* Increased by 'additional benefits' (averaging 3s 3d a week sickness benefit) for nearly two-thirds of insured men; about one-quarter of insured women have additional sickness benefits averaging 2s 3d a week.

† The Beveridge proposal for married women is 20s for health and unemployment and 15s for pension (but 25s if she has retired from a gainful occupation and her husband is not a pensioner).

‡ The allowances for second and later children in family would be payable under a scheme of universal children's allowances.

§ Under the Beveridge proposals allowances for all children would be payable under a scheme of universal children's allowances.

233

interest from the accumulated investment funds (viz: National Health Insurance funds, about £220 million; balances of the pensions accounts over £50 million; and balances of the unemployment funds about £130 million) thus leaving a net cost of £334 million. On the basis of contributions of 6s a week (men) and 4s a week (women) payable jointly by insured persons and their employers, the annual income from contributions would be £223 million, or exactly two-thirds of the cost of the contributory services, leaving a contribution to these services from the Exchequer of £111 million.

(8) If to this contribution from the Exchequer there be added the cost of the non-contributory services, namely £100 million in round figures, the total net cost falling to the Exchequer would be about £40 million a year more than at present.

(9) Thus the effect of the above analysis is to produce a bedrock scheme, the cost of which does not exceed the present cost by more than a moderate figure, and at the same time to indicate the additional cost of each successive extension of the scope of the scheme and improvement of the scale of benefits which might become financially possible hereafter.

(10) The comparative weekly rates of benefits are given in an Appendix [above, pp. 232–3]: (*a*) pre war; (*b*) now; (*c*) as proposed above for the first stage; (*d*) the full Beveridge proposals.

10 August 1942

After the first meeting of the committee, Keynes reported.

To SIR HORACE WILSON, *11 August 1942*

THE BEVERIDGE PLAN FOR SOCIAL SECURITY

We paid our first visit to Sir William Beveridge yesterday and spent two hours with him. It was arranged that we should meet him again in a fortnight's time and that he would probably have

a further conversation with myself in the interval. We came away feeling that there had been quite as much progress as we could have hoped for.

I began by handing him the enclosed paper, which I had prepared on the basis of material supplied by Epps and which had been agreed by him, and we went through it clause by clause. I pointed out that I was partly concerned to suggest ways in which expense could be economised, but was also concerned with the method of presentation, so as to distinguish what one might call the bedrock scheme from further extensions of it or increases in rates of benefit and pension, so as to indicate what could be detached from the rest, if the scheme as a whole is financially impossible.

Taking the suggested methods of economy in turn, Sir William Beveridge's first reaction was as follows:

To 4(i), namely the proposal not to extend the scheme beyond the present insured categories, his feeling was adverse. I pointed out that this was not merely a question of saving money, the sum involved not being very large. It was a case where by taking two bites at the cherry he could immensely reduce his initial administrative complications. Would it not be wiser to unify the existing insurance schemes before taking on the further task of extending them to new classes? I also pointed out that pensions were already provided for civil servants and for most of the other 'excepted' classes, so that he was in danger of throwing money away for no very substantial purpose.

As to 4(ii) he was ready to agree that something might be saved here and that he had not come to a final conclusion that the standard rate of benefit need be quite so high as 25s. In the same way he agreed that his full proposal for pensions was capable of being abated, but not so low as the figure mentioned in my text. He thought, however, that he could certainly save £35 million on these two heads together.

As to 4(iv), namely children's allowances, he agreed to the first saving, namely the exclusion of the first child, but not to

the reduction of the rate of benefit from 6s 3d to 5s. He added that we should be lucky if we got away with anything so low as 6s 3d and that this might well be 7s 6d before he had finished.

The net result of the above is a saving of £100 million, or a little more, compared with the saving of £250 million in my paper. At the same time, Sir William Beveridge expressed himself as agreeing that the additional cost to the Exchequer compared with the present cost must be kept below £100 million. He proposed to effect this by raising the 6s contribution, for which I had taken credit, to 7s and adding a further 1s for health services in particular, making 8s in all. Thus he would be saving the Exchequer, including contributions, £205 million compared with my £250 million, so that the net additional cost to the Exchequer would still be kept at not more than £85 million. He asked us to agree that this was not an unreasonable expense.

I replied to this that it made all the difference whether the saving was arrived at by methods that were politically possible and politically stable. Proposals which seem to have some measure of finality (at least for the time being) and political stability in them would have to be regarded quite differently from proposals which reached a given result on paper but were of such a character that they were very unlikely to last, even if agreed to temporarily. That led us to a discussion of the objections to the way in which Sir William Beveridge proposed to bring his result about:

(1) We all pointed out to him emphatically that a contribution of 8s would be extremely difficult to obtain and that the contributory system pushed to such a length was in fact a bad form of taxation, inasmuch as it was a poll-tax related neither to the amount of wages earned nor the the amount of profits earned. We thought that so high a contribution would be unpopular and could not be relied on. To this Sir William Beveridge had two replies. The first was that, if the existing heavy expenditure by the working classes on industrial insurance

and outside medical benefits could be brought to an end, they would not be paying any more than at present. We agreed that this was so, but rejoined that that did not affect the employers' contribution; and in so far as the employees were concerned the termination of the existing outside contributions could not at best be brought to an end for several years to come. Secondly he argued that he was strongly in favour of making the high rate of benefit proposed by him contingent on the high rate of contribution. He was strongly of the opinion that the benefits must be paid for. In that case, I said, the scheme should be put forward in an alternative form, showing that contributions of 8s a week would provide a certain level of benefit, and contributions of 6s a week a lower scale, closely linking the one with the other and making it apparent that, if the lower rate of contribution was preferred, that carried with it the lower rate of benefit. Sir William Beveridge did not react strongly against that suggestion.

(2) We pointed out that the exclusion from children's allowances of the first child, although that was also a feature of my suggested economies, was politically unstable; that there was in fact a much stronger case for bringing in the first child than for very high pensions for the old; that public opinion might justifiably prefer to spend more on the young and less on the old; and that, if we gave priority to expenditure on the old, contrary both to the merits of the case and to popular sentiment, we should very soon have to concede the additional expenditure on the young as well. He was not entirely unmoved by this, but is himself decidedly against children's allowances to the first child on its merits.

(3) We pointed out that his pension proposals, taken in conjunction with his transitional clauses, were likely to be very unpopular, and that he had devised a pension scheme which would succeed at the same time in spending the largest amount of money and obtaining the smallest amount of popular satisfaction. In particular, we argued that to have for twenty years

to come, different classes of people having the same degree of need receiving widely different pension scales would not be felt tolerable. According to his proposals, those in the present contributory scheme would receive the full pension rate of 25s, even when they had not paid the additional rate of contribution for anything approaching enough years to pay for it; whereas the new classes brought in would have as a class to pay contributions for twenty years before they had any pensions at all. He had made a particular point of the hardship to persons not in the employee class and yet he proposed to do nothing for them, except exact contributions, for twenty years. Thirdly, he did nothing whatever for non-contributory pensioners and did not provide, for example, a single penny to satisfy the demands made in recent debates in the House of Commons. He proposes to leave the non-contributory pensioners with a basic 10s a week, with the existing system of supplementary pensions unchanged. Finally, in order to have his retirement provision, he introduces for the first time what is in effect a drastic means test for contributory pensioners, who have to sacrifice out of their pensions half of any of their future earnings. This means test is particularly objectionable in that it would apply only to earned income and not to unearned income. For these reasons we did not believe that those pension economies he himself was taking credit for were practicable. You could not leave the non-contributory pensioners where they are. You could not have such inequitable treatment between those who are now in the contributory class and those who will in future be in the contributory class. Indeed, it was hard to see how one could avoid having the same basic pension rate for everyone. Surely public opinion would demand that and, in that case, all his economies had gone west, and the total cost would be at a level which he would agree is appalling.

On the other hand, in favour of the economies suggested in my paper is the argument that all pensioners would then have the same basic pension at an improvement of 50 per cent above

the present figure *plus* supplementary pensions when required. (He himself does not get rid of the system of supplementary pensions for at least 20 years in any case). If hereafter we had more money to spend on social services, we could gradually raise the basic rate to everybody. But it was a hopeless system to try and get your economies by different basic rates to classes whom the public would rate as equally deserving or undeserving.

It was evident at the end of the discussion that Sir William Beveridge was considerably impressed by these arguments, and he promised to think over the whole case again carefully in the next fortnight. Obviously the major point, and we all agreed about that, is the future level of contributory pensions. If Sir William Beveridge could bring down his rate to the neighbourhood of what is proposed in 4(iii) above, there would not remain a great deal between us on the financial issue. The real reason why he is reluctant to agree to this is that the high basic rate of pension is connected with his proposed retirement clause. If we could wean him from the retirement clause, he would, I think, readily give up the excessive basic rate of pension. This is the point we must concentrate on. There is no evidence that anyone except Sir William Beveridge is in favour of the retirement clause, which is plainly unworkable. His own adviser told us afterwards that he himself was in disagreement with Beveridge over this. The proposal by which whenever anyone over 65 does the slightest stitch of work he has to hand over half of his income to the state is about as fully charged with unpopularity as anything one could well conceive.

Perhaps I should add that the highly provisional estimate of the cost of the full health service is about £80 million above the medical items in the above paper. But this is a highly unreliable estimate, and such a scheme could, in any case, only come into force very gradually through lack of personnel to work it.

KEYNES

Keynes saw Beveridge again on 21 August and the informal sub-committee met him again on 24 August and 12 October. On each occasion, Keynes minuted the results.

To E. HALE, *21 August 1942*

SIR WILLIAM BEVERIDGE'S SOCIAL SECURITY PROPOSALS

1. I had a further conversation with Sir William Beveridge this morning. Professor Robbins, Sir George Epps and I will be having our final conversation with him on Monday. Meanwhile he has made various changes with a view to reducing the initial financial cost of the scheme. The most important of the revised provisions are the following:

(1) The classes not at present subject to insurance are to be brought into the scheme forthwith. But, as they will receive no benefits for six years, this will serve to reduce the financial cost of the scheme during the early period, as compared with my suggestion that this part of the proposals should be deferred for the time being. Under Sir W. Beveridge's revised scheme it will be some time before there is a net outgoing in respect of this class.

(2) The children's allowance is now increased to 9s a week less the estimated present cost of what children are receiving in kind (which might reduce the figure to 8s 6d or a little less). But this allowance is not to be given to the first child.

(3) The estimated cost of medical treatment in the early years is now put at £m100.

(4) The contribution is put at 7s.

(5) The standard benefit for unemployment, sickness, etc. is 24s for a single man and 40s for a married man.

(6) Pensions for those already in the contributory class are raised to 14s for a single man and 25s for a married couple. This is not increased hereafter for those already in receipt of pensions,

but those retiring after having paid two years of the higher contribution will have their basic pensions increased by 1s each, this figure remaining constant for the rest of their lives. Those who have paid four years of contribution will have a pension 2s higher than the minimum, and so on for each further two years. This will continue until pensions are at the same level as unemployment etc. benefits, subject to a discretion on the part of the Government to stop the increases when they have reached 20s a week, i.e. in that case they would not go up to the full figure of 24s.

(7) Persons within the present contributory scheme will only receive a pension in excess of the existing rate of 10s subject to a retirement condition, which means that 'from one-half to two-thirds of the excess of any earnings above £3 a month will be deducted from his pension for the ensuing quarter'.

(8) The scheme thus amended is estimated to cost the Exchequer £m100 more than the existing scheme in the first year. It is not yet clear how fast the cost will rise or to what maximum figure. But it would appear likely that the final cost of the scheme will be not less than £m150 in excess of the initial cost.

2. It will be seen that the retirement condition is retained in spite of the initial rate of pensions being at a reduced level. It will also be seen that as time goes on pensions will be in force at all kinds of different rates, dependent partly upon the year in which the pension starts and partly on the operation of the retirement condition. The treatment of existing pensioners is not clear, but it would seem that those in receipt of non-contributory pensions will remain at 10s, subject to supplementation. Those in receipt of contributory pensions will either remain at 10s or rise to 14s, subject to supplementation, but will neither now nor in the future go above that.

3. Sir William Beveridge had an interview with the T.U.C. a few days ago and believes that they will support his revised scheme as it stands. They did not quarrel with a contribution

of 7s nor with the proposal that pensions should start at a low level and only rise gradually towards full subsistence. But how far they fully appreciated the details of a very complicated scheme must remain uncertain.

(4) Sir W. Beveridge has also seen, or will be seeing, a number of other bodies with a view to securing their support for his scheme before publication. He is seeing Friendly Societies at Oxford this Sunday. Later on he is meeting the Social Research Section of the Conservative Party, also groups of the Liberal and Labour Parties.

5. He tells me he is asking permission to reprint his Report as a Penguin as soon as it is out.

6. The scheme is still subject to revision in detail. But I do not think Sir W. Beveridge will change his mind on the four questions of—

(a) bringing in the whole population forthwith;

(b) the high level of children's allowances (which will, by the way, also apply to the first child in the case of unemployment or sickness);

(c) a contractual right to a rising level of pension as time goes on; and

(d) a retirement provision.

But the costs of the different parts of the scheme are, I think, now adequately disentangled, and it is fairly easy to see the financial effect of taking only part of the scheme in the first stage or of applying benefits at a reduced level until we know better than we do now the scale of our future resources. Sir W. Beveridge regards the general principles of the scheme as independent of the exact rates of contribution and benefits. He would, I think, be prepared to agree within limits that the figures he inserts for these in his scheme are to be regarded as illustrative, the definitive figures to be fixed nearer the time in the light of the cost of living etc. at that date. He also holds that the rates of contribution are closely associated and should move together if there it to be any change.

KEYNES

To E. HALE, *24 August 1942*

A FURTHER NOTE ON SIR WILLIAM BEVERIDGE'S
SOCIAL SECURITY PROPOSALS

Professor Robbins, Sir George Epps and I had our final conversation for the time being with Sir William Beveridge this morning, though he may be asking us to go again for a final talk in about a month's time.

There can be no doubt, I think, that Sir William Beveridge has made a manful effort to meet the financial criticisms which have been made, with the result that his proposals in their present form are not, in my judgement, open to serious criticism purely on financial grounds, provided one assumes that the paper scheme is politically practicable and stable.

On most of the points at issue I have nothing to add to my note of August 21st. But it is now easier to sum up the total effect, and there are also some further concessions to report.

(1) The initial cost to the Exchequer would be £m115 in excess of the present basis. But this includes an additional expenditure on the health service of £m100 (making £m170 on the health service altogether), although it is most unlikely that this figure can be in fact attained in the first year. Since the children's cash allowance will cost £m110, this means that the burden on the Exchequer will not exceed the cost of children's allowances, the whole of the rest of the additional cost, including all pensions and an additional £m100 for the health service, being met out of the additional contributions. To have made the scheme self-supporting, apart from children's allowances, seems to me as much as one could well have hoped.

(2) The transitional arrangements now appear to involve the Exchequer in a very slow rate of increase. For the classes which are not already contributory no pensions are proposed for six years, whilst he is willing to suggest that, if need be, the deferment of the grant of these pensions might be for ten years.

The contribution of 7s is to go up to 7s 6d (worth £m25) after six years in view of the health service being more complete by that date. The proposal by which the initial rate of pension depends on the number of years paid at the high rate of contribution and is never afterwards raised means that a very great number of years will have passed before the full cost of the scheme is reached. Even twenty years hence the increase in the cost above the initial figure will have only attained about half its eventual total. Put in figures, the increase in the cost after twenty years will be £m140 a year, from which has to be deducted the additional £m25 of contribution from the further 6d, making a net addition of £m115. This has not yet been divided by Epps between the first and the second decade. But I think the major part of it is in the second decade. So that, even ten years after the inception of the scheme, the cost to the Exchequer will not be very seriously increased.

(3) Thus, it is obvious that very large concessions have been made from the first version of the scheme. The main criticism to which it is open is that the proposal to saddle pensioners for life at the rate of pension prevailing in the year in which they first became pensionable is not politically stable. It will be interesting to know how much it would cost to substitute for this a progressive scale by which all pensions went up by stages over a period of years. Obviously there would be much advantage in this, but the cost would be materially greater and, if it were contractual, the risk of excessive cost that much more serious. But it is one thing to say that the Beveridge scheme costs too much, and another to say that a more expensive scheme is likely to be substituted for it by the politicians.

(4) The major part of the economy has, of course, been achieved by accepting pensions at the greatly reduced rate of 14s single and 25s double in the initial year. This rate of pension to those particular persons will never be increased subsequently. It is, I think, of great value that Beveridge should not be raising higher hopes than this in the early period. He will propound his

scheme as being a scheme for pensions of 24s single and 40s double, but in fact no one who is now above 45 years of age will receive pensions at this rate, and this will not be the generally prevailing rate of pension for thirty or forty years.

(5) The main extravagance of the scheme is in putting children's allowances at 8s a week in cash in addition to a further 1s a week through allowances in kind. I pointed out that it was entirely illogical to apply subsistence standards to all children, since it had not been intended even by advocates of allowances to remove the totality of expense from the parents. The arguments which might make a subsistence level appropriate to old-age pensioners or to the unemployed and their dependents are clearly not applicable. Beveridge agreed that this was so. He had no justification for going to so high a figure except that he must give the subsistence figure to the children of the unemployed and, if he did not give it all round, he was afraid that the earnings of a family man out of work would approximate too closely to what he could earn when in work. He agreed, however, to put in a clause pointing out that the children's allowances, except in the case of the unemployed, might be reduced to 6s instead of 8s without jeopardy to the main principles of the plan, which would save £m25. This is important if it is held that the withholding of children's allowances from the first child is politically unstable, since the cost of an 8s allowance to all children would be enormous. Many people might hold that it would be better to include the first child rather than have so high an allowance for further children, if the money runs to one or the other. I think the scheme would be greatly improved if the allowance were to be reduced to 6s, if not to 5s, since this would make it so much less prohibitive to include the first child subsequently, if public opinion were to press strongly for this.

(6) I should add that the scheme provides a discretion to stop pensions from rising above 20s if in 1960 the further increase to 24s looks too expensive.

We had no further discussion about the retirement provision.

I cannot believe that this will survive. But I do not think it makes a significant difference to the financial cost of the scheme whether or not it is included. It was much more important from the financial point of view when it was being used as a main justification for starting pensions at a high initial figure.

(7) Sir William Beveridge has promised to put emphatic passages in his report calling attention to the financial difficulties, arguing that the finance of the scheme stands or falls as a whole and that there is no room for further concessions except in return for increased contributions, and generally emphasising the contributory character of the plan so that the rights of those who have not contributed in the past will be legitimately limited.

There are, of course, innumerable details and complications which I have not touched on, some of them being in themselves of the first order of importance. Sir George Epps and Sir William Beveridge have, I think, a legitimate complaint against the difficulties caused by the statistical inadequacy of the Ministry of Health's information. One's impression is that this requires drastic reorganisation. It has not yet been possible to obtain a firm estimate from them of the existing expenditure of public authorities on the health services.

KEYNES

To SIR RICHARD HOPKINS, *13 October, 1942*

SIR WILLIAM BEVERIDGE'S PROPOSALS

I

At my last meeting with Sir William Beveridge yesterday (at which Professor Robbins, Mr Hale and the Government Actuary and his Assistant were also present). I mainly emphasised three points where some re-drafting of the proposals might help us:

(1) It is stated in the Report that the scale of reliefs and contributions proposed is illustrative and based on the assump-

tion of a price level 25 per cent above that of 1938. I pointed out that prices were almost certain to be 30 per cent above pre-war and might easily be as high as 35 per cent before we had settled down to equilibrium. Sir William Beveridge agreed that he would not in fact in this case and if prices did not rise higher than that wish to revise his proposed scheme of benefits and contributions. That being so, I pointed out to him that it might cause trouble to emphasise so much the 25 per cent, since it might be held that there was a case for having the scale automatically lifted if in fact 30 to 35 per cent proves to be nearer to the facts. As usual with his calculations, he is being dragged at the heels of the subsistence experts, and the calculation based on 25 per cent above the 1928 figure goes deep into all the quantitative aspects of his Report. He agree, however, that he would do his best to speak less precisely and to make it clear that he would not be in favour of any revision of the scale unless prices were materially higher than they are now.

(2) I pointed out that, whilst the ultimate benefits to those who would have paid the higher contributions for a long period were necessarily on a contractual basis, this did not apply to the proposed biennial increments during the next twenty years, since the recipients of such increments would be receiving something for which they would not have paid. He agreed that this was so and that it was the essence of his plan to make a sharp distinction between benefits which had been paid for and transitional benefits which had not been paid for. He promised to make this clearer. It ought to be made plain from the outset that there is no final commitment to the proposed scale of biennial increments, which might be temporarily suspended or spread over a longer period than at present proposed, if the financial situation seemed to make this inevitable.

(3) Sir William Beveridge proposes no allowance in respect of the first child except in the case of a man who is out of work, but for all subsequent children the allowance is to be 8s a week. This figure is based on the estimated actual subsistence cost for

food, clothing, fuel and light, etc., but not rent, for each additional child. I argued that, whilst there was force in this subsistence argument for all unemployed men, few, if any, advocates of children's allowances had argued that the parents should be relieved of all expense whatever, and that there was no sufficient argument on subsistence grounds for giving the full amount to parents in employment. Sir William Beveridge agreed with this, which, indeed, fits in very well with his general argument on children's allowances. He said that he had in effect recognised this by providing no benefit for the first child, thus the average benefit per child for two children was 4s under his scheme and for three children 5s 4d, thus falling short of the full subsistence level. On the other hand he had to admit that he was giving full subsistence in respect of each additional child. Profesor Robbins pointed out to him that it would be fully in accordance with his principle and, indeed, more fully in accordance than his actual proposal, if he was to reduce the allowance for the second child (in the case of employed men) to 5s, retaining his 8s figure for subsequent children. This would mean an average allowance per child of 2s 6d for each of two children, 4s 4d for each of three children, 5s 3d for each of four children, and so on. At a rough shot it looked as if this modest amendation would save no less than £m20 a year on the cost. I doubt if Sir William Beveridge will actually adopt this amendment, but he will probably amend his draft so that it could easily be introduced, and he may mention it as one of the alternatives. I should add that the estimates of financial cost take no credit for any gain in income tax, either through the abolition of existing children's rebates or through treating the new children's allowances as part of taxable income. The proposals expressly reserve the taxation aspects. But, unless there is some change on the taxation side, the effect would be to allow in respect of additional children an actual profit to the parents, since the income tax rebates would be superimposed on the Beveridge subsistence allowance.

II

As set forth in the Report, the net additional cost to the Treasury is £m100. (It is not quite clear whether this comparison is with 1939 or with the present cost, but I believe it to be with 1939). The following notes on what lies behind this figure may be useful:

(i) As mentioned above, it takes no credit for gain in income tax as an off-set to children's allowances.

(ii) A reduction of benefit to employed persons in respect of the second child from 8s to 5s would be worth about £m20 a year.

(iii) There appears to be a large margin in the early years in respect of the figure put down for health services, namely, £m170. The present cost is about £m50. The increase has been arrived at by assuming that the whole of the incomes of the medical profession are received through the state under the health scheme, and that these incomes will be 25 per cent greater after the war than they were before. It seems most unlikely that so great a transformation of the medical services can be achieved immediately on the inception of the new proposals (assumed to be 1945). This figure is also bound up with the proposal to bring the whole population within the scheme. Certainly it would be a most surprising thing if the new proposals, even if they are accepted as desirable, could be brought so completely into force within a brief period. On the other hand, the figure of the cost 20 years hence is put at only £m10 above the initial cost. On my asking for the explanation of this, I was told that the practice of preventive medicine in the same period would have been so great as to abate illness sufficiently to off-set the otherwise growing cost. This seems optimistic, since, even assuming that the premises are fulfilled, standards of medical treatment will certainly rise proportionately.

(iv) If full allowance had been given to these possible savings, the cost to the Treasury in the early period might perhaps seem

too small. This would not remain so in the long run, since the cost will rise at the rate of about £m7 a year during the first decade and £m10 during the second decade, whilst, even after 20 years, the maximum cost will not have been attained. Moreover, there are certain, perhaps inevitable, modifications of the scheme, referred to below, which would have the effect of increasing the cost to the Treasury in the early years.

(v) It may be thought advisable, quite apart from the merits of the case, and purely on administrative and legislative grounds, to limit the scheme in the first instance to the existing contributory classes. In the early years this would add to the cost of the scheme, since the financial provisions assume contributions from the new classes to be paid in whilst giving them less than equal benefits. I cannot estimate how much extra the scheme would cost at the outset if this part of it were deferred. It cannot be a large sum, but it is nevertheless sufficient to be worth mentioning.

(vi) Sir William Beveridge's retirement provisions are likely, in my opinion, to be unpopular, and it would not be surprising if they have to be dropped. They do, however, provide a fairly substantial economy, again especially in the early years; so that to drop them would somewhat increase the initial cost. At first I was opposed to the retirement provisions on merits and apart from their probable unpopularity. On second thoughts I begin to think there may be something in them, especially in connection with other features of the scheme as they have now developed. The retirement provisions are as follows:

If a man notifies that he desires to retire, half of the excess of any future earnings over 15s are deducted from his pension. If, on the other hand, he decides not to retire when he reaches pensionable age, the rate of his ultimate pension increases by 2s each year for a married man and 1s each year for a single man. This is a valuable inducement to keep men at work, and it fits in well with the other transitional arrangements for the following reasons: Take the case of a married man, who reaches

pensionable age in the first year of the scheme. If he retires at once, he will receive 25*s* a week, rising by 1*s* 6*d* every other year. If, on the other hand, he puts off retirement for four years, his initial rate of pension will be 32*s* instead of 25*s*. Thereby he will have benefited both himself and the State.

(vii) The finance of the scheme essentially depends on the increased rates of contribution proving acceptable. These are 4*s* 3*d* for the employee and 3*s* 3*d* for the employer, making 7*s* 6*d* in all. Sir William Beveridge produces powerful arguments why this increase should be acceptable. He is able to point out that the increase is of the same order of magnitude as the sums which the average wage-earner is already expending voluntarily to obtain similar advantages to those now promised by the scheme. One may add that the children's allowance side of it (and that is an argument perhaps for bringing in the children's allowance simultaneously with the increased contribution, and not earlier or separately) means that any man with more than one child is actually from the outset substantially better off than he is now, the children's allowance being much larger than the increased contribution. I believe Sir William Beveridge is right in believing that this will not prove unacceptable to the employee. It is the very large sums obtained in this way which make so far-reaching a proposal practicable at such modest cost to the Treasury.

One must, however, face the fact that the employer's contribution is an ingredient in cost and must, sooner or later, be reflected in prices. Very roughly it would seem likely that it would raise prices by something like 1 per cent. This is not to be neglected. But it is really very small relatively to the advantages obtained and means no more than that scale of increase of wages which might happen any day for most insignificant reasons.

III

I have not seen the final version of more than mere fragments of the proposals as a whole. But they have been greatly improved as the result of discussion. From what I have seen, it looks to me that the document is a very fine one and will impress public opinion as at the same time moderate and far-reaching and argued in the most convincing and striking manner.

The question remains what can be done with it. I do not think it has to be regarded as an independent whole to the full extent that Sir William Beveridge himself believes and would argue. The central part of his scheme is a great simplification of what happens already and, whilst a great deal of existing legislation would have to be repealed, I should have thought that what would replace it would be so much simpler that it would not be a very overwhelming task to work it out or to get it through Parliament. This does not apply, however, to certain completely new features of the proposals,—in particular, the extension of the social security benefits and contributions to the whole population, and not merely to the present contributory classes. Worked out in detail, this will raise all kinds of personal difficulties and special cases. The legislator would be treading a new field with not nearly so much experience to guide him. The drafting would be far more difficult and the legislation (I should have supposed) much more contentious.

Moreover, it is from this extension of the services to the whole population that the immediate socialisation of the medical profession follows. If this further step was postponed, the medical profession could be dealt with by much more gradual and much less violent means.

Thus, irrespective of the merits of extending the benefits and contributions to the whole population (I should agree that there is a great deal to be said in favour of it), the postponement of this side of the scheme deserves the most serious consideration. The rest of it is so much a simplification of the familiar that the task should be relatively easy.

I daresay the same applies to the proposals about industrial insurance. I have not yet seen the final draft of this and do not clearly know what they amount to.

If some substantial parts of the Report were to be approved in principle by the Government, the question then arises what interim measures may be necessary. Probably it would be necessary to raise pension rates to the new minimum of 14s forthwith. It may be that there is also something to be said for raising unemployment, but perhaps not sickness, benefits to the new figure. Unemployment, at any rate, would cost very little currently and the provision of substantial unemployment relief might facilitate the demobilisation proposals. Indeed, the increase would have to be explained and justified on the ground that it would ease the transition arising out of demobilisation. If these increases are made, unquestionably they should be accompanied by a substantial increase in contributions. This would not be so easy pending the consolidation of the existing contributions into a single figure, but no doubt something could be worked out.

KEYNES

13 October 1942

On reading the final version of the Beveridge Report on its way to the printer, Keynes wrote to its author.

To SIR WILLIAM BEVERIDGE, *14 October 1942*

Dear Beveridge,

I have now read your Part VI and have no crititisms worth making, beyond such modifications of drafting here and there as you might be willing to make to meet the points I raised at our meeting, the other day. On the whole, the phrasing of this part of the Report seems to me to fit in well with what we were talking about. Now I see your whole discussion of children's allowances, it would seem very easy to graft Robbins's suggestion on to it. Indeed, it closely follows the lines of your own

argument, and only means a certain modification of scale. Here certainly seems to me to be a case where we can start on the moderate side without any injury to the main principles of the scheme, whatever we may be able to afford later.

On the question of the post-war level of prices, your paragraph 38 seems to be put perhaps the wrong way round. It is certainly not the policy of the Treasury to allow prices to break loose after the war, and it is only if the continuation of the stabilisation policy now under consideration breaks down that anything of the short could happen. I should like to put the passage in question the other way round, somewhat as follows:

The question of how the plan should be financed in terms of money can only be determined in the light of the level of prices after the war. If the present stabilisation policy is maintained, with the result that the post-war level of prices is not seriously in excess of what it is today, the money values used in the earlier parts of this report might be taken as definitive, for, although they are based on the assumption of a subsistence level costing no more than 25 per cent above 1938 prices, there are various uncertain elements, and it is certainly not the recommendation of this report that the scale of benefits and contributions should be thrown into the melting pot except in the event of a serious disturbance to the established level of prices. It should, however, be emphasised that, in any case, the plan for social security set out in this report is not primarily concerned with fixing in terms of money the precise level of benefits and contributions. It is concerned primarily, etc.

The same point arises in paragraph 46. This seems to me greatly to overstate the possibility of putting off decisions of the third kind. Surely they would have to be embodied in any Bill. Admittedly they would need revision in the event of a serious change in the level of prices, but it would be impossible to expect Parliament to discuss the scheme on a purely hypothetical basis of benefits and contributions. I should have thought that, if the reference to this matter is amplified in paragraph 38, you could be content in paragraph 46 with referring back, simply saying in paragraph 46:

Decisions of the third kind as to rates of benefits and contribution must depend on the considerations mentioned in paragraph 38.

After reading this further instalment of your Report, I feel confirmed in the feeling I expressed the other day, that it is a grand document. You can scarcely expect it will be adopted just as it stands, but it seems to me that you have got it into an extremely workable shape, and I should hope that the major and more essential parts of it might be adopted substantially as you have conceived them.

On further reflection I find myself becoming a bit more sympathetic than I have expressed myself hitherto about your retirement provisions. I do see that there is a good deal to be said for them. I still think that they are likely to prove unpopular and difficult to get through the House. But, on second thoughts, I should on the whole prefer to start off the proposals with the retirement provisions included on your lines. It will be worth emphasising when the Report comes up for consideration, that these retirement provisions do fit in extremely well with the latest version of your transitional provisions. There are important groups within the wage-earning classes where 69 is quite as plausible an age for retirement as 65. Take the case of a married man who reaches 65 in the first year of the scheme. If he retires forthwith he starts off with 25s. If he waits until he is 69, both sets of increments work in his favour and he starts off with 32s. Thus the postponement will have served to benefit both himself and the state. Nevertheless, there remains the difficulty of the abatement of pension to those who retire and continue to earn anything substantial. I cannot but believe that there will be a good deal of difficulty in getting that through.

Yours ever,
KEYNES

All this is, of course, my purely personal views.

After the Beveridge Report was published on 1 December 1942, the Government treated it with reserve. This reserve showed up clearly in the House of Commons debate of 16–18 February 1943. Keynes proposed to make his maiden speech in the Lords debate on the Report on 24 February. However the day before he warned his mother.

From a letter to F. A. KEYNES, *23 February 1943*

Do not be disappointed when you see no speech from me in the papers of Thursday. Great pressure has been put on me not to speak, and on Catto also. They have all got themselves into a hideous mess over this Report, and it has become a very sore political spot. They think, perhaps truly, that, if I make a candid statement of the position, it will not redound to their advantage,...[and] my general relations with the Treasury might become somewhat embarrassed. I am not convinced by all this. I think a few honest words generally do more good than harm; all the same, I have given way and agreed not to speak. Whilst I believe that my intervention on this occasion would have done good rather than harm, I do see that there are great advantages in making my first speech on some constructive, positive, good-tempered occasion rather than as part of the present imbroglio. Also I value too highly my present relations with everyone in the Treasury to want to run the risk of disobliging them.

Draft for House of Lords on 24 February 1943

My Lords,

I hope for the indulgence your lordships are accustomed to grant to those who address you for the first time. And, since I am closely associated with a Gov^t Dep^t, I ought, perhaps, to emphasise that anything I say to your Lordships to-day or on any other occasion is a purely personal expression of opinion. I speak because as a member of your Lordships' House who happens to be a close student of the matters under discussion

I feel it to be a duty to express the views I have formed for what they may be worth.

I shall not attempt to cover the very wide field opened up by this Debate. I propose to confine myself to a single aspect, the question whether the country can afford what we most of us agree to be desirable. It is this financial aspect, I think, which is the chief cause of anxiety to those whom apart from this the Beveridge proposals greatly attract.

I view the Budgetary prospects after the war with great concern. It is impossible to say how constrained the position will be until we know the cost of post-war defence. And it may be a considerable time before we know that with any confidence. We must therefore be very slow to burden the Budget with any avoidable and unnecessary charges especially in the early post-war period.

On the financial side, therefore, I approach the Beveridge proposals with the question whether there is a reasonable alternative before the country which would during this period cost the Exchequer significantly less. The strange thing is that during the lengthy debate in another place no one, neither Ministers nor their critics, seems to have asked this simple question—except on the special matter of children's allowances. On that matter the Gov^t, prudently in my opinion, proposed to substitute 5s for the 8s in the plan. 5s, particularly if it is supplemented as the Lord President foreshadowed by increased services in kind, is quite enough to begin with in a new social policy which if it is a success we may carry much further when our means increase.

But assuming that the plan is amended in this way, what *other* variations does anyone propose which would save a significant amount of money? In the early period, that is to say—I will consider later on in my remarks the position twenty years hence. —I know of none.

What are the economies open to us? To slow down the development of the National Health Service? The pace of

progress will be limited for reasons outside our control by the shortage of available personnel. But neither the Gov^t nor anyone else proposes to make any economy here by proceeding more slowly than we need. By offering lower rates of benefit for unemployment and sickness? I have heard no suggestion of this kind from Ministers or from anyone else. Indeed the Lord President was careful to make it clear that the Gov^t have in mind 'rates not widely different from those in the Report'. By fixing a lower initial rate for pensions than the Beveridge figure? The Lord President has indicated that the Gov^t contemplate a higher rate. These are the provisions which cost the money. There is only one other way of saving the Budget, namely by fixing higher contributions than those of the plan. No-one has suggested this, though it would be easy to risk the existing readiness to peg these increased contributions, and thus increase the charge on the Budget, if too much of the scheme is put into the melting pot. I am, therefore, at a loss to known how it is proposed to save money from the Budget by *not* having the Beveridge Plan. This is a very obvious question to ask. No-one so far has dropt even a hint how to answer it.

Allowing for the proposed economy on children's allowances and the inevitable delays in the development of the Health Service, it is not true that the Beveridge proposals involve the Exchequer in any serious expense beyond what is already inevitable.

It is, therefore, precisely because I am deeply concerned about the Budget position in the early years after the war that I welcome the Beveridge proposals. For these years there is no cheaper scheme on the map. On the other hand, it would be very easy, if we proceed piecemeal, to slip into a more expensive scheme with higher benefits in certain directions, and with a danger of some loss of the proposed contributions.

What I am saying is not a paradox. That Sir William Beveridge's scheme is a relatively cheap scheme for the early period is not an accident. He has deliberately designed it this

way and that, in my judgement, is one of the great merits of the scheme which has not attracted the attention it deserves. That the Plan achieves its results at a low budgetary cost follows from one of its fundamental principles, namely that we collect to-day's pension contributions from a working population larger than corresponds to the number of today's pensioners, and we use these contributions, which are paid in return for future pensions, to defray a smaller number of current pensions. This means that the immediate financial problem is greatly eased.

But it also means that the future cost will increase progressively. The right question to ask therefore, is not whether we can afford the Beveridge Plan now, but whether the Plan brings immediate financial ease at the cost of future commitments which will prove too heavy.

This takes us into a speculative field where, admittedly, nothing can be proved certain. Speaking for myself, I can only affirm that I am not worried about the remotest future if only we can surmount our immediate post-war difficulties. On the average the cost of the Beveridge scheme will increase cumulatively by about £8 million a year as time goes on. But with merely normal technical progress such as we have experienced for many years past, the national income out of which to meet this should increase cumulatively by more like £100 million a year. Personally I expect a much greater growth of national income even than this. When the future looks black, I comfort myself with the thought that British industry can scarcely be more inefficient than it was before the war. I am confident that we could increase output both in industry and in agriculture by at least 50 per cent compared with 1938 merely by putting to work modern methods and techniques that already exist. Indeed in agriculture I fancy we have done it already. By taking on burdens we force ourselves to face the problems of organisation which it is our duty to face anyhow.

Nothing but a major reversal of fortune which would upset a great deal more than the Beveridge Plan can prevent our

national income from increasing several times as fast as our obligations under the Plan.

The Gov^t has, therefore, done well to accept the Report. I have read carefully the speeches of the Gov^t spokesmen in another place. It is a gross travesty of what they said to represent it otherwise than as a substantial acceptance of the Plan. Nor do I see any indications of avoidable delay in putting it into force. Indeed it is obvious that we shall urgently need the Plan in operation to help us to get through the difficult period of transition from war activities. We can go into the demobilisation period without the higher contributions. We cannot go into it without the higher benefits. So how is delay going to help the Budget? I agree that there was a good deal of what the lawyers call 'without prejudice' about the Gov^t statements. But if I am satisfied with the substance of a statement, I do not bother too much whether it has pencilled at the bottom the letters O.K. or whether the family solicitor has recommended E. and O.E. The difference between the two sets of letters is more a matter of style and temperament than substance. I hope that the noble and learned Viscount on the Woolsack will, if he can frame his lips to so convey an expression, give us a little more of the O.K. and a little less of the 'without prejudice'.

My Lords, a refusal, if it had been made, to commit later years to this modest extent would have raised the whole question of our attitude to the future. The future will be what we choose to make it. If we approach it with cringing and timidity, we shall get what we deserve. If we march on with confidence and vigour the facts will respond. It would be a monstrous thing to reserve all our courage and powers of will for War and then, crowned with victory, to approach the Peace as a bankrupt bunch of defeatists.

Moreover, to make a bogey of the economic problem is, in my judgement, grievously to misunderstand the nature of the tasks ahead of us. Looking beyond the immediate post-war period, when our economic difficulties will be genuine and must

take precedence over all else—perhaps for the last time—the economic problems of the day [that] perplex us, will lie in solving the problems of an era of material abundance not those of an era of poverty. It is not any fear of a failure of physical productivity to provide an adequate material standard of life that fills me with foreboding. The real problems of the future are first of all the maintenance of peace, of international co-operation and amity, and beyond that the profound moral and social problems of how to organise material abundance to yield up the fruits of a good life. These are the heroic tasks of the future. But there is nothing, My Lords, in what we are discussing today which need frighten a mouse.

However, Keynes did speak on the finance of the Beveridge scheme to the Watching Committee of both Houses at a private meeting at the Treasury on 23 March.[7]

Keynes's final involvement with the Beveridge proposals came in May 1944, as the authorities were drafting their White Paper on Social Insurance, in response to a letter from D. N. Chester.[8]

To SIR B. GILBERT *and* SIR RICHARD HOPKINS, *15 May 1944*

This letter from Chester is the outcome of a conversation he had with me last week. He came round to say how much upset he was at the line which the draft White Paper on Social Insurance was now taking. I have not myself seen this White Paper but am assuming that Chester has rightly understood it.

The reasons for his dismay are as I understand him the following:

1. The Treasury criticised Beveridge for extravagance and

---

[7] The Watching Committee was a group of peers and M.P.s of influence and seniority, which met confidentially on matters before Parliament.

[8] Daniel Norman Chester (b. 1907); Lecturer in Public Administration, University of Manchester, 1936–45; member, Central Economic Information Service and Economic Section of War Cabinet Secretariat, 1940–5; Fellow of Nuffield College, Oxford, 1945, Warden, 1954–78.

with some effect. Beveridge having been persuaded to produce as economical a plan as possible, then finds that it is not merely the distant cost but the immediate cost for 1945 which is inflated by £49 million by concessions which, when he was disposed to make them, were declared to be financially impossible. Chester feels that this inconsistency will need some defending and that the passage relating to it should be drafted with particular care.

2. The late Chancellor of the Exchequer, having strongly endorsed the contributory principle, and this having been regarded as the sheet anchor of the proposals, the Government now throw this principle entirely to the winds. So much so that they actually treat a man who has made no contributions whatever, better than they could treat future contributors. For the former will get the £1 without question whilst the latter will only get it if his contributions have been sufficient. Chester feels that the abandonment of the contributory principle will make the whole finance of the scheme vulnerable. In particular a further increase in the basic pension of 40s would be very difficult to resist.

3. Whilst the new proposals are exceedingly lavish on pensions, they are exceedingly mean in the matter of children's allowances, where the absolute minimum is given. He thinks that this will lead to great criticism and that the Treasury, having shown by their treatment of pensioners that money is no object will find sooner or later that they have a very weak case on which to resist further children's contributions—the case for which, on merits, many people will think vastly superior. (This particular point came out more clearly in conversation I think than in the attached note.)

Chester appreciates I think that Ministerial decisions have gone too far for it to be any use to criticise them. He is concerned that the relevant passages should be drafted with a full awareness of the above points of weakness so that at any rate the criticisms are anticipated and the case is presented in a way that will leave the case against further concessions as strong as possible.

My own feeling is that so great a concession on pensions is lamentable. But I do not think it would prove easy for Beveridge or anyone else to criticise them on the ground that they go beyond the original Beveridge proposals. On the other hand I do feel that the inconsistency between the lavishness on pensions and the meanness on children's allowances would prove very difficult indeed to defend. I also agree with him that what amounts to the abandonment of the contributory principle leads us into uncharted seas.

I always thought, it will be remembered, that the Beveridge scheme was by far the cheapest we ever had a hope of getting and I several times represented this to the late Chancellor. I am not therefore much surprised that a readiness to depart from these proposals immediately leads to largely increased expense.

KEYNES

Chapter 5

EMPLOYMENT POLICY

Discussions of post-war employment policy began in the course of 1941. While Keynes was in America, the Treasury had preliminary discussions on post-war internal economic problems, but these petered out before his return as other matters were more pressing. However, the Economic Section of the War Cabinet kept up the momentum. As early as February 1941, James Meade, in the first of a long series of memoranda, had turned to the subject. A later memorandum by Meade, dated 8 July 1941 and entitled 'Internal Measures for the Prevention of Unemployment', along with the preliminary Treasury discussions, played a part in the organisation of an inter-departmental Committee on Post-War Internal Economic Problems in October 1941. This Committee was charged with ascertaining what would be the chief internal problems facing post-war economic policy makers, arranging for memoranda to examine these problems and recommending to Ministers the considerations that they should have in mind in framing policy. Meade's July memorandum was one of the first documents circulated to the Committee.

During the early stages of the Committee's work, Keynes himself made a foray into the shape of the post-war world, not for internal Treasury consumption, but as part of a series of BBC broadcasts on post-war planning.

From The Listener, *2 April 1942*

HOW MUCH DOES FINANCE MATTER?

For some weeks at this hour you have enjoyed the day-dreams of planning. But what about the nightmare of finance? I am sure there have been many listeners who have been muttering:

'That's all very well, but how is it to be paid for?'

Let me begin by telling you how I tried to answer an eminent architect who pushed on one side all the grandiose plans to rebuild London with the phrase: 'Where's the money to come from?' 'The money?' I said. 'But surely, Sir John, you don't build houses with money? Do you mean that there won't be

264

enough bricks and mortar and steel and cement?' 'Oh no', he replied, 'of course there will be plenty of all that'. 'Do you mean', I went on, 'that there won't be enough labour? For what will the builders be doing if they are not building houses?' 'Oh no, that's all right', he agreed. 'Then there is only one conclusion. You must be meaning, Sir John, that there won't be enough *architects*'. But there I was trespassing on the boundaries of politeness. So I hurried to add: 'Well, if there are bricks and mortar and steel and concrete and labour and architects, why not assemble all this good material into houses?' But he was, I fear, quite unconvinced. 'What I want to know', he repeated, 'is where the money is coming from'. To answer that would have got him and me into deeper water than I cared for, so I replied rather shabbily: 'The same place it is coming from now'. He might have countered (but he didn't): 'Of course I know that money is not the slightest use whatever. But, all the same, my dear sir, you will find it a devil of a business not to have any'.

A question of pace and preference

Had I given him a good and convincing answer by saying that we build houses with bricks and mortar, not with money? Or was I only teasing him? It all depends what he really had in mind. He might have meant that the burden of the national debt, the heavy taxation, the fact that the banks have lent so much money to the Government and all that, would make it impossible to borrow money to pay the wages of the makers of the raw material, the building labour, and even the architects. Or he might have meant something quite different. He could have pointed out very justly that those who were making houses would have to be supported meanwhile with the means of subsistence. Will the rest of us, after supporting ourselves, have enough margin of output of food and clothing and the like, directly or by foreign trade, to support the builders as well as ourselves whilst they are at work?

In fact was he really talking about money? Or was he talking about resources in general—resources in a wide sense, not merely bricks and cement and architects? If the former, if it was some technical problem of finance that was troubling him, then my answer was good and sufficient. For one thing, he was making the very usual confusion between the problem of finance for an individual and the problem for the community as a whole. Apart from this, no doubt there *is* a technical problem, a problem which we have sometimes bungled in the past, but one which today we understand much more thoroughly. It would be out of place to try to explain it in a few minutes on the air, just as it would be to explain the technical details of bridge-building or the internal combustion engine or the surgery of the thyroid gland. As a technician in these matters I can only affirm that the technical problem of where the *money* for reconstruction is to come from can be solved, and therefore should be solved.

Perhaps I can go a little further than this. The technical problem at the end of this war is likely to be a great deal easier to handle than it was at the end of the last war when we bungled it badly. There are two chief reasons for this. The Treasury is borrowing money at only half the rate of interest paid in the last war, with the result that the interest paid in 1941 on the new debt incurred in this war was actually more than offset by the relief to national resources of not having a large body of unemployed. We cannot expect that the position will be so good as this at the end of the war. Nevertheless if we *keep* good employment when peace comes (which we can and mean to do), even the post-war Budget problem will not be too difficult. And there is another reason also. In 1919 public opinion and political opinion were determined to get back to 1914 by scrapping at the first possible moment many of the controls which were making the technical task easier. I do not notice today the same enthusiasm to get back to 1939. I hope and believe that this time public opinion will give the technicians a fair chance by letting them retain so long as they think necessary many of the controls

over the financial machinery which we are finding useful, and indeed essential, today.

What can we afford to spend?

Now let me turn back to the other interpretation of what my friend may have had at the back of his head—the adequacy of our resources in general, even assuming good employment, to allow us to devote a large body of labour to capital works which would bring in no immediate return. Here is a real problem, fundamental yet essentially simple, which it is important for all of us to try to understand. The first task is to make sure that there is enough demand to provide employment for everyone. The second task is to prevent a demand in excess of the physical possibilities of supply, which is the proper meaning of inflation. For the physical possibilities of supply are very far from unlimited. Our building programme must be properly pro-portioned to the resources which are left *after* we have met our daily needs and have produced enough exports to pay for what we require to import from overseas. Immediately after the war the export industries must have the first claim on our attention. I cannot emphasise that too much. Until we have rebuilt our export trade to its former dimensions, we must be prepared for any reasonable sacrifice in the interests of exports. Success in that field is the clue to success all along the line. After meeting our daily needs by production and by export, we shall find ourselves with a certain surplus of resources and of labour available for capital works of improvement. If there is *insufficient* outlet for this surplus, we have unemployment. If, on the other hand, there is an *excess* demand, we have inflation.

To make sure of good employment we must have ready an ample programme of re-stocking and of development over a wide field, industrial, engineering, transport and agricultural—not merely building. Having prepared our blue-prints, covering the whole field of our requirements and not building alone—and

these can be as ambitious and glorious as the minds of our engineers and architects and social planners can conceive—those in charge must then concentrate on the vital task of central management, the *pace* at which the programme is put into operation, neither so slow as to cause unemployment nor so rapid as to cause inflation. The proportion of this surplus which can be allocated to building must depend on the order of our preference between different types of project.

With that analysis in our minds, let us come back to the building and constructional plans. It is extremely difficult to predict accurately in advance the scale and pace on which they can be carried out. In the long run almost anything is possible. Therefore do not be afraid of large and bold schemes. Let our plans be big, significant, but not hasty. Rome was not built in a day. The building of the great architectural monuments of the past was carried out slowly, gradually, over many years, and they drew much of their virtue from being the fruit of slow cogitation ripening under the hand and before the eyes of the designer. The problem of pace can be determined rightly only in the light of the competing programmes in all other directions.

The difficulty of predicting accurately the appropriate pace of the execution of the building programme is extremely tiresome to those concerned. You cannot improvise a building industry suddenly or put part of it into cold storage when it is excessive. Tell those concerned that we shall need a building industry of a million operatives directly employed—well and good, it can be arranged. Tell them that we shall need a million-and-a-half or two million—again well and good. But we must let them have in good time some reasonably accurate idea of the target. For if the building industry is to expand in an orderly fashion, it must have some assurance of continuing employment for the larger labour force.

I myself have no adequate data on which to guess. But if you put me against a wall opposite a firing squad, I should, at the last moment, reply that at the present level of prices and wages

we might afford in the early post-war years to spend not less than £600 million a year and not more than £800 million on the output of the building industry as a whole. Please remember that this includes repairs and current painting and decorations and replacements as well as all new construction, not merely on houses but also on factories and all other buildings. That, for what it is worth, is my best guess. It covers the activities of private citizens, of firms and companies, of building societies, as well as of local authorities and the central government. Now these are very large sums. Continued, year by year, over a period of ten years or more, they are enormous. We could double in twenty years all the buildings there now are in the whole country. We can do almost anything we like, *given time*. We must not force the pace—that is necessary warning. In good time we can do it all. But we must work to a long-term programme.

Not all planning is expensive. Take the talk of two months ago about planning the countryside. Nothing costly there. To preserve as the national domain for exercise and recreation and the enjoyment and contemplation of nature the cliffs and coastline of the country, the Highlands, the lakes, the moors and fells and mountains, the downs and woodlands furnished with hostels and camping grounds and easy access—that requires no more than the decision to act. For the community as a whole the expense is insignificant. Or take the question of compensation, which Mr Osborn discussed so clearly and so fairly a fortnight ago. Compensation uses up no resources. It is out of one pocket into another and costs nothing to the community as a whole.

Even the planning of London to give space and air and perspective costs nothing to the nation's resources and need not involve a charge on the Budget. There is heaps of room, enough and more than enough, in a re-planned London. We could get all the accommodation we need if a third of the present built-up area was cleared altogether and left cleared. The blitz has uncovered St Paul's to the eyes of this generation. To leave it

so will cost nothing to the community as a whole. To build may be costly. Let us offset that expense by a generous policy, here and there, of *not* building.

Where we are using up resources, do not let us submit to the vile doctrine of the nineteenth century that every enterprise must justify itself in pounds, shillings and pence of cash income, with no other denominator of values but this. I should like to see that war memorials of this tragic struggle take the shape of an enrichment of the civic life of every great centre of population. Why should we not set aside, let us say, £50 millions a year for the next twenty years to add in every substantial city of the realm the dignity of an ancient university or a European capital to our local schools and their surroundings, to our local government and its offices, and above all perhaps, to provide a local centre of refreshment and entertainment with an ample theatre, a concert hall, a dance hall, a gallery, a British restaurant, canteens, cafés and so forth. Assuredly we can afford this and much more. Anything we can actually *do* we can afford. Once done, it is *there*. Nothing can take it from us. We are immeasurably richer than our predecessors. Is it not evident that some sophistry, some fallacy, governs our collective action if we are forced to be so much meaner than they in the embellishments of life?

Yet these must be only the trimmings on the more solid, urgent and necessary outgoings on housing the people, on reconstructing industry and transport and on re-planning the environment of our daily life. Not only shall we come to possess these excellent things. With a big programme carried out at a properly regulated pace we can hope to keep employment good for many years to come. We shall, in very fact, have built our New Jerusalem out of the labour which in our former vain folly we were keeping unused and unhappy in enforced idleness.

As part of the Committee's programme of enquiry, the Treasury prepared a memorandum entitled 'The Post-War Relation between Purchasing Power

and Consumer Goods'. This memorandum was largely the work of Sir Hubert Henderson. It spent more space discussing the immediate post-war transitional period and drawing parallels with the position of the United Kingdom between 1919 and 1924 than considering appropriate policy measures, despite the fact that it was deeply pessimistic as to the long-run level of demand. Keynes's role in the preparation of this paper, as later, was largely that of a critic at a late stage, as the following comments indicate.

To SIR HUBERT HENDERSON *and* SIR RICHARD HOPKINS, *8 April 1942*

MEMORANDUM ON THE POST-WAR RELATION BETWEEN PURCHASING POWER AND CONSUMERS' GOODS

I am not at all happy with the new ending provided for this paper from paragraph 25 onwards. If Mr Bevin was to look on this with as jaundiced an eye as on the Clearing Union, he would say, I think, that the author was scared to death lest there might be some date at which the figure of unemployment would fall below three million! It seems to me to be too pessimistic all along the line under the three headings—(*a*) interim unemployment, (*b*) risk of inflation and (*c*) difficulty in maintaining the standard of life.

(*a*) The last sentence of paragraph 25 seems to me too pessimistic, as paragraph 26 really shows. It might be well to emphasise the rapidity with which the problem will be on us this time owing to the release of civil defence workers. On the other hand, if the army is serving in distant theatres of war or if hostilities in some theatres terminate before hostilities in others, the demobilisation of the army proper may be more easily spread over a period than was the case last time. I should much prefer to put the emphasis on the importance of making early provision and fairly cut-and-dried plans for the transition and particularly in those fields where, with adequate preparation, peace-time employment can be provided quickly, and point out

271

that, *unless this is done*, the problems indicated in the present draft will arise.

(*b*) If we manage our affairs properly, I do not believe that the prevention of inflation will be to slow down the process of reabsorption. The process of manufacturers bidding against one another for supplies which are not there was not particularly helpful last time. I should agree, however, that it may be necessary to provide other incentives than the hope of speculative gains, particularly perhaps by underwriting orders,—a subject which I should like to develop. But here again I should like to put the emphasis on the positive side of the matter and say that if we maintain, as we shall have to, control of prices to prevent an undue rise, it will be particularly important to see that manufacturers have markets opened to them promptly and on attractive terms, such as will be likely to stimulate them into reasonably rapid action during the interim period.

(*c*) The passage about the standard of living comes in paragraph 33. I do not at all share the pessimism here expressed. In line 6 I should like to substitute 'short' for 'considerable'. I think the memorandum greatly under-estimates the consequences of full employment and of the improvement in technical production, which will not cease to take place but will in some directions have been even accelerated during the war period. In this connection I call attention to some studies which are being made by the Economic Section. In their provisional studies of the post-war period they are assuming that we can reduce unemployment to 5 per cent and that technical progress between 1938 and 1946 will amount to 10 per cent. Their figures, which have been agreed by Leak, are as follows:

	(*a*) Home production	(*b*) Exports	(*c*) Retained home production	(*d*) Imports	(*e*) Total, (*c*) +(*d*)	(*f*) Total (pre-war = 100)
Pre-war	100	15	85	26	111	100
Post-war	119	22	97	28	125	113

This shows that, even though we have to increase our exports by 50 per cent, with a very small corresponding increase in imports, we can nevertheless afford an increase of standards as compared with pre-war of 13 per cent. It may be that this is too optimistic, that our memorandum is thinking of a date less distant than 1946 and that the Economic Section is assuming that we can attain that volume of exports. Nevertheless, it is going very much to the other extreme to suggest that 'a considerable interval must elapse before it is possible to restore the standard of living to its pre-war level'. At any rate, I should like to utter the warning that we shall be speaking with an entirely different voice from the Economic Section and in terms which would certainly excite Mr Bevin, if he reads so far on in the memorandum. Here, for the third time, I should put the emphasis on the positive side and point out that our capacity to restore our standard of living and raise it in the measure which technical progress should prompt is to an important extent contingent on the satisfactory development of our exports, a programme which we shall have to further by every possible means open to us, orthodox or unorthodox.

I object not less to the latter part of this paragraph. Of course, it is dangerous to exclude any possibility, but this does seem to me to be seriously overdoing it. Similarly, I do not like, for reasons already given, the whole of paragraph 34. The cumulative effect of paragraphs 33 and 34, although worded in polite language, almost amounts to saying that unemployment and reduced standards are necessary, inevitable and even desirable —of course this is unfair, but it is the impression.

I have another objection to coming down so early in the debate so violently on the negative side, apart from not sharing this view. It seems to me that it is premature and unjustifiable to reach such conclusions until we have made some attempt at quantifying the prospects and relating our general ideas to the statistical facts, so far as we know them. When we can make some progress towards quantifying, this will have the further

advantages that it enables us to give the more favourable and more pessimistic prognosis on different assumptions. For the quantifying, if we can accomplish it, will not be in the nature of a prophecy, but an analysis of the consequences of various alternative assumptions. After showing such consequences, we can then emphasise the importance of adopting that policy which has some chance of making those assumptions come true which lead to the more favourable conclusions.

[copy initialled] J.M.K.

To SIR RICHARD HOPKINS, *15 April 1942*

MEMORANDUM ON THE POST-WAR RELATION BETWEEN PURCHASING POWER AND CONSUMERS' GOODS

Your emendations help me here so far as they go. But I am still not at all happy about the concluding sections:

(1) I must warn you that when we come to the attempt to quantify the problem the results are at least as likely as not to lead to a contrary conclusion to those set forth here, except as regards the very early period. As at present drafted, there are several passages indicating that the inflationary tendency 'is likely to be considerably longer than two or three years'.

(2) It is noticeable that where statistical investigations have already been made the statements in the document are definitely not borne out. For example—

(*a*) I agree with the Bank's criticism on 16 (iv). The reference to hoarding of currency overstates the real situation. At one time we thought this might be the explanation of the increase of currency. Subsequent enquiry shows that there is little or no reason for supposing that the wage-earning classes are carrying about a holding of currency increased appreciably more than the increase in their incomes.

(*b*) The statement that a large and sudden increase in the cost

274

of living is to be expected after the war unless we continue with large subsidies is quite contrary to the last statistical indications. It is certainly the case that the agricultural subsidies will have to be borne by the general taxpayer. But practically the whole of the rest of the subsidies is required to off-set war risks on sea and on land, which will come to an end immediately the war is over. I should say there is no reason to expect a rise in the cost of living unless prices rise overseas (which, of course, they may do) or domestic wages increase for reasons not justified by the cost of living or by increased efficiency.

(c) Surely, in the light of the last Budget figures, it is overstating it to talk of the difficulty of restoring the Budget to a balanced condition at an early date. It may well be the case that we shall have to go slow in abating war taxation. But to suppose that the regular Budget after the war will for a long time to come exceed £m2,400 is scarcely reasonable. No account is taken of the separation between the normal Budget for expenditure out of income and the so-to-speak capital budget, which surely we shall have to set up after the war.

(3) I still feel that it is much better to put the matter positively, namely, that the difficulties envisaged will surely come to pass unless we take constructive steps to solve two or three outstanding problems. In my judgement, far and away the most important and most difficult of these is the sufficient expansion of exports. But here also I do not like the way this is put in paragraph 6. This suggests that the supply of goods for the home market will be rendered insufficient by the requirements of the export trade. I agree that this will assuredly be the case in the short period. But I do not think that we lack the physical capacity to produce adequate exports. We can take this in our stride without interfering with the home supply. So far as exports are concerned, the essential difficulty will not be in producing them but in finding a satisfactory market for them. The second outstanding condition is that we should have a planned capital programme so that the capital demands are

released at the right pace. The third overriding condition is that we control consumption expenditure for what I should hope would be a very limited period.

This is my impression of the results which the attempt at quantification will lead to. But it is very possible that I may have to change my mind when I see them. My warning remains that it is unwise to be so dogmatic when we have it in view to produce a second document about the contents of which we are still very much in the dark.

[copy initialled] J.M.K.

P.S. Since writing the above I have had a word with Stone, who has already given a day or two's thought to analysing the relevant statistics. I find he is prepared to go further than I in doubting whether the statistics, when fully analysed, will justify the more pessimistic forecast. It is, of course, much too soon to prejudge the statistical outcome, when we have it, one way or the other. But it is easy to see how much room there is for optimism if one merely considers the proportion of current resources now being devoted to government purposes and the margin which will exist when these purposes are no longer required. This margin has to be divided between (*a*) doing less work (*b*) consuming more and (*c*) increasing gross investment. At first sight, on any reasonable hypothesis, it looks as if each of the three would get a good share.

[copy initialled] J.M.K.

The Treasury memorandum on purchasing power and consumer goods went to the inter-departmental Committee on 26 May. Before it was complete, however, Treasury discussion turned to other issues. On 14 May 1942 Sir Richard Hopkins circulated a memorandum to Keynes, Sir Hubert Henderson, Lord Catto and others suggesting that the remaining business of the inter-departmental Committee might involve a consideration of budgetary policy and national debt questions. At this stage, he suggested that there was wisdom in saying little more than previously on the transitional period,

beyond raising the question of the budgetary accounting treatment of war remanets. On the longer-term issues, he believed that the Treasury would have to take decisions on the meaning of a balanced budget, the role of sinking funds, public works expenditure and budgetary accounting. On this last matter, he argued that, in normal circumstances, so much occurred on the accounts of local authorities and government-guaranteed bodies that the need for a special capital budget in the central government's accounts was minimal. Hopkins saw the role of the central budget as consisting of variations, about a norm of £100 million, in the size of the sinking fund for the retirement of the national debt, these variations being reflected in changes in taxation (primarily death duties). He saw counter-cyclical public works as hindered by administrative and other practical problems, while changes in most direct and indirect taxes would prove slow in operation and politically difficult and might not help the situation when they did occur. Hopkins concluded his memorandum with rejection of equalisation funds operated over the trade cycle in which the surpluses of booms covered the deficits of slumps.

Hopkins' memorandum drew written replies from S. D. Waley, Sir Hubert Henderson and Keynes. Waley's reply emphasised the absence of any sense in balancing budgets as such, given that their role in economic stabilisation was more important. He also raised such matters as semi-annual budgets for improved economic management and the integration of budgetary and monetary policy. Sir Hubert Henderson, for his part, raised the question of post-war interest rates in relation to sinking fund policy, supported a capital budget to aid the process of inter-departmental co-ordination, and agreed with Hopkins' line on equalisation funds within the budget proper, but not with respect to extra-budgetary funds.

Keynes's reply, which was rather brief, ran as follows:

To SIR RICHARD HOPKINS *and others, 15 May 1942*

BUDGETARY POLICY

I. *A sinking fund*

It depends on what you mean by it. I should aim at having a surplus on the ordinary Budget, which would be transferred to the capital Budget, thus gradually replacing dead-weight debt by productive or semi-productive debt on the lines which the Government of India have successfully pursued for many years.

But this would not involve repayment of debt, since I should expect for a long time to come that the government debt or government-guaranteed debt would be continually increasing in grand total.

It is probable that the amount of such surplus would fluctuate from year to year for the usual causes. But I should not aim at attempting to compensate cyclical fluctuations by means of the ordinary Budget. I should leave this duty to the capital budget.

In this connection Mr Meade will be putting forward a proposal, which I think deserves consideration, namely, that the amount of the contribution from employers and employed to the Social Security Fund should vary according to the state of employment, rising when unemployment falls below a critical figure and falling when it rises above it. He points out that the advantage of this is that it is not subject to the time-lag which applies to direct taxation, but can be brougbht into operation at the shortest possible notice and should have a very rapid effect. If, under a Beveridge consolidated scheme, the income of the Social Security Fund is of the order of £200 million a year, which could vary according to circumstances from zero to £400 million a year, there is a fairly large sum to play with, quite free from the objections to interfering with the normal tax system for such a purpose.

I do not agree that death duties are a special argument for sinking funds. Death duties are in effect a tax on savings, and therefore indirectly on income, though in individual cases they may be paid, just as income tax may be paid, out of capital. This is brought out rather clearly by the way in which we have handled it in the White Paper; the net savings in any year available for new investments are gross savings in the sense in which the ordinary man would understand it *minus* death duties.

II. *The capital budget and war remanets*

No special objection to keeping war remanets in a separate account. But I should prefer to merge them in the capital Budget.

The following are characteristic examples of what might properly be regarded as war remanets:

On the credit side—(*a*) proceeds of war disposals; (*b*) war damage contributions. On the debit side—(*c*) post-war credits; (*d*) post-war E.P.T. repayments; (*e*) war damage payments; (*f*) war risk payments. There is also something to be said for regarding post-war E.P.T. as a war remanet, taking it out of the ordinary Budget, crediting the net proceeds, so long as there are any, to the capital Budget and, when these are succeeded by net repayments, debiting such repayments.

If this were merged with the capital Budget, then as additional credit items I should show—(*g*) the surplus on the Social Security Fund in the surplus years; (*h*) the surplus on other extra-budgetary funds; (*i*) the surplus on the ordinary Budget in surplus years; (*k*) net new borrowings from the public; and on the debit side—(*l*) net redemption of debt (should there ever be such); (*m*) the deficit on the Social Security Fund in deficit years; (*n*) expenditure or advances on capital account.

The last item, namely, expenditure or advances on capital account, raises the question whether public boards and local authorities should borrow after the war either on their own credit, for what it is worth, or with a government guarantee; or whether we should substitute something more on the lines of the Local Loans Fund, by which all borrowings would be by the Treasury, direct advances then being made out of the pool for various capital purposes. I much prefer the latter alternative. (i) It will allow cheaper borrowing; (ii) it will avoid the present undefined and anomalous position, by which there is a sort of implied government guarantee, e.g. to municipal loans or to the Central Electricity Board, without the full advantage of this

implied guarantee being realised in the price of the loans; and (iii) it will facilitate the management of conversions and the management of the market generally, if all borrowings are under the same title. We have seen during the war what great advantages there are in having a single borrowing programme.

III. *Interest rates in the early post-war period*

Sir H. Henderson has raised this very important question. But it is rather a different issue from the above on which, at greater leisure, I should like to write separately.

[copy initialled] J.M.K.

During the discussion of budgetary policy, in collaboration with Dick Stone, Keynes was attempting to estimate the post-war national income to provide guidance for post-war planning. On 28 May, when Stone's detailed estimates were ready, Keynes circulated them with a covering note.

NATIONAL INCOME AND EXPENDITURE AFTER THE WAR

1. This paper is an attempt to project the figures of the Budget White Paper into the post-war period, with the object of ascertaining in round figures the resources likely to be available for various alternative and competitive purposes. The figures given are based on what seem *prima facie* to be plausible assumptions, but they should be regarded as illustrative rather than prophetic. They have been set forth in an Appendix somewhat elaborately and in such a form that different assumptions can be easily substituted and the result calculated.

2. The upshot is that 'standard' post-war national income at factor cost with White Paper definitions can be taken (see Appendix §12) at £m6,500 (±200), increasing thereafter by £m100 annually, on the assumptions stated, of which the most important are the following:

(1) One million men in H.M. Forces. Each 250,000 above or below this figure would make a difference of about £20 million, this figure being the result of the conventional method adopted to measure the contribution to the national income of men in the Forces.

(2) 800,000 men unemployed (or a somewhat larger aggregate of men and woman together, 10 women reckoning as the equivalent of 7 men for the purpose of this calculation). Each 250,000 above or below this figure would make a difference of about £100 million.

(3) Wage cost at a level 30 per cent above 1938 in round figures. (Current wage cost is 28·4 per cent above 1938.) Each 2·5 per cent movement in wage-cost above or below this figure would make a difference of about £145 million.

(4) The margin of ±£m200 around £m6,500 is provided to allow for different assumptions as to the loss of skill of labour on account of the war and the gain in technical efficiency, compared with 1938, when the war is over. No separate allowance has been made to cover the loss of ultimate product resulting from a deterioration in the terms of foreign trade, this being regarded as one element in the factors on which depends the technical efficiency of the national productive resources.

3. The method adopted for the computation of the national income assumes that all factor costs, other than house rents, have increased to the same extent as the assumed increase in wage cost (i.e. 30 per cent). Gains in productive efficiency are assumed for the purpose of statistical comparison, to show themselves in an increased return to the factors of production, over and above the increase of 30 per cent in their cost, though, if they occur, they may in fact show themselves partly in lower prices and only partly in higher returns.

If market prices in fact exceed this index because they also reflect an excess profit due to scarcity, the national income measured in terms of money is increased by the amount of such excess profit. There is, however, a further reason of quite a

different kind why the index number of market prices, including foreign as well as domestic produce, may differ from the index of wage cost. For if the price of imports has risen relatively to the price of exports, this is reflected in market prices, but obviously not in calculations relating to the amount of domestic output.

4. Does our figure of £m6,500 (±200) look reasonable on general grounds?

At a level of factor costs 30 per cent higher than in 1938, the national income of 1938 would have been about £m6,000; and the national income of 1941 about £m6,700. But the latter figure was somewhat reduced by the method adopted for computing the output of men in the Forces, namely as being measured by their pay and allowances in cash and kind, which works out at less than the net output per wage earner in industry. If they had been employed in industry, in addition to those already so employed, the value of the national income in 1941 would have been nearly £m7,000. Thus our post-war estimate assumes a substantial falling off from war-time productivity.

5. The most difficult and problematic of our assumptions relates to the measure of industrial efficiency after the war compared with 1938. As pointed out in the Appendix, a fairly large proportion of the labour force is employed during the war on the same or similar work to that on which they will be employed after the war. The progress of electrification, the improvements in the internal combustion engine, the greater familiarity with mass-production methods acquired by many manufacturers, the introduction of a wider range of American-designed machine tools, the standardisation of product and the cutting out of redundant and unnecessary variations of type, the concentration of industry, the elimination of middlemen and many unnecessary costs of distribution, the pruning of 'extras' which do not add to the value of product proportionately to their expense, the dilution of fully skilled men, the acceleration of training, the revolution in agriculture,—surely much or most of

all this will remain as a permanent gain. Moreover the loss of skill on the part of men absent in the Forces must have been partly offset by the great numbers trained in industry for the first time and the benefit to individuals by 'up-grading' and the advantage of experience on high-grade jobs which they might have waited for years to get or might never have had in peace-time conditions.

It can, therefore, be argued that, so far from industrial efficiency having stood still during the war years, we shall find ourselves with at least the usual secular improvement in hand as soon as the special war-time difficulties of black-out and of transport and of the shortage of certain materials and of excessive strain and overtime are removed. If so, the calculation in § 12 of the Appendix would justify the higher limit of £m6,700 for £m6,500 as our standard estimate of post-war national income; and we might adhere to this figure even after allowing for deterioration in the terms of foreign trade. The lower limit of £m6,300 assumes a very modest gain from the above war-time changes after allowing for a possible deterioration of labour skill.

We shall find in the sequel that if, after a short interval of transition, the state of industrial efficiency allows us to take £m6,700 in place of £m6,500 as our standard estimate (reckoned at a price level 30 per cent above 1938), this will make all the difference between comfort and discomfort in the early post-war years.

6. In the first two years after the war it would be prudent to assume a larger army, heavier interim unemployment, and temporarily reduced efficiency as compared with our 'standard' estimate of £m6,500. On the other hand, it is inevitable— —particularly if the above factors are operating—that we should have a heavy adverse balance of trade during these two years, i.e. a continuance for the time being of overseas disinvestment.

It seems not unlikely that these two factors may be of the same order of magnitude, thus roughly offsetting one another and leaving disposable resources at a fairly constant figure around

£m6,500. For example, in the first year national income might be as low as £m6,150 and the adverse balance £m350; in the second year national income £m6,300 and the adverse balance £m200; in the third year national income £m6,450 and the adverse balance £m50; in the fourth year national income £m6,550 and the favourable balance £m50,—thus leaving the domestically disposable resources at around £m6,500 throughout this period; i.e. about 8 per cent in volume above the domestically disposable resources in 1938, although we should not be earning this increment from our own resources until the fourth year after the war.

7. It is to be doubted if we can get much closer to the prospects than this. As we have seen in §5 above more optimistic, but far from extravagant, assumptions as to efficiency, would allow us another 3 per cent improvement. It would need very pessimistic—and, surely, highly unplausible—assumptions to bring us out significantly worse off in disposable resources than in 1938. Such a result could only come about in practice through an absolute inability to import either in exchange for exports or on credit and its equivalent. An absolute inability to import necessary food and raw material would constitute a breakdown in our national economy of which this survey does not attempt to take account.

8. Can we forecast how this aggregate might be divided between (*a*) personal consumption, (*b*) government expenditure on goods and services and (*c*) domestic investment?

Let us begin with government expenditure (central and local) on goods and services. Pre-war expenditure corrected for higher costs and a larger army (we need not assume that additional munitions will be required—at least for a time!) might be put at £m1,300. Let us raise this to £m1,400 to allow a margin for unavoidable new services (other than new transfer payment services). After deducting expenditure by local authorities and adding (say) £m650 for transfer payments, this would correspond to an ordinary budget of about £m1,750. But, obviously,

government expenditure would not fall to this figure until demobilisation had proceeded far enough to reduce the size of the Forces to our 'standard' assumption. The discharge by the Government of all arrears of payments in respect of war contracts, which do not involve any current expenditure on goods and services, are, on the other hand, in the nature of transfer payments. Altogether, perhaps we might take ordinary government expenditure on goods and services (including local authorities) at £m1,800 in the first complete post-war year, £m1,600 in the second and £m1,400 thereafter. (These figures are exclusive of the budgetary cost of transfer payments.)

9. For what level of personal consumption must we provide as indispensable?

In 1941 consumption, adjusted for indirect taxes on consumption, was £m3,863 at the prices then ruling; which for reasons explained above, were somewhat above the level of wage costs in this year. Adjusting to a uniform price level 30 per cent above 1938, consumption may have been about £m3,900 in 1941, and about £m4,650 in 1938.

Let us begin by assuming a consumption of £m4,000 in the first post-war year (which would probably mean a significant improvement on 1942 consumption which is likely to be appreciably below 1941). How much is left over for net investment?

To begin with, a small adjustment has to be made. National income as calculated excludes *all* indirect taxes. Expenditure, whether personal, government or investment, is not easily adjusted for indirect taxes on *production*, as distinct from consumption, amounting to about £m200. The above estimates of expenditure include indirect taxes on production. Thus in order to reckon how much is left for investment, the cost of which will also be inclusive of indirect taxes on production, we have to start by adding on £m200 to our estimated £m6,500 of disposable resources, in order to reach a total which includes indirect taxes on production.

Thus, on the basis of £m4,000 personal consumption and a government expenditure of £m1,800 on goods and services, we are left with £m900 for investment. If in the second and third years we allow the reduction of government expenditure first of all to £m1,600 and then to £m1,400 to be balanced by an increase of personal consumption first of all to £m4,200 and then to £m4,400, we have a steady figure of £m900 available for investment in each of the first three post-war years.

10. This represents a high, but not impossible, standard of austerity; for even in the third year after the war period consumption would be 5 per cent below 1938. How high a level of saving does it imply? To ascertain *total* saving, we have to deduct from £m900 the amount of overseas disinvestment, leaving £m550 in the first year, £m700 in the second year and £m850 in the third year. To ascertain personal gross saving we have to deduct government and business saving and add on death duties.

In view of the pressure of deferred personal expenditure and the natural reaction from war-time restrictions, it seems unlikely that total saving would reach these figures in the early post-war period except with the assistance of a level of taxation sufficiently high to allow substantial government saving and a somewhat strict direct control of consumption through rationing, etc.

If, however, we were content with a balance of £m600, instead of £m900, available for net investment in each year, thus reducing the demand on total saving by £m300, this result might be attainable with less strain; for we should have reached the pre-war level of consumption by the third year, and have got nearly half-way back to pre-war consumption in the first year.

Also if post-war industrial efficiency proves high enough to allow the substitution of £m6,700 for £m6,500 as our standard, that would permit £m800 as the rate of annual investment and also a satisfactory relaxation of restrictions on personal consumption. There might also be a further economy in the amount expended by government on goods and services below

the assumed estimate. And unemployment might turn out to be less than 800,000, which is a pessimistic assumption.

11. The chief demands on the pool of resources available for net investment are, in the early period, the following: (a) re-stocking; (b) working capital; (c) costs of change-over to peace-time production including the liquidation of war contracts; (d) deferred repairs and maintenance; (e) war damage to buildings; (f) rebuilding the mercantile marine; (g) strictly new investment. Towards (a) and (b) we have the liquidation of government-owned stocks and other proceeds of the War Disposals Board. The other items can be met either at a slower or a faster pace. At a first glance it would appear that £m600 a year (equivalent to £m460 at pre-war prices) available for net investment would do no more than provide at a minimum pace for the items other than strictly new investment. But £m800 to 900 should be a fairly comfortable allowance. It should be remembered that these figures are calculated on the basis of a price increase of 30 per cent over 1938, and would be correspondingly higher if a higher level of prices in fact prevails. (It is apparent what an important difference £m200–300 of national output, more or less, will make in mitigating or aggravating the difficulties of the post-war situation, when we come to the final analysis.)

It would be useful if the appropriate Departments would make estimates of their capital requirements under each of the above headings in each of the first three post-war years.

12. It would seem likely that, in the first two or three post-war years, demand for goods and services on the part of the government, private consumers and investment, might be sufficient to absorb disposable resources of as much as £m7,250 if they were available and in the absence of any controls. This compares with £m6,500, increased by £m200 if we take the more optimistic assumptions, as the measure of the disposable resources likely to be available.

If this is correct, the necessity of controls both on consumption

and on investment is evident. On the other hand, the restricted standards of consumption and investment which should be physically possible are not intolerable; and the higher limit of £m6,700, if attainable as the national output, should prove very tolerable indeed.

13. If it is permitted to draw morals from the above, the two following emerge clearly—

(a) The continuance of controls is indispensable since the existence of potential excess demand is indisputable and outside the limits of possible error.

(b) But the curtailment (or slackened pace) of investment should be left to be decided by actual physical impediments and not by an attempt to lay down beforehand a programme reduced to the procrustean bed of a predetermined figure such as £m600 or any other amount; for the range of uncertainty is too great to allow prior determination. No harm in having ready a programme considerably larger than we can carry out.

The amount available for investment is, within wide limits, necessarily and properly a *residue* and is subject to the wide range of error inevitable in estimating residues. The above suggests a range of £m600 to £m900 as reasonably probable; this is very wide, yet it would not be safe to assume that the true figure will certainly lie within it. Since inflation and not deflation is clearly the danger in the early post-war years, there is perhaps, some risk of our becoming too precautious about it. There should be only those limitations on *production* (as distinct from consumption) which are made physically inevitable by the shortage of materials or suitable labour.

The continuance of controls should clearly include the raw material controls in particular. These are the lynch-pin of the whole system, since rationing and price stabilisation and priority allocation all depend on them. But raw material control must not become a means, or a pretext, for hoarding raw materials. Consumers of raw materials must be prevented from hoarding them. But available raw materials should not be withheld from

actual use unless for exceptional reasons. The maintenance of security stocks must not become a habit or stand in the way of *use*, particularly in the early years. When we again reach the era of surpluses, the time for re-building them will return.

J.M.K.

28 May 1942

Statistical appendix

1. The method adopted is to express the income from current production as a function of employment, labour productivity, factor prices etc., and then to make certain additions to this amount for items, such as the net income of dwelling houses, which do not depend on these variables. To avoid confusion in the main analysis it will be convenient to dispose of these special items first.

2. There are three items which it is convenient to exclude in this way and they will be denoted as follows—A = net income from dwelling houses etc., B = net income from foreign investments, C = income in cash and kind of H.M. Forces and Auxiliary Services.

It is evident that none of these items form part of the current net output of labour. C, which might at first sight seem an exception, cannot conveniently be so treated since the net output of the forces is treated as being equal to their income. They are therefore in a very different position from workers in industry for whom income represents about one-half of net output.

These three items have been estimated as follows—

	1938	1940	1941	1944
		(£ million)		
A	265	265	265	265
B	200	175	150	100
C	85	450	710	210
Total	550	890	1,125	575

The value of A is the same as the figure implicit in the White Paper. B for 1938 has been taken from the Board of Trade's estimate and for later years has been roughly estimated. C is the cash pay, allowances and income in kind of H.M. Forces and Auxiliary Services. The average income in this sense of all officers and other ranks of H.M. Forces in 1941 was £208. The

estimate of C for 1944 assumes therefore that H.M. Forces are approximately one million in number.

We shall now estimate the remaining and more important part of the national income. The first factor to be considered is employment.

3. An estimate of employment involves the following steps

(*a*) An estimate of the number of gainfully occupied male and female wage earners. It will be convenient here to treat shop assistants as wage earners although in the White Paper they were treated as salary earners. From this figure an allowance must be made for unemployment.

(*b*) An allowance for the difference in the average productivity of men and women.

(*c*) An allowance for changes in hours of work.

(*d*) An allowance for the fall in the average productivity of wage earners due to bringing into industry of progressively less efficient workers.

In short, writing

N_m = number of male wage earners (including shop assistants) in work,

N_w = number of female wage earners (including shop assistants) in work,

s = the ratio of the productivity of the average female wage earner to the average male wage earner,

h = the proportionate addition to the labour force over 1938 resulting from the increase in hours worked,

z = the proportionate reduction in the labour force due to the fall in average productivity resulting from bringing less efficient labour into industry,

then employment is equal to

$$(N_m + sN_w)(1+h)(1-z).$$

Each of these variables must now be considered separately.

4. A rough estimate of the order of magnitude of the ratio of men's to women's productivity (s) may be made as follows. It may first be assumed that the ratio is not greater than unity nor less than 0·5 which is the ratio of earnings. Indeed, it is likely that the ratio is greater than 0·5 which is the ratio of earnings. Indeed, it is likely that the ratio is greater than 0·5 owing to the preference of employers for the employment of men and to the monopoly position of men's trade unions. On the other hand, in the case of similar work the average ratio is likely to be less than unity on account of the greater sickness rate among women; let us put it at 0·9. But again, over the whole of industry the average woman has a less skilled job than the average man, so that the ratio must be further reduced. In the absence of a lengthy investigation into the occupational grouping of the two sexes, we

shall assume that the true ratio is approximately the mean of 0·9 and 0·5, i.e. that $s = 0·7$.

5. The information in paragraph 4 together with data on unemployment, an assumption about the post-war level of unemployment, and an assumed rate of growth of the wage earning population, may be used to make an estimate of wage earners in employment in 1944. Writing j for the annual proportionate growth of the wage earning population and k for the post-war unemployment proportion, it will be assumed that

$j = 0·002$

$k = 0·05$,   i.e. the equivalent of 800,000 male wage earners unemployed (see below).

The position in 1944 can be worked out either from 1938 or from 1941. Provided we adopt the same assumptions in both cases and provided that any constants used are accurate, we should reach the same conclusion from each starting point. The two calculations for 1944 are as follows:

(1) Beginning with 1938		millions
Male wage earners		
in work	10·53	
unemployed	1·41	
	11·94	11·94
Female wage earners		
in work	4·39	
unemployed	0·46	
	4·85	
$4·85 \times s$		3·40
		15·34
$15·34(1+jt)j = 0·002, t = 6$		15·52
Assumed permanent increase in female labour force resulting from the war	0·25	
$0·25 \times s$		0·18

Less

Wage earners retained in H.M. Forces on the assumption that these consist of 1·00 million men	0·40

Occupied wage earners in 1944	15·30
15·30(1 − k): k = 0·05	14·53

On these assumptions the employed wage-earning labour force in 1944 will be equivalent to 14·53 million men.

(2) Beginning with 1941

Male wage earners

in work	9·69	
unemployed	0·21	
in H.M. Forces	2·11	
	12·01	12·01

Female wage earners

in work	5·31	
unemployed	0·21	
	5·52	
5·52 × s		3·86
		15·87
15·87(1 + jt): j = 0·002, t = 3		15·97

Increase in female wage earners in work between 1938 and 1941 *less* decrease in unemployment of female wage earners over the same period   0·67

Less

s(0·67 − 0·25)	0·29
Wage earners retained in H.M. Forces on the assumption that these consist of 1·00 million men	0·40

Occupied wage earners in 1944	15·28
15·28(1 − k): k = 0·05	14·52

On these assumptions the employed wage-earning labour force in 1944 will be equivalent to 14·52 million men.

6. It will be convenient at this point to set out the method for arriving at the number of wage earners in the Forces given the size of the Forces. This is important since in the light of plans for demobilisation it is probably possible to make an estimate of the size of the Forces at various intervals after the war in place of the round figure used above.

It appears from a comparison of unemployment books surrendered and entrants into H.M. Forces that about 75 per cent of all entrants since the beginning of the war have been wage earners. At the beginning of the war there were about 468,000 men in H.M. Forces. Hence writing

T = all members of H.M. Forces in millions

W = peace time wage earners in millions

we have
$$W = 0.75(T - 0.468).$$

It is of course possible that the figure 0.468 is unduly swollen by abnormal additions to the forces in the period just before the war. If this be so, a figure smaller than 0.468 should be taken, in which case W would, of course, be larger for any given value of T.

7. It is possible to construct an index of hours worked in the following manner:

Let E_0 = average actual hourly earnings in year o, i.e. 1938

W_0 = average hourly wage rates in year o

H_0 = average normal hours in year o

g = average ratio of overtime to normal rates of pay, and e_0, w_0, h_0 and n_0 be the values of E, W, H and N in a single industry in year o. Then

$$E_0 = \frac{S(e_0 n_0)}{S(n_0)}$$

$$W_0 = \frac{S(w_0 n_0)}{S(n_0)}$$

$$H_0 = \frac{S(h_0 n_0)}{S(b_0)}$$

where S is a summation sign.

The proportionate change in hours between year o and year 1 is equal to

$$\frac{1}{g}\left(\frac{E_1}{W_1} - \frac{E_0}{W_0}\right) + \left(\frac{H_1}{H_0} - 1\right)(g - 1).$$

In order to evaluate this expression we shall assume that average normal hours have remained unchanged, i.e. that $H_1 = H_0$; that $g = 1.5$; that, in view of the first assumption above, an index of weekly wage rates can be taken to represent the series W; and, finally, that on the average hours were normal

in 1938. This being so, current hours as a proportion of the hours worked in 1938 are given by

$$0\cdot3 + \frac{0\cdot505 \, E_c}{W_c},$$

where

E_c = average current earnings

W_c = average current wage rates as measured by Bowley's wage index on the base August 1939 = 100.

We thus obtain as an index of hours of work on the base of 1938 = 1·000 the figure of 1·059 for 1940 and 1·089 for 1941.

It appears from studies on hours of work and fatigue that the weighted average of production in an hour of overtime is approximately 88 per cent of production in a normal hour. Accordingly, it would appear that additional working hours added some 5·2 per cent to the labour force in 1940 and about 7·8 per cent in 1941. The assumption that in the post-war period there is a return to the average hours worked in 1938, that is that $h = 0$, can therefore be seen to imply a considerable reduction in effective employment.

8. No data are available on z, the fall in the average productivity of wage earners due to bringing into industry progressively less efficient workers, but it does not seem likely that a reduction of more than 5 per cent of the labour force should be made to take account of the fact that new recruits to industry are less efficient than the average peace time worker. This is very roughly equivalent to assuming that the productivity of the average recruit is about 75 per cent of that of the normal peace time worker. Any fall in efficiency through time due to the necessity of tapping sources of labour with lower and lower productivity is assumed to be offset by the increasing efficiency of past recruits resulting from greater experience at their work.

We need to consider the probable level of z after the war. No doubt z will tend to return to zero, but against this must be set the loss of skill of many of those who have served in H.M. Forces, which will be felt at any rate in the short run, and also the fall in productivity due to a partial return in the short run, at any rate, to the restrictive Trade Union practices which have been abandoned during the war. Two calculations will therefore be made; one on the assumption that $z = 0$ and the other on the assumption that $z = 0\cdot025$, which should make adequate allowance for loss of skill during the war.

9. The second factor is productivity. In 1938 this may be estimated as follows:

$$p_m = \frac{Y - (A + B + C)}{(N_m + sN_w)},$$

where p_m is the net output per head of male wage earners. The value of this

constant is £298. This productivity may be assumed to increase at a rate r per annum, so that at the end of t years productivity will be—

$$p_m(1+r)^t$$

Under peacetime conditions it is usual to assume that productivity increases at the rate of about 1·5 per cent per annum so that r would normally be 0·015. On the other hand it is argued that wartime gains in efficiency will not be fully retained in the change from wartime to peacetime output. It is not altogether easy to see why this should be so to any great extent since throughout the war, production of consumption goods still remains a fairly large part of total production and it is not unreasonable to suppose that it will be possible to apply most of the wartime technical advances to peacetime production. This process of re-organisation may however take time, so two calculations will be made with $r = 0·010$ and $0·015$ respectively. For the sake of interest a third calculation will be made on the assumption that $r = 0$.

10. Finally allowance must be made for changes in factor costs. To measure this an index of wage rates has been used. Although this is clearly inadequate in theory its use may perhaps be justified by the fact that while the earnings of the various factors of production have moved differently, the general movement may not have been very different from that of wages.

Bowley's wage rate index, denoted by c, has been used to measure changes in wage rates. The proportionate increase in 1941 over 1938 was 0·224. It is now nearly 0·3 and it will be assumed that $c = 0·3$ in what follows.

11. The estimate of the net national income at factor cost may now be summarised thus—

$$Y = A + B + C + (1+c)(1+h)(1-z)(N_m + sN_w)p_m(1+r)^t$$

12. The foregoing data and assumptions lead to the following results:

Estimated net national income in 1944 at present factor cost

	$r = 0$	$r = 0·010$	$r = 0·015$
$z = 0·025$	6,051	6,388	6,563
$z = 0$	6,192	6,537	6,717

13. The chief assumptions on which these estimates are based may be summarised as follows:

(1) The estimate that the employed wage-earning labour force will be equivalent to 14·5 million men requires the following main assumptions:

(a) that there will be 1·00 million men of all ranks in H.M.Forces in 1944 and that 400,000 of these will be wage earners (see paragraph 5). It may well be that this is too low a figure for the first full post-war year but, if this is so, other factors (particularly (1)(b) and (2) below) are likely to diverge from

295

what is here assumed in a way which will produce a contrary effect on the estimate of the national income.

(*b*) that unemployment among wage earners will be equivalent to 800,000 men (see paragraph 5). This is very considerably higher than the level of 1941 and as much as half a million higher than the present level.

(*c*) that of all the women who have entered industry or the Auxiliary Services from wartime motives or direction, 250,000 will represent a permanent addition to the wage-earning labour force (see paragraph 5). This does not seem extravagant and in any case is of minor importance.

(*d*) that the ratio of the productivity of the average female wage earner to the average male wage earner (*s*) is 0·7 (see paragraph 4). This is not of great importance, particularly in conditions where the sex composition of industry is not greatly changed, since an alteration in *s* would to some extent be offset by the value obtained for p_m.

(2) The average hours worked by wage earners are assumed to fall back to the level of 1938, that is, it is assumed that $h = 0$ (see paragraph 7). It is easily possible that this may not come about at once.

(3) The two assumptions about z (see paragraph 8) are set out in the main table (see paragraph 12).

(4) The three assumptions about r (see paragraph 9) are set out in the main table (see paragraph 12).

(5) The net income from foreign investments is assumed to be £100 million in 1944 (see paragraph 2).

(6) The calculations are based on a level of factor costs 30 per cent higher than those ruling in 1938 (see paragraph 10). At this higher level, the national income of 1938 would have been some £5,980 million and that of 1941 some £6,734 million.

14. The estimates in section 2 of the foregoing paper require a knowledge of the effect on the net national income of variations in (i) the number of men in H.M. Forces, (ii) the number of wage earners in work reduced to an equivalent number of men, and (iii) the level of factor costs. The calculations made in section 2 were derived from the following equations from which the effect of assumptions other than those adopted can easily be seen.

(i) Write Y' for the change in the net national income due to the transference of one man from civil life to H.M. Forces. Then

$$Y' = 210 - 0.75(1+c)(1+h)(1-z)(1-k)\,298(1+r)^t$$

Assuming that $c = 0.3$, $h = 0$, $z = 0.025$, $k = 0.05$, $r = 0$, $t = 6$, we have

$$Y' = 210 - 0.75 \times 1.3 \times 1.0 \times 0.975 \times 0.95 \times 298 \times 1.0$$
$$= -59,$$

whence each 250,000 men transferred to H.M. Forces would reduce the net national income by

$$\pounds 59 \times 250,000 = \pounds 15 \text{ million approximately.}$$

If these assumptions regarding z and r are replaced by the other extreme, namely that $z = 0$ and $r = 0.015$, then

$$Y' = 210 - 0.75 \times 1.3 \times 1.0 \times 1.0 \times 0.95 \times 298 \times 1.03$$
$$= -92,$$

whence each 250,000 men added to H.M. Forces would reduce the net national income by $\pounds 23$ million.

It may therefore be said that according to the assumptions made each 250,000 men transferred from H.M. Forces will increase and each 250,000 men allowed to remain in H.M. Forces will decrease the net national income by some $\pounds 15$ million to $\pounds 23$ million.

(ii) Write Y'' for the change in the net national income due to the re-employment of one unemployed male wage earner. Then

$$Y'' = (1 + c)(1 + h)(1 - z)\,298\,(1 + r)^t.$$

On the same assumption as before we find that this expression lies between 378 and 423, whence the reduction of unemployment by the equivalent of 250,000 male wage earners would increase the net national income by some $\pounds 95$ million to $\pounds 106$ million.

(iii) Write Y''' for the change in the net national income due to a 1 per cent increase in factor costs. Then

$$Y''' = \frac{Y - (A + B + C)}{100},$$

from which it can be seen that, according to the assumptions made, a 2·5 per cent increase in factor cost would increase and a 2·5 per cent reduction would decrease the net national income by between

$$\pounds 5,476 \text{ million} \times 0.025 = \pounds 137 \text{ million approximately}$$
and $\qquad \pounds 6,142$ million $\times 0.025 = \pounds 154$ million approximately.

15. The problem in the last paragraph of section 4 in the foregoing paper can be treated by the same method as was used in 14(*a*) above. For, in the conditions assumed

$$Y' = 203 - 0.75 \times 1.3 \times 1.078 \times 0.95 \times 298 \times 1.044$$
$$= -83$$
$$W = 2.11,$$

so that if all the men who had joined H.M. Forces since the war began were to have returned to their civil occupations, the net national income would have been increased by

$$£103 \times 2,110,000 = £217 \text{ million approximately,}$$

that is, the 1941 net national income at factor costs 30 per cent above 1938 would have been £6,951 million.

16. The table in paragraph 12 suggests the following broad conclusions. It seems likely that immediately after the war the net national income may not be greatly in excess of the level in 1938. But in a short space of time, perhaps not more than a year or two, it should rise to as much as £6,500 million or more in terms of present factor costs and thereafter rise at a more moderate rate, perhaps about £100 million per annum, depending largely on improvements in industrial technique, organisation, etc. J.R.N.S.

The Keynes–Stone exercise drew comments from Dennis Robertson, Sir Hubert Henderson and Sir Richard Hopkins. Most of the comments dealt with the assumptions concerning unemployment, which most found very optimistic, efficiency or productivity, and post-war frictions. Keynes's replies to the comments set out more completely his view of the post-war world.

To SIR HUBERT HENDERSON, *3 June 1942*

NATIONAL INCOME AND EXPENDITURE AFTER THE WAR: SIR H. HENDERSON'S CRITICISMS

1. *Unemployment*

The calculations are in terms of equivalent men and probably represent about 900,000 men and women, if they are unemployed in the usual relative proportions. The main points here are, however, the following:

(i) It is assumed that, compared with 1938, 650,000 additional men are in the Forces. This can be regarded as a completely new demand for labour and might be, therefore, a partial answer to the question, what reason is there for expecting better employment than before the war. It is assumed that 1,800,000

equivalent men will be either in the army or unemployed. This is quite high, even on pre-war standards.

(ii) But it is a misunderstanding to suppose that the 5 per cent is a prophecy of what will happen if nothing is done and pre-war methods, generally speaking, are continued. Mr Stone and I chose as our basic assumption 800,000 equivalent men out of work, chiefly on the ground that it seemed to us that this was about the highest that the public would stand in post-war conditions without demanding something very drastic to be done about it, coupled with the fact that it did not seem to us impracticable to take drastic steps which would bring down the figure to this total. If one was to put in, as Sir H. Henderson suggests, a figure approaching 2 million men normally out of work after the war, I should have expected the rejoinder that we were wasting our time in assuming a situation which could not possibly be allowed to happen.

(iii) Sir H. Henderson has misunderstood the reference to the 'heavier interim unemployment in the first two post-war years'. This means heavier than the 800,000 men assumed in the basic year. In fact I took the income in the first year after the war at £m6,150, which allows for additional unemployment of 875,000 equivalent men, making 1,675,000 altogether.

(iv) Sir H. Henderson says that in this connection wartime experience is entirely irrelevant. But none of these figures is based on wartime experience.

2. Growth in working population

The casualties up to 1941 have been implicitly taken care of. If there are heavy casualties hereafter, a necessary adjustment to allow for this would have to be made. The assumed value of j, namely, the annual rate of growth of the wage-earning population, is exceedingly low, namely $\frac{1}{5}$ of 1 per cent. There is probably a margin here to offset, except in the very early years, some increase in casualties. j is so small as to make very little

difference one way or the other unless a big alteration is to be made in its evaluation.

3. *Efficiency*

Admittedly, two views can be taken about this. This was emphasised in the paper. I remain of the opinion, especially after reading what Sir H. Henderson has to say about economies in distribution, that the assumption is not too optimistic, especially if one regards it as relating to the third year after the war rather than earlier. Here again, however, one can certainly emphasise that the forecast is not meant to be a prophecy of what will happen if we do nothing about it or pursue a passive and reactionary policy. In this sense we are dealing in what Sir H. Henderson calls 'a potentiality of increased production'. The figure is meant to be an estimate of a potentiality, which there should be no particular difficulty in realising, if we bestir ourselves to make sure that we lose no valuable part of the wartime economies and take the best advantage of wartime innovations.

4. *Post-war friction*

We have assumed an effective 7 per cent reduction, not merely of industrial hours, but over the whole of activity, compared with 1941. It is true that no further reduction of hours of work as compared with 1938 is assumed. One might well expect a further reduction of hours in conditions of abounding prosperity. But is it not paradoxical to expect a reduction of hours in circumstances which, on Sir H. Henderson's assumptions, will be extremely severe in most respects?

5. *Expenditure on the Armed Forces*

Perhaps my wording here was misleading. I am not assuming no expenditure on the output of munitions, but have allowed for the continuance of the pre-war output of munitions,

aeroplanes and men-of-war at post-war prices, which would be, I think, of the order of £m150.

6. *Recalculation on Sir H. Henderson's assumptions*

The material for a recalculation on his less optimistic hypotheses is provided in the paper. The result is £m5,766 or £m5,636 according as $z = 0$ or 0.025. Let us take the mean figure of £m5,700.

7. The meaning of the question as to the 'extent of the increase in productivity per employed person required to put matters reasonably right' is not quite clear to us. A 16 per cent rise in productivity per employed person would be necessary to restore income to £m6,500, which is our basic figure.

Working on Sir H. Henderson's figure of £m5,700 plus £m200 for indirect taxes on production and taking off our standard assumption of £m1,300 for government expenditure on goods and services, which Sir H. Henderson has not questioned, we have £m4,600 left for consumption and investment. This is slightly below the consumption figure of £m4,650 of 1938. Thus a return to 1938 standards would mean that there could be no investment whatever, not even re-stocking, repair of houses, overtaking of arrears, etc. If we regard £m600 as the minimum figure for post-war investment at post war prices, we are left with £m4,000 for consumption in the standard year. This is very nearly equal to the actual consumption of 1941, which was £m3,900. In my paper I started off in the first year after the war with consumption at £m400 below the basic assumption, and in the second post-war year at £m200 below the basic assumption. With Sir H. Henderson's hypotheses, these figures become £m3,600 in the first year and £m3,600 in the second year, rising to £m4,000 in the basic year.

Thus he is supposing that we have a standard of consumption very greatly below anything we have suffered hitherto in the first two post-war years, returning in the third year to a little better

than 1941 standards. This is with a bare minimum of investment. I do not find it plausible to suppose that we shall put up with this in circumstances in which 2 million men are normally unemployed. It would cross someone's mind that it was not very sensible to suffer these severe privations with all that labour available to make something useful. [copy initialled] J.M.K.

From a minute to SIR ALAN BARLOW, *4 June 1942*

(2) *800,000 men unemployed.* I shall be dealing with this at greater length in answer to Sir H. Henderson's comments. The main point to bear in mind seems to me to be that we shall be operating in an atmosphere of potential boom, with overwhelming demands which we are not in a position to meet. Our only previous experience of such a situation has been during the war, when the number of unemployed males has been reduced to 79,000, and the number of equivalent males and females to about 120,000. I still think an estimate more than six times as large as this in circumstances of unsatisfied demand is not an optimistic assumption, but a very pessimistic one. Sir Alan Barlow's reference to labour-saving technological improvements would be all on the right side, since they would bring us a little nearer satisfying the demand for labour. They do not seem to me to be relevant to the numbers of the unemployed, if, in the special conditions of the post-war period, there are still unsatisfied demands for labour.

(3) The current wage cost includes, I think, all the wartime accretions to wage rates, as distinct from overtime. It does not, however, make much difference in this context whether we assume 30 per cent or some higher figure, such as 40 or 50 per cent. It means that all the measures of the national resources in terms of money are that much higher. The substantial consequences of a higher wage cost will be:

(*a*) a smaller effective burden of the national debt and of

certain other transfer payments, if they are not raised proportionately;

(*b*) greater difficulty in obtaining the necessary volume of exports, unless there is a similar further increase in other countries.

(4) This seems to me to be true, but it only serves to confirm the probability of unsatisfied demand for labour for some time to come, since the only thing which will hold back reconstruction will be shortage of labour (unless there is also a shortage of imports).

From a minute to SIR RICHARD HOPKINS, *4 June 1942*

NATIONAL INCOME AND EXPENDITURE AFTER THE WAR
(YOUR NOTES)

(1) Our unexpressed fundamental assumption does not go so far as to suppose that 'everything that could humanly be done has been done by the state'. That, I should say, would produce a reduction of the unemployed to the sort of level we are experiencing in wartime, when we are trying to do everything humanly possible, that is to say, an unemployed level of 120,000. As you will see in my comment on Sir Alan Barlow's note, I consider 800,000 rather on the pessimistic side. It certainly does not assume a continuance of the pre-war situation. But, since we shall be in an environment of potential boom with enormous unsatisfied demands, the main change will be forced on us by circumstances and will not require any surprising energy or intelligence on our part, except not to put unnecessary obstacles in the way of this potential demand being satisfied. That is to say, we are assuming a reasonable government policy in the face of the actual circumstances and the change which has taken place in public opinion in the light of war experience as to the practical possibilities of keeping unemployment at a reasonable figure.

I am afraid I am quite impenitent after having read the

comments up to date about our assumptions being too optimistic. Indeed, further reflection is leading me, if anything, rather in the other direction.

J.M.K.

P.S. I see that I have not dealt in the above with your query how 1 million in the army could be an offset to 1 million unemployed: 1 million in the army is in effect an additional demand for labour on that scale and, therefore, in so far as unemployment is due to an inadequate demand for labour, it ought to cure the problem nearly as well as any other additional form of activity.

In the light of criticisms, Keynes then circulated a list of corrections and amplifications.

NATIONAL INCOME AND EXPENDITURE AFTER THE WAR

I propose the following amendments to this paper in the light of the criticisms which have reached me:

I. For paragraph 2 (1) substitute the following:

(1) *One million men in H.M. Forces.* Each 250,000 above or below this figure would make a difference of about £m50, apart from munitions, to the expenditure by the Government on goods and services; but a difference of no more than £m20 to the national income calculated by the conventional method adopted to measure the contribution to the national income of men in the Forces. A margin has been provided below in the first two post-war years to allow for higher figures during this period. A higher figure than 1 million after the transitional period is perhaps best regarded as one of the competing demands on our resources of which we have to take account in estimating the 'standard' expenditure on goods and services by the Government.

II. For (2) substitute the following:

(2) Unemployment is due to—

(*a*) the hard core of the virtually unemployable (100,000);

(*b*) seasonal factors (200,000);

(*c*) men moving between jobs (300,000);

(*d*) misfits of trade or locality due to lack of mobility (200,000); and

(*e*) a deficiency in the aggregate effective demand for labour. Pre-war statistics are not a useful guide, because at all recent dates before the war (*e*) played a significant part, whereas the probable heavy demands for labour in excess of the supply indicated below suggest that the most convenient 'standard' assumption for the post-war period is the virtual absence of this factor. An attempt which was made by an official committee in 1935 to estimate the probable minimum level of unemployment, excluding factor (*e*), arrived at a figure of 760,000 or 6 per cent. Subsequent experience suggests that this survey may have overestimated the number of the virtual unemployables, an actual count of insured persons who have been classified as unsuitable for ordinary industrial employment made on 16 March 1942 having brought out a figure below 25,000 compared with 150,000 *plus* 50,000 casuals' unemployment assumed by the Committee. In view of this a 'standard' assumption of 800,000 men unemployed (or a somewhat larger aggregate of men and women together, 10 women reckoning as the equivalent of 7 men for the purpose of this calculation), which is about 5 per cent of the insured population, seems quite sufficient made up as indicated above between brackets. It compares with about 120,000 equivalent men, or less than 1 per cent, unemployed at the present time, when factors (*b*) and (*c*) above are virtually inoperative. Experience after the last war shows that, apart from a brief transitional period in the spring of 1919, the above estimate would have been more than enough to cover the facts up to the end of 1920, although Professor Pigou reckons that the slump must be regarded as having commenced in the summer of 1920. This should, however, be regarded as a

standard assumption rather than as a prophecy; and it can be adjusted to any other assumptions by reckoning that each 250,000 above or below would make a difference of about £m100.

III. Add at the end of paragraph 2 (3): a higher estimate of wage cost would make little substantial difference to the estimates below, since most of the figures given would go up proportionately, the most substantial consequences of such higher cost being—

(a) a smaller effective burden of the national debt and of certain other transfer payments, if they are not raised proportionately; and (b) greater difficulty in marketing the necessary volume of exports, unless there is a corresponding increase in cost in other countries.

IV. At the end of paragraph 2 add—

(5) In the first post-war year national income is taken at the reduced figure of £m6,150. It is also assumed that Government expenditure on goods and services exceeds the standard assumption by £m400. It is not easy to judge the adequacy of these allowances. But the reasonableness of their order of magnitude can be checked as follows:

In 1941 there were 3,500,000 men in H.M. Forces and auxiliary services and about 500,000 men in the munition industries proper in excess of June 1939. This leaves us with an aggregate of 4 million men to be dealt with, a figure which is not likely to be much greater at the end of the war, after allowing for wastage. In addition to these 4 million there will be a further number to be reckoned during the period of the transition of the works in which they will be employed to peacetime activities. As against this, there will be some demands for labour, now unsatisfied, which can become effective immediately at the termination of hostilities. The above assumptions would allow for about 2,500,000 men either remaining in the Forces or in unwanted munitions and 1,250,000 men out of work. This is on the average of the first year and is, therefore,

compatible with much worse conditions in the first half of it, and does not seem to involve too optimistic an assumption as to the rate of absorption.

(6) In the second post-war year income is taken at £m6,300 and government expenditure on goods and services in excess of the 'standard' at £m200. It will be seen that this still allows for a considerable delay in demobilisation and in the absorption of the unemployed.

V. Before the concluding sentence of paragraph 5 add:

It should be noticed that the 'standard' income of £m6,500 is not reached until the third year after the war, so that two years of peace is added to the period of war experience in which to acquire the assumed increase of efficiency, thus providing a further margin for pessimism.

VI. In paragraph 8, bottom of page, for '(we need not...)' substitute: '(we can assume that current output of additional munitions on the pre-war standard should suffice—at least for a time!)'.

VII. For 13 (*b*) substitute:

(*b*) But the curtailment (or slackened pace) of investment should be planned in the light of the actual availability of different kinds of resources when the time comes and not by an attempt...than we can carry out.

The above estimate of the amount available for investment on certain assumptions is arrived at as a statistical residue and is subject...

VIII. In the Appendix substitute 'standard year' for '1944' throughout.

IX. An attempt will be made to simplify the form and language of the draft before it receives more general circulation.

J.M.K.

9 June 1942

In the course of the summer of 1942, although on the Treasury's recommendation the Beveridge social insurance proposals had ceased to contain a detailed discussion of them, Keynes and James Meade continued to discuss the latter's idea for the counter-cyclical variation of national insurance contributions.[1]

To J. E. MEADE, *20 August 1942*

Dear James,

Thank you for sending me your paper no. 20 on the effect on employment of a change on the employers' social security contribution and Fleming's rejoinder in paper 21.

My feeling is that both of you, though in differing degrees, are too willing to assimilate the effects of a change in the employers' contribution to the effects of a change in the employees' contribution. For you are both of you, so it seems to me, allowing yourselves to use an essentially long-term argument for what is essentially and by hypothesis a short-term contingency.

If the effect of the reduction of the employers' contribution is to affect prices, then to the extent of this effect Fleming's original argument is correct. But I should have supposed that no effect, or a negligible effect, on prices is the correct assumption to make. The reduction comes about by hypothesis when output is well below capacity. The reasons why in such circumstances prices do not fall to prime costs are well known. The reduction of costs is by hypothesis a highly temporary one. I should have thought, therefore, that the reduction would operate almost entirely to the relief of the employer and would serve to bring his income that much nearer normal. No great harm in that, perhaps, and in some cases it might help to steer him clear of bankruptcy. But I should not expect that the immediate effects on employment would be noticeable.

I suggest, therefore, that you might give some consideration to the question whether the proposed fluctuations in the rate of

---

[1] For the earlier discussions and their upshot see above pp. 207–19.

contribution should not be limited to the employees' contribution. I believe that you could by that means get the greater part of your results at half the cost. From the point of view of the stability and solvency of the Fund, it would be much easier to work out a scheme, if the employers' contributions were not subject to the proposed fluctuation. I should have thought that one might find other ways in which the Treasury could use the same sum to the better advantage of employment than by allowing this concession to employers which is likely to be passed on to such a very limited extent in increased immediate expenditure.

Yours,

KEYNES

From J. E. MEADE, *21 August 1942*

My dear Maynard,

Many thanks for your letter of August 20th on the subject of changes in employers' social security contributions. We had just finished a redraft of our paper before I got your letter, and I enclose a copy of this redraft. We are agreed that changes in employers' contributions will be less useful than those in employees' contributions, (though there may be some difference of opinion as to the extent of this difference). You will see from paragraph 22 of the enclosed redraft that the only reason why we have continued to suggest that employers' and employees' contributions should be subject to equal variations is because we considered that any other proposal would be politically impracticable. It seems to me that the practicability of a scheme in which only the employees' contribution varied is a point which should most certainly be raised in any departmental discussion of the scheme which may follow.

On the question of economic analysis, may I put the point this way? In so far as the reduction in employers' contribution causes a reduction in selling price, it will be comparable to a reduction in employees' contribution. Such a reduction in price is, however, in many cases likely to be delayed. In the meantime, I agree, the increased profit income is very unlikely to lead to any significant increase in expenditure on consumption by profit makers. But may not the increased margin between prices and prime costs, at least in certain trades, lead directly to some increase in output and employment?

Yours sincerely,

J. E. MEADE

To J. E. MEADE, *25 August 1942*

My dear James,

I have your letter of August 21st about changes in employers' social security contributions.

Why do you say that you consider a different treatment for employers' and employees' contributions politically impracticable? I agree that the opposite proposal, namely to fluctuate the employers' contributions and not the employees', might give rise to such difficulties. But is the actual proposal likely to?

On the question of economic analysis I agree with you that 'in so far as the reduction in employers' contributions causes a reduction in selling price, it will be comparable to a reduction in employees' contribution'. But I do not think you put it strongly enough in saying that such reduction is likely to be 'delayed'. My point is that it is likely not to happen at all precisely because the reduction in question is by hypothesis temporary. If there were a permanent reduction in employers' contributions, then, after a time lag, one might expect it to be passed on in prices. But in this actual case the change will have been reversed before the time lag has been overcome.

I should agree that the increased margin between prices and prime costs might conceivably lead to some increase in output in certain directions, but I should have supposed that this would certainly not be large and, taking everything into account, I should be surprised if a given reduction in employers' contributions would have more than one-fifth at most of the effect of an equal reduction in employees' contributions.

Apart from these questions of substance, couldn't you make your draft shorter and clearer for the outside reader? I should have thought that the whole thing could be expressed in half the number of words actually used. If I were drafting it, I should turn it inside out, starting off with an explanation of the proposal, then point out its advantages and, if necessary, but at no great length, explain why you reject alternatives. It is

generally rather a waste of time to rebut arguments which have in fact not yet been advanced by anyone, because the critics are sure to find different objections to make. Although this is an important and interesting contribution to a vital problem, in the course of drafting it you seem to me to have got it into a shape which will confuse and perhaps deter the non-expert reader.

Yours,

KEYNES

It was with these discussions with Meade and his colleagues behind him that Keynes entered the Treasury's consideration of the proposals as a part of its examination of post-war budgetary policy.

To SIR WILFRID EADY, *3 September 1942*

I feel that you and Gilbert have not done full justice to the great potentialities of the Meade proposals, for the following reasons:

(1) That part of your argument which relates to special unemployment applies to any remedy against unemployment which relies on an increase in general purchasing power. It is quite true that a general increase of purchasing power is not equally efficacious in all circumstances. But it is easy to underestimate the contribution it can make, even where special unemployment is the trouble, since by providing a good demand for labour elsewhere it greatly facilitates labour transfer out of the industries suffering from special unemployment. At any rate, Meade was not concerned to argue this. He was assuming that measures of increased general purchasing power as a cure for unemployment were now widely approved, both by experts and the general public, and he was considering the best technique for injecting purchasing power, assuming one wishes to do so.

(2) I think that you greatly under-estimate the quantitative efficacy of what he proposes. You point out that he would be

releasing about £m60 a year on each 2 per cent decline of employment. This is not far short of 1 per cent of the national income. The multiplier is generally taken as being, in this country, a trifle above 3. But, of course, it is not a constant figure at all levels of employment or in all circumstances. If, however, we assume the very conservative figure of 2 or a shade better, it follows that the release of £m60 would increase the national income, and therefore employment, by 2 per cent. This is exactly in the same order of magnitude as the evil it is endeavouring to remedy. If the circumstances were predominantly those of special unemployment, some people might want to put the multiplier a little lower. But then neither Meade nor anyone else has suggested that his proposal is in fact adequate *by itself* to maintain a constancy of employment. But he can argue, I think, that its quantitative effect is highly significant relatively to the evil it attacks. Moreover, if the contribution is 7s rather than 5s, the amount of the fluctuation might be greater than what Meade is assuming.

(3) Since Meade wrote the paper below, there has been a domestic discussion inside the Economic Section, in which I have taken part, as to whether the short-period efficacy of a reduction in the employers' contribution is anything like as great as a reduction in the employees' contribution. We all agree that it is less, and I go so far as to say that it is so much less as perhaps not to be worth while. I may be overstating my point and have not quite convinced the others. Nevertheless, I think it is well worth considering whether the proposals should not be restricted to the employees' contribution. This would mean upsetting the Fund very much less, since the sum involved would be only half as great. I should put the multiplier resulting from money injected through a reduction in the employees' contribution at least as high as 3. So at a conservative estimation you would get three-quarters of the effect at half the cost by restricting the fluctuation in this way.

(4) Unless I have misunderstood Beveridge, he is proposing

only a notional fund. That is to say, he would not be actually accumulating its actuarial liabilities. I agree, therefore, with Gilbert that the Treasury contribution should remain constant. As I understand, the contributions and benefits are to be such that there would be the desired degree of balance over a period of time if there were a fund. Indeed, if the Treasury contribution were to vary to make good the fall in the others, it might work the wrong way. For it would increase the size of the budgetary deficit without in fact increasing purchasing power at all. Unless the Treasury becomes more cynical about budgetary deficits than is likely, this will make more difficult a budgetary deficit for other reasons which would be more helpful and might lead to an increase of taxation, which would be actually harmful.

If I understand rightly, the relationship of Meade's proposal to the Beveridge scheme is as follows. When Beveridge first heard about it from Meade, he was extremely bitten by it and was anxious to make rather a feature of it. Hopkins felt that it did not really belong to the Beveridge scheme, but might possibly form one of the proposals to be considered in a memorandum on the general issue of remedying unemployment by the release of purchasing power. He, therefore, urged Robbins and myself to withdraw it so far as possible from Beveridge's attention, and that we have done. Beveridge is quite conscious of this and agrees that probably he had better content himself with not much more than a passing reference. At least that was the position last time I heard about it. If Meade and I can persuade you that it is as good as we think, it might well form a feature of the Treasury memorandum on the relationship of public finance to unemployment, which we ought to contemplate sooner or later.

[copy not initialled]

Keynes received the 'final' draft of Meade's proposals on 28 September 1942. At this stage, his suggestions were of a minor drafting order and are not reprinted here.

Early in 1943, James Meade attempted to get Keynes more actively involved in the employment policy discussions with the following letter.

From J. E. MEADE, *8 January 1943*

My dear Maynard,

The great public support which the Beveridge Report has received has suggested to me that there ought really to be a similar publication on the subject of post-war unemployment. The enthusiastic public reception of the social security proposals shows that there is an exceedingly strong feeling in the country about post-war internal reconstruction and that people are in such a mood as they have never been before for the reception of imaginative ideas for social reform. At the same time everything goes to show that there is a real feeling of uneasiness that nothing much can, or perhaps rather that nothing much will in fact, be done to prevent the re-growth of large-scale unemployment. People do not realise that the Government is giving any serious attention to this problem and it would be my guess that a really imaginative approach to this problem would now have such a reception as permanently to influence the course of post-war policy.

An exploration of the possibilities in this connection would no doubt cover the topics which are now generally familiar to economists, such as the use which can be made of our new national income statistics for the purpose of stabilisation and the various ways in which Government expenditure, private investment and private consumption can be controlled or influenced in order to prevent general depression. A public investigation and report on this topic should not be politically very controversial, but would put new heart into the public and would probably ensure once and for all that a sensible policy in this field would in fact have to be adopted by any post-war Government.

It would, moreover, provide an admirable opportunity for clearing up certain misunderstandings on this subject. For example, there is little understanding outside Government circles that the immediate post-war problem may be rather to prevent inflation than deflation; or that the immediate post-war unemployment that may result from demobilisation is one that cannot suitably be cured by general expansive policies. It requires, of course, rather policies of retraining, labour transference and general adjustment of production to peacetime uses. Moreover, this would present an admirable opportunity for making reference to the importance of international conditions and of economic relations with other countries that are suitable to an internal policy of stabilisation and expansion in this country.

It may be that there are better methods of getting these ideas across, but it occurs to me, to be quite frank, that what we really require is a Keynes Report to follow up the Beveridge Report. People cannot be enthusiastic about too many things at the same time. Personally I think the Keynes Report should have come before the Beveridge Report, but I do not want to see it postponed until a dozen other reports on matters of relative unimportance have anaesthetised the public.

Yours sincerely,
J. E. MEADE

Keynes's reply, which was part of a longer letter also dealing with agriculture, was brief.

From a letter to JAMES MEADE, *11 January 1943*

I am afraid, however, that there are essential differences between the Beveridge proposals and the post-war unemployment programme, particularly the following:

(1) Post-war unemployment is far less a question of a really concrete plan and would involve little, if any, definite legislation;

(2) it is very much more mixed up with external policy; but

(3) above all, all sorts of aspects of it are already being worked out by different Departments and by various Hurst Committees. It seems to me impossible to have a new commission working alongside all the present activities. Moreover, it is much too soon to decide that those activities are not being quite well and fruitfully conducted.

Despite Keynes's lack of enthusiasm, the Economic Section continued to attempt to force the pace on what had become by then an inter-departmental Committee on Reconstruction Priorities with a study by James Meade on the various measures which might be taken to preserve full employment.

Professor Robbins sent Keynes a first draft of the Meade paper in March 1943, and drew the following comment.

To PROFESSOR L. C. ROBBINS, *29 March 1943*

My dear Robbins,

James Meade tells me that he is now wanting to get on with re-writing the paper on the maintenance of full employment. Apologies for not letting you have sooner my comments on the draft of March 11th. But it was only this week-end that I was able to get down to it.

I have very few criticism of substance. The main one is perhaps that the multiplier effect needs more emphasis. There is very little reference to this before paragraph 57. One of the things I feel it important to impress on Ministers is that much less effort is required to prevent the ball rolling than would be required to stop it rolling once it has started. This is of the first importance. After the slump has fully developed, the relevant figures get dreadfully large. I feel there is some reason to hope that remedies on a much smaller scale would be sufficient to maintain the balance, if they are all ready prepared and are applied in good time. Indeed, I am confident that this is so, apart from international repercussions.

On the question of form I have much more criticism. But I appreciate that this is a very early draft. In its present shape I find it terribly indigestible. To begin with there is the language. A great deal could be cut out. There is far too much of 'In this connection there is one suggestion which merits close examination', etc. etc. Moreover, I should have thought there was a good deal which could be taken for granted. For example, do Ministers want the existence of unemployment in the past to be elaborately demonstrated to them? (If it is to be demonstrated, some interesting figures, which I have seen in a recent draft on a similar sort of subject by Loveday about fluctuations in incomes in 24 different countries, seem to me newer and more impressive than the figures for U.K. and U.S. given in paragraph 11.)

At the other end of the paper I should have thought that

the section on industrial and labour market conditions might be omitted. You emphasise that this paper is primarily for Ministers. I should like to offer a prize for any Minister who reads it through without his attention wandering. Possibly John Anderson would win it, but there would be no *proxime accessit*. Since, in the main, this does not purport to be an original contribution, the form is above all what matters.

I should, therefore, make it much less expository. It is aiming too much at abbreviated completeness and is like the bare bones or reasoned index of a book. This would make it possible to concentrate on those things which ought to be done. I should plunge straight into that with the least possible preamble. On further reflection, I still very much like Appendix E.[2] I am not so much struck by Appendix F. I doubt if one could have the proposals both of E and F, and of the two E seems to me much the better and more likely to touch the spot.

Yours sincerely,
[copy initialled] K

As Meade re-drafted his paper for the Reconstruction Committee, he raised a further issue with Keynes.

From J. E. MEADE, *19 April 1943*

My dear Maynard,

I am at the moment redrafting our paper on the maintenance of full employment. As a result of the suggestion which you made to me in conversation, I have tried my hand at introducing a reference to the possibility of dividing the budget into a capital budget and a current budget. On consideration, however, I am now against the introduction of such a reference. We argue in our paper that one should try to control investment in such a way as to prevent violent fluctuations in national income, but we suggest that this may not alone be successful:

(i) because it is not always easy to control sufficient home investment promptly enough to prevent all variations in total investment, and

---

[2] This appendix contained Meade's scheme for counter-cyclical variations in social insurance charges. Appendix F contained an income tax credit scheme in which taxes collected to damp down booms would be refunded in the ensuing slump.

(ii) because there may be fluctuations in other items of national expenditure (e.g. in foreign investment) which need offsetting and which it would not be possible to compensate fully and promptly by immediate fluctuations in home investment.

The conclusion which we draw from this is that, in certain circumstances, it will be wise to operate on other forms of expenditure by a tax policy which stimulates (or restricts), say, personal expenditure.

This, however, involves unbalancing (or overbalancing) the current budget. It is my fear that if the budget is divided into a capital and a current budget, this will reinforce the orthodoxy of an annual balance for the current budget. We may, therefore, lose more than we gain from dividing the budget in this way.

It may be suggested that in so far as there is a case for operating through taxation on personal consumption, this is provided by our proposal for variations in social security contributions. But we should not urge the division of the budget on the assumptions that we shall get the social security scheme, because we may not get that scheme and may, therefore, need to fall back upon variations in ordinary taxation. There is, however, a logically more potent point. The great merit of a scheme like that for variations in social security contributions is that it acts as what I will call an 'instantaneous automatic stabiliser'. In other words, if plans go wrong and *if unemployment develops*, there is an automatic instantaneous adjustment stimulating demand to prevent the multiplier from doing its evil work of exaggeration. We may, however, foresee a slump in demand and to offset this we may wish to stimulate demand by a reduction in taxation *before unemployment develops in order to prevent such unemployment from appearing*. For this purpose, we must be free to plan taxation (and so the deficit of the current budget) ahead. I conclude, therefore, that we want both a potent 'instantaneous automatic stabiliser' such as the social security scheme and freedom to plan ahead year by year for a deficit or a surplus in the current budget; and I fear that the latter freedom would be prejudiced by a division of the budget.

Yours sincerely,

J. E. MEADE

To J. E. MEADE, *25 April 1943*

My dear James,
The Maintenance of Full Employment
I am not quite happy about the line of argument you set forth
in your letter of April 19th. I doubt if it is wise to put too much
stress on devices for causing the volume of consumption to
fluctuate in preference to devices for varying the volume of
investment.

In the first place, one has not enough experience to say that
short-term variations in consumption are in fact practicable.
People have established standards of life. Nothing will upset
them more than to be subject to pressure constantly to vary them
up and down. A remission of taxation on which people could
only rely for an indefinitely short period might have very limited
effects in stimulating their consumption. And, if it was
successful, it would be extraordinarily difficult from the political
angle to reimpose the taxation again when employment improved. On this particular tack your proposal about varying the
insurance contribution seems to me much the most practicable,
partly because it could be associated with a formula, and partly
because it would be pumping purchasing power into the hands
of the class which can most easily vary its expenditure on
consumption without radically altering its general standards.
This seems to me quite enough as a beginning. I should much
deprecate trying to superimpose on this proposals to reduce
taxation on drink and tobacco with a view to making people
drink and smoke more when they were tending to be out of work,
or to dealing with income-tax, where there is a huge time lag
and short-run changes [are] most inconvenient.

In the second place, it is not nearly so easy politically and
to the common man to put across the encouragement of
consumption in bad times as it is to induce the encouragement
of capital expenditure. The former is a much more violent version
of deficit budgeting. Capital expenditure would, at least partially,

319

if not wholly, pay for itself. Assuredly it is much the easier of the two to put across. These ideas are too young and tender to be put to the strain which your present line of thought would require.

Moreover, the very reason that capital expenditure is capable of paying for itself makes it much better budgetwise and does not involve the progressive increase of budgetary difficulties, which deficit budgeting for the sake of consumption may bring about or, at any rate, would be accused of bringing about. Besides which, it is better for all of us that periods of deficiency expenditure should be made the occasion of capital development until our economy is much more saturated with capital goods than it is at present.

I recently read an interesting article by Lerner[3] on deficit budgeting, in which he shows that, in fact, this does not mean an infinite increase in the national debt, since in course of time the interest on the previous debt takes the place of the new debt which would otherwise be required. (He, of course, is thinking of a chronic deficiency of purchasing power rather than an intermittent one.) His argument is impeccable. But, heaven help anyone who tries to put it across the plain man at this stage of the evolution of our ideas.

Yours sincerely,
[copy initialled] K

The circulation of the final version of the Meade memorandum on 18 May led to renewed discussions of the issues in the Treasury. On 20 May, Sir Hubert Henderson circulated a pessimistic 'Note on the Problem of Maintaining Employment'.[4] This naturally drew a comment from Keynes.

THE LONG-TERM PROBLEM OF FULL EMPLOYMENT

1. It seems to be agreed to-day that the maintenance of a satisfactory level of employment depends on keeping total expenditure (consumption *plus* investment) at the optimum

[3] A. P. Lerner, 'Functional Finance and the Federal Debt', *Social Research*, February 1943.
[4] Reprinted in *The Inter-war Years and Other Essays* (ed. H. Clay) (Oxford, 1955).

figure, namely that which generates a volume of incomes corresponding to what is earned by all sections of the community when employment is at the desired level.

2. At any given level and distribution of incomes the social habits and opportunities of the community, influenced ([as] it may be) by the form and weight of taxation and other deliberate policies and propaganda, lead them to spend a certain proportion of these incomes and to save the balance.

3. The problem of maintaining full employment is, therefore, the problem of ensuring that the scale of investment should be equal to the savings which may be expected to emerge under the above various influences when employment, and therefore incomes, are at the desired level. Let us call this the *indicated* level of savings.

4. After the war there are likely to ensure three phases—

(i) when the inducement to invest is likely to lead, if unchecked, to a volume of investment greater than the indicated level of savings in the absence of rationing and other controls;

(ii) when the urgently necessary investment is no longer greater than the indicated level of savings in conditions of freedom, but it still capable of being adjusted to the indicated level by deliberately encouraging or expediting less urgent, but nevertheless useful, investment;

(iii) when investment demand is so far saturated that it cannot be brought up to the indicated level of savings without embarking upon wasteful and unnecessary enterprises.

5. It is impossible to predict with any pretence to accuracy what the indicated level of savings after the war is likely to be in the absence of rationing. We have no experience of a community such as ours in the conditions assumed, with incomes and employment steadily at or near the optimum level over a period and with the distribution of incomes such as it is likely to be after the war. It is, however, safe to say that in the earliest years investment urgently necessary will be in excess of the indicated level of savings. To be a little more precise the

former (at the present level of prices) is likely to exceed £m1000 in these years and the indicated level of savings to fall short of this.

6. In the first phase, therefore, equilibrium will have to be brought about by limiting on the one hand the volume of investment by suitable controls, and on the other hand the volume of consumption by rationing and the like. Otherwise a tendency to inflation will set in. It will probably be desirable to allow consumption priority over investment except to the extent that the latter is exceptionally urgent, and, therefore, to ease off rationing and other restrictions on consumption before easing off controls and licences for investment. It will be a ticklish business to maintain the two sets of controls at precisely the right tension and will require a sensitive touch and the method of trial and error operating through small changes.

7. Perhaps this first phase might last five years,—but it is anybody's guess. Sooner or later it should be possible to abandon both types of control entirely (apart from controls on foreign lending). We then enter the second phase which is the main point of emphasis in the paper of the Economic Section. If two-thirds or three-quarters of total investment is carried out or can be influenced by public or semi-public bodies, a long-term programme of a stable character should be capable of reducing the potential range of fluctuation to much narrower limits than formerly, when a smaller volume of investment was under public control and when even this part tended to follow, rather than correct, fluctuations of investment in the strictly private sector of the economy. Moreover the proportion of investment represented by the balance of trade, which is not easily brought under short-term control, may be smaller than before. The main task should be to *prevent* large fluctuations by a stable long-term programme. If this is successful it should not be too difficult to offset small fluctuations by expediting or retarding some items in this long-term programme.

8. I do not believe that it is useful to try to predict the scale

of this long-term programme. It will depend on the social habits and propensities of a community with a distribution of taxed income significantly different from any of which we have experience, on the nature of the tax system and on the practices and conventions of business. But perhaps one can say that it is unlikely to be less than $7\frac{1}{2}$ per cent or more than 20 per cent of the net national income, except under new influences, deliberate or accidental, which are not yet in sight.

9. It is still more difficult to predict the length of the second, than of the first, phase. But one might expect it to last another five or ten years, and to pass insensibly into the third phase.

10. As the third phase comes into sight, the problem stressed by Sir H. Henderson begins to be pressing. It becomes necessary to encourage wise consumption and discourage saving,—and to absorb some part of the unwanted surplus by increased leisure, more holidays (which are a wonderfully good way of getting rid of money) and shorter hours.

11. Various means will be open to us with the onset of this golden age. The object will be slowly to change social practices and habits so as to reduce the indicated level of saving. Eventually depreciation funds should be almost sufficient to provide all the gross investment that is required.

12. Emphasis should be placed primarily on measures to maintain a steady level of employment and thus to prevent fluctuations. If a large fluctuation is allowed to occur, it will be difficult to find adequate offsetting measures of sufficiently quick action. This can only be done through flexible methods by means of trial and error on the basis of experience which has still to be gained. If the authorities know quite clearly what they are trying to do and are given sufficient powers, reasonable success in the performance of the task should not be too difficult.

13. I doubt if much is to be hoped from proposals to offset unforeseen short-period fluctuations in investment by stimulating short-period changes in consumption. But I see very great attractions and practical advantage in Mr Meade's proposal

for varying social security contributions according to the state of employment.

14. The second and third phases are still academic. Is it necessary at the present time for Ministers to go beyond the first phase in preparing administrative measures? The main problems of the first phase appear to be covered by various memoranda already in course of preparation. Insofar as it is useful to look ahead, I agree with Sir H. Henderson that we should be aiming at a steady long-period trend towards a reduction in the scale of net investment and an increase in the scale of consumption (or, alternatively, of leisure). But the saturation of investment is far from being in sight to-day. The immediate task is the establishment and the adjustment of a double system of control and of sensitive, flexible means for gradually relaxing these controls in the light of day-by-day experience.

15. I would conclude by two quotations from Sir H. Henderson's paper which seem to me to embody much wisdom.

Opponents of Socialism are on strong ground when they argue that the State would be unlikely in practice to run complicated industries more efficiently than they are run at present. Socialists are on strong ground when they argue that reliance on supply and demand, and the forces of market competition, as the mainspring of our economic system, produces most unsatisfactory results. Might we not conceivably find a *modus vivendi* for the next decade or so in an arrangement under which the State would fill the vacant post of entrepreneur-in-chief, while not interfering with the ownership or management of particular businesses, or rather only doing so on the merits of the case and not at the behests of dogma?

We are more likely to succeed in maintaining employment if we do not make this our sole, or even our first, aim. Perhaps employment, like happiness, will come most readily when it is not sought for its own sake. The real problem is to use our productive powers to secure the greatest human welfare. Let us start then with the human welfare, and consider what is most needed to increase it. The needs will change from time to time; they may shift, for example, from capital goods to consumers' goods and to services. Let us think in terms of organising and directing our productive

resources, so as to meet these changing needs; and we shall be less likely to waste them.

KEYNES

25 May 1943

On reading Keynes's note, Sir Wilfrid Eady commented.

From SIR WILFRID EADY, *26 May 1943*

I see no objection to the circulation of your note on the Maintenance of Employment. It is a voyage in the stratosphere for most of us.

We are proposing in the first stage to ask Ministers to endorse the stabilisation and control policy for the early transitional period in detail: so far they have approved it in principle.

When we all know what is to happen in the transition period we can begin to look at the next phase. You will find your official colleagues obtuse, bat-eyed and obstinate on much of this!

W.E.

Keynes replied

To SIR WILFRID EADY, *27 May 1943*

THE LONG-TERM PROBLEM OF FULL EMPLOYMENT

Very sorry, but it does seem to me quite essential that all of you should become accustomed to the stratosphere—if that is really what it is! For, if the argument which I have tried to bring into the open in my paper is not understood by those responsible, they are understanding nothing whatever. It seemed to me advisable to make explicit the argument which underlies both Meade and Henderson. If you do not understand that, you are, as I say, understanding nothing, certainly neither Henderson nor Meade.

And, after all, it is very easily understood! There is scarcely an undergraduate of the modern generation from whom these truths are hidden. And, once they have been digested and have

325

entered into the apparatus of the mind, it is possible for most people to move fairly safely over a terrain otherwise most dangerous.

KEYNES

Keynes's memorandum also led to further correspondence with James Meade.

To J. E. MEADE, *27 May 1943*

My dear James,

I enclose a brief note which I have written on the Long-Term Problem of Full Employment. You will notice that I do not directly traverse your paper. Indeed, I have no wish to do so. My criticisms are not of substance but of emphasis. And they really boil down to two points—(1) I think you lay too much stress on cure and too little on prevention. It is quite true that a fluctuating volume of public works at short notice is a clumsy form of cure and not likely to be completely successful. On the other hand, if the bulk of investment is under public or semi-public control and we go in for a stable long-term programme, serious fluctuations are enormously less likely to occur. I feel, therefore, that you do a little less than justice to investment under public auspices by emphasising the deficiencies of this method in the short period, whilst under-estimating their efficacy for preventitive purposes and as a means of avoiding the sharp fluctuations which, once they have occurred, it is so difficult to offset.

(2) I have much less confidence than you have in off-setting proposals which aim at short-period changes in consumption. I agree with Henderson that one has to pay great attention to securing the right long-period trend in the propensity to consume. But the amount one can do in the short period is likely to be meagre. I think it may be a tactical error to stress so much an unorthodox method, very difficult to put over, if, in addition to its unpopularity, it is not very likely to be efficacious.

It did not seem to me that Henderson's document was really very inconsistent with yours. It was largely concerned with a more distant period. Both of you, I think, are in danger of getting a little too academic for the purpose of Ministers. The only matters about which it is necessary that they should take immediate decisions relate to the first phase, whereas you, as it seems to me, are largely concerned with the second phase, and Henderson with the third phase.

However, I must not accuse you of being academic, since Eady tells me that my own paper moves in the stratosphere and will be entirely unintelligible to any civil servant,—to which, however, I am replying that he really must try to understand it, since the theory which I have brought out into the open underlies both your paper and Henderson's. If he does not understand this, he understands nothing. And, if, not understanding this, he thinks he understands either you or Henderson, he is deceiving himself.

Yours,
[copy initialled] K.

From J. E. MEADE, *31 May 1943*

My dear Maynard,

Thank you for your letter of 27th May and for your note on 'The Long-term Problem of Full Employment'.

I am glad that in the main you sympathise with the substance of our paper. On the question of substance I have only one comment to make on your letter. In the present draft of our paper we do not, I think, lay any very great emphasis on controlling the propensity to consume except through such schemes as that for variations in social security contributions, with which I understand you agree. Paragraphs 45 and 46 of our paper tend to rule out the use of ordinary fiscal policy for this purpose and lead up merely to the proposal of the social security scheme (or possibly as an alternative a deferred credit scheme) as 'stop-gap' to prevent the multiplier from getting under way. I should have thought, therefore, that the present draft (although not, I agree, earlier drafts) of our paper was not open to criticism on the grounds of stressing this unorthodox method.

I confess, however, that I cannot so readily assent to your suggestion that Ministers need not at the moment take decisions relating to anything later

than the first post-war period in which supplies will be scarce and effective demand will be high. There are a number of reasons for taking the opposite view:

(i) I will not deny that the period of excess demand *may* last as long as five years as you suggest in your note, but I should have thought that it was at least possible (in my opinion more probable) that it would not last longer than two to three years. After all the amount of physical damage in relation to total capital stock is really not so huge, and there have been great increases in productive equipment and in productive efficiency etc. here and in the United States. The actual replacement of deficiencies so that we get back to where we were in, say, 1938 may not take much longer than a couple of years, particularly in view of the spurt that may occur in output per head as a result of wartime progress in technique. But if it is *possible* (even if it were not probable) that we shall, after two years of peace, be back where we were in the 1930s, Ministers should by the end, say, of the first year of peace have taken more or less final decisions on the broad lines on which they intend to deal with the situation. In view of all the complex problems they will have to deal with in the post-war period and of the hectic political situation in which they will have to operate, it is certainly not too soon for them to start work on this subject now in the calm of war.

(ii) Much work *has* already been done and many decisions by Ministers *have* already been taken on the immediate post-war problems. It is not as if Ministers were being asked to neglect these immediate post-war problems in order to build a distant Utopia. Having taken general decisions on the first stage, and having started detailed work on that stage, they are being asked now to prepare to take general preliminary decisions on a stage only a little further on.

(iii) What we plan to do in the immediate post-war transitional period should be related to our rather longer aims. There is a grave danger that Whitehall will plan to deal with these immediate transitional problems as if the problems were completely separate from the subsequent problems. For example, Civil Servants always treat the problems of 'physical reconstruction' and of 'public works policy' as if they existed in separate universes. In your note you properly show that, fundamentally, the same analysis applies to each of the three periods which you analyse; and the same should be true to a certain degree in our administrative mechanisms for dealing with them. In fact, some of the immediate post-war mechanisms which will be useful for restricting an excess demand would be useless as a means of stabilising or stimulating demand in a future period; these mechanisms should naturally be temporary. But other mechanisms can be used to stabilise and stimulate as well as to restrain, and it might be wise to turn these into more or less

permanent features of our economy from the start. Is it, for example, really political wisdom to suppose that we shall have any chance of success if we put off discussing the scheme for variations in social security contributions until the close of the first transitional period, when the social security plan as a whole will be not only determined but actually in operation, when political wrangling will have started again, and when the willingness on the part of politicians and the public to consider radical changes will have passed? This is the surest way to assure that we shall get no such scheme.

(iv) The above arguments, in my opinion, provide solid economic reasons for the view that we ought to be concerned with these problems as soon as possible. There are, in addition, equally convincing political reasons. The public are, I am told, more concerned about employment prospects after the war than about any other major post-war issue. As the prospects of victory become clearer, this public interest will become more and more marked. Already Beveridge has set up his bureau to deal with the problem. He will probably get the answer wrong; but if his is the only answer in the field, and if the Government has not its own answer ready (and an answer which does not refer merely to good prospects of employment for a year or so after the war) there will be another first-class political row.

(v) Finally, I feel that it would be truly tragic if this opportunity were lost. The policy which is advocated is one which is to the interest of all classes and all political parties; it is one for the success of which intellectual enlightenment rather than a change of heart is required; and we have at the moment the unique opportunity of all political parties in a government which is seriously willing to consider social innovations. The opportunity is unlikely to recur. Perhaps you will allow me to add the personal note that, in these matters of a full employment policy, I have always regarded you as the guiding intellect and the moving force; and I believe that in this I am typical of the younger generation of economists.

Yours sincerely,

J. E. MEADE

To J. E. MEADE, *2 June 1943*

My dear James,

The Problem of Full Employment

I should find it easier to say whether I agree with you that there are further decisions which Ministers ought to take in the near future if you would tell me what the decisions are which you think they ought to take.

You will have noticed that in my paper I deliberately excepted your social security contributions proposal from deferment. I agree with you that this deserves early consideration. But I am not clear what else there is, which does not too much depend on the actual progress of events for it to be ripe for ministerial decisions at this stage.

Yours,

[copy initialled] J.M.K.

From J. E. MEADE, *3 June 1943*

My dear Maynard,

The Maintenance of Employment

Thank you for your letter of 2nd June. The following are the main points on which, in my opinion, Ministers might fruitfully take decisions in the near future—

(i) We are agreed that the social security contributions proposal falls into this category. In this connection I would only add that, if for one reason or another it should be rejected, Ministers should then proceed to consider the possibility of continuing into normal times of peace a scheme of deferred income tax credits on the principles outlined in Appendix F of our memorandum. Personally I vastly prefer the social security scheme. But the income tax scheme would be better than nothing; and in this case also the golden opportunity might be missed, if a decision was postponed until after the transitional period when the principle of deferred credits will have been forgotten.

(ii) There are decisions which should be taken now on the control of investment. It should be realised that the forward planning, control and timing of public investment is important both in the immediate transitional period, in order to restrain and spread out the demands for physical reconstruction, and also in the longer period for the stimulation of such investment. For example, it might be decided, in principle, that public authorities should prepare and revise annually a five-year plan for their future capital works, and this should be reviewed periodically by a central body for the purpose of the proper timing of expenditure. Certain inducements might be considered to persuade local authorities to keep in step with such a plan, e.g. by varying the rate of state grants for different types of works, according to the period in which they were undertaken. Here surely is a field of action and of administration, which is equally relevant to the immediate post-war period of restraint and to the subsequent period of stimulation. The danger

is that if Civil Servants and Ministers concentrate exclusively on *ad hoc* mechanisms for restraint immediately after the war, they will fail to have built their controls in a way which will also be useful for stimulation later on. In that case we may well be caught napping again.

(iii) I am pretty sure that the same principle might be applied in perhaps a lesser degree to the control of private investment. Various measures will be used immediately after the war for its restraint. Which of these measures of control will, and which will not, be useful later on to stimulate private investment? This question should be considered now, since it should influence the way in which the controls are instituted or developed in the immediate post-war transitional period.

(iv) A minor matter. We have suggested in our paper (paragraph 44) that it may be worth while controlling the terms of hire-purchase finance in such a way as to impede such purchases when restraint is needed and to ease them when stimulation is required. Here again is a mechanism which might be usefully employed to restrain buying in the immediate post-war period, but could subsequently be readily used to stimulate buying. This would be much preferable to the employment, during the former period, of an *ad hoc* and temporary measure of restraint which will have no subsequent use.

(v) There are broad issues on which Ministerial decision should be sought for the purpose of dealing with 'structural' unemployment. For example, the problem of labour transfer (occupational and geographical) should not be regarded as merely a question of shifting labour during the immediate post-war period from war-like to peaceful occupations. Labour movement must be regarded as a continuing need, and decisions should be taken now to perpetuate, and, in certain cases, to develop so much of the Ministry of Labour machinery for this purpose as is considered desirable. Here, in my view, is an outstanding case of the need for considering the long-term problem when decisions are being taken on the maintenance of controls in the transitional period. I am one of those who think that it would be useful to offer two rates of unemployment benefit, a specially favourable rate being offered to those who are willing to be moved about. But whether or not this particular device is desirable, the subject wants discussion and decision as a long-run as well as a short-run problem.

(vi) The same is true of the location of industry. The problem of bringing work to the men (as a supplement to bringing men to the work) should be regarded as a continuing one; and decisions should be taken now with this in mind, and not merely with a view to improvising a temporary means of getting industry going in black spots after the war.

The above are examples of important economic issues on the long-run aspects of which discussions and decisions should be started now. I have tried

331

above to outline the substantive economic reasons why decisions on these matters should be taken at once. You will see that one of my main reasons is that the decisions which are taken about the short run will be relevant to long-run policy and should, therefore, be taken after a consideration of the needs of the longer run. But I have also a subsidiary 'political' reason which I mentioned in my earlier letter, namely that many of these things will require considerable legislative or administrative changes and that these changes may be politically possible now or immediately after the war, and impossible later on.

The overriding argument, in fact, for taking decisions now, in my opinion, is yet another political consideration. The public are demanding plans for post-war employment policy; and if the Government have not fairly soon reached preliminary decisions on the matter (extending well beyond the immediate post-war transition) there will be another political explosion.

May I end by an *argumentum ad hominem*? In the international sphere you have advocated an International Clearing Union. In the immediate post-war years the principles of such a Union could not be fully applied. We shall need to continue all sorts of exchange controls on current payments for a period of years; we must hope that the principles of Mutual Aid in international commerce will be continued at least for some time at least for some purposes such as relief; and a whole series of *ad hoc* measures will be required to keep international monetary and commercial relations in balance. The Clearing Union scheme is, in essence, a longer-term measure for more normal times. Why, in this case, did Ministers need to take these decisions of long-term principle *before* they considered all the detailed hugger mugger of the process of adjustment? The answer, in my view, is clear: it was in order that they might see where they were going before they started to go there. Is not this true of internal policy also?

Yours sincerely,

J. E. MEADE

To J. E. MEADE, *7 June 1943*

My dear James,

The Maintenance of Employment

Substantially there is nothing with which I disagree in the list given in your letter of June 3rd of the main points on which Ministers might take early decisions. Indeed, the first page and a half of your letter seems to me to give much more suitable

material for a brief memorandum for Ministers than the documents actually in their hands.

When I said that there was nothing on which Ministers could take early decisions, I did not mean to rule out these various important matters. My point—not clearly expressed—was that it did not seem to me that any matters arose either out of yours or out of Henderson's memorandum which led up to decisions which ought to be taken now.

None of the points in your letter of June 3rd seem to me to depend in the least either on the academic argument set forth in the Economic Section's memorandum or in Henderson's. None of the disputed points of fact, or prognosis, or prescription, or theory, implicit in these documents affects to any significant extent the six points in your letter of June 3rd. Nor do I think—though that is dangerous matter on which to prophesy— —that any of them would meet with much difficulty or controversy from Henderson. These points have the great advantage of bringing the issues back to practical matters and away from a debate, which seemed to me was getting academic and might be endless.

Yours,
[copy initialled] K

Meade's paper came before the meeting of the Ministerial Committee on Reconstruction Priorities on 31 May. At the meeting, the Chancellor argued that it went too far and that he would like to make his own contribution in the future in a Treasury note. The meeting agreed to ask the Lord President to formulate proposals for future work on post-war problems, especially the transitional period, industrial location, labour mobility and public works. The upshot was the appointment in July of a Steering Committee on Post-War Employment, under the chairmanship of Sir Richard Hopkins, to carry out and co-ordinate the investigations.

Before the Steering Committee began its deliberations, Keynes was involved with other members of the Treasury, Economic Section, and Central Statistical Office in preparing another estimate of the post-war national income. In the early drafts, Keynes provided a chapter on the

probable range of fluctuation of the estimates around a central estimate of just over £7,000 million for the national income at factor cost in 1948.

From 'Influences Affecting the Level of the National Income',
June 1943

CHAPTER III: THE PROBABLE RANGE OF THE POST-WAR NATIONAL INCOME

30. Some of the factors analysed above are known with some precision; others are likely to change during the period in view, but have been assumed to remained stable because there is no sufficient evidence for predicting any particular degree or direction of change; others again cannot affect the final result significantly even if they vary somewhat widely. The gap between the more optimistic and the more pessimistic expectations which can reasonably be held, depends almost entirely on the view taken about three main factors: (*a*) the number of employed wage-earners; (*b*) the increase of productivity; (*c*) the terms of international trade.

31. The number of employed wage-earners may come to differ from that assumed in the table of reference for the following reasons:

(i) The number of women, who would not have been 'occupied' before the war but remain in employment as a result of the war, has been taken at 500,000. The Ministry of Labour believe that this is the lowest likely figure. The actual figure may conceivably prove to be as much as 250,000 higher.

(ii) The table of reference makes no allowance whatever for casualties, either military or civilian, not even for those which have occurred up-to-date. So far deaths from all causes in the forces amount to about 300,000 and deaths to civilians by enemy action to about 75,000. Not the whole of the resulting aggregate of 375,000 falls to be deducted from the estimate of the 'occupied' wage-earners, since not all the casualties are at the expense of the wage-earning class and since an allowance has

334

already been made for normal mortality. Casualties up-to-date are, perhaps, sufficient to require a reduction of 250,000 from the estimate of 'occupied' wage-earners assumed in the table of reference. To this there has to be added a conjectural allowance for the casualties yet to come.

(iii) Taking (i) and (ii) together it is evident that the basic assumption for the numbers of the occupied population is likely to be somewhat too high. But a more important cause of divergence (either way) from the basic figure is the unemployment percentage which it is appropriate to apply to the occupied wage-earners to obtain a figure for the employed wage-earners. The assumption in the table of reference is an average unemployment of 1,200,000 or approximately $7\frac{1}{2}$ per cent of the total wage-earning population. (This is a mean figure and does not assume that unemployment will never rise above this or fall below it.) If we expect a return to more or less the same conditions which obtained in the ten or twelve years before the war, this is an optimistic figure. It might be argued that, even if we are more successful in handling cyclical unemployment, structural unemployment may prove a problem still more intractable than before in a free enterprise society which cannot direct (in peacetime as distinguished from wartime) either enterprise or labour to the desired activities or locations. On this more pessimistic view it might be prudent to look forward to an average unemployment of not less than (say) 1,500,000.

Against this it may be argued that even 1,200,000 is a pessimistic assumption in the light of the greater knowledge and experience of these problems and, above all, of the greater will to grapple with them and to regard their solution as one of our primary responsibilities, which exists today in all quarters. We cannot, on this view, regard the unemployment problem as substantially solved so long as the *average* figure is greater than 800,000, namely 5 per cent of the wage-earning population, or rest content without resort to drastic changes of policy so long as it exceeds 1 million. Those who feel confidence in the

335

accuracy of current diagnoses of the problem and of our will-power to apply the appropriate remedies, would think it justifiable to assume an outcome more favourable than an average figure of 1,200,000, though they would readily admit that a higher figure is easily realisable on the basis of pre-war experience, if we adopt no new policies and are no more energetic and enterprising than in the decade of the thirties; and equally so if we are quite on the wrong lines in our new policies and ideas.

32. Taking one thing with another and allowing for all the considerations under (i), (ii) and (iii) above, it is likely that the optimists would not wish to improve on the basic assumption and would agree that it would be rash to rely on anything much better than this; while the pessimists might claim that this assumption may over-estimate the numbers of the employed population (including a substantial allowance for future casualties) by as much as (say) 750,000. Since, according to the ready-reckoner (§27 above), each reduction of 250,000 reduces the national income by £100 million, the net effect of this would be a reduction of the estimated national income by £300 million.

33. The other main assumption, capable of leading to a wide divergency of estimates, relates to the increase of productivity and of efficiency in production and distribution. The basic assumption in the table of reference supposes that the experience of the war has made no difference whatever, neither one way nor the other, to our efficiency and to our knowledge of new methods. It allows for the normal peace-time rate of progress of $1\frac{1}{2}$ per cent per annum, but nothing extra for the shake-up of the war experiences of industry, for the intensive training of labour, for the widespread introduction of the fruits of the best American experience, for necessity being the mother of invention, or for the long-overdue discarding of much dross and waste which clogged the pre-war system of production and distribution in this country. It assumes that industry will immediately relapse into doing exactly what it would have been

doing, or rather into that state of efficiency (or inefficiency) which it would have attained (or maintained), if the war had not occurred.

34. It is possible that the pessimistic school may rest content with this and not argue that the effect of the war on industry and distribution has been to deprive it of the normal progress which it would have made in the absence of the war. In this case it will be satisfied with the assumption in the table of reference, just as the optimistic school might accept the table's assumption concerning the numbers of the employed population.

35. On the other hand, there are substantial reasons for reaching a widely different conclusion. These reasons are partly statistical and are partly based on common observation of a number of separate facts. They can be conveniently reviewed under the following heads,—somewhat at length, since the crucial question in forecasting the national income is that of the right conclusion on this head.

36. (i) Apart from the adoption of new methods and inventions which the pressure and experience of the war have brought into existence, there was in 1938 great scope for the introduction into this country of methods and machinery which had been already adopted elsewhere, particularly in the United States. Details have lately become available (*Economic Journal*, April 1943, pp. 39–54, 'Industrial Production, Productivity and Distribution in Britain, Germany and the United States' by L. Rostas) for comparing physical output per head in certain manufacturing industries and mining based on the 1935 Census of Production in the U.K. and the 1937 Census of Manufactures in the U.S. These show that output per head in the U.S. ranged from four times greater (or even more) in iron and steel products, motor cars, and radio sets, and nearly three times greater in machinery, down to no more than 20 or 30 per cent greater in cotton textiles. Over the whole range of manufacturing industry American output per head averaged about double the British output. (On the other hand, there was little to choose

337

between British and German output per head.) Output per hour showed an even greater superiority than this, since American hours of work were appreciably less than the British. Some part of this superiority may have been due to natural advantages of size of market and in other respects. But a major explanation of it must also have been the use of more modern machinery, methods and factory layout, which were quite capable of being introduced into this country. Can we not expect, and indeed decide, to overcome some part at least of this avoidable inferiority? If so, we are entitled to anticipate a once-for-all addition to the normal rate of progress as a result of our having taken advantage, not of new technical inventions, but of those which have been already employed for some time in the U.S.

37 (ii) Is there not some evidence that considerable progress has in fact been made during the war in the direction of gaining ground on the U.S. over a wide front? An important piece of such evidence is to be found in the enquiries made by the Ministry of Production into the relative prices of production of the leading types of munitions of war which are being currently produced both here and in America. These indicate that on the average of such products our money prices of production in terms of money are less than two-thirds of the costs of similar products in the United States.* Having regard to the much higher level of money wages, the wider margin of profit and the larger allowance in the price for writing down capital expenditure in the U.S., this still indicates an appreciably higher output per head there than here. But, if allowance is made for these factors it would appear that American superiority in current output per head is not more than 25 to 50 per cent greater than here, which is a very great improvement on the pre-war position as indicated above. Moreover the comparison is in precisely those fields where American superiority used to be most marked. It would seem that our relative efficiency, over and above the current

* Ministry of Supply products—British prices 66 per cent of American; M.A.P. products, 57 per cent ship-building, 40 per cent.

improvements common to both countries, can scarcely have improved by less than 50 per cent on the average of the output covered by the Ministry of Production, and must have gained a great deal more than that in certain directions. Admittedly these figures cover only a part of the whole field. They provide in themselves no evidence of a relative gain in such important industries as, for example, textiles, building and coal. Moreover these industries have experienced in wartime the signal advantage of working to full capacity on the optimum technical scale of output. Nevertheless material gains should surely survive the war. The industries in question are amongst those which traditionally have been regarded as most suitable for this country, but which happened to have reached a dangerous age in the period before the war when they were tending to become fossilised in old practices and had fallen seriously behind America through a failure to adopt the best modern methods and machines. The whole of our engineering industry, both heavy and light, has been violently shaken out of its old habits and has been forced in a brief period to learn the use of the best modern precision tools, of factory layout, and, when suitable, of mass-production methods. There is evidence, as we have seen, that they have learnt their lesson well and have gone a long way towards overtaking American practice. Once the general ideas which lie behind the best modern practice have been learnt, they are easily applied to types of product different from those in the production of which the lesson was first learnt. Also the native capacity and originality of this country's designers and inventors has been fully confirmed by this war's experience. With modern methods of application behind them they should again be able to lead the world. No doubt such cheerful words will cause the heads of the very wise to wag with alarmed precaution. Nevertheless to suppose that all the above has gone for nothing would be an extreme assumption.

38. (iii) Some statistical evidence covering a much wider field than that of the Ministry of Production can be derived from the

conclusions of the latest statistical White Paper. The table of reference is based on 1938 and takes no account of what may have already happened to the growth of efficiency between 1938 and 1942. The adoption of this method has been inevitable in view of the abnormal conditions of 1942 and the difficulty of measuring with precision the comparative efficiency of that year and of the last pre-war year. But this does not mean that no relevant evidence about what has been happening can be obtained from the White Paper figures for 1942. The main difficulty is in calculating the price of the large proportion of total output which was produced for the Government. The White Paper estimated the increase in net factor cost of civilian consumption at 36 per cent, but did not attempt a figure for Government output. The price increase for such output was certainly much less than 36 per cent. Perhaps it would be safe to say that the increase in net factor cost for output as a whole was not greater than 30 per cent. If the growth of efficiency is worked out on this assumption, it is found to be about 12 per cent for the four years 1938 to 1942, instead of 6 per cent ($1\frac{1}{2}$ per cent for four years) as assumed in the table of reference. If we were to assume that this gain of efficiency will be retained and keep all the other assumptions (i.e. as to the hours of work in 1948 and the gain in efficiency between 1942 and 1948) the same, the estimate of net national income in 1948 would be about £m7,500, compared with £m7,087 in the table of reference. Now in some important respects we must expect that the gains of efficiency in wartime will be lost in peace-time conditions, if only because a large part of production will be changed over from directions where we have learnt maximum efficiency into directions where we still have much to learn. On the other hand, there are also important respects in which wartime production is at a grave disadvantage. The handicaps of the black-out, of transport difficulties, of inability to obtain delivery of necessary supplies, of rapid changes in type of product, of the loss to the armed forces of a large proportion of the most efficient labour

in the prime of life, of using unskilled labour for skilled jobs, of excessive hours of work, of wear and tear not made good, of lack of opportunity to overhaul and repair plant and machinery— all these things mount up in the aggregate to a very great loss of efficiency which will certainly be recovered and made good when peace returns. It is paradoxical to maintain that productive efficiency per hour of work (not *aggregate* output which is the result of intensive hours of labour for the loss of which we have already made full allowance) will be very greatly less than it is now, when all the handicaps mentioned above have been removed.

39. (iv) We turn, finally, to a short catalogue of some facts of common observation which may be held to confirm, rather than question, the broad indications of the statistical evidence marshalled above:

(*a*) Many new factories with modern layout have been constructed, and there has been much capital expenditure of permanent value in manufacturing industry.

(*b*) A vast quantity of the most modern machine tools, are in the hands of every engineering firm, large or small, throughout the country. Some of these tools are general purpose, others can be adapted, but chiefly the users have learnt what can be done with this type of tool.

(*c*) There has been a very large increase in electrification.

(*d*) Wartime concentration has led to a great reduction of unnecessary types and much greater standardisation.

(*e*) Similarly it has led to the elimination of unnecessary processes and packing and useless extras.

(*f*) Also to the elimination of unnecessary labour and services both in production and distribution. Firms have been forced to give attention to what can be eliminated without disadvantage such as they might never have given except under pressure.

(*g*) The enormous economies of straight-run production to the maximum optimum capacity have been made abundantly clear to all producers.

(*h*) Necessity really has been the mother of invention in tens of thousands of cases.

(*i*) Successful experiments have been made in mass-production methods of what are called 'utility goods', which are of particular value because they are perfectly suitable to be carried over and indeed extended in peacetime production.

(*j*) British agriculture has enjoyed some revolutionary changes of method which may well increase its permanent efficiency by (say) 30 per cent.

(*k*) The experience of the Ministry of Food in the production, purchase and distribution of what constitutes more than a quarter of national consumption should have immensely valuable permanent results.

Again, it seems pessimistic to suppose that all this will have gone for nothing, which is what the table of reference assumes, and that we shall immediately relapse in all these respects to pre-war practices.

40. There remains the question of the post-war terms of international trade; that is to say, the question whether the prices of what we import are likely to rise more or less than the prices of what we export. In this respect the table of reference assumes no change in 1948 compared with 1938. In fact there has been no significant change during the war—partly as the result of the success of the Food Ministry and the Supply Departments, greatly aided by their control over shipping and by the shortage of shipping, in retarding the rise in the prices of what we buy, and partly because we can sell our restricted volume of exports for anything, within reason, that we choose to ask. But it would be unjustifiably optimistic to assume a continuance of this state of affairs after the war. The relationship of the prices of primary to manufactured products in 1938 was exceptionally in our favour. There is a widespread movement throughout the world in favour of improving the position of primary producers. If the relationship were to return to what it was in 1924, it would cost us £220 million a year, whilst a

return to the conditions of 1911 would cost us something of the order of £500 million. In fact, it was the progressive change of the terms of trade in our favour since 1911 that enabled us to surmount the difficulties arising from the loss of our foreign investments in the last war and of much of our staple textile exports between the wars. A large part of this improvement was due to changes in productivity on the continuance of which we can rely. But we must certainly be prepared for some reversal of the trend, and a reduction on this account of the estimate in the table of reference by less than £100 million (which would allow our imports to rise in price by 8½ per cent compared with our exports) would not be reasonably prudent.

41. Taking all these matters into consideration and making allowances for the many difficulties of the post-war years—adopting, in fact, what the optimists would regard as a sufficiently cautious view—an estimate of £m7,250 for the net national income in 1948 rising to £m7,700 in 1952 might be suggested as suitably conservative. This is considerably short of what might be reached in all-round favourable conditions.

42. If, on the other hand, it is thought more prudent not to assume that we shall solve the new problems of post-war unemployment before we have done so, and not to assume that we shall retain wartime improvements in efficiency until this is proved to be the case,—if, in short, it is better to base ourselves on our pre-war experience rather than on hopes engendered by the energies and will-power of wartime before these hopes have been actually fulfilled in the slacker times of peace, then an estimate of (say) £m6,800 for 1948 rising to £m7,200 in 1952 is to be preferred. Even the lowest of these figures represents a substantial increase, namely about 12 per cent, in the real national income compared with 1938, whereas the estimate of £m7,250 for 1948 assumes an improvement of no less than 22 per cent over 1938 in real terms (though chapter II above shows that in the light of past experience there is nothing very unlikely in this).

42. In conclusion, an assumption (or method of presentation), which underlies all the estimates of these three chapters, needs to be emphasised. Prices in 1948 are assumed to have jumped 35 per cent over the 1938 level, which supposes that average hourly wages and other costs, including the increased cost of imports through a worsening of the terms of trade, have risen over this period by that much in excess of any improvement in efficiency. This allows room for an improvement in hourly earnings in 1948 by more than 35 per cent compared with 1938, the exact amount of the permitted excess depending on the growth of efficiency, the degree of deterioration in the terms of international trade and the growth of certain other costs such as the share of social security contributions falling on employers. After 1948 prices are assumed to remain unchanged. This means that hourly money-wages and other costs (including any further deterioration in the terms of international trade) will be free to rise cumulatively by the amount of the improvement in efficiency without disturbing the price-level. If efficiency rises by $1\frac{1}{2}$ per cent per annum, then (provided there is no reduction in hours of work) it is assumed that this will be absorbed by higher wages, etc, not by lower prices leaving the average price-level unchanged.

43. There is a certain trap in this method of presentation which needs to be exposed. The term 'efficiency' is not clear and unambiguous and needs to be defined. Human services directly applied, as for example in domestic service or in education, are assumed to have a constant efficiency, since there is no measurable change in the quantity of the product, though there may be in its value. Thus in order to attain an increase of efficiency of (say) $1\frac{1}{2}$ per cent per annum averaged over the whole of output, it is necessary to have an appreciably larger increase than this in the manufacturing industries where progress makes itself measurably felt in the quantity of a given product per unit of human labour. Nevertheless increases in the remuneration of services directly applied must obviously keep step, more or less, with increases in other wages. It follows that the

344

fruits of a quantitative increase in output in manufacture have to be shared by the producers of this output with those otherwise employed whose services are equally indispensable to society. Thus if manufacturing efficiency increases by 3 per cent, this may mean an over-all increase of 'efficiency' interpreted as above by no more than 2 per cent; and if an increase in hourly wages in manufacture is to be accompanied, as it should be, by an equal increase elsewhere in fields of necessary activity not equally susceptible to the gains of technical progress, the increase in wages must not exceed 2 per cent. It follows that the prices of manufactured products will tend to fall and the cost of direct services, etc to rise, thus keeping stable the price level as a whole. This assumption (which is an assumption for convenience of exposition and is not intended as a prophecy of what will happen) underlies the particular monetary measurement of the prospective national income which has been adopted in this memorandum.

Between Keynes's draft and the draft, dated 25 June 1943 which went to the Reconstruction Priorities Committee, the central estimate fell to £6,800 million and the discussions of the possible range of fluctuations became more pessimistic.[5] As a result, the final draft contained a note of dissent by Keynes.

NOTE OF DISSENT BY LORD KEYNES

In my opinion the conclusion that the effect of war experience on efficiency has gone for nothing cannot be sustained. If this is superimposed on other assumptions which are not very optimistic, the result reached is unnecessarily depressing. To expect a range of £m7,000 to £m7,400 would not be indulging exaggerated hopes—the position might well be better than the higher of these figures. This leads to a minimum figure of £m7,000, and this is the lowest estimate, in my judgement, on which we should base our plans. This will represent (after price adjustment) a very great reduction in the national income as it

[5] The Chancellor was prepared to take £7,000 million as a working basis.

will be at the end of the war, in spite of the return of some 3 million men from the forces into industry and the escape from the many handicaps which industry suffers in war conditions.

Whilst we may be overtaken after the war by many misfortunes, it is important to base policy on a consistent approach, even though this assumes hopes which are not certain of fulfilment. The figure of £m7,000 already assumes a state of affairs which many people will think disappointing. For example, it supposes that, if we have gained 5 per cent in efficiency as a result of the war, this will have been offset by average unemployment running up to 2 million. Moreover, if the national income falls significantly below £m7,000 this will probably mean a reduction of something like 20 per cent in the real earnings (including overtime) of wage-earners compared with what they are now, either because of unemployment or because of a reduction of real wages (though not more than 5 per cent need come off real wage rates), and that savings will not be sufficient to look after the building and other capital developments now in contemplation.

This memorandum approaches the problem from the *supply* side. If we approach it from the *demand* side, it soon becomes apparent that an estimate of less than £m7,000 makes no sense at all. I am preparing a brief supplementary memorandum giving what seems (to me at least) to be compelling reasons for this view—provided we accept the scale of capital investment which Departments are believed to have in view.

KEYNES

24 June 1943

At the time of these discussions, Josiah Wedgwood, a fellow director of the Bank of England,[6] gave Keynes another opportunity to spell out his view of post-war prospects.

[6] Hon. Josiah Wedgwood (1899–1968); Chairman (1947–67) and Managing Director (1930–61), Josiah Wedgwood & Sons, potters; Director of Bank of England, 1942–6.

From JOSIAH WEDGWOOD, *6 July 1943*

Dear Keynes,

I apologise in advance for this, but I am full of perplexity, and it is important to educate business men and bank directors. As you say, most people do not assimilate new economic or philosophic ideas after 25. I am trying to do a little better than that by reading (7 years late) your *General Theory of Employment* [, *Interest*] *& Money*. I am partly handicapped in understanding the definitions, detailed argument, and mathematical expression by having been brought up in the school of Cannan, who disliked the mathematical developments of the Marshallian School, and, like some other Johnsonian de-bunkers over-simplified and probably ridiculed too much.

(1) As far as I understand the argument of the *General Theory* and of your *Treatise on Money*, it is that if general unemployment is to be avoided, savings must find expression in 'real investment', and that the best way of ensuring this is to keep the rate of interest low enough for both state and business men to embark on a sufficient volume of additions to real capital. This involves state control of investment (similar to that exercised in wartime?).

(2) Alternatively or additionally the 'propensity to consume' must be increased, if employment falls off, but, despite remarks on pages 324–5, the main theoretic and practical emphasis seems to be laid on control of investment and the rate of interest as a necessary means of sustaining 'full employment'. Now I do not quite understand why keeping up the volume of investment and keeping down the rate of interest should necessarily have such a paramount importance in the anti-slump offensive—though perhaps some of your disciples give these measures a higher degree of all-importance than you do.

(3) Your example (page 129) *of avoiding unemployment and increasing real income and capital of the community by burying bottled bank notes in mines and digging them up again*: Since what we want is a 'full belly' rather than 'full employment', would not an equally good or better effect have been obtained (during the slump) by presenting the notes to the needy without the necessity for digging? I came to think in the '30s that if Government, instead of cutting the dole, had increased it, there would have been less unemployment, provided there were adequate safeguards against large scale 'lead swinging' and excessive trade union rigidity regarding swapping jobs and dilution etc. Is that true?

(4) More generally—does it not follow from your general argument that a guaranteed weekly minimum in sickness and health, in work or out of work (based on the known facts about existing national productivity and contingent only on the recipient's readiness to undertake any sort of work within his

347

mental and physical capacity) would help considerably towards 'full employment' in the desired sense? and that in so far as the Beveridge plan provides this, it helps to guarantee the employment assumption? (Always provided that (*a*) we are not tied to a system of fixed exchange rates and (*b*) Government and public are prepared to retain any controls and other war expedients necessary to stabilise the cost of living?).

(5) Returning to my lack of understanding of the paramount importance of the rate of interest—

(*a*) As you say in various passages, there are many ways (other than a low rate for borrowing) in which the community can get sufficient fresh capital (real investment) to maintain or increase its income.

(*b*) Again (as before) is it not often as easy and proper to increase consumption as to increase investment?

(*c*) I agree that in housing and public works 1 per cent in the rate of interest may make a good deal of difference. But it seems to me that in most manufacturing business one does not make decisions on extensions or improvements depending on 1 per cent or 2 per cent in the rate of interest. Certainly if one thinks one will be able in two or three years to borrow at 4 per cent, one may defer capital expenditure when the available rate is 6 per cent—but if one thought the rate would remain 6 per cent for a generation, I doubt if that would be a deterrent. Estimates of output, saving in costs, and future returns are open to too large a margin of error. So are estimates of upkeep, depreciation and obsolescence risk. The margin of error in all these items is far higher than the rate of interest itself. In my business, unless as careful an estimate as possible shows a minimum *net* return of 15 per cent to 20 per cent after deducting normal depreciation, I don't usually feel that capital expenditure on new equipment is likely to be economically justified—and I believe other business men think along the same lines.* If pressed as to why, I should say because one should usually allow at least 10 per cent to 15 per cent for optimistic error, risk of the unexpected, and obsolescence. That is when one is making a fair profit with existing equipment. Of course, if one is making little or no profit or a loss and capital expenditure on fresh equipment or building seems to offer the chance of working at a profit, then I agree that one might embark on it (if one could) for an estimated net return of as low as 10 per cent, or say 5 per cent over the rate of interest payable on borrowed money—because the alternative would be ultimate extinction. But I cannot think that the margin of error on the net return estimated from new buildings or plant could usually be

---

* My Railway uncle says the Railways used to stipulate 10 per cent net return on fresh capital normally and 20 per cent in bad times! Things are more cut and dried in railways than in manufacturing. J.W.

safely put at less than 5 per cent either way on the capital involved. There is so much inevitable guess work; the imponderables are usually pretty important; and e.g. I know that in the case of our new Works the cost saving hitherto has been greater on the un-budgeted than on the budgeted items. It seems to be like estimating walking times in mountainous country from an un-contoured or imperfectly contoured map!

(6) But, apart from any pre-war theoretical argument, it does seem to me that the rate of interest should be kept low after the war—in fact, kept as it is now—for many years by capital rationing (*a*) in order to enable Government and public authorities and others to borrow cheap and build cheap for essential works and priority goods, and (*b*) to enable short-term debt to be funded cheaply and (*c*) to safeguard the legitimate interests of Government bondholders. Is that correct theory and policy?

(7) Presumably, if home investment is to be stimulated by an 'artificially' low rate of interest, foreign investment must be strictly controlled also (and perhaps differential taxation on it introduced?) This alone means continuance of national Government Exchange Control, doesn't it?

(8) If, after the war, we decide to maintain and develop the measures and controls necessary to safeguard a healthy minimum income for all, to stabilise the internal price of necessaries, and to develop internal reconstruction with a low rate of interest, does it really matter greatly what happens to international Exchange rates? Those countries which follow our example will achieve stable exchange with the £, others not. Is this not better than being tied by the leg to the dollar, or to gold—or even to Bancor? That seems to the layman to be the fair deduction from the Keynes doctrine of the '30s and from Keynes practice in wartime. Is not 'Bancor' just an ingenious compromise to induce America to 'play ball' in the settlement of war debts and the reconstruction of Europe?

Again apologies for so long a letter and so many questions, which betray, I fear, not only colossal ignorance and 'rustiness' but also colossal optimism in hoping that a busy man is going to answer them! At any rate I hope it will not be long before we laymen have another pamphlet from you. I begin to realise why you want to get back to Cambridge after the War, for, as someone said, the world progresses by a series of calculated indiscretions, but institutional loyalty makes that difficult.

Yours sincerely,

JOSIAH WEDGWOOD

To JOSIAH WEDGWOOD, *7 July 1943*

Dear Wedgwood,

I am afraid that your questions are too long and searching for me to deal with them by correspondence. We must have a talk about it all sometime. In replying, I will limit myself to a point, which I think runs all through your letter. It is not quite correct that I attach primary importance to the rate of interest. What I attach primary importance to is the scale of investment and am interested in the low interest rate as one of the elements furthering this. But I should regard state intervention to encourage investment as probably a more important factor than low rates of interest taken in isolation.

The question then arises why I should prefer rather a heavy scale of investment to increasing consumption. My main reason for this is that I do not think we have yet reached anything like the point of capital saturation. It would be in the interests of the standards of life in the long run if we increased our capital quite materially. After twenty years of large-scale investment I should expect to have to change my mind. Even in the meanwhile it is a question of degree. But certainly for the first ten years after the war—and I should expect for another ten years after that—it would not be in the interests of the community to encourage more expenditure on food and drink at the expense of expenditure on housing. For that broadly is what it would come to.

There is also a subsidiary point that, at the present stage of things, it is very much easier socially and politically to influence the rate of investment than to influence the rate of consumption. No doubt you can encourage consumption by giving things away right and left. But that will mean that you will have to collect by taxation what people would otherwise save and devote to investment,—all of which would be a stiff job in the existing political and social set-up. Perhaps you may say that that is a reason for getting rid of the existing political and social set-up.

But is it clear that expenditure on housing and public utilities is so obviously injurious that one ought to attempt a social revolution in order to get rid of it?

Yours sincerely,

[copy initialled] K.

From JOSIAH WEDGWOOD, *10 July 1943*

Dear Keynes,

It was nice of you to bother with my letter, which clears up to a large extent my uncertainty as to your views on the rate of interest and your reasons for emphasising the desirability of more investment. I think I follow and agree with your first and second paragraphs, and the application of the second paragraph to post-war industrial problems has indeed been stressed by me in a memorandum on the pottery industry.

But I am not so certain that I follow your third and last paragraph, which leaves me guessing at the answer to my questions 3 and 4. For example, in the circumstances of 1930–3, if we assume that neither the plans nor the organisation for large scale public investment were ready, might not a short run policy of bread and circuses without additional taxation have been both possible and desirable? Or what are the implications of your treasury notes in bottles?

No—so pale an orange as myself does not deserve to be crushed by the steam hammer of your last two sentences! I am all for 'reform that you may preserve' (the proper motto for an old-established family business), and I also agree with the social philosophy of pages 374 and 380 of the *General Theory*.

I shall take seriously your kind suggestion of a further talk, and I hope you will really let me give you a return lunch on some convenient day, when cares of State are not too pressing. I look forward to seeing you at the Bank on Thursday.

Yours sincerely,

JOSIAH WEDGWOOD

During the summer of 1943, the Treasury also began to prepare a reply to the Economic Section memorandum by James Meade on the maintenance of employment for the Steering Committee. Keynes provided various comments on the Treasury draft written by Sir Wilfrid Eady.

To SIR WILFRID EADY, *10 June 1943*

MAINTENANCE OF EMPLOYMENT: THE DRAFT NOTE FOR THE CHANCELLOR OF THE EXCHEQUER

My comments on a first reading of your draft are the following:

1. Paragraph 6: Two distinct conceptions seem to be confused in this paragraph. There is the proposal for a capital budget. In a sense this is no more than a matter of presentation. But, from the point of view of the Budget Speech, it would be much more than that. Recent Budgets have attempted to adjust the amount to be borrowed on all heads to the amount of savings which we can reasonably hope to collect during the year. The Chancellor has aimed at covering any gap that would otherwise exist by increased taxation. There will have to be an analogy to this in peace-time budgets through the Chancellor making a forecast of capital expenditure under all heads, and comparing this with prospective savings, so as to show that the general prospective set-up is reasonably in accordance with the requirements of equilibrium. The capital budget will be a necessary ingredient in this exposition of the prospects of investment under all heads. If, as may be the case, something like two-thirds or three-quarters of total investment will be under public or semi-public auspices, the amount of capital expenditure contemplated by the authorities will be the essential balancing factor. This is a very major change in the presentation of our affairs and one which I greatly hope we shall adopt. It has nothing whatever to do with deficit financing.

Quite apart from this is the proposal that if, for one reason or another, the volume of planned investment fails to produce equilibrium, the lack of balance would be met by unbalancing one way or the other the current Budget. Admittedly this would be a last resort, only to come into play if the machinery of capital budgetting had broken down.

Thus the capital budgeting is a method of maintaining

equilibrium; the deficit budgeting is a means of attempting to cure disequilibrium if and when it arises.

The proposals for deficit budgeting were, in my opinion, rather overstressed in the first version of the Economic Section's document, but they are not overstressed in the final version. Personally I like Meade's social security proposal. It is not open to many of the objections to other forms of deficit finance. Indeed, it can be defended on the ground that it will actually promote stability in the size of the social security fund itself. It is arguable, that is to say, that in periods of increasing unemployment the fund will actually make up a significant part of what it loses through reduced contributions through having to pay out less unemployment relief than would otherwise be the case.

About other forms of deficit financing I am inclined to lie low because I am sure that, if serious unemployment does develop, deficit financing is absolutely certain to happen, and I should like to keep free to object hereafter to the more objectionable forms of it. Assuredly the Chancellor of the Exchequer is entitled to take up at least as cagey a line to it as that. But I doubt if he need trail his coat by going into it in so much detail.

2. Paragraph 6 might also be criticised in the form of presentation on the ground that, particularly towards the end, it mixes up politics and merits. It is one thing to dispute Meade's proposal or alternative proposals on merits, and another thing to point out that they will present considerable political and psychological difficulties. It is not sufficiently clear when the objection is on one ground and when on the other. There is also superficial inconsistency whether in the immediate post-war period employment is expected to be good or is expected to be bad. There is an appearance that each of the two alternatives is adopted according as it suits the argument of the moment.

So very decidedly I should cut down all this and not lead the critics to think that the Chancellor is confusing the fundamental

idea of the capital budget with the particular, rather desperate expedient of deficit financing.

3. I do not agree with the history of the first paragraph of 7 on structural unemployment. It is one thing to say that substantial structural unemployment continued all those years, quite another thing to suggest that, except in 1931/3, there was no deficiency in aggregate effective demand. I should have said that in almost every year of the pre-war decade there was a deficiency of effective demand, the actual level of unemployment being the result of a combination of this and of structural unemployment. You would certainly bring a hornet's nest about your ears in suggesting that structural unemployment was the whole trouble.

I agree that the problem of structural unemployment needs emphasising and that the memorandum of the Economic Section is open to criticism on the ground that it did not stress this sufficiently. But I wonder if the Chancellor of the Exchequer appreciates into what deep water the adoption of the more pessimistic expectation on this heading leads him. The optimistic view on this, and also on some other matters, which I am charged with maintaining is by no means intended as a prophecy of what is certain to happen. I regard it much more as the only hypothesis on which the kind of economic future which the Chancellor and probably most other people in the Treasury envisage as desirable really has a chance. It might turn out to be true that anything at all closely resembling free enterprise is incapable of dealing with the problem of structural unemployment. If so, I feel sure that free enterprise will go by the board to the necessary extent. I have not abandoned the view that something like free enterprise can be made to work. I think we ought to have a good try at it. And that try ought to be based on the assumption that the underlying conditions are not such as to make it impossible.

Now I suggest that the Chancellor gets into somewhat deep water if he hints at a chronic return to the sort of troubles we

experienced before the war and leads his readers to feel that he is extremely sceptical as to the capacity of a free enterprise system to deal satisfactorily with the problem. I fancy he will find himself open to some rather unexpected rejoinders if he takes a defeatist line about the possibility of free enterprise dealing satisfactorily with the outstanding problem of the age. Much safer, I should have thought, to adopt a more optimistic line until the case is proved to be otherwise. But, of course, it is no good adopting the optimistic line unless one is prepared at the same time to give it a chance of coming true.

That leads me to my other criticism on the section about structural unemployment. Is not it rather futile to suggest an enquiry from the Departments into the 5/7 years prospects of certain critical industries? How can we possibly expect the Departments to give a confident answer? All they can say, surely, is that on the optimistic hypothesis it is so-and-so, and on the pessimistic so-and-so. Are we any further on?

Would it not be much better to end up with a recommendation for the preparation of detailed proposals how to handle structural unemployment in a free enterprise environment?

More generally, I feel considerable doubt whether you will have succeeded in your aim of avoiding provocation, if you consider into whose hands this paper will go. It will be read by a number of advisory economists, more particularly by some of those who advise Labour Ministers. I feel quite sure that the document will be interpreted by them, and they will so inform their masters, that the Treasury is intending to stone-wall on everything to the last, and would much rather be found drowned than learn to swim. This view would be reached, not so much as a result of anything positive that is said, but by the generally negative implications of the paper as a whole.

I suggest, therefore, that something which at least looks much more constructive in intention would be safer. Do I interpret rightly that the Treasury official policy at this stage is to be rather non-committal and lacking in positiveness until proposals

from elsewhere have crystallised a bit more? If so, I do not lack sympathy with this approach. But if this is the policy, my recommendation would be that much the safest line to take is to invite Ministers to come down to brass tacks and rub their noses in the practical difficulties of the case, rather than envelop them in an all-embracing wet blanket.

I fancy you could get moderately near to what I am suggesting without very enormous changes in the draft. Something like this:

The first five paragraphs might stand practically as they are, though I suggest the omission of the last sentence of paragraph 5, which seems in that particular context to confuse the question whether Clyde Canals etc. are desirable as a long-term proposition when capital investment seems to be approaching saturation point and the quite different issue whether the sort of thing is suitable as a short-term make-weight to offset cyclical depression in other directions.

I should, however, supplement paragraph 3 by bringing in a reference to the capital budget in the first of the senses I have distinguished above. It would come in quite conveniently there. It could be explained that long-term stability of employment may largely depend on having a stable long-term investment programme; that we shall, therefore, have to have a periodic survey of the investment prospects of which the capital budget may be an important ingredient; and, if we can find ways of retarding or accelerating the long-term programme to offset unforeseen short-term fluctuations, all the better. No reason, surely, why the Treasury should not be fairly constructive and optimistic on this heading.

I should then cut down Section 6 and make it much more concerned with its title, which is 'Maintenance of Consumers' Demand' and much less with the objections to deficit financing as such. Why not ride this all rather lightly? 'Deficit budgeting' the Chancellor might say 'may well turn out to be a last resort, from which some of my successors will not in practice escape.

But a Chancellor of the Exchequer can scarcely be expected to bless it in advance as a general principle'—and let it go at that.

Paragraph 7 would then emphasise the importance and significance of structural unemployment and perhaps chip the Economic Section a bit for not paying more attention to it. The Chancellor could agree with the President of the Board of Trade that it requires special attention. I hope the passage about new industries will be kept and even emphasised. But structural unemployment could be treated as something to be handled forcibly and not something to be defeatist about.

The Chancellor could then conclude by saying that the problem really seems to divide itself into two main headings. The first is the means of ensuring stability in the long-term investment programme coupled with proposals for adjusting its tempo to unforeseen changes. He could say that the Departments concerned with building had provided first-class material so far as they are concerned in this problem. But there are many other types of long-term investment, examination of which has made nothing like as much progress. Is not the next thing to get down to dealing with these other types in the same comprehensive way as building has been treated?

The second aspect is the problem of structural unemployment. This comprises the question of the location of industry and inducements of private enterprise to come here rather than go there. It also involves the issue of the mobility of labour with particular reference to social security. Finally it is particularly concerned with the question of our new industries, where we start with a fairly free hand as to location. *Pari passu*, therefore, with the study of the investment programme should be a study of structural unemployment under the above headings.

This sort of approach would give a cheerful and constructive air to the whole thing without committing the Chancellor or the Treasury to any of the more dubious experiments and without getting involved in academic or ideological controversies.

KEYNES

357

To SIR WILFRID EADY, *30 June 1943*

THE MAINTENANCE OF EMPLOYMENT

I think I had better refrain from commenting in detail on your latest draft. There are substantial parts of it with which I do not disagree, and there are passages in the memorandum of the Economic Section which are not entirely to my liking. Nevertheless, I think that their approach is fundamentally much more sound, and on the general issues involved I am whole-heartedly on their side. I disagree fundamentally with the underlying theory of your paper. It seems to me to be in the last analysis not much more than Neville Chamberlain disguised in a little modern fancy dress.

I wonder whether the Chancellor will wish to expose so much surface in an academic controversy. Rightly or wrongly, this paper would provoke the deepest suspicions in nearly all the circles of the younger economists, and the Treasury would be regarded as past praying for. It would be said that the forces of deflation and contractionism after the war are going to shelter themselves behind the respectable barrier of 'maintaining controls', and the inevitability of structural unemployment. Indeed it is not unlikely, I begin to think, that there will be too much rather than too little control at the outset. Controls over demand, as distinct from prices, will have to be exercised with great elasticity and sensitiveness, if we are to avoid making the controls unpopular by giving colour to the conclusion that they themselves are actually creating unemployment. If the controllers overdo it and the level of unemployment is attributed to them by the public, with indeed some measure of reason, it will end in the controls being prematurely abolished. We shall then have too little control, and for the ensuing inflation it is the cautious souls who will really be guilty.

At the same time it is such a gentle and urbane statement of the point of view that for the purpose of fighting a controversy intended to win it has not a chance.

With the positive recommendations of your paper, as distinct from the analysis and the prognosis, I am in complete agreement in, I think, almost every case—complete and hearty agreement. Would it not be much better for the Chancellor to concentrate on these positive suggestions expressing, if he is so minded, some gentle cynicism about the brave hopes of the new world but putting the emphasis on the real point that, if these hopes are to be realised, there are some highly concrete matters, which need urgent attention and where action is necessary?

[copy initialled] K.

He also commented on a Treasury reply to an Economic Section paper on the maintenance of investment.

To SIR WILFRID EADY *and others, 9 July 1943*

In my opinion the first three pages of this memorandum totally misunderstand what the Economic Section is driving at. It is apparently supposed that, when they speak of the stabilisation of investment, they mean keeping investment at a constant figure, year in, year out, for a considerable number of years.

I am sure that this is not what the Economic Section mean. I should expect them to recognise that we may have to facilitate an exceptionally high level of investment in the early post-war years by encouraging saving and discouraging consumption. They would presumably desire these controls to be removed as soon as seemed advisable, with the result that investment would taper off. And, if one is looking forward to a much longer period—10 or 15 or 20 years—then, if it seemed that investment was becoming saturated, they would surely favour the stimulation of consumption and the discouragement of saving, so as to make a steady volume of investment at a gradually lower level compatible with stability of incomes.

What they are concerned with are two main theses:

(1) The maintenance of the national income at a stable level,

either by influencing consumption or influencing investment, as a long-term problem.

(2) The avoidance of the trade cycle and short-term fluctuations, for which they recommend primarily, though not exclusively, what they describe as the stabilisation of investment. But this would be entirely compatible with having investment at a higher level in the initial period than it would taper down to eventually.

I share the view, and I think they would, that, sooner or later, we shall be faced, if not with saturation of investment, at any rate with increasing difficulties in finding satisfactory outlets for new investment. It is very difficult to predict when this will come about. When it does come about, we shall then have to start on very important social changes, aimed at the discouragement of saving and a redistribution of the national wealth and a tax system which encourages consumption and discourages saving.

It may be that the Chancellor's official advisers are right in thinking that this period of impending saturation of investment is rather nearer than I personally think it is. But surely the Chancellor will appear in rather an odd light in taking up the line that those who press for a steady investment policy are in the wrong, whereas what we ought to be doing is getting ready in good time for discouraging saving to the utmost extent that we know how and can devise changes in social institutions to facilitate.

For that is what it comes to. If you accept the view of the Economic Section that we want to stabilise the national income, you have to do it either by encouraging investment or by encouraging consumption. We most of us, not only expect that we shall reach a point where the encouragement of consumption is the thing to put first, but we hope for it. All this, however, is in the future. The immediate task is to make good the losses of the country and equip the country with all the new investment it requires to be properly housed and thoroughly productive. When that task is complete, then we can turn our minds to

encouraging in every way a higher standard of current expenditure. But, as I have said, the Chancellor surely looks a little odd in wanting to emphasise the aim of getting ready in good time to discourage saving.

When we come down to strictly short-term fluctuations, such as those which arise out of the trade cycle, the alternative remedies are to try to off-set fluctuations of general demand by increasing investment, or to try to off-set it by stimulating consumption. Personally I favour the first alternative. The Economic Section is fairly well balanced between the two, but gives more favour to the second alternative than I do. In other words, I am nearer to what I gather to be the Treasury view about this than the Economic Section is. Nevertheless, the discussion of this matter appears to me to be extremely confused and not to fit in too well with what has appeared in the first part. In the first part the Chancellor declares himself against the stabilisation of investment, misunderstanding, as I think, what is meant by this term. In the second part he appears to reject the alternative, namely trying to get the off-setting factor by encouraging consumption.

So you will see that, taken in its entirety, the document appears to me to darken counsel rather than otherwise and is likely, like all things based on misunderstanding, to lead to a good deal of fruitless controversy. Does not the very short draft flagged 'A' below meet the case sufficiently pending further more far-flung discussions, which are now to follow?[7]

KEYNES

By the time the Steering Committee got down to business at the end of September 1943, Keynes was in America (*JMK*, vols. XXIII and XV). Partially as a result, the main Treasury memorandum to the Committee, 'The Maintenance of Employment: Prefatory Note by the Treasury',

[7] Not printed (Ed.).

circulated on 16 October, was a pessimistic document emphasising the problems of structural employment and adjustment as being as fundamental as the aggregate problem raised by the Economic Section, challenging the financial bias in the Economic Section's proposals, especially as regards investment, emphasising that 'it would be wrong and dangerous in the Treasury's view to look to financial policy as the chief instrument for averting fluctuations' and raising difficulties over tax changes and unbalanced budgets.

While Keynes was in America, another proposal concerning employment policy came his way, as he reported to Sir Wilfrid Eady.

To SIR WILFRID EADY, *14 October 1943*

I was invited to lunch by Mr Lubin, Economic Adviser in the White House. When I arrived the other guest was Mr Carter Goodrich[8] of the I.L.O.

They alleged that when the Prime Minister was at the White House he and the President had a conversation (I gather, which is extremely likely, on the latter's initiative) on the question of preparing proposals to deal with the problem of possible post-war unemployment. The President mentioned with favour the use of the forthcoming I.L.O. conference as the preliminary platform from which to prepare public opinion for various measures. The Prime Minister is alleged to have encouraged him.

They then told me that it was proposed to appoint a small committee for the purpose of preparing an agenda for the I.L.O. conference, and they tried to make me believe that the names suggested for this committee had emerged under the above high auspices. I was not at all clear, however, exactly where high auspices ended and less high auspices began. It was felt, they said, that the I.L.O. itself was not capable of preparing the agenda. Moreover, the agenda should be more than the word

---

[8] Carter Goodrich (1897–1971); Professor of Economics, Columbia University, from 1931; U.S. Labour Commissioner, League of Nations, Geneva, 1936–40; Special Assistant to U.S. Ambassador, London, 1941; U.S. Government member of I.L.O. Governing Body, 1936–40, Chairman, 1939–45.

indicates, and should be a general guide as to the sort of resolutions which the conference should be asked to carry.

The names suggested for this committee, I was told, were those of T. V. Soong, Mr Van Zeeland, Mr Nash[9] of New Zealand, Mr Lubin himself for U.S., and myself for U.K. I fancy there was another name, which I have forgotten—I think it must have been Dr Schacht,[10] but am not quite sure!

I inferred that T. V. Soong had received the invitation with reserve and without commitment. I am afraid that I poured cold water, which was more definitely water and more definitely cold, on the suggestion that I should play a part. I said that I could well see that the President may think some such conference a good sounding-board from which to launch proposals or outlines of proposals which had been worked out in detail in the proper quarters. But I doubted whether that would be possible so early as January, and I was not much inclined to turn aside from taking an interest in what is going on behind the scenes in official circles, nor waste my own breath and my poor fountain pen's ink, and Mrs Stephens' carbons, on the quixotic enterprise they offered me.

They did not press the matter unduly and we passed on to other topics.

I seem to recognise in the above an echo from what we had already learned through other channels. Mr Van Zeeland's name, in particular, rings familiar in this context. Also the idea that there was to be an I.L.O. conference on unemployment in January or thereabouts. How far the President (much less the Prime Minister) has really blessed and encouraged all this I remain very much in the dark. I should not have believed a word of it had it not been for the presence of Mr Lubin, who after all is the President's principal personal adviser on such matters.

[9] Walter Nash (1882–1968), G.C.M.G. 1965; member New Zealand Parliament, 1929–68; Minister of Finance, Customs etc., 1935–49; Minister in the United States, 1942–4; Member, War Cabinet, 1934–45; Deputy Prime Minister, 1940–9; Prime Minister, 1957–60.
[10] Hjalmar Horace Greely Schacht (1877–1970); President of Reichsbank under Dawes Plan, 1924; resigned, 1930, reappointed President, 1935–9; Reichsminister of Economics, 1934–7.

However this may be, the infant did not strike me as a sturdy one. Neither Mr Lubin nor Mr Goodrich opposed my lukewarm and deprecatory observations, and I thought it was pretty obvious that in their minds they agreed with them. But there were certain motions which they had to go through, and gone through them they had.

KEYNES

When he returned from America, he remained relatively uninvolved in the work of the Steering Committee's discussions, either directly or indirectly, beyond keeping a protective eye on the Meade scheme. However, after the Steering Committee reported in January 1944, he turned to its consideration.

POST-WAR EMPLOYMENT: NOTE BY LORD KEYNES ON THE REPORT OF THE STEERING COMMITTEE

1. I am in general sympathy with the line taken in this Report and with its recommendations. It is, indeed, an outstanding State Paper which, if one casts one's mind back ten years or so, represents a revolution in official opinion. At this late date, I limit myself to some short notes on chapter II, Professor Robbins' note of dissent, and the appendices.

2. §46 provides an easy answer to the wrong question. No one really supposes that the Government can go on spending £14 million a day in conditions of peace. The right question is why we cannot continue to produce a net national product worth £8,000 million a year at present prices. It is true that hours of work have been excessive, but in all other respects this total has been reached in spite of extraordinary handicaps. The answer, if there is one, is not nearly so easy but would be more to the point.

3. §§81–83 dismiss rather lightly the possibility of directly influencing the pace of private investment. I notice that several

364

members of the Reconstruction Committee (Minutes of the 8th Meeting (*d*)) take the same view. A private Conservative Committee has made some proposals which at least deserve consideration. It might be wise in what is to be published to pay a little more attention to this. Something might be done if the major, private firms were brought to regard it as their duty to pay attention to the indications of the official barometer.

4. §87 calls attention to the delays to investment caused by the present complicated parliamentary procedure. This is very important. Should there not be a specific recommendation for the improvement of the existing expensive and out-of-date machinery of the private bill?

5. After seeing the evidence on which it is based, I believe that §101 under-estimates the maximum limits within which public investment can be made to fluctuate. More should be made of the point that early action on the comparatively modest scale which is possible at short notice may be enough to stop deterioration, but in the event of the deterioration continuing over a long period measures on a larger scale should be practicable.

6. §§105–117 bless the most original and (perhaps it may prove) one of the most powerful of the offsetting expedients brought before them, namely variations in social insurance contributions. It is all the more disappointing that in §117 the majority of the Committee recommend that the method should not find an early place in the Statute Book. This has too much the air of fighting a rearguard action. The Steering Committee remind me of Lord Balfour who, when he was asked if he believed in progress, replied that of course he believed in progress but it should be as slow as possible. I hope that the alternative suggested in §115 will be adopted by Ministers.

7. §§118–122 on Hire Purchase do not mention what has always seemed to be the most promising method of regulation, namely that there should be a prescribed minimum down payment and maximum period over which instalments may be

spread appropriate to each class of goods, and that these conditions should be stiffened up in good times and relaxed in bad times. (In this connection see item (*j*) of the Minutes of the 8th Meeting of the Reconstruction Committee.)

8. There seems to be some confusion of thought in the section on Budgetary Considerations (§§ 123–139) No objection can be taken to the warning in the earlier paragraphs against an undue growth of dead-weight debt, coupled, as it is, with an explanation that the proportion of such debt arising from the present proposals is likely to be neither large in itself nor out of proportion to the growth of the national income. In so far as the dead-weight debt is increased, the normal level of taxation must clearly provide for this. But the latter part of the argument, which seems to suggest that the tendency of the proposals is to unstabilise the national budget, is surely topsy-turvy. It would be a *failure* to adopt a remedy for severe cyclical unemployment which might have that effect. There appears to be no glimmer of a recognition that measures to stabilise the national income are *ipso facto* measures to stabilise the national budget. The additional charges falling on the budget in years of bad employment as a result of the Committee's proposals are, in fact, almost negligible; whilst the effect on the revenue of maintaining the national income should be obvious. The Committee give the impression that, whilst the measures they propose to avoid unemployment are admittedly necessary and advisable, a price has to be paid for them in the shape of budgetary deficits and perhaps a consequent weakening in international confidence in our position. Exactly the opposite is the truth. It would be a failure to take such measures which would inevitably unstabilise the budget and weaken confidence. Is it supposed that slumps increase the national wealth?

Moreover, the full strength of the case has been in this section entirely overlooked. In this part of the Report (though it is to be found elsewhere) there is no hint of the operation of what economists call 'the multiplier', that is to say the effect of

injecting additional demand into the system in increasing the national income by at least double its own amount. Suppose for example that additional investment of £100 increases the total national income and output by £200 (which is probably an under-statement), and that the additional investment will not have a genuine permanent value in excess of £80 (which, one may hope, will also be an under-statement) it follows that the net result to the nation's production, strictly valued, will not be a loss of £20 (as some once argued) but a gain of £180. It follows that, if the increment of revenue exceeds one ninth of the increment of national income (which it certainly does), the transaction taken as a whole positively benefits the Exchequer there and then. The additional taxes, collected as a result of the induced investment in that very year in which it takes place, should be more than enough to write off the excess of the investment's cost over its true value. How slow dies the inbred fallacy that it is an act of financial imprudence to put men to work! If the Minister of Labour were found praising periods of cyclical unemployment on the ground that they gave the workers a much-needed rest and improved the nation's proficiency in the matter of darts, it should be for the Chancellor of the Exchequer to protest against such idling and to demand the present proposals for providing employment on the ground that they were essential to the solvency and stability of his Budget. This section has the air of having been written some years before the rest of the report. There are some acute outside critics who are well on the look-out for what they will regard as budget humbug, and it would be unfortunate to offer them so rich a feast. By all means emphasise the importance of maintaining budget equilibrium. But let this be represented as an important argument in favour of the rest of the proposals, as it most truly is, and not as an argument against them.

9. I find this particular section of the Report open to criticism for what it omits as well as for what it includes. Proposals have been before the public for some years under the description of

a *capital budget*. Something of the kind is included in most recent programmes and booklets for the cure of unemployment. They are not discussed in the Report or even mentioned. Yet they embody, not perhaps very clearly, a notion which is most desirable and useful. The failure to mention this matter will be interpreted to mean that the Treasury has turned it down, and the demand for it may well become the slogan of those who choose to regard this excellent Report as too timid and not going far enough. This would be particularly unfortunate, because the capital budget proposal is not merely consistent with the recommendations of the Report but is, in fact, not much more than a formal or regular embodiment of policies and calculations which permeate it throughout.

The term *capital budget*, though very convenient rightly understood, is liable to create misunderstanding because it suggests a closer connection with the Chancellor of the Exchequer's Budget than really exists and an interference with the latter which might result in a clouding and impairment of its soundness. In fact the adoption of a capital budget in the sense intended would leave the regular Budget practically the same as at present. The utmost that might be involved would be a slight tidying up of a few items as between (in technical language) 'above' or 'below the line' of the Exchequer Accounts, and even this would not be really necessary. A capital budget, in the sense in which I understand it, means a regular survey and analysis of the relationship between sources of savings and different types of investment and a balance sheet showing how they have been brought into equality for the past year, and a forecast of the same for the year to come. If aggregate demand gave signs of being deficient, the analysis would indicate a deflationary gap exactly corresponding to the inflationary gap which we have so often discussed during the war. This survey and balance sheet might well be presented on the occasion of the regular Budget Statement and form a part of the Budget White Paper. It would give an annual opportunity for examining

whether the state of demand during the ensuing year looked like being adequate to maintain employment and national income at the desirable level and for the Government to explain to Parliament what steps it had in view to remedy a prospective disequilibrium in either direction. Such a procedure as this might give greatly increased confidence to the public that the maintenance of employment and national income was now an avowed and deliberate aim of financial and economic policy. I forbear to enter into details as to its precise form. But its silent suppression is much to be regretted and will be severely criticised.

10. I am in strong agreement with Professor Robbins' Note of Dissent on Restrictive Developments in Industry, and with his recommendations in §6. I am confident that he speaks here—and most effectively, if I may say so—for the great majority of responsible economists in the whole of the Anglo-Saxon world. For those who believe that it will be the role of this country to develop a middle way of economic life which will preserve the liberty, the initiative and (what we are so rich in) the idiosyncrasy of the individual in a framework serving the public good and seeking equality of contentment amongst all, Professor Robbins' admonitions go to the heart of things. The majority of the Committee attempt no serious rebuttal of his arguments. The Report would be much enriched and its balanced effect on public opinion enhanced, if Ministers were to approve the substitution of his Note for the parched and desiccated passages of the Report which correspond to it.

11. *Appendix A*. This appendix recommends *two* new financial institutions, one for small businesses and one for reorganisation. As regards the former, I suggest that it would be better to establish the principle that each of the clearing banks should regard a certain proportion of its resources as available for this type of business, rather than that there should be a combined institution for handling it. When the amount required is relatively small, the business might be better handled by an

individual bank than by a consortium, with the added advantage
that this would allow for a desirable element of competition
between the banks to show success and enterprise in the task.
Consortiums of the kind suggested have not always in the past
proved very lively affairs. Under the alternative here suggested
an applicant turned down in one quarter can still try his luck
in another. Moreover the accommodation in question would
naturally merge in the provision of banking facilities generally.
Under the consortium he would be at the mercy, with no appeal,
of the lowest discoverable common factor of response without
the bait of winning what might prove a loyal, life-long and
valuable customer. This type of business should be made as
personal as the size and character of our financial institutions
permit.

12. *Appendix B.* §14 rightly emphasises the importance of
stressing statistics of the volume of *total employment* rather than
of unemployment (conventionally estimated). This will be
particularly significant and instructive during the demobilisation
period. The point is not overlooked in the body of the Report.
But in presentation to the public I should like to see more
lime-light directed on to it.

§22 rightly stresses the need to obtain better statistics of the
level of profits. In this field the present state of our information
is particularly defective, and deliberate obscurantism has pre-
vailed. Important figures bearing on this, collected by the Board
of Inland Revenue some years before the war, are still being
withheld from students and from the public on the ground (so
one is told) that, although the Board would welcome publication,
this is a matter on which the F.B.I. is entitled to the last word.
It would at least make a beginning of progress in a difficult field
if Ministers would give an instruction for this material to be
released.

I should like to call particular attention to the key position
which the Board of Inland Revenue could occupy if, after the
war, its methods were to be mechanised and its statistical staff

greatly strengthened. The Board is already giving invaluable assistance within the limits of its wartime resources, and without this aid the preparation of the Budget White Paper would have been impossible. But its present methods were not devised to produce statistical by-products. If the Board's statistical staff were on the scale of the statistical staff of the Bank of England, extraordinary improvements in fiscal policy and in general administration, as well as in knowledge, diagnosis and forecast, would become possible.

With the Ministry of Labour handling labour statistics on the lines proposed, the Board of Trade conducting a continuous census of production (here the Report is weak-kneed and unambitious and hence, in my judgement, inadequate), the Inland Revenue digesting and analysing the vast body of information which passes through its files, and the Bank of England continuing and improving its running analysis of our external position, the new era of 'Joy through Statistics' (I do not write ironically) can begin.

Theoretical economic analysis has now reached a point where it is fit to be applied. Its application only awaits the collection of the detailed facts which the economist, unlike the scientist, cannot collect in a laboratory by private enterprise. The authors of the Report would, I think, have written with more confidence about their plans for the future and in a spirit of more buoyant hope, if they had fully appreciated what knowledge is capable of doing in making the future different from the past as soon as we decide to furnish the social sciences with *data* comparable to the *data* of the other sciences, appendix B is the clue to the whole business. I should almost have made it (somewhat strengthened up) the body of the Report, relegating the rest to appendices in small print which no-one would have been expected to read, for the excellent reason that, until appendix B has done its work, no-one can quantify his recommendations or say except in the most general terms what ought to be done, and that, when appendix B has done its work, it will all be

371

obvious and as clear as daylight with no room left for argument.

KEYNES

14 February 1944

Keynes's paper brought a strong rejoinder from Sir Hubert Henderson entitled 'Lord Keynes and Employment Policy'[11] and a further note early in March 'Lord Keynes on Budgetary Considerations'. This last was the first of a long series of critical comments on the process of transition of the Steering Committee's report towards White Paper form.

As the White Paper, the product of many hands, moved towards completion, Keynes made comments on particular aspects of particular drafts.[12] However, his illness during March and April, the main period of drafting, and his concurrent concern with post-war international economic arrangements prior to Britain's agreeing to an international financial conference at Bretton Woods meant that Keynes's involvement was relatively limited, and that his drafting comments had little effect on the tone of the White Paper. The sections into which he appears to have put the most effort, those on the financial aspects of the proposals, cost of living stabilisation and the conclusion, survived only in small pieces.

Throughout the discussions, Keynes continued an intermittent exchange of memoranda with Sir Hubert Henderson, in many ways the White Paper's strongest critic. For example, on 27 March, in a memorandum called 'The Employment Policy', Henderson argued that the White Paper would result in external difficulties owing to the facts that unemployment in Britain normally came from a decline in demand for British exports and resulted in a deterioration in the balance of payments and that, in these circumstances, especially with the large sterling balances left behind by the war, budgetary policy of an unorthodox type would prove difficult to pursue. Thus, he suggested, the White Paper's ignoring of the external sector led those involved to overestimate the possibilities of a successful internal employment policy. To this memorandum, Keynes replied.

---

[11] Reprinted in *The Inter-War Years and Other Essays*.

[12] There was some pressure to get on with the White Paper at the time owing to the progress of Sir William Beveridge's private enquiry, eventually published as *Full Employment in a Free Society* (London, 1944).

To SIR WILFRID EADY *and* SIR RICHARD HOPKINS, *28 March 1944*

Sir H. Henderson has sent me a copy of his paper of March 27th on 'The Employment Policy', and I should like to comment on it briefly.

I share his pessimistic view about our prospective external financial position. I agree, therefore, that what he says under this heading, though not comfortable, is wholesome. I think it very probable that those Ministers who are mainly concerned currently with the post-war domestic front are living in a fool's paradise. Indeed, all this would form part of the theme of a paper which I hope to produce myself in the course of the next two or three weeks.[13] Nevertheless, I am sure that the advice which he bases on these prognostications should be most unhesitatingly rejected. Some of the reasons against it are briefly summarised below.

The fact that the maintenance of our exports is going to be a matter of life and death to us is surely a reason for expecting that the primary impulse to unemployment will not, and simply cannot be allowed to, come from that source. By whatever expedients may be necessary we shall have to maintain our exports. I consider that the seriousness of this position is a positive safeguard as compared with what was formerly the case. At one time we could pursue *laissez-faire* in this matter and just acquiesce in a declining trend of exports. Henceforward that will be simply out of the question. On this heading, therefore, I draw the opposite conclusion from Sir H. Henderson.

Much the same applies to the question of import restriction. I agree with him that we may very likely find ourselves in a position where this is unavoidable. It will mean that the working class will not be able to spend their earnings on imports just as they please. In other words, the position may have important resemblances to what is going on now. But the very fact that

[13] See *JMK*, vol. XXIV, pp. 33–65.

we shall have, not too reluctantly, to restrict imports when we see ourselves getting into difficulties will, of course, be very good for domestic employment, since the expenditure of earnings will necessarily be canalised to a greater extent into what we can produce at home. So here again I derive the opposite conclusion from the same premises.

Thirdly, the view, to which he obviously attaches a good deal of importance, that it will be good for our external credit if we allow large-scale unemployment to develop without attempting to use the remedies recommended in the White Paper seems to me a plain delusion. There may have been a time when that sort of policy attracted the approval of foreign financiers. Indeed, such financiers are still be found here and there. But the world changes. It will improve our external credit if we are seen tackling the problem of internal unemployment vigorously, and just to stand aside will have the opposite effect.

Finally, Sir H. Henderson does not appear to expect, or does not at any rate attach any importance to, the social and political consequences of deliberately using domestic unemployment as a remedy for external disequilibrium. Even if this policy had its advantages, it is surely obviously out of the question and might easily mean the downfall of our present system of democratic government. If, therefore, the evils which Sir H. Henderson fears develop (and I do not deny that they may), we must discover some other way out.

KEYNES

To put it briefly, Keynes's reply did not satisfy Sir Hubert Henderson. When the White Paper appeared on 26 May, three days after Keynes had defended the draft proposals for Bretton Woods in the House of Lords (*JMK*, vol. xxvi), Keynes provided a series of possible notes for the Chancellor's speech in the subsequent House of Commons discussion.

To SIR ALAN BARLOW, *15 June 1944*

WHITE PAPER ON EMPLOYMENT POLICY

You asked me if I had any notes I would care to put down for possible use in connection with the Chancellor's opening speech. Perhaps the most useful thing I can do is to note down a few points where it seems to me criticism is most likely to arise, and then endeavour to provide an answer to the criticism where I think there is one.

1. *Criticism.* It could be said that the policy is of the right kind, but that it does not go far enough; and that the concrete measures proposed are inadequate to solve the probable dimensions of the actual problem.

Answer. It is true that the figures mentioned are on the cautious side. They are not really to be taken as more than illustrative, since it is quite impracticable at the present date to quantify measures which have not yet been worked out in detail, and probably relate to a date 3 to 5 years hence at the least. It is proper, therefore, that at this stage members should concentrate on the quality of the policy and consider whether that is right. Quantities will have to be filled in at a much later date. Moreover, the figures prepared by Departments naturally take account in the main only of policies already within their knowledge. They cannot take account of future developments, which, even when they are in quite definite prospect, are still too indefinite in detail to be reduced to figures. I should add that in my own opinion—an opinion which I have frequently put forward during the course of the discussions—the White Paper considerably under-estimates the quantitative effect of the measures it actually proposes. That is only to say once again that the figures used are deliberately on the cautious side, and we have preferred to risk under-statement than over-statement.

2. *Criticism.* It could be argued that the proposals are too much of a thermostatic character; that is to say they are more

375

concerned with stabilising the level of employment than making certain that the level of employment will not only be stable, but will be high. It will be pointed out that many of the measures are of a nature accelerating this or that on one date, and balancing this by an opposite movement at some other date. Thus, the critic may say that this is a policy of having a steady level of unemployment rather than a high level of employment.

Answer. I think it has to be admitted that the actual text of the White Paper is somewhat open to this misrepresentation, but it is largely a matter of presentation. It is an implied premise that the general level of investment, etc., must be maintained at a suitable average aggregate. In considering practical measures one is of course inevitably concerned with fluctuations around the average; but it would be an entire misunderstanding to suppose that it is not a high level of employment that the Government policy is aiming at.

3. *Criticism.* It could be said that the emphasis on budgetary equilibrium is excessive, and that more stress ought to be laid on the advantages to be obtained from deliberately unbalancing the Budget in bad times.

Answer. It may be that some phrases intended to sound piously in some ears, tend to produce the wrong reaction in others; but in fact this is not a sensible criticism. As I have argued before now, the whole effect of stabilising employment will be on the receipt side to maintain the buoyancy of the revenue. Measures to increase investment and to maintain incomes will of course help the Budget on the receipt side. On the other hand it is the nature of our national accounting that practically nothing of the expenditure contemplated will fall on the normal Exchequer Budget. Neither modifications of the Social Security contributions, nor increased capital expenditure by Local Authorities and public bodies, nor inducements to Local Authorities, which will be spread over a period of years, will cost the Exchequer, narrowly interpreted in the budgetary sense, anything whatever. A forward employment policy is

therefore entirely compatible with budgetary equilibrium; and not only so, but it is in fact the best way of ensuring budgetary equilibrium. Thus the criticism boils down to a complaint that proposals for taking off taxes in bad times have been rejected. These have been rejected for pretty good and obvious reasons, of which the Chancellor is fully cognisant. The criticism only becomes plausible, I think, by mixing up these specific proposals with the general impression abroad that a budgetary deficit, as such, is the inevitable accompaniment of public works.

4. *Criticism.* Reference to interest rates in Paragraph 59 has been subjected to criticism in some quarters of the Press. It is said that whilst we are promised a continuance of the cheap money policy for the time being, we are threatened with a reversal of it at some later date.

Answer. I have never myself been able to make much sense of that paragraph. If it relates to the short-term rate of interest I am very doubtful how much it will help. If it relates to the long-term rate of interest, then the practical and fiscal difficulties in the way of significant fluctuations over a short period, have not been sufficiently examined and are, in fact, overwhelming. Perhaps the only way of making good sense of this paragraph is to hint that the second sentence about the variation of interest rates need not be taken to mean fluctuations of the long-term rate of interest over short periods, but rather a policy of aiming at a long-term equilibrium rate, which helps to maintain average capital expenditure at the right figure, even if this requires a progressive change in the standard rate from time to time, a change which is more likely to be in the downward than the upward direction. I think it is the supposed suggestion of short-term changes in the long-term rate of interest, which in my opinion is quite unworkable, which has occasioned the criticism.

5. *Criticism.* I fancy that in Sir William Beveridge's proposals, when we have them, the capital budget will take a much more prominent part. The Government will be asked whether or not

it accepts the general principle of the capital budget, and if not, why not?

Answer. It is quite true that the White Paper does not adopt the term 'capital budget' as one of its slogans; but this does not mean that the actual policy lying behind this phrase has been rejected. In fact it has been most definitely adopted. There is a particular reference in paragraph 84; but the whole of chapter 5 is really concerned with the substance of what is popularly called the 'capital budget', namely a policy of surveying the whole field of capital expenditure and then acting one way or the other in order to keep it at the optimum level.

6. *Criticism*. It may be said that the part which can be played by private enterprise is insufficiently emphasised.

Answer. There may be something in this. The difficulty of laying more stress on it at this stage is that concrete measures are not easily proposed until the time comes. The principle of influencing private enterprise to accelerate and decelerate in accordance with national policy is accepted. Here I should have thought the Chancellor might ask for concrete suggestions. He could point out that the Government had entirely accepted the advisability and desirability of this, but it is a matter on which those concerned with private enterprise are in a much stronger position than Whitehall to make useful and practicable suggestions. He could invite aid rather than claim that the White Paper has said, or attempted to say, the last word on the subject.

Generally speaking, the attitude to the White Paper which I have found to prevail in Beveridge circles, is that in fact the Government have gone a very long way forward. They appreciate that the acceptance of this type of policy is the essential thing just now, and that it must be the future which will take care of the detailed working out. Some of the sentences in the foreword are declared by some, who otherwise might be critical, to be worth more than all that follows. It seems to me that this is the line which the Chancellor can quite well accept for himself. All that the Government is attempting to lay down at this stage is the general line and purpose of policy, the basic

378

assumptions on which it proposes to act, and the general analysis of the problem which it proposes to accept as correct. The quantitative and detailed working out can only be done satisfactorily over a period of time. It would be quite premature to attempt something of that sort now and any attempt that might be made would almost certainly be proved inaccurate by events. As soon, however, as the general policy has been laid down, then it will be the duty of the various Departments and all other authorities concerned, to work out the details, with far greater particularity than has been done, or could be done, up to this point. The object of the White Paper is to choose the pattern of our future policy. This must not be confused with the technical working out of the very extensive blue prints, which will be needed to implement this policy, when it has been approved by Parliament. To the preparation of these blue prints, those concerned will of course proceed, as soon as the general line has been definitely laid down by the Government and approved by Parliament.

Finally, perhaps the Chancellor might consider whether he could safely, without entering into premature explanations about the sterling area, give some explanation of how the repayment of our war debt, in the shape of sterling balances, can prove a useful adjunct to the full employment policy. He could say, for example, that we shall clearly have to meet our accumulated liabilities to overseas creditors out of British exports. As regards some part at least of this, the rate of repayment will have to be adjusted to our capacity, and plans might well be worked out by which, in times of declining employment, particularly unemployment arising in the export trades, the position could be helped by a more rapid repayment of our obligations. This would meet the point made by some critics that if, as is very likely, the source of unemployment will sometimes be found in a declining level of exports, the existing remedies proposed do not touch the right spot.

KEYNES

After the events of the spring of 1944 which culminated in the White Paper, Keynes continued to take an interest in employment policy. At one level, his views were reflected in his correspondence. The first letter concerned Beveridge's *Full Employment in a Free Society* whose preparation had encouraged rapid publication of the official White Paper in May 1944.

From a letter to SIR WILLIAM BEVERIDGE, *16 December 1944*

I was able to borrow a copy of your book just before sailing so had a chance of looking at it on the voyage. Very warm congratulations on it. I thought it extremely good and found myself in general agreement with by far the greater part of it—as perhaps you would expect.

I was particularly fascinated by Table 18 on page 139 and the summary you give of Kaldor's appendix. If one could get people in the Treasury (and elsewhere) thoroughly to understand that table, knowing as well as you and I do just what it means and what lies behind it, and then decide which of the alternative rates they prefer or what compromise between them, and could stand an examination on this matter and themselves explain it, if necessary, to a chap like a Minister,—then, indeed, we should have made some progress.

The only weak spot in the volume was, I thought, the chapter on international implications. I do not pretend to have thought through this thoroughly, but have to confess that I did not find [it] much help to doing so. Clearly, if there is a big slump in U.S.A., the problem of maintaining employment here is made more difficult. But I looked in vain for even a shadow of an explanation of how the mysterious system known to me only by its name, namely bilateralism, is supposed to help or to prevent this situation.

My own private opinion is that you will find on further examination that bilateralism is merely a blessed word,—something that does not even begin to make practical sense. Ask some of your friends who seem bitten that way to tell you just how our relations with, to take two examples, India and Canada,

will work out under this system, if there be any such system, and what would happen in the event of a slump in U.S.A.

On a very small point, page 267, either Oliver Lyttelton was talking through his hat, which is, of course, quite possible, or you have misunderstood his meaning. The 40 per cent he speaks of must, I think, have been in tons and not in value and relates almost entirely to our having to do without our usual imports of timber, paper, iron ore and scrap. As regards timber, having cut down everything ripe in the country, that obviously cannot continue. I fancy that the iron and steel industry do not believe they can be competitive without imports of iron ore and scrap, but whether they are right about this I do not know myself...

Yours ever,

K.

P.S. Two points of criticism. No harm in aiming at 3 per cent unemployment, but I shall be surprised if we succeed. I entirely fail to understand how you can avoid making public investment a counterweight to fluctuations of private investment. But perhaps this is not really what you intend.

To M. KALECKI, *30 December 1944*

Dear Kalecki,

Thank you for *The Economics of Full Employment*[14], which reached me as it were as a Christmas present. I found it a most excellent and instructive volume. When one gets a book like this, one feels that economics is really making progress. With one qualification, mentioned below, I found it all very good indeed, and there is scarcely a thing with which I do not agree.

Your own contribution seems to me most striking and original, particularly pages 44–46; also most beautifully compressed. It is a great comfort to read something so short and so much to the point. I am very much taken with your modified

[14] (Oxford, 1944).

income-tax. It will be alleged, I am afraid, that the difficulties of transition would be excessive, since it would mean that a new business might have next to no tax to pay for years, which would appear to give it a great competitive advantage. Nevertheless, there is, I think, a good answer to this, and such criticisms, which would be certain to arise, would be based on a fallacy.

Why don't you apply it, however, to working capital also? That would have the great advantage of mitigating the effect of taxation in impairing real capital when there is an inflation and presenting windfalls when there is a deflation. Indeed, I think you can claim it as an additional merit for your plan that it goes a long way to getting over the inequities which will arise when the level of prices at the time when depreciation is allowed is different from the level of prices when the outlay was originally incurred.

Apart from your own contribution, there is hardly an article which has not something interesting and even new. The one exception I make to this, as perhaps you will have guessed, is the section on International Aspects. This seems to me a frightful muddle, which leaves the reader more in a fog and stupider than when he began. It does not even make a beginning at the basic analysis needed to tackle this rather difficult and intractable problem. I wish I had time to think it properly through myself. It is not so difficult that it is impossible to write sense about it.

On a point of detail; I have not a copy of my House of Lords speech by me, but I find it difficult to believe that I said any such thing as is attributed to me in the footnote on page 145. I think I might have been given the credit of not being quite so foolish as that! The point I intended to make, and the point which I think I probably did make, was that we should be no worse off with the Plan than without it. If, as is alleged, I said that the International Monetary Plan 'would ensure the conditions necessary to maintain full employment at home, irrespective of conditions abroad and without further direct

control of foreign trade', I must have been out of my mind. What is happening to Balogh? He has done some excellent stuff in the past, but much of what I have seen of his lately strikes me as extremely confused.

> Yours sincerely,
> [copy initialled] K

The third letter came in an exchange with T. S. Eliot.[15]

From T. S. ELIOT, *23 March 1945*

My dear Maynard,

I have no doubt that you are in San Francisco, but I cannot refrain from sending to you two copies of the *Christian News Letter*, the first containing an article on Full Employment by *Civis*—an economist who must remain anonymous, but whom I dare say you know; and the other a reply by *Metoikos* who is myself. It seems as odd to me as it will to you that I should be writing on this subject; and certainly it would have surprised me to be told that I should some day do so, at any time between the age at which I was keeping a scrap-book of the Boer War, and a month ago. But I hope that I have stuck to my own weapons on my own ground; and what I want to know is, if you ever get this and have the time to read the stuff, whether I have taken your name in vain.

But if you and Lydia are in town—I wonder if you have deserted Antoine's. I lunched there yesterday, and it seemed to me to have deteriorated appallingly.

> Yours ever,
> T. S. ELIOT

To T. S. ELIOT, *5 April 1945*

My dear Tom,

No, I am not in San Francisco, thank God, nor going to be. It should prove the biggest monkey house yet.

I am on your side against Civis.

Not long ago I was at a Conference where the Australians urged that all the Powers in the world should sign an international compact in which each undertook to maintain full employment

---

[15] The references are to *The Christian News-Letter*, 7 and 21 March 1945.

in their own country. I objected on the ground that this was promising to be 'not only good but clever'. Civis, like the Australians, takes exactly the opposite line. He thinks that we can reach the goal by promising to be 'not so much clever as good'.

It may turn out, I suppose, that vested interests and personal selfishness may stand in the way. But the main task is producing first the intellectual conviction and then intellectually to devise the means. Insufficiency of cleverness, not of goodness, is the main trouble. And even resistance to change as such may have many motives besides selfishness.

That is the first, ought-to-be-obvious, not-very-fundamental point. Next the full employment policy by means of investment is only one particular application of an intellectual theorem. You can produce the result just as well by consuming more or working less. Personally I regard the investment policy as first aid. In U.S. it almost certainly will not do the trick. Less work is the ultimate solution (a 35 hour week in U.S. would do the trick now). How you mix up the three ingredients of a cure is a matter of taste and experience, i.e. of morals and knowledge.

But, of course, the really fundamental point is what you say on your last page—and that does not go only for Christians.

Finally, there is a most definite smell of humbug about Civis, infecting his style as well as his mind.

Will you lunch with Lydia and me at Antoine's on Wednesday, April 18, at 1 o'clock?

Yours ever,
[copy initialled] M.K.

The fourth came in a comment on the Australian government's full employment proposals.

From a letter to S. G. MACFARLANE, *5 June 1945*

I expect that both of our countries incline to under-estimate the difficulty of stabilising incomes where exports play so large a part. One is also, simply because one knows no solution, inclined to turn a blind eye to the wages problem in a full employment economy.

A final letter covered more general ground, but best appears here. On his way to America for the Bretton Woods negotiations, Keynes read Hayek's *The Road to Serfdom* (London, 1944). When he reached Atlantic City, Keynes wrote to the author.

To PROFESSOR F. A. HAYEK, *28 June 1944*

My dear Hayek,

The voyage has given me the chance to read your book properly. In my opinion it is a grand book. We all have the greatest reason to be grateful to you for saying so well what needs so much to be said. You will not expect me to accept quite all the economic dicta in it. But morally and philosophically I find myself in agreement with virtually the whole of it; and not only in agreement with it, but in a deeply moved agreement.

Turning to a few special points, I think you strike the wrong note on page 69 where you deprecate all the talk about plenty just round the corner. No doubt this is partly due to my having a different view to yours about the facts. But apart from this, would it not be more in line with your general argument to urge that the very fact of the economic problem being more on its way to solution than it was a generation ago is in itself a reason why we are better able to afford economic sacrifices, if indeed economic sacrifices are required, in order to secure non-economic advantages? It seems to me that it is in this particular matter above all that the Communist doctrine is so desperately out-of-date, at least in its application to U.S.A. and Western Europe.

They ask us to concentrate on economic conditions more exclusively than in any earlier period in the world's history precisely at the moment when by their own showing technical achievement is making this sacrifice increasingly unnecessary. This preoccupation with the economic problem is brought to its most intense at a phase in our evolution when it is becoming ever less necessary.

The line of argument you yourself take depends on the very doubtful assumption that planning is not more efficient. Quite likely from the purely economic point of view it is efficient. That is why I say that it would be more in line with your general argument to point out that even if the extreme planners can claim their technique to be the more efficient, nevertheless technical advancement even in a less planned community is so considerable that we do not today require the superfluous sacrifice of liberties which they themselves would admit to have some value.

One point which perhaps you might have pressed further is the tendency today to disparage the profit motive while still depending on it and putting nothing in its place. The passage about this on page 97 is very good indeed; could not be better; but I should like to have seen this theme a little more expanded.

On the moral issue, I also find the last paragraph on page 156 extraordinarily good and fundamental.

I come finally to what is really my only serious criticism of the book. You admit here and there that it is a question of knowing where to draw the line. You agree that the line has to be drawn somewhere, and that the logical extreme is not possible. But you give us no guidance whatever as to where to draw it. In a sense this is shirking the practical issue. It is true that you and I would probably draw it in different places. I should guess that according to my ideas you greatly under-estimate the practicability of the middle course. But as soon as you admit that the extreme is not possible, and that a line has to be drawn, you are, on your own argument, done for, since you are

trying to persuade us that so soon as one moves an inch in the planned direction you are necessarily launched on the slippery path which will lead you in due course over the precipice.

I should therefore conclude your theme rather differently. I should say that what we want is not no planning, or even less planning, indeed I should say that we almost certainly want more. But the planning should take place in a community in which as many people as possible, both leaders and followers, wholly share your own moral position. Moderate planning will be safe if those carrying it out are rightly orientated in their own minds and hearts to the moral issue. This is in fact already true of some of them. But the curse is that there is also an important section who could almost be said to want planning not in order to enjoy its fruits but because morally they hold ideas exactly the opposite of yours, and wish to serve not God but the devil. Reading the *New Statesman & Nation* one sometimes feels that those who write there, while they cannot safely oppose moderate planning, are really hoping in their hearts that it will not succeed; and so prejudice more violent action. They fear that if moderate measures are sufficiently successful, this will allow a reaction in what you think the right and they think the wrong moral direction. Perhaps I do them an injustice; but perhaps I do not.

What we need therefore, in my opinion, is not a change in our economic programmes, which would only lead in practice to disillusion with the results of your philosophy; but perhaps even the contrary, namely, an enlargement of them. Your greatest danger ahead is the probable practical failure of the application of your philosophy in the U.S. in a fairly extreme form. No, what we need is the restoration of right moral thinking—a return to proper moral values in our social philosophy. If only you could turn your crusade in that direction you would not look or feel quite so much like Don Quixote. I accuse you of perhaps confusing a little bit the moral and the material issues. Dangerous acts can be done safely in a community which

thinks and feels rightly, which would be the way to hell if they were executed by those who think and feel wrongly.

Yours ever,

KEYNES

Keynes became more involved in one particular aspect of post-war employment policy early in 1945. As a result of a request from Mr Attlee asking for a paper on a post-war capital levy and a suggestion from James Meade of a wider enquiry into the measures available for reducing the post-war burden of national debt interest, the Government in January 1945 set up a National Debt Enquiry. Its members were Sir Edward Bridges (Chairman), Sir Richard Hopkins, Sir Herbert Brittain, Sir Cornelius Gregg, Paul Chambers,[16] James Meade, Professor Robbins and Keynes.

At the second to the fourth meetings of the Enquiry, on 8, 22 and 27 March 1945, Keynes gave an exposition of his theory of the relation between savings and investment, the nature of and effects of changes in the structure of interest rates and his proposals for post-war interest rate and debt management policy. For these meetings, whose summary minutes also survive, Keynes used a set of hand-written notes as the basis for his exposition.

NATIONAL DEBT ENQUIRY: LORD KEYNES' NOTES

I

Rate of interest determines equilibrium between savings and investment. If people become more willing to save and therefore willing to accept a lower rate of interest, a corresponding increase of investment takes place. Thus a greater willingness to save causes and is indispensable to more investment. Here virtue of saving. Doubt about this due to

(a) It did not fit the facts. For in this case there could never be general, as distinct from frictional and seasonal unemployment, i.e. there would always be a sufficiency of jobs offering

---

[16] Stanley Paul Chambers (b. 1904); member, Indian Income Tax Enquiry Committee, 1935–6; Income Tax Adviser to Government of India, 1937–40; Assistant Secretary and Director of Statistics and Intelligence, Board of Inland Revenue, 1942–5; Commissioner of Inland Revenue, 1942–7; Chief of Finance Division, Control Commission for Germany, British Element, 1945–7; Director, Imperial Chemical Industries, 1947.

for it would mean that whatever was earned was spent so that business as a whole would always cover its costs (subtleties here, I will not stop to explain)

(*b*) It was logically pure nonsense for $S = I$ at all rates of investment. Y either definable as $C + S$ or as $C + I$. S and I were opposite facets of the same phenomenon they did not need a rate of interest to bring them into equilibrium for they were at all times and in all conditions in equilibrium.

This was a paradox because decisions made by different people. What was the mechanism by which they were led to the same result.

The amount of savings is a function of income; the amount of income is determined by the volume of production; i.e. by the volume of consumption plus investment. Thus if investment falls, i.e. that part of output which is not consumed, off, income falls off, and therefore savings fall off and they always fall off by exactly the right amount to an exact farthing.

Now see what a reversal this meant. Instead of saving determining investment, it is much truer to say that investment determines saving—though this is in fact too simple.

War conditions make this obvious.

If this is the case, what brake is on investment and consumption exceeding what is possible.

The Price Level

Suppose decisions to consume and decisions to invest add up to more than what can be produced at the existing price level, competition causes prices to rise.

When investment $\left. \begin{array}{l} \text{falls off} \\ \text{rises} \end{array} \right\}$ profits $\left\{ \begin{array}{l} \text{fall} \\ \text{rise} \end{array} \right.$

Thus volume of investment *plus* consumption determine both the price level and the profit level and hence the volume of employment. Thus changes in prices and employment depend on the propensity to consume and the inducement to invest. Now we begin to get back to the rate of interest and to seeing how much that there was in the old theory. The rate of interest does not determine the absolute amount of savings but it is one of the influences affecting the propensity to consume. Nor does it determine the volume of investment, but it is one of the influences affecting the inducement to invest.

Experience shows, however, that whilst a high rate of interest is capable of having a dominating effect on inducement to invest, it becomes relatively unimportant at low levels compared with the expectations affecting the inducement. The optimum rate of interest depends on (*a*) how much investment one wants, (*b*) how much reward to saving is socially desirable. The monetary authorities can have any rate of interest they like. Up to the point when inflation begins (and there are, as we have seen, other efficient ways besides the rate of interest to control that), a lower rate of interest tends to increase employment. Below a certain point other considerations may begin to prevail. But see how we are standing on our heads, a fall in the rate of interest increases investment and therefore increases saving. Thus a fall in r. of i. decreases propensity to save but nevertheless increases saving.

If, after the war, we need more saving to provide more investment, we have to reduce the rate of interest up to the point of full employment. Thereafter the old rules apply we have to raise the rate of interest to prevent inflation. We come back to our first point—the previous theory is what works in conditions of domestic full employment.

After the war we may have inflationary conditions for what is probably only a short time. So here is a 3rd reason affecting our immediate policy. The object of a high rate of interest after the war will be to prevent Kindersley [National Savings] from

getting so much. The higher the rate of interest the less K will get. It is quite true that the propensity to save will be increased but the absolute amount of saving will be reduced.

But there remains another function of the r. of i. or rather of the short term of rates of interest. I have been speaking so far as if there was a single rate of interest. Obviously there is not. If you keep your money fully liquid in cash in current account, you [do not] get, and never have got, any rate at all. Obviously therefore it is not the reward of saving. You only begin to get a rate of interest in so far as you depart from liquidity. What determines the reward the individual requires to surrender his liquidity for a long or short period. In practice, of course, what some stockbroker who knows nothing about it advises him, or convention based on old dead ideas or past irrelevant experience. But assuming enlightened self-interest (which probably influences convention) it is your expectation of or a lack of expectation and temporary uncertainty about the future *changes* in the r. of i.

If it was certain that there would be no change in present short-term, longer-dated would always be best. If it was certain that they would fall rather than rise *a posteriori*.

But suppose, you just don't know and are chiefly interested in protecting yourself from possible loss in the event of your desiring liquidity, then the shorter are preferable and you need to earn a risk premium to lock yourself up longer.

Present position is a mixture of ignorance (when the C of E says cheap money is Gov^t's long-term policy, then this plays a lesser part) and of expectation of higher rate (both before the war and now again after the war). This is based on the false belief that it will be necessary to stimulate and encourage saving and that cheap money during the war has been the result of controls.

Now the authorities are only fettered in their policy if they themselves have a counter-liquidity preference. If they are indifferent about funding they can make both the short and long-term whatever they like, or rather whatever they feel to be right

having regard to possibilities of under or over-employment and other social reasons.

If, however, they are not indifferent their motivation comes into play.

Historically the authorities have always determined the rate at their own sweet will and have been influenced almost entirely by balance of trade reasons and their own counter-liquidity preference.

All four reasons are relevant. The new school rationality itself.

2. *Relation to Unemployment: The Multiplier*

Continuous injection would cause instability if people spent the whole at home

    Savings   Transfer Exp.—buying sites

    Expenditure abroad

    Effect on prices—you do not get equivalent real expenditure

Temporarily run down stocks; also new investment, not always equal new *net* investment

    Multiplier between 2 and 3

    Meade's Social Services contribution—if people spent all the relief, you would always cure unemployment by taking $1d$ off income tax.

Authorities make rate what they like by allowing the public to be as liquid as they wish.

Suppose Tr^y say half the debt must be more than 25 years off *or* floating debt must not exceed £xm then it is the public which set the rate of interest. If they require a great inducement to become so illiquid, then rates have to be higher. However it is a vicious circle, dear money provokes expectation of dearer money.

It is the technique of the *tap* issue that has done the trick.

Thus it is only if the Tr^y get rid of the Funding Complex that cheaper money is possible.

The Funding Complex originated in a situation

(*a*) when there was a fixed fiduciary issue

(*b*) Bank rate was the means of preserving the balance of payments

(*c*) the rate of interest was used as an instrument of deflation. With the abandonment of both [*sic*]^{17} it becomes completely meaningless. I am not aware of *any* argument in its favour. On the contrary it is expensive

> it is inconsistent with the avowed policy of cheap money
>
> (as Hoppy pointed out) it means losing control of the rate of interest.

Thus the reason for offering 3 per cent Savings Bonds are

(*a*) an inducement to saving as an offset to inflation (the Kindersley reason)

but chiefly

(*b*) a wider complex of the social reasons why the euthanasia of the rentier should not take place just yet.

But one offers these bonds, not in the hope that the people will subscribe, but in the hope they will not.

For the above reasons it is desirable to offer them the opportunity, but the less they accept the better and the cheaper for the Tr^y.

Now let me begin to apply this policy

I have a major proposal to make which entails the 3 per cent offer to be available but not indefinitely. It is, in fact, a proposal to return to what was ideally the perfect security. At present our offers are dominated by the Funding Complex. We offer 3 per cent Savings 1955/65 and then pretend we are worsening the

---

^{17} (*c*) was added at a later stage in the drafting.

offer by putting out ditto 1960/70 and then 1965/75. In fact each issue is worse and more expensive than its predecessor for the Tr^y. For we end by promising the continuance of 3 per cent for ten years longer. As soon as people believe that the long rate will not rise above 3 per cent and may fall below, Redemption 3 per cent become the market for they and they alone promise 3 per cent until 1986. Yesterday you could buy them at par.

The ideal security is old 2½ per cent Consols or 3 per cent local loans redeemed at the option of the Treasury at any time. We pay the stipulated interest for so long as we choose and no longer.

Probably it is going too far to start a new security on these lines. But should offer a 3 per cent Bond repayable say in 1955 or after at the Treasury's option, though I should not much mind a compulsory date of redemption if that helps the market. 1955/75 might be the best variant. One could start a new series annually, which would be available for all borrowing purposes including local loans i.e. after Jan. next the new series would be 1956 or after; or if you prefer 1956/76—thus never promising more than 30 years ahead. A permanent tap issue, with power at any time, of course, to revise the terms of the next series.

Turn next to the other end

Brittain's table How much is overseas? I think it is directly and indirectly

approx   £2,000 millions
another   2,250
public [sector] incl. B of E
    J S Banks 2,000
    ———
    6,250
Broadly speaking no one else holds any
This now costs £62.5m
    of which   £20 goes overseas

£22.5 is out of one pocket into another

£20 goes to J. S. Banks

of latter   £10 comes back in income tax

J. S. Banks are now clearly overpaid, but there is only about £m5 in it. Main point is we are worsening balance of trade by £10 as compared with reducing to $\frac{1}{2}$ per cent. Also when we come funding overseas debt, a part[icular] advantage if we can offer them a little more interest than they get now.

Thus   Bill Rate $\frac{1}{2}$ per cent

      T.D.R. $\frac{5}{8}$ as being six months

Can a use be found for Bank Rate?

How does one fill in the gap?

Short-dated securities should have a single redemption date. As they approach it they become shorts, and rise to par. Thus effective rate is higher than the nominal rate

Five year Exchequer bond $1\frac{1}{2}$

Ten year Exchequer bond 2

3

What we shall want in the future materially different from what we want now. Thus important to keep our hands free. At present we want to encourage prudence in the sense of distributing income through a man's life. When that time comes all sorts of fancy devices possibly with a counter-life insurance element in it e.g. annuities on joint lives which assume a nil rate of interest.

A deposit fund or Savings Bank for statutory charities at a suitable rate say $2\frac{1}{2}$ per cent per annum.

Also devices rewarding *de facto* illiquidity. Savings certificates and 3 per cent Defence Bonds existing types which may have a future. There is a great variety of fancy devices one could suggest. But the time for them is not yet. The essence of our interest policy should be to give a sufficient immediate reward

to saving, so not to run prematurely against public psychology, and meanwhile to keep a free hand.

Bridges said game was up when everyone understood it. In fact the game is only up when the public believe that the Treasury understands it.

The system does not depend on controls and importance of extreme short-term stability in new issue market can be exaggerated. The controls are required to prevent inflation, and are probably the wrong way to prevent it. I should like to return to controls later.

Meanwhile, as run at present, the controls are the ideal way of persuading the outside expert that the authorities do not know a thing about it. From this point of view Lord Kennet of the Dene and Mr Brittain probably impress more confidence than almost any possible alternatives.

U.S. 2 per cent for 10 years
$2\frac{1}{4}$ for 15 years

After a further discussion of his views on 5 April, Keynes submitted a summary of his proposals to the Committee.

NATIONAL DEBT ENQUIRY: SUMMARY BY LORD KEYNES
OF HIS PROPOSALS

I

1. The technique of tap issues, by which the preferences of the public rather than of the Treasury determine the distribution of the debt between different terms and maturities, should be continued into peace-time.

2. That is to say, the funding of the debt on long term should not be considered a primary Treasury interest.

3. No dogmatic conclusions should be laid down for the future about the rates of interest appropriate to different maturities, which should be fixed from time to time in the light

of experience and should pay attention primarily (*a*) to social considerations in a wide sense, (*b*) to the effects of Government policy on the market for borrowing by the private sector and on the problem of controlling and maintaining the desired rate of investment at home and abroad, and (*c*) to the burden of interest charges on the Exchequer and other funds.

4. The terms of the issues should, therefore, be such as to preserve the maximum degree of flexibility and freedom for future policy. But continuity of policy and gradualness of changes should be ensured unless in exceptional circumstances and for grave cause.

5. If, at any time, the terms offered result in an increasing preference on the part of the public for the shorter-dated securities, this need not, in general, be regarded as a cause for alarm; on the contrary, the resultant saving in the interest cost should be welcomed, and, unless the ruling conditions at the time indicate a different conclusion, opportunity should be taken for a further economy in interest cost by a lowering of short-term rates, with the result of a widening of the gap between short-term and long-term rates.

6. If, on the other hand, the terms offered result in an increasing preference for the longer-term securities, consideration should be given whether the social and administrative advantages of the existing terms outweigh the cost to the Exchequer; and, if not, the rate of interest on them should be reduced if it appears that these market conditions are likely to continue.

7. Changes in the complex of interest rates, with a view to controlling the trade cycle and to offset inflationary or deflationary trends, should not be precluded, but should affect the shorter-term, rather than the longer-term, issues, and should, as a rule, be regarded as secondary to the technique of rationing the volume, rather than altering the terms of credit by the machinery of e.g. the Capital Issues Committee by influencing the volume of bank advances.

8. The short-term rates on the Floating Debt in the hands of domestic holders should be no higher (except on the occasions when a stiffening of short-term rates is deemed to be a useful adjunct to a policy of rationing the volume of credit) than is required to give a return adequate to meet the costs of market and banking machinery.

9. A special short-term rate might be allowed on overseas funds in London, which could be the new meaning of Bank rate without any break in the continuity of tradition.

10. If the previously prevailing long-term tap rate, say 3 per cent, becomes chronically too high, in the sense that it attracts to the Exchequer an excessive volume of funds in that form and the supply of new investments expected to yield a corresponding return is running short, the rate should, in general, be reduced and other means could be sought, if necessary, to provide the social incentives and advantages which a lower rate might be inadequate to afford.

11. Such means (which would be suitable whenever the long-term rate appropriate to investment policy was too low for social purposes) might include—

(a) the further development of the existing facilities already available up to a limited amount for an individual holder, such as Post Office and Trustee Savings Bank deposits, Savings Certificates and Defence Bonds;

(b) the acceptance by the Treasury of deposits from charities and the like (perhaps including Life Offices) at a preferential rate;

(c) the offer of annuities on joint lives, calculated on the basis of a low rate of interest, but favourable to the holder in other respects, especially the principle on which the annuity is taxed.

12. If the prevailing long-term tap rate becomes chronically too low, in the sense that it encourages new capital formation on a scale tending to inflation, the rate should, in general, be raised.

13. Tap issues of short- and intermediate-term debt should

be, in general, on terms of repayment at a fixed date; and, where optional dates of redemption exist, advantage should be taken of the option to repay if, otherwise, the bonds would be standing at a premium (thus indicating that the rate of interest they carry has become too high to be appropriate to the term of maturity they have now reached), unless there appear to be special reasons at the time to the contrary. (As an immediate matter this might be put off until a 5 year Bond at $1\frac{1}{2}$ per cent is available and Treasury bills are reduced to $\frac{1}{2}$ per cent. If the $2\frac{1}{2}$ per cent stocks optionally repayable were paid off at that moment, a considerable part might be expected to go into the new five year bonds or Treasury bills, thus saving at least 1 per cent in interest.)

II

14. The progressive application of the above general principles to the situation after the end of the German war would aim at the following results:

(*a*) Bank rate to be reduced to 1 per cent and to govern the rate payable on overseas money in the hands of the Bank of England, so that this rate would remain unchanged;

(*b*) Treasury bills rate to be reduced to $\frac{1}{2}$ per cent and Treasury Deposit Receipts to carry $\frac{5}{8}$ per cent;

(*c*) Subject to action on (*b*), 5 year Exchequer Bonds at $1\frac{1}{2}$ per cent and 10 year Bonds at 2 per cent on tap, a new series to be started annually;

(*d*) 3 per cent Savings Bonds on tap, a new series to be started annually, with an option to the Treasury to repay after 10 years and with, preferably, no final maturity (or, if necessary, a fixed latest date of repayment 35 years hence);

(*e*) No change in the present terms affecting Tax Reserve Certificates, Savings Bank Deposits and Savings Certificates, (but a reduction of the rate on Defence Bonds to $2\frac{1}{2}$ per cent).

15. The justifications for maintaining the offer of a 3 per cent bond, certain for 10 years, are—

(i) that it would be premature to move to a lower rate at a time when the opportunities for investment are exceptionally abundant and before the conditions normal to the post-war epoch have been established;

(ii) that the return to the investor and the cost to the Exchequer of a 3 per cent bond is modest so long as direct taxation remains at or near its present level;

(iii) at the same time, the option of early redemption safeguards a future liberty of action;

(iv) and, if the effect is to cause a famine of bonds carrying a longer fixed term, this may help industry and Public Boards to float off bonds successfully which compete with the Exchequer issues on terms of maturity, whilst involving no immediate additional burden of interest and being sometimes appropriate to a long-lived physical investment, as well as in the rate of interest—for a counter-liquidity preference has more meaning for the private borrower than for the Exchequer.

16. There are arguments for introducing the changes piecemeal and also arguments for introducing the new debt structure as a connected whole. If it is thought better to defer major changes until (say) the occasion of an Autumn Budget and after the General Election, this position could probably be held for the next six months by withdrawing the $1\frac{3}{4}$ per cent bonds of 1950 and replacing them by 2 per cent bonds of 1955. (Or, if this is felt to be too sharp a move, 2 per cent bonds of 1953). The new 3 per cent Savings Bonds should probably be introduced, and the existing issue withdrawn, without notice, if a flood of money into the existing issue is to be avoided.

17. The new structure, if announced in an Autumn Budget, might be accompanied by the introduction of revised criteria for the New Issues Control suitable to the commencement of re-conversion and by the opening of the doors for business of the two new Finance Institutions.

KEYNES

18 April 1945

APPENDIX A: THE FLOATING AND SHORT-TERM DEBT AS AT 31 DECEMBER 1944

	£ million
Treasury bills	
Home banks, including Bank of England	620
Overseas banks*	1,175
Discount market	344
Other non-public holders	95
Total non-public	2,234
Public Departments	1,572
Total	3,806
Treasury Deposit Receipts	1,794
Ways and Means Advances	
Banking Department	59
Public Departments	588
Total	647
Total floating debt	6,247
Tax Reserve Certificates	760
Total floating and short-term debt	7,007

In round figures the total floating debt is probably held approximately as follows:

	£ million
Overseas holders (direct and indirect)	2,000
Home banks and discount market	2,000
Public Departments	2,250

* Direct holdings; other overseas debt is covered indirectly by Treasury bills and Treasury Deposit Receipts.

APPENDIX B: MATURITIES 1945–1955 (INCLUSIVE)

(Amounts shown as at 31 December 1944)

	Assuming all options exercised		Final maturities only	
	Security	£m	Security	£m
1945	2% Conversion 43/45	245	2% Conversion 43/45	245
	2½% National War Bonds 45/47	444		
	2½% Conversion 44/49	207		
	2½% National Defence Bonds 44/48	80		
1946	2½% National War Bonds 46/48	493	—	—
1947	—	—	2½% National War Bonds 45/47	444
1948	3% Conversion 38/53	302	2½% National War Bonds 46/48	493
1949	2½% National War Bonds 49/51	714	2½% Conversion 44/49	207
1950	1¾% Exchequer Bonds [£202 m at 31.3.45]	37	1¾% Exchequer Bonds 1950 (£202 m at 31.3.45)	37
1951	2½% National War Bonds 51/53	522	2½ National War Bonds 49/51	714
1952	3½% War Loan (option)	1911	—	—
	2½% National War Bonds 52/54	809	(N.B. War Loan option opposite)	
	2¾% Funding 52/57	101		
1953	—	—	3% Conversion 48/53	302
			2½% National War Bonds 51/53	522
1954	3% National Defence Loan 54/58	321	2½% National War Bonds 52/54	809
1955	3% War Loan 55/59	303	—	—
	3% Savings Bonds 55/65	713		

Total   £m7,202

APPENDIX C: LONG-TERM AND UNDATED MATURITIES

	£ million
Funding 2½% 1956/61	200
3% 1959/69	364
4% 1960/90	320
Victory 4% (average term 1962)	179 (net)
Savings 3% 1960/70	1,009
1965/75	99
Consols 2½% etc. after 1923	299
Conversion 3½% after 1961	739
Consols 4% after 1957	401
Total	3,610

APPENDIX D: SUMMARY

	£ million
Floating and short-term debt	7,007
Intermediate debt	7,202
Long-term debt	3,610
Miscellaneous non-marketable debt (N.S.C., Defence Bonds etc.)	2,954
Total	20,773

APPENDIX E: YIELDS ON TYPICAL SECURITIES AS AT 13 APRIL 1945

The yield to a holder on the same security varies according to the way in which he is taxed—i.e. whether

(a) both interest and capital gains (or losses) on redemption are exempt from tax, e.g. a charity;

(b) both interest and capital gains (or losses) on redemption are brought into taxable profit, e.g. a bank or finance house or insurance other than life;

(c) interest but not capital gains (or losses) on redemption is brought into taxable profit, e.g. ordinary business or a private holder.

The gross yield before tax is the same to holders (a) and (b) if it is assumed that income tax is unchanged throughout the term of the bond. The gross equivalent yield, as compared with the yield on a security selling at its redemption price, to holders (b) and (c) depends on assumptions about the future rate of tax.

In the following table the gross equivalent yield is calculated on the assumption of a standard rate of tax at 10s throughout the term of the bond. If income-tax falls through time, the average yield over the whole period to holders (b) will prove lower than in the table on bonds standing above par, and the

403

yield on bonds standing below par will be higher; whilst the opposite will be true in the case of holders (*c*).

The earliest date of redemption is assumed when the price is at or above par and the latest date when below par.

(Approximate figures)

	(*a*) and (*b*)	(*c*)
Optional date of redemption 1945 or earlier	negative	negative
Optional date of redemption 1946 or earlier	$1\frac{1}{8}$	negative
Years to run:		
three	2	$1\frac{1}{4}$
four	2	$1\frac{1}{2}$
five (current tap issue)	$1\frac{3}{4}$	$1\frac{3}{4}$
six	$2\frac{1}{4}$	2
seven	$2\frac{3}{8}$	$2\frac{1}{8}$
nine	$2\frac{5}{8}$	$2\frac{3}{8}$
ten*	$2\frac{5}{8}$	$2\frac{3}{8}$
fourteen	3	3
twenty (current tap issue)	3	3
forty-one (Redemption Stock)	3	3
Undated (old $2\frac{1}{2}$% Consols)	3	3

Sir Richard Hopkins was then asked to prepare a report for the Chancellor on cheap money using Keynes's proposals as a basis. This report, after further discussion, went to the Chancellor on 15 May 1945.

At its other meetings, the Enquiry discussed capital issues control, issues control, the problem of an externally caused deflation,[18] financial policy and employment policy—where it appears from the summary note that Keynes

* These are 3% stocks with a final date of maturity 14 years hence. There is no stock with a final date 10 years hence. N.W.B. with a final date 9 years hence yield £2 6s 6d and £2 3s 4d to the two classes of holders.

[18] Keynes remarked, according to the minutes, that the risk of this eventuality made Beveridge's target of 3 per cent unemployment too ambitious, as the authorities would be unable to offset completely the loss of external markets through internal expansion and devaluation was unlikely to prove completely effective. Therefore, he emphasised in serious situations the role of import controls, official encouragement of the consumption of domestically produced goods, and, as a last resort, state trading and bilateralism.

was still attracted by Lerner's notion of functional finance—post-war anti-inflation policy,[19] capital taxation or 'capital levity' as Keynes called it, and capital budgeting. This last subject brought another memorandum from Keynes, along with a memorandum from Sir Herbert Brittain entitled 'Proposals for a Capital Budget'

NATIONAL DEBT ENQUIRY: THE CONCEPT OF A CAPITAL BUDGET (MEMORANDUM BY LORD KEYNES)

1. This question is essentially a question of *presentation*. It does not enable anything to be done which could not be done without it by means of the existing technique and in conformity with the existing form of the Exchequer Accounts. Nevertheless presentation may be of great importance by bringing out clearly the relevant criteria for policy and by high-lighting what it is desirable that Parliament and the public, and also officials, should understand.

2. The name has been used for at least four distinct concepts, all of which deserve examination, namely—

(i) a clearer segregation of capital items paid for out of, and received into, the Exchequer and a budgetary forecast of them for the coming year;

(ii) a compilation and budgetary forecast of *all* capital expenditure under *public* control, including local authorities and public boards;

(iii) a compilation and budgetary forecast of capital expenditure for the economy of the country as a whole, including the private sector;

(iv) as a temporary convenience during the post-war transitional period what might be termed a separate *remanet* budget to deal with items of Exchequer receipts and outgoings which do not properly belong to the income and expenditure of the current year.

[19] Here Keynes placed great emphasis on controls and reductions in taxation. Keynes advocated tax cuts because he believed that the addition to demand would not be that large as compared to their psychological effect on individuals' saving behaviour.

3. I will call these respectively (i) Exchequer Capital Budget, (ii) Public Capital Budget, (iii) Investment Budget, (iv) Remanet Budget.

4. It is important to emphasise that it is no part of the purpose of the Exchequer or the Public Capital Budget to facilitate deficit financing, as I understand this term. On the contrary, the purpose is to present a sharp distinction between the policy of collecting in taxes less than the current non-capital expenditure of the state as a means of stimulating *consumption*, and the policy of the Treasury's influencing public capital expenditure as a means of stimulating *investment*. There are times and occasions for each of these policies; but they are essentially different and each, to the extent that it is applied, operates as an *alternative* to the other.

5. An Exchequer Capital Budget should cover both the capital expenditures which are now entered 'above the line' and included in the estimates to be paid for out of the normal Budget, and also the capital expenditures which are now entered 'below the line' and are financed by loans specially authorised for the purpose. Sir H. Brittain's analysis indicates that the former comprise at present a number of miscellaneous items which are individually small, adding up to £12m in 1936 and £21m in 1945 on Civil Votes; whilst the latter consist almost exclusively of Post Office capital expenditures. (In 1936 there were quasi-capital items of £60m on Defence Votes, a corresponding item in 1945 being, of course, outside the scope of reasonable calculation.) Sir H. Brittain explains that this is in conformity with the existing criterion for charging 'below' or 'above' the line according as the expenditure does or does not bring in a cash return in subsequent years. This seems to me wrong. The criterion should be whether the real return in meal or malt is spread over a period. If so, it is reasonable that the charge on revenue should be similarly spread. Moreover the present criterion leads to meaningless anomalies. A new G.P.O. is charged 'below', a new Somerset House 'above'. A capital

contribution to school buildings is 'above' in the Exchequer Accounts and is paid for out of Revenue, and is 'below' in the Local Authority Accounts and is paid for out of loans. The cost of a road is 'above', of a railway is 'below'. And so on. (I am not burdening this paper with a discussion of the treatment of defence expenditure, especially on ships, which presents a special problem, to the solution of which we were finding our way before the war.) Hitherto the matter has been, it appears, of small importance. But it may not be so in future. Forestry, national parks, contributions from the Exchequer to the capital costs of town and country planning etc. will present larger-scale issues than formerly. The existing practice is an unnecessary deterrent to capital expenditure. With a full employment policy, we should not be biassed as between two useful capital projects because one will bring in a direct cash return and the other a social or indirect cash return. In both cases, of course, the subsequent service of the loan should be charged on the Revenue Budget and the income from the investment (if any) brought in as Sundry Revenue; the Sinking Fund element, whether in respect of the dead-weight or productive debt should be carried down as a contribution from the Revenue Budget to the Capital Budget, to provide finance for new investment or to reduce debt in the event of the Exchequer Capital Budget showing a net reduction of central borrowing.

6. The Exchequer Capital Budget should comprise *inter alia* such items as the following:

(i) the surplus or deficit of the Unemployment, Health and other similar extra-budgetary funds;

(ii) the growth or loss of funds in the hands of the N.D.C. and other public accounts;

(iii) changes in the fiduciary issue;

(iv) the net receipts of the Post Office and Trustee Savings Banks;

(v) net receipts (or repayments) of public debt held by the private sector;

(vi) net receipts (or repayments) of overseas Government loans;

(vii) the profits of the E.E.A.;

(viii) sinking Funds charged to the Exchequer Revenue Budget;

(ix) new capital expenditure on Exchequer Account;

(x) advances to the Local Loans Fund. (But see below §§14 *et seq.* the transitional arrangements perhaps convenient in Stage III.)

7. It has been the practice of this country hitherto to entrust most capital expenditure of a public character to Local Authorities or Public Boards. I am not aware of any intention to change this. If so, the significance of the Exchequer Capital Budget will be incomplete if taken in isolation, and it should be regarded rather as an item required in building up the Public Capital Budget, which should also comprise the capital expenditure of all bodies, boards, authorities and institutions which are scheduled as belonging to the public, as distinct from the private, sector of the national economy.

8. It is an integral part of the Government's full employment policy, as I understand it, that some authority will exist (the Treasury I hope) charged with the duty of examining and reporting on the state of the Public Capital Budget as a whole, not merely after the event but also prospectively. At one time I had conceived that this should be the task of a semi-independent statutory authority to be called the National Investment Board. But with modern developments of policy, decisions on such matters have become so much a part of the Government's economic programme as a whole that they should not be dissociated from the Chancellor of the Exchequer as the responsible Minister and his official Department.

9. Nevertheless, in this event the Treasury will have to be as self-conscious and publicly explicit as a National Investment Board would have been. The best means of public presentation and parliamentary discussion will no doubt be discovered

ambulando. The summary figures of the previous calendar year will, of course, be incorporated in the annual statistical Budget White Paper. But it will, I think, overload the Budget proper if the attempt is made to present this issue to Parliament at the same time as the Revenue Budget. I suggest that the Public Capital Budget should be presented to Parliament more on the lines of the Departmental Estimates. An estimate of the net public investment of the coming financial year might be presented as early as possible in the calendar year, accompanied with a statistical White Paper setting out the realised results of the previous calendar year. (It would be advisable on all grounds—for we must watch the trend closely—to keep the statistics in the Treasury month by month on the basis of monthly returns by all the investing public bodies to be delivered within a week of the end of the month, so that a sufficiently accurate summary of the past year should be available very soon after its close.)

10. The Public Capital Budget should comprise such items as the following: (i) the receipts and expenditure of the Exchequer Capital Budget; (ii) sinking funds and amortisation of Local Authorities; (iii) ditto of other Boards etc. included in the public sector; (iv) the gross new investment of the public sector not already included in the Exchequer Capital Budget.

11. As one of the principal purposes of the Public Capital Budget will be to balance and stabilise the Investment Budget for the national economy as a whole, the need for current up-to-date information about net investment in the private sector, with a separate division for changes in stocks, is a necessary corollary of or (if you prefer) prolegomenon to the above. I suggest that the continuous current collection both of the statistics of current performance and of prospective plans by the private sector should be entrusted to the Ministry of Trade and Production (if that is to be its name), which would be charged with the duty of passing on absolutely up-to-date information to the Capital Budget division of the Treasury. The

best and latest information on this aspect would, of course, be reported to Parliament along with the estimates of the Public Capital Budget.

12. In the years in which the Capital Budget division in the Treasury found itself in a position to report to the Chancellor that the prospective private investment coupled with the prospective public investment which it was not convenient to retard or postpone looked like being fully adequate or excessive, the Chancellor would recommend in his Revenue Budget an increase in the Sinking Fund towards the extinction of the dead-weight debt. And contrariwise.

13. It is contemplated here that the annual amortisation of the productive debt would always be charged to the Revenue Account of the authority responsible, including the Exchequer in the case of projects financed out of the Exchequer Capital Budget. It would also be a good plan, I suggest, to include in the Revenue Budget a modest normal contribution, say £25,000,000 a year, towards the extinction of the dead-weight debt, or rather, as I would prefer to put it, towards the conversion of the dead-weight debt into productive debt. This would mean, of course, that the normal programme of the Public Capital Budget would have to aim at providing sufficient total investment to cover the dead-weight Sinking Fund of the Revenue Budget, in addition to current amortisation, public and private, and to the current net savings of the private sector. This would have the advantage of making it possible to offset a modest unforeseen disturbance of investment-savings equilibrium by reducing the normal sinking fund to zero, avoiding to this extent the necessity of budgeting for an actual Revenue deficit. This seems to me to be the correct doctrine of the Sinking Fund when taken in conjunction with a full employment policy. In fact, on the assumption that the outlets for public investment are not yet nearly saturated and that we are, for the time being at least, more concerned with increasing the capital equipment of the nation than with raising the immediate standards of private

consumption, the larger the 'normal' Sinking Fund of the Revenue Budget the greater will be the latitude possessed by the Treasury for quickly offsetting unforeseen disturbances without budgeting for an actual deficit. One's qualms about pushing this very far, pending further experience, are due to doubts about the prospective outlets for public investment for more than a short period ahead and to the possibility that more durable results (in stabilising full employment) may be attained by allowing a fairly high priority to creating habits of more liberal standards in private consumption.

14. There remains the Remanet Budget, which is a question of purely temporary interest and importance. The point is that various large items, involving both receipts and expenditure, arising out of the liquidation of the finance of the war, will be in danger for the first three years or longer after the war of so swamping the normal Revenue Budget as to obscure the relevant criteria of a permanent character. There may result, through the difficulty of sufficient clarity of exposition, a serious lack of rational discussion and understanding of the critical problems of the post-war Revenue Budgets. This might be avoided by setting up an extra-budgetary *War Liquidation Fund* to which such items would be credited or debited.

15. There will be room for legitimate differences of opinion where to draw the line. But the following are some examples of items which might be suitable candidates for such a Fund:
Receipts

(i) Disposals of Government-owned stocks of commodities (including, e.g., the new wool disposals body).

(ii) Ditto of military surplus.

(iii) Ditto of lend-lease material whether received freely or covered by a loan.

(iv) Receipts from the expiring or diminishing E.P.T.

(v) Profits emerging from various war-time sub-funds of Departments, particularly Ministry of Food and Ministry of Supply.

(vi) Profits of the E.E.A.

(vii) Receipts from assistance towards the reduction or cancellation of overseas war debt.

(viii) The proceeds of overseas loans required to balance the international payments account in Stage III.

Expenses

(i) Refund of E.P.T. post-war credits

(ii) Refund of income tax post-war credits

(iii) Refund of E.P.T. to cover deficiencies and end-of-war adjustments

(iv) War gratuitites

(v) Demobilisation expenses overseas

(vi) War Damage compensations

(vii) The subscription of capital to the Bretton Woods Plans.

16. The above items will amount altogether to some thousands of millions sterling and are, no doubt, incomplete. Some of the above might be carried direct to the Exchequer Capital Budget (e.g. (viii)) and others might be carried direct to the extinction of domestic debt. Indeed, the difficulty of drawing the line might make it convenient to amalgamate the Remanet Budget with the Exchequer Capital Budget. The point is to exclude as many as possible of these large abnormal items from the normal Revenue Budget, with a view to getting into good habits about balancing the latter on permanent lines at as early a date as possible.

17. I take this opportunity to remind the Committee what is in danger of being overlooked that, if we have to raise abroad as Exchequer receipts the large sums which we are anticipating as necessary to cover the adverse balance of trade in Stage III, it is quite certain (even after allowing for the proposed centralisation of the borrowings of Local Authorities) that there will be no net borrowing by the Treasury on the domestic market during Stage III, and even a large reduction of market Government debt is quite probable. This probability is increased by the prospect that the bulk of small savings will, no doubt,

continue to reach the Treasury. We may all of us have been rather short-sighted about this. Large overseas loans on the anticipated scale, unaccompanied by corresponding investment, are liable to produce a colossal deflationary pressure. The Investment Budget in Stage III will have to be large enough to absorb the whole of the excess of the receipts over the expenses set forth in §15 above as well as current savings and amortisation. Otherwise severe unemployment is bound to result. Just as overseas investment helps to maintain employment, so equally overseas borrowing for consumption purposes serves to impair it. This is one reason why it is dangerous to delay in relaxing control of the capital issue market. At present it beats me to see how the market is to be nursed back quick enough into sufficient absorptive power. The remedy may have to come through applying to the borrowing of all public and semi-public bodies the centralised technique which is to be used henceforward for Local Authorities.

19. I would urge on the Committee that enough has been said above to prove the tremendous importance, which I began by emphasising, of a method of presentation, both to officials and to Ministers and to Parliament, which facilitates clear thinking on matters at the same time so complicated and so novel and yet so essential to the effective implementation of accepted policies.

20. I believe that the announcement by the Chancellor of a presentation on the above lines would have an enormous public success, since it would greatly increase confidence that the Full Employment policy is intended seriously. Moreover under cover of the novel presentation it might be possible to get through some wholesome matter which otherwise would have to face stiffer opposition.

KEYNES

21 June 1945

The Enquiry discussed Keynes's and Brittain's papers at its last meeting on 28 June 1945. It agreed on the desirability of retrospective publication each March of surveys of total national investment on a calendar year basis, on the desirability of preparing forecasts of capital expenditure (but not their publication), on the desirability of annual and quarterly surveys of government capital expenditure, with forecasts appearing in the Budget Statement, and on the need for changes in the Budget accounts with the inclusion of items under capital ('below the line') expenditure depending on their size and benefits over a period of years and with a separate unpublished wartime remanet account. Finally the Enquiry agreed that the sinking fund should not exceed £25 million per annum for the time being.

Keynes's final contribution to discussions of post-war economic management came somewhat later. Richard Kahn found the following notes on his table at Tilton after his death in April 1946. They were circulated within the Treasury.

POST-BUDGET REFLECTIONS (LORD KEYNES)

The level of prices and wages and the cost of the Stabilisation Policy the key to the situation.

External prices already round 200.

Wholesale prices (largely governed by external prices) 175 (Feb).

Wages 160

Cost of living 131 (when stabilisation policy began in 1941 cost of living 128

wages 122).

A recent calculation in *The Economist* puts normal Budget expenditure in (say) 1948 at £2,750 million or rather more than £1,000 million reduction on this year. Would anyone put it at less?

Colin Clark's 25% argument—pseudo-scientific; but with some sound empirical basis.

This indicates a net national product of £12,000 million (since expenditure would also rise somewhat).

W. P. puts last year at £8,500 million at a price level of about 150 for consumption and probably higher for investment.

If this was revised to 200 income would be by 1948 or 9 say £11,500 which is within striking distance of the target.

I venture to predict that the Budget will never be balanced except at a prices and wages level in the neighbourhood of 200.

I urge that, very secretly and behind the scenes, we should be preparing for a movement in that direction.

It will not interfere with foreign trade, since almost all other countries are in the same boat. It may even help by preventing the terms of trade moving against us. Indeed by that time external prices are likely to be well above 200 (which will facilitate payment of external debt) and the subsidy might easily approach £500 million. Prices are going to break loose everywhere in the world.

If allowing the cost of living to rise causes some inevitable repercussion on wages, this will not matter, since there is room for it. Moreover wages, as experience clearly shows, will rise anyhow.

During 1947 cost of living should be allowed to rise gradually to 150, first of all by withdrawing as many individual subsidies as possible and concentrating on a few articles and then by reducing it on the remaining articles. Wages should, of course, not be *encouraged* to go up. But, naturally, we must expect that this will be used as a pretext for some rises. Our wage policy should be to get the wage rises *in the right places*. One of the advantages of the proposed policy is that it allows a margin for this.

Publicly we should talk in terms of a price level of 150. Any prices or wages in excess of this should require special justification, e.g.

in the case of prices external movements or justifiable wage increases

in the case of wages increased productivity (as indicated by continuous census of production)

a low pre-war base

or relatively low net advantages as indicated by unpopularity of an industry.

It is better to reduce subsidies and reduce taxation than to increase subsidies and increase taxation. And that is the choice before us. A gradual and controlled rise—or a collapse of policy and a crisis.

I suggest that these reflections should be remitted to the Budget Committee for study, both from the statistical and from the policy angle.

STATISTICAL FORECASTS

Direct estimation of investment ex post and comparison with forecast

At present you can tell only by direct estimate what investment will be next year, but not what it was last year.

Also of depreciation* which has become very arbitrary.

Also work in progress.

Inland Revenue with Hollerith cases.

Continuous censuses of production and distribution.

Collaboration with firms on investment forecasts and output forecasts generally.

Concentration on chronicles and let Habakkuk wait. Fortunately we have—probably three years for improving the statistical apparatus.

For investment forecasting is primarily needed against a deflation.

No harm in some fighting for supplies, which will be dealt with at the physical, not the overall end, in an inflation phase.†

Physical controls in the over-investment phase.

Overall programming in the underinvestment phase.

Thus Habakkuk is not urgent.

---

* It is net investment (including work in progress) which comes out as a residue. But it is gross investment which will be directly estimated. Depreciation is what is deducted in reckoning profit.

† Investment in excess of physical supply cannot happen. Investment in deficit of physical supply can happen.

Post-Budget Reflections

I

We have been using 'inflation' to mean pressure of demand to raise prices above current cost of production, e.g. in Budget Speech. Quite a useful practice. But inflation of this sort a temporary factor, I think, and one which we have learned to keep under good control.

The real question is the price level which is going to be determined by costs of production, internal and external. If the costs can't be controlled, it is futile and dangerous to attempt to exercise any general control over the price level. Subsidies in special cases have to be kept in strict control and in reasonable relation to the general price level. This does not mean that it is necessarily a mistake to use taxes *plus* subsidies—e.g. to make bread and milk cheap, tobacco and beer dear. But a prudent policy needs to be based on a clear view as to what the general price level, as determined by costs and apart from temporary scarcities, is likely to be.

II

Current and prospective price levels. Very likely imports 250, wages 175.

III

Key position of this in Budget estimates: 2,750 is 32 per cent of 8,500.

An increase of 25 per cent would make income 11,000.

But expenditure would also rise, though not so much, and revenue would rise more.

417

Direct Taxes

Capital Tax ½ per cent.

Corporation Tax on all Schedule D profits 3s.

Earnings: personal tax on income earned 5s deducted at source in excess of £2 a week.

Allowances applied, first to social security contributions.

Personal Tax

At present	1,000		500	
earned	166		83	
	834		417	
Personal	110		110	
	724		307	
			115	27
3s on	50	7. 10s		
6s on	65	19. 10s	182	81
9s	609	270		108
		297		

An initial notional book value of all real estate and assets.

This book value to be written down appropriately for depreciation and scrapping and added to by new investment in the business quinquennial valuation.

The initial value to be declared by the taxpayer. He cannot claim more on compulsory acquisition. His depreciation allowance cannot be calculated on more.

New investment to be exempt from Corporation Tax.

In lieu of N.D.C. Capital tax ½ per cent, Interest Tax 8s 6d deducted at source.

Profits tax 6s in the £ deducted at source.

All money reinvested in business exempt from profits tax but
no depreciation allowances hereafter.

Standard earnings tax 5s.

Surtax on excess of net incomes over £1,000 ranging from 1s
to 15s.

Allowances on deficiency of net incomes below £1,000.

A capital tax on real estate and business assets.

An initial book value for different classes of asset.

A depreciation writing off allowance for each class.

A realised profit and loss allowance on disposal.

No depreciation on allowance on outside assets.

Investment in business exempt from profits tax (on previous
investment depreciation as at first).

The initial book value on depreciable assets to be the book value
as now accepted by I.R.

Value of real estate not subject to depreciation to be declared
at 25 times Schedule A.

PART III
CONCLUSION

Chapter 6

LAST THINGS

On 11 June 1945 Mr Rowe-Dutton proposed 'a full enquiry into the future of our silver coinage'. Keynes supported it, emphasising that it should be secret to avoid alarming American silver interests.

When the report of the enquiry emerged in October 1945, it was forwarded to Keynes in Washington. His reply, written at the end of the Loan Negotiations drew the following comment from E. Rowe-Dutton.

To SIR HERBERT BRITTAIN, *12 December 1945*

I attach letter from Keynes about the silver proposals, together with copies which you may well like to send to the other members of the party.

You will see that he raises two questions of definite importance, namely the use of 5/- notes, and the speed at which silver might return from circulation.

The remainder of the letter is an incredibly brilliant piece of fireworks when you consider that it was written under the strain of the conclusion of the Anglo-American Loan Agreement.

E.R.D

Keynes's comments ran as follows.

To E. ROWE-DUTTON, *6 December 1945*

My dear Rowe-Dutton,

Silver

We have all studied with great interest your letter of November 14th and its enclosures. This reply is after discussion with Brand, Lee and Harmer and represents our collective views.

1. We all like the idea of the cupro-nickel coinage, especially for the small denominations. But we are none of us convinced, or, indeed, in the slightest degree impressed, by the arguments in paragraph 10 against the five shilling note. We can understand that you might not gain much by this in the immediate future

if it presents greater labour difficulties than the proposed new coinage. But with normal conditions we all believe that the case for a five shilling note is overwhelming. Is there any other country in the world which has not been able to overcome without, so far as one is aware, any complaint whatever, the difficulties mentioned in that paragraph? After living here with dollar bills, honestly we are left gasping at this passage, which we cannot but regard as a product of conservatism rather than experience.

We much hope, therefore, that so far as the long term policy is concerned, the five shilling note will not be given up. If this was combined with cupro-nickel for the small denominations, we might have the ideal system; though this would not be fully attained until the penny had also been dealt with by reduction of its preposterous size and weight.

2. There seems to be a serious discrepancy between the estimate in paragraph 13 that we shall eventually recover 200 million ounces of silver from circulation and the prediction that we can only rely on getting this back at the rate of five million ounces a year. In other words, it will take forty years to withdraw the existing silver. One can easily believe that a long time might elapse before the last coin had found its way home; but one would have supposed that in the early years the rate of recovery should enormously exceed five million ounces.

3. The answer to the question whether the above prediction about only recovering five million ounces a year is correct is very important. If it is correct, the proposed new move would enable us to economise in the use of new silver in currency, but it will not make any sufficient contribution within the next five years to our restoring the 80 million ounces which we have to return to the U.S.A. during that period. If, on the other hand, as we should have thought ought to be the case, we can recover the greatest part of the 80 million ounces during that period, then our tactical position will be much stronger. We would add in this context that the use of five shilling notes as well as the cupro-

nickel coins for small denominations might greatly accelerate the return of half-crowns and florins if, as may well prove to be the case, the notes are popular.

4. As regards timing, we think it would be unwise to disregard the possible reactions of the silver Senators when the measure is introduced. We should prefer, therefore, not to make the change until the new loan is past Congress, a date which we now hope will be not later than next March. Even if the change were made immediately thereafter, an unfavourable impression might be created inasmuch as critics might say that the British had waited until the credit had been passed by Congress before introducing a change which was deterimental to important American interests. Therefore we think it would be best – despite the difficult outlook for silver supplies – to postpone the change for, say, four to six months. Admittedly this delay will involve a continued drain of the silver to coinage and would be open to the objections mentioned in paragraph 19 of the report. We do not think that the same reasons for so long a delay apply with equal strength to India. From a political standpoint, therefore, it might well be better to let India take the first step towards demonetisation and so receive the first brunt of criticism from the silver interests in this country.

Brand hopes that a decimal system will be brought into existence as soon as possible. He feels that what we now have might have been all very well when the pound sterling was thought to have a sort of divine character and was untouchable. But those days have passed and it seem absurd that we should lag behind the rest of the world for many decades before making such a necessary change so that we seem to run with the 'traditional' countries like Saudi Arabia and Abyssinia, who can't change at all. What an immense saving in time, trouble and expense would be made. Personally I have no answer to all this but confess to some emotions of duo-decimal conservatism. I have always thought that the decimalisation which the Aryans brought in was a trifle vulgar and that the Sumerian origins of

our civilisation were more distinguished when they duo-decimalised the fundamental concepts for measuring time and money which they invented. Bradbury who, like me, had no answer to the arguments of the decimaliser, used to say that he could always defeat them by asking the question whether they proposed to decimalise the pound sterling or the penny. In other words, would the pound remain as it is and the penny be altered, or vice versa? By this means he considered the decimalisers would be divided into equal halves and be defeated by the fact that the sumerian fundamentalists would always include at least one-third of the population.

Your sincerely,

KEYNES

Over and above the arrangements for Savannah (*JMK*, vol. XXVI) and his involvement in budgetary policy, Keynes did not drop completely out of Treasury activities after his return from the Loan negotiations in Washington. However, he did try to keep his commitments down, 'to slip out of the Treasury, if not suddenly, at least steadily' as he told Lord Halifax on 1 January (*JMK*, vol. XXIV, p. 628). He also raised the possibility with Sir Richard Hopkins at the same time as writing to Sir Edward Bridge from Tilton.

To SIR EDWARD BRIDGES, *6 January 1946*

My dear Edward,

I am coming back to London tomorrow and will be in the Treasury in the course of the day. I shall be grateful if the next two or three days you could give me time for a talk about what happens next. I am pretty clear that we ought to take advantage of the break which has happened so to arrange that I do not come back any more to the Treasury for whole-time work. Experience shows that half-and-half arrangements are not at all easy, at any rate for any length of time, but that is what I should like to talk over with you thoroughly before one finally makes up one's mind.

After a little more than a fortnight here, I am feeling completely recuperated in health. The time has not been free from work, since after four months there was an immense amount of accumulations, mostly non-Treasury, to clear up. But at least one has been free from *worry*, and that is what really matters.

Yours ever,
[copy not signed or initialled]

One of his first contributions of the new year did not, in the end, appear until after his death in the June 1946 issue of the *Economic Journal*. The article had its origins in a paper entitled 'Will the Dollar be scarce?' which he prepared with F. E. Harmer and David McCurrach[1] in Washington the previous October for communication to London. On his return, Keynes, with official permission, worked it up into a full-dress piece for the *Journal*, sending it to Roy Harrod, the editor, at the end of January with a request that it not appear before the Loan was through Congress. In the end, Congressional delays meant that it missed the March issue of the *Journal*, but the delays also allowed him to revise the article in the light of additional statistics and comments from Harry White and David McCurrach.

From the Economic Journal, *June 1946*

THE BALANCE OF PAYMENTS OF THE UNITED STATES

The recent proposals for financial and economic agreements with the United States have raised doubts in many quarters on two largely distinct matters. The first relates to our capacity to achieve an adequate increase in the volume of our exports. The second relates to America's capacity to accept goods and services from the rest of the world on a scale adequate to secure a reasonable equilibrium in her overall balance of payments. Both these issues relate to the position of ourselves and of the United States respectively in relation to the rest of the world taken as

---

[1] David F. McCurrach, company director and chairman of the Alliance Trust Company; seconded by the Bank of England to Washington.

a whole. On the assumption, however, that the International Monetary Fund and other supporting arrangements will be successful in establishing multilateral clearing of current transactions over a wide area, bilateral equilibrium will be achieved between the United Kingdom and the United States, if the two conditions are fulfilled that British exports of goods and services to the rest of the world as a whole reach an appropriate level and that American imports of goods and services from the rest of the world as a whole reach an appropriate level. If these conditions are satisfied, there will be no necessity for a strictly bilateral balance between the two countries taken in isolation.

This article is solely concerned with the available statistics relating to the second of these two problems—namely, the balance of payments of the United States. It is dangerous in this, as in many other contexts, to project pre-war statistics into the so greatly changed post-war world. But some current conclusions on the matter may be based too much on general impressions and too little on an examination of the details, with the result that the problem is not seen in the right perspective, that the orders of magnitude involved are not rightly apprehended, and, as a result, that the difficulties ahead of us are exaggerated. The object of this article is not to make definite predictions, but to bring out some of the data which are required for an informed judgement, as the prospects of the future gradually unfold themselves.

Let us begin with the figures of the pre-war position. The favourable balance of the U.S. year by year from 1930 to 1938 on all current transactions ran as follows:

	$ million		$ million
1930	+735	1935	−156
1931	+175	1936	−218
1932	+159	1937	− 31
1933	+108	1938	+967
1934	+341		

Thus it is a mistake to suppose that the United States had an enormously favourable balance on current account. If the nine-year period is broken up into three-year periods, the average favourable balance works out at $356 million, $98 million and $239 million. The average for the whole period—namely, $231 million—is very much the same as it was for the latest triennium. Moreover, if the first and last years of the period are left out, it will be seen that during the intervening seven years, which included the slump, the United States current balance of trade broke about even. Even with the inclusion of the first and last years the average favourable balance of the United States on current account before the war was much less than the favourable balance earned by the United Kingdom (at a much lower price level) at the time when we were building up our overseas investments; and it was about the same as our own favourable balance as recently as 1923–9, when our own average surplus was $374 million. The general impression to the contrary is based partly perhaps on the figure of the most recent pre-war year—namely, 1938—but mainly, I think, on a confusion between current movements and capital movements. The pressure on the rest of the world from 1930 onwards was due to a large-scale capital movement from Europe to America being superimposed on a substantial, but not unwieldy, balance on current account. The serious consequences to the rest of the world flowed from the anomaly of a country with a substantial favourable balance being simultaneously the recipient of invesible funds from abroad. Most countries, however, have now armed themselves with precautionary powers against the repetition of undesirable and useless capital movements of this character. The influence of the Bretton Woods plan is, of course, against a future repetition of this experience. Surely we now have means to avoid it.

Nor is it the case that in times of depression in America imports always fall off on a great scale relatively to exports. The statistics of the decade before the war show that, on the whole,

Table I. *Indices of U.S. industrial production, imports and exports* (1935–39 = 100)

	1930	1931	1932	1933	1934	1935	1936	1937	1938	1939
Industrial production	91	75	58	69	75	87	103	113	89	109
Imports	129	89	56	61	70	87	102	130	83	98
Exports	134	85	56	59	74	80	86	117	108	110

Notes. Figures for industrial production are the Federal Reserve Board unadjusted index (1935–39 = 100). The import and export indices have been calculated on the same basis.

industrial production, exports and imports tend to move together. The common opinion of this matter is based too exclusively on the experience of 1938 (1939, being a war year for the rest of the world, cannot be used as a basis for the argument) compared with 1936 and 1937. The movements are shown in Table I.

All that can be said on the other side is that these figures do not show what would happen in a period of slump in the United States and of full employment in the rest of the world. This, however, involves an *a priori*, not a statistical, argument, which would lead us on to the question just what difference in such circumstances the proposed financial and economic agreements would make. I am limiting myself here to the statistical evidence and to conclusions purporting to be based on it.

Perhaps the most mistaken and most prevalent delusion relates, however, to the creditor position of the United States to-day in relation to the rest of the world. It is commonly believed that the end of the war has left the United States in a strong creditor position, in addition to her large gold reserves. How many people are aware that apart from her gold holdings, which do not, of course, represent an undischarged claim on the rest of the world, the United States was a debtor country on balance at the end of 1945? The details are as follows:—

Table II. *International investment position of the United States, 31 December 1945**

	$ billion
Assets (United States investments abroad)	
Long-term†	
Direct	7·0
Foreign dollar bonds	1·9
United States Government‡	2·7
Miscellaneous private	1·0
Total long-term	12·6
Short-term:	
Private	0·3
Official	0·1
Total short-term	0·4
Total assets	13·0
Liabilities (foreign investments in the United States)	
Long-term†	
Direct	2·3
Preferred and common stocks	3·7
Corporate and government bonds	0·9
Miscellaneous	0·6
Total long-term	7·5
Short-term	
Private	4·5
U.S. Government§	3·1
Total short-term	7·6
Total liabilities	15·1
Net creditor (+) *or debtor* (−) *position of the United States*	
On long-term account	+5·1
On short-term account	−7·2
Net position	−2·1

* Preliminary Estimates. The preceding table, prepared by the U.S. Department of Commerce, appears in Part 2 of the Eighth Report of the U.S. Congressional Committee on Postwar Economic Policy and Planning dated 7 February 1946.

† Basis of valuation: Direct investments at book value; all other at market values where available, otherwise par or estimated values.

‡ Includes estimated amounts due under lend lease credits and military civilian supply programmes; outstanding Export-Import Bank Loans and the R.F.C. Loan to the U.K.; and the $650 million due by the U.K. under the lend lease settlement of 6 December 1945.

§ Includes holdings of United States currency and of short-term Government securities as well as certain foreign deposits within the U.S. Treasury.

Table III. *U.S. Gold Holdings ($ million)*

	U.S. gold reserves at end of period	Net gold import	Decrease or increase (−) in ear-marked gold on foreign account
1938	14,512	1,974	−333
1939	17,644	3,574	−534
1940	21,995	4,744	−645
1941	22,737	982	−408
1942	22,726	316	−458
1943	21,938	69	−804
1944	20,619	−845	−460
1945 Jan.–Nov.	20,030	−125	−352
1945 Oct.	20,036		
1945 Jan.–Dec.	20,065		−357

Source: Federal Reserve Bulletin, January 1946.

Table IV

Short-term foreign liabilities reported by banks in U.S.		$ million
	1938	1,997
	1939	3,057
	1940	3,785
End of December	1941	3,482
	1942	3,987
	1943	5,154
	1944	5,269
End of October	1945	6,397

Of the amounts outstanding on 31 October 1945, $3,748 million represented official balances and $2,649 million other balances.

Notes. Other capital movements in the period December 1941 to October 1945 were comparatively small and partly equalising in effect, as follows:

(i) Decrease in U.S. banking funds abroad	$84 million
(ii) Return of U.S. funds in foreign securities	150 million
(iii) Inflow of foreign funds invested in securities	168 million
(iv) Inflow of brokerage balances	33 million

Source: Federal Reserve Bulletin

Table V. *Analysis by countries of short-term foreign liabilities reported by Banks in U.S.A. at 31 October 1945*

$ million

I. Europe		
U.K.	740	
France	360	
Netherlands	228	
Switzerland	284	
Belgium	196	
Norway	183	
Sweden	213	
Other European	341	
	———	2,545
II. Canada		1,552
III. Latin America		
Brazil	179	
Cuba	145	
Mexico	164	
Argentine	77	
Colombia	83	
Panama	64	
Chile	90	
Venezuela	40	
Other Latin America	248	
	———	1,098
IV. Asia		
China	592	
Netherlands East Indies	104	
Other	312	
	———	1,008
V. All other countries		194
		6,397

Source: Federal Reserve Bulletin.

After she entered the war, the net short-term position of the United States deteriorated substantially; so much so that by October 1945 she had dissipated by far the greater part of her large gains from ourselves and others in 1939, 1940 and 1941 before she entered the war, and was only very slightly stronger, after deducting her increased foreign liability from her increased gold reserve, than at the end of 1938, an increase of $5,524 million in gold holdings and of about $200 million in currency holdings abroad being offset by an increase of $5,175 million in foreign liabilities, as is shown in Tables III and IV.

433

Gold held under ear-mark for foreign account at December 31, 1945, represented $3,994 million.

The fact that the U.S. Administration blocked the resources of a number of foreign countries during the war, and that these assets remained blocked throughout the war period, has made available fairly accurate statistics of the very large dollar holdings of the countries in question, which stood at the end of the war as follows:—

Table VI. *Distribution of blocked property by nationality of owner*
(*as of 14 June 1941*)

	$ million
Netherlands, including Netherlands (East) Indies	$1,800
Switzerland	1,500
France and Monaco	1,400
Belgium	400
Sweden	600
China	300
Norway	100
Japan	150
Germany	150
Italy	100
All others	750
Blocked nationals resident in the United States (other than business enterprises owned abroad)	500
Holdings of American citizens in blocked enterprises	750
Total	$8,500

Distribution of blocked property by type of property
(*as of 14 June 1941*)

	$ million
Short-term funds, including ear-marked gold	$4,000
Securities	2,000
Direct investments and miscellaneous	2,000
Holdings of blocked nationals resident in United States	500
Total	$8,500

Note. The above tables appear on page 223, Report on Hearings before the Subcommittee of the Committee on Appropriations, House of Representatives, Seventy-ninth Congress, First Session on the Treasury Department Appropriation Bill for 1946.

At the same date (14 June 1941) a general census was taken of all foreign-owned United States assets, showing a grand total of $12,739 million, exclusive of ear-marked gold, which has been brought up to date in Table II above. A detailed analysis of this census was published by the U.S. Treasury in 1945 under the title 'Census of foreign-owned assets in the United States'.

If the figures are restricted to the more or less liquid reserves of foreign countries held in the United States at the end of the war in the shape of ear-marked gold, bank balances and market securities, the aggregate is of the order of $15 billion, and has *increased* since the end of 1938 by some $9 billion. This huge movement, most of which represents a gain by foreign countries at the expense of the United States, has been largely overlooked by commentators in this country.

Table VII

	$ billion
(a) Short-term assets held in the United States (Table IV)	6·4
(b) Ear-marked gold (Table III)	4·0
(c) Market Securities (Table II) (compared with $3,825 billion at the end of 1938)	4·6
	15·0

So far we have been concerned with firm statistics relating to the present position and the most recent pre-war experience. How materially has this been changed by what there is good reason to expect in the immediately ensuing period?

The sterling prices of goods entering into foreign trade are running at the present time at not much less than double pre-war. This ratio is rather too high for dollar prices. But for convenience of calculation an assumption of double pre-war prices will be used in what follows. The results can be easily adjusted to alternative assumptions. (A lower figure for prices would probably ease the eventual problem on balance.)

On this price assumption the average level of imports immediately before the war would be worth rather less than $5 billion. American experts are expecting a considerably higher figures than this after the war, even as much as 50 per cent higher, on account of the greatly increased activity of the American industrial machine and its increased consumption of imported raw materials as soon as they are available in the required volume. The American view may perhaps be regarded as in part a reflection of the vivid consciousness of the need for maintaining domestic prosperity currently in evidence in the United States; for, as appears from Table I above, an index of imports shows annual changes in the period 1932–8 as a magnified reflection of changes in the level of U.S. industrial production, or rather, as it should be read in this context, in the level of internal prosperity. Whatever vicissitudes one may foresee for American prosperity, it is certain that the public demand for vigorous Government action to meet any serious or prolonged unemployment will be intense. When the outside world has recovered its capacity to supply, imports of $6 to $8 billion on the above price assumption would seem quite reasonable. U.S. imports averaged $4 billion in the decade 1920–9 at the prices and level of national income *then* prevailing. They are running currently in the neighbourhood of $5 billion at present prices.

Exports, at the average level immediately before the war, on the same price assumption would be a little more than $6 billion. Here also the American experts expect a higher figure, various estimates up to as high as $10 billion being current. In the second half of 1945 American exports, which were still dominated by lend lease, were running at an annual rate of $8 billion. The U.S. Secretary of Commerce, Mr Henry Wallace, in his evidence to the Senate Banking Committee during the hearings on the British Loan on 12 March 1946, estimated the total foreign requirements from the U.S. in 1946 at $10,728 billion. A figure of $10 billion might well be reached in the early years, when overseas lending by the United States in the shape of tied

loans is on a large scale; for the loans in many cases create, and are the necessary condition of, the exports. It is not clear, however, that this figure will be easily reached without the assistance of tied loans or subsidies, in view of the fact that the prices of American agricultural produce and raw material now stand over a wide field above world prices. Moreover, industrial wages in the United States are already two and a half times the British level, and are rising more rapidly. There is certainly a potential danger from a policy of export subsidies. But extensions of this policy are frowned upon by the State Department, and will be strictly regulated if the proposals of the projected International Trade Organisation come into operation.

Perhaps the reader may be left for the moment to form his own judgement, in the light of the above, of the most probable order of magnitude of the American favourable balance of visible trade in the post-war environment. An average of $2 to $3 billion a year over a period of years beginning in 1947 looks to me fully high [enough] on the basis of present expectation.

What about the invisible items other than interest (which it will be convenient to deal with separately)? Apart from interest charges and dividend income, the United States had before the war an adverse balance in excess of $500 million, the principle items of which are given in the following table:

Table VIII. *U.S. balance of payments on invisibles* (*other than dividends and interest*) (Average 1936–9)

	Receipts	Payments	Net
Shipping and freight	241	321	− 80
Travel	129	309	−180
Personal remittances	31	159	−128
Institutional contributions (net)	—	—	− 35
Government aid and settlements	2	22	− 20
Other government items	34	83	− 49
Silver	10	131	−121
Miscellaneous adjustments and services (net)	—	—	+ 85
Net total	—	—	−528

American statisticians are expecting a substantial increase in this adverse balance, and rely on this, more than on any other factor, for the maintenace of equilibrium. The pre-war adverse balance in respect of shipping may be reversed, but not perhaps by as much as some people think. The great increase of American-owned tonnage is mainly concentrated in a few specialised types, and a very great part of it will, according to present plans, be scrapped, laid-up or otherwise disposed of. American costs, both of building and of running ships, are very high compared with our own. Overseas government expenditure, on the other hand, will certainly be much greater.

American forecasters are, however, mainly influenced in reaching their conclusion by the expectation of a very great increase in tourist expenditure. Before the war their gross payments out on this ground were of the order of $300 million. It is believed that after the war this expenditure will reach at least $1 billion, and even such figures as $2 billion are spoken of. Those who know the present state of hotel accommodation here and in Europe are likely to consider these figures greatly over-estimated in the short run. But in the long run, if we take adequate measures to develop the tourist industry up to its full potentialities, this source of overseas income, both here and in Europe, may be very great. Moreover, even in the short run American tourist expenditure nearer home in Canada, Mexico and the West Indies may be substantial.

An important item to complete the balance sheet of current receipts and expenditure still remains for examination—namely, the growth of income from the new foreign loans now in prospect. We start off with an estimate of net receipts of $300 million at the end of 1945 in respect of interest and dividend receipts.* It is the prospective increase in this item which looks most alarming to the outsider, and it is therefore particularly

---

* That this is a positive, and not a negative, figure, in spite of U.S. being a net debtor on capital account, is explained by the large amount of her external liabilities held at short term at a very low rate of interest. It follows that this figure will be increased correspondingly less when foreign countries begin to draw on their dollar balances.

important to clear our minds about its possible order of magnitude in relation to the other figures in the balance-sheet.

An estimate of American commitments, actual and prospective, up to date has been given in the January Bank Letter of the National City Bank of New York as follows:

Table IX

	$ million
U.S. subscription to the International Monetary Fund	2,750
Ditto to the International Bank	3,175
Authorised lending power of the Export–Import Bank	3,500
Proposed British credit—new money	3,750
Ditto for lend lease settlement, etc.	650
Credit for lend lease settlement with France	575
Ditto with Russia	400
First contribution to UNRRA	1,350
Second proposed contribution	1,350
	17,500

This table is, of course, a very imperfect guide to the final situation. But it may help to give us a clue to the orders of magnitude in relation to the other figures in the balance sheet. those commitments already approved by Congress or recommended to Congress by the Administration. In this respect, therefore, the total of the ultimate commitment is presumably under-estimated. In particular it may be noted that in a message to Congress on 1 March 1946, President Truman endorsed the recommendation of the National Advisory Council on International Monetary and Financial Problems that the lending authority of the Export–Import Bank be increased by $1·25 billion. In the second place, on the other hand, it looks some way ahead. It assumes, for example, that the whole of the American subscription to the Bretton Woods Fund has been drawn upon. It also assumes that the whole of the present resources of the Export–Import Bank have been utilised. Nor does the amount of the American subscription to the Inter-

439

national Reconstruction Bank accurately measure what really matters in this context—namely, the volume of loans which the new Bank will be able to raise in the American market, a figure which may, in the long run, either exceed or fall short of the amount of the American subscription as a member. Moreover the contributions to UNRRA can be neglected for our present purpose; for they are a free gift which will help to preserve equilibrium in 1946 but will have no effects on the balance of payments in later years.

The actual, as distinct from the potential, state of commitment as at the end of January, 1946, was stated by the President in his Budget statement at that time as follows:—The loans and commitments of the Export–Import Bank then stood at $1·3 billion out of its total authorisation of $3·5 billion. The President 'anticipated that net expenditures of the Export–Import Bank and expenditures arising from the British credit and the Bretton Woods Agreement will amount to $2,614 million including the non–cash item of $950 million for the Fund in the fiscal year 1946 and $2,754 million in the fiscal year 1947'.

What is the annual burden of interest which the rest of the world will have undertaken on the basis of the present programme? Current interest receipts from the International Monetary Fund will depend not only on the amount drawn upon, but also on the dividend policy of the Fund. It is not yet possible to enter any figure under this head. The Export–Import Bank rates of interest have varied between $2\frac{3}{8}$ per cent and 3 per cent. The Lend-Lease settlements with France and Russia are at $2\frac{3}{8}$ per cent. The British credit is at 2 per cent, beginning on 31 December 1951. The terms on which the International Bank will be able to borrow are quite uncertain. To fix a base for our impression of the order of magnitude, let us leave out UNRRA and the subscription to the IMF and assume that the rest costs 3 per cent on the average (which one may hope is an outside estimate). The result is an annual interest burden of $360 million. It will be seen, contrary perhaps to expectation, that

the total is small compared with the other main items in our calculation. Treble it, and you have only just exceeded $1 billion. And if you treble it the corresponding increase of new loans would be sufficient to clear the overall position for another decade or two. Moreover, it should be repeated that the figure of $360 million looks some way ahead. For we have included interest on the British credit which does not begin to fall due for nearly six years, and the calculation assumes loans of $3,175 million on the American market through the International Bank, which will take some doing.

In addition to the interest payment, there is the annual amortisation of capital. The British credit is spread over fifty years, the Export–Import Bank and other lend lease credits over twenty to thirty years. But it is easiest to assume, what is not unreasonable, that new American loans hereafter will be at least equal to the annual amortisation payments. If not, of course the aggregate interest payments will, after a time, fall off appreciably. In their statement of Foreign Loan Policy of the United States Government published on 21 February 1946, the National Advisory Council on International Monetary and Financial Problems assert that the annual interest *and* amortisation on the entire present and contemplated Export–Import Bank programme (that is, presumably, including the proposed additional $1·25 billion), the British Loan and the International Bank loans floated in U.S. markets would be less than $1 billion.

There are far too many uncertainties in the position to allow of any clear-cut summing up. I am content to leave the reader to reach his own tentative conclusion in the light of the above. Very broadly, however, it looks as if the invisible balance of the United States on current account, including interest, is more likely to be adverse than favourable, and, if tourist traffic fulfils expectations, substantially adverse. For visible trade to assume an excess of exports over imports by as much as $2 to $3 billion as an average over a period of years allows, from the point of

view of the outside world, a considerable, one should hope an excessive, measure of pessimism. If American commercial policy is successful in directing itself with any degree of conviction to the preservation of equilibrium in the overall balance of payments, the final outcome might be appreciably better than the above.

It may be worth while to record the experience of the United States after the last war. The U.S. balance of payments from 1924 to 1930 inclusive showed a merchandise excess of almost $800 million a year on the average. But shipping and travelling expenditure cut the above favourable balance almost in half whilst cash remittances from the United States (no longer relatively so important to-day) almost eliminated the remainder; with the result that the net annual balance on capital account was not more than $100 million.

It is obvious that no country can go on for ever covering by new lending a chronic surplus on current account without eventually forcing a default from the other parties. The above estimates show, nevertheless, that the United States can continue foreign lending on a substantial scale for many years to come before the interest due becomes a major and burdensome element in the balance of payments taken as a whole. Anyway, the above estimates are certainly not, for better or for worse, going to continue valid for an indefinite time. Much will happen which we cannot foresee. It is sufficient to cast one's prognosis a moderate distance forward. If we look forward a moderate distance, what resources will the outside world possess to discharge what, in the light of the above, it may find itself owing to the United States on annual current account?

These resources fall under three headings:

1. *Existing resources in the US*

We have seen above that foreign-owned liquid resources in the United States in the shape of ear-marked gold, bank balances and market securities amount to at least $15 billion. It appears

from Table V that the more liquid resources are well spread between a number of countries. Nevertheless, the countries most needing dollars are not necessarily those holding the largest balances; and some of the countries with the largest amounts regard their dollar balances as part of their ultimate reserves (e.g., Canada) and are not likely to draw upon them fully except in extreme circumstancs. Thus only a portion of the above aggregate can be regarded as easily available to cover a balance of payments favourable to the United States.

2. *The new projected loans themselves*

If we omit from Table IX the contributions to UNRRA and the credits for lend lease settlements which have been already, or shortly will be, spent, we are left with a total of $13 billion; this will rise to $14·25 million if the Export–Import Bank's lending powers are increased, and it is presumably not the end, if we are looking five or ten years ahead.

3. *Gold reserves and current production*

The 1937–40 average output outside the USSR was in excess of $1 billion a year. In 1942–45 this fell to about $700 million, on account of shortage of man-power and material. A large increase is now expected in Canada, and an increase, rather than a decrease (perhaps a substantial increase a little later on), in South Africa. Moreover, Russia presumably intends to make some use some day of her presumed large reserves and current output. The most recent report of the Bank for International Settlements estimates the gold reserves of central banks and governments other than the United States (excluding gold in the United States ear-marked on foreign account of which we have already taken account above) at about $10·4 billion. $2·7 billion of this was accumulated in 1942–45; whilst the total increase in gold stocks outside U.S. after America came into the war was considerably greater than this. It would seem, therefore, that

the rest of the world could, if necessary, spare upwards of $1 billion a year, for a time at any rate, without suffering great embarrassment.

Putting one thing together with another, and after pondering all these figures, may not the reader feel himself justified in concluding that the chances of the dollar becoming dangerously scarce in the course of the next five to ten years are not very high? I found some American authorities thinking it at least as likely that America will lose gold in the early future as that she will gain a significant quantity. Indeed, the contrary view is so widely held, on the basis (I believe) of mere impression, that it would be a surprising thing if it turns out right.

In the long run more fundamental forces may be at work, if all goes well, tending towards equilibrium, the significance of which may ultimately transcend ephemeral statistics. I find myself moved, not for the first time, to remind contemporary economists that the classical teaching embodied some permanent truths of great significance, which we are liable to-day to overlook because we associate them with other doctrines which we cannot now accept without much qualification. There are in these matters deep undercurrents at work, natural forces, one can call them, or even the invisible hand, which are operating towards equilibrium. If it were not so, we could not have got on even so well as we have for many decades past. The United States is becoming a high-living, high-cost country beyond any previous experience. Unless their internal, as well as their external, economic life is to become paralysed by the Midas touch, they will discover ways of life which, compared with the ways of the less fortunate regions of the world, must tend towards, and not away from, external equilibrium.

Admittedly, if the classical medicine is to work, it is essential that import tariffs and export subsidies should not progressively offset its influence. It is for this reason that one is entitled to draw some provisional comfort from the present mood of the American Administration and, as I judge it, of the American

people also, as embodied in the *Proposals for Consideration by an International Conference on Trade and Employment*. We have here sincere and thoroughgoing proposals, advanced on behalf of the United States, expressly directed towards creating a system which allows the classical medicine to do its work. It shows how much modernist stuff, gone wrong and turned sour and silly, is circulating in our system, also incongruously mixed, it seems, with age-old poisons, that we should have given so doubtful a welcome to this magnificent, objective approach which a few years ago we should have regarded as offering incredible promise of a better scheme of things.

I must not be misunderstood. I do not suppose that the classical medicine will work by itself or that we can depend on it. We need quicker and less painful aids of which exchange variation and overall import control are the most important. But in the long run these expedients will work better and we shall need them less, if the classical medicine is also at work. And if we reject the medicine from our systems altogether, we may just drift on from expedient to expedient and never get really fit again. The great virtue of the Bretton Woods and Washington proposals, taken in conjunction, is that they marry the use of the necessary expedients to the wholesome long-run doctrine. It is for this reason that, speaking in the House of Lords, I claimed that 'Here is an attempt to use what we have learnt from modern experience and modern analysis, not to defeat, but to implement the wisdom of Adam Smith.'

No one can be certain of anything in this age of flux and change. Decaying standards of life at a time when our command over the production of material satisfactions is the greatest ever, and a diminishing scope for individual decision and choice at a time when more than before we should be able to afford these satisfactions, are sufficient to indicate an underlying contradiction in every department of our economy. No plans will work for certain in such an epoch. But if they palpably fail, then, of course, we and everyone else will try something different.

445

Meanwhile for us the best policy is to act on the optimistic hypothesis until it has been proved wrong. We shall do well not to fear the future too much. Preserving all due caution in our own activities, the job for us is to get through the next five years in conditions which are favourable and not unfavourable to the restoration of our full productive efficiency and strength of purpose, of our prestige with others and of our confidence in ourselves. We shall run more risk of jeopardising the future if we are influenced by indefinite fears based on trying to look ahead further than any one can see.

(Invaluable help has been given by Mr David McCurrach in the preparation of the above tables.)

Within the Treasury, as well as keeping his eye on the evolution of payments agreements, especially the French, he turned once more to the eventual settlement of the sterling balances problem envisaged in the Loan Agreement[2] with a memorandum dated 23 January. He followed this up after internal discussions in the Treasury with further comments.

NOTES ON STERLING AREA NEGOTIATIONS

I. *The corpus*

1. I favour the technique proposed by the Bank of England in §§1–6 of their memorandum. It should not be overlooked that where private balances make up an important part of the statistically unavailable sterling, there will be a heavy duty on the exchange control of the S.A. country in question. This, however, seems to me to be inevitable and the *other* exchange control is the right quarter on which to place the responsibility. The proposal for reinstatement through the I.M.F. of any

[2] See *JMK* vol. XXIV, pp. 571–7, 639–40. See also *Financial Agreement between the Governments of the United States and the United Kingdom dated 6th December 1945* (Cmd. 6708). Section 10.

deficiency of sterling below the statistical datum line strikes me as a particularly bright idea, which should lighten the burden of policing any agreed arrangements.

2. I should define as follows the *corpus* on which the operation of 'adjustment' etc. is to take place:

(i) The sterling resources as shown and defined in the quarterly returns of the Bank of England at zero hour *minus* an estimate of the corresponding figure as it stood at the beginning of the war (so that we are dealing with the wartime increment);

(ii) *plus* official repatriations and redemptions of securities by governments since the beginning of the war;

(iii) *minus* (or *plus*) the final settlement of obligations on both sides arising out of the war, including military expenditure up to an agreed date which might be later than zero hour.

3. All these items may require further and more precise definition. But we should aim at ending up with a round figure on which to operate. It is not necessary that it should be statistically exact. For the Bank of England technique provides in effect that any sterling resources, which, after 'adjustment', lie outside the figure fixed for the unavailable sterling from time to time, are *free*. It is not necessary that we should know exactly what the *available* balances amount to. It will be the round figures fixed for the adjustment and for the statistically *unavailable* sterling which alone matter.

4. There are, however, a few further observations which can be made at once. What is to be zero hour? It will suit us that it should be as late as possible. A year after the effective date of the Washington Agreement, or anyhow 31 December 1946, would suit our book best. Nevertheless I doubt whether we can insist on so late a date. There will be great trouble and difficulty about what happens meanwhile. Moreover, it is unlikely that the aggregate of sterling balances will continue to increase after 30 June 1946, apart from the military expenditure, the amount of which we are entitled to strike at later date. Thus, apart from the continuing military expenditure (and, of course, the final

wartime settlements under 2 (iii) above), I would accept 30 June 1946, as zero hour for the statistical calculation. Nor, I believe, would there be much objection from our point of view to taking 31 March 1946, which would have the advantage that the figures would be known and unalterable during the course of the negotiations, whereas we should know the figures as at 30 June rather too late in the day. On the other hand, we should, I think, resist a date so early as 31 December 1945, which would antedate the effective operation of the Washington Agreement and exclude a period during which sterling balances may perhaps increase apart from military expenditure. (According to the latest Bank of England estimate, which is admittedly very precarious, the aggregate S.A. balances during 1946 as a whole will increase by about the same amount as the military expenditure during the year.)

5. It would be very unfair not to bring the repatriations of government debt and the like into the hotch-potch. But I do not think we need try to trace the movements of market securities, though in the cases of South Africa and Eire this may have been fairly important.

6. The wartime settlements under 2 (iii) should be limited to wartime and should not include such adjustments as, for example, the Indian pensions, which should be brought in at a later stage. Moreover it is not clear how far they should cover disposals of war surplus which will represent a post-war asset to the recipient. In particular dollar payments for lend lease settlements due from S.A. countries to the U.S. for pipe-line, inventory and war surplus should probably be brought in at a later stage, 'below the line' so to speak, 'the line' being intended to determine, broadly speaking, the order of magnitude of overseas financial increment arising out of the war.

7. This concept should also require us to take account of gold movements and gold reserves. In the case of India and the Middle East sales of gold to them should certainly be brought into hotch-potch, just like repatriations of securities. Strictly

speaking, the increase in the South African gold reserves should be brought into the picture. And so, in discussion, it should be. But South Africa presents, of course, a special case where we are not in a position to get any more than is, strictly voluntarily, proffered.

8. It would be helpful if an estimate could now be made of the various ingredients which might be brought into the settlement which determines the initial weight of the *corpus*. For convenience of calculation and to fix our ideas, I shall assume in what follows that the *corpus* determined according to the above principles will work out at £3,500 million of which £3,000 will consist of actual outstanding balances at zero hour (if zero hour is later than 31 December 1945, and with the inclusion of military expenditure, the latter figure should be, in fact, rather higher than this).

II. *The operation*

9. It is evident that *any* solution which lies within our power will be highly distasteful to, and strongly resisted by, the other parties concerned. There is no means whatever by which, in the case of certain countries, we can avoid political difficulties of a high order. If appeasement were practicable, I do not doubt we should adopt it. But in fact this is not one of the alternatives open to us; so, fortunately perhaps, temptation is removed.

10. Our object, therefore, must be to offer our creditors the choice of two alternatives so devised that the alternative most acceptable to us is also the alternative most acceptable to them. One of the alternatives must be of such a character that it involves no cancellation of debt, though in this case we should have to be left free to repay what we owe, whilst ultimately in full, nevertheless at our own pace and time. To this extent the settlement will be voluntary, that is to say there will be no forced cancellations. But in the last resort, since we can only pay what we can pay, the final settlement must inevitably be, in a sense,

imposed. The question what happens if both the offered alternatives are rejected is dealt with in Section IV of this paper.

11. We have to start from the end of what we can afford. The American loan will cost us £35 million a year after five years. The Canadian loan may cost us £10 million a year after a similar delay. The American Agreement provides that, in calculating the waiver formula, up to £43·75 million a year can be taken into account for the service of war-time sterling balances (outside, as well as inside, the S.A.). This figure was based on general indications we ourselves gave in the course of discussions about how we might handle the sterling balances, and it was mentioned at a time when we were hoping that the Americans might specifically help us in this direction. I suggest that it represents about the outside maximum of what it would be prudent for us to accept as an absolute obligation, subject only to a waiver clause similar to the American. Let us then take £40 million a year as our maximum annual obligation for capital repayment and interest on S.A. balances, reserving a little for non-S.A. balances (including any part of the Canadian loan which may relate to wartime debts) and as a margin.

12. Now if the settlement is a very tight one there are bound to be individual cases, especially perhaps amongst the Crown Colonies, where from time to time it is almost inevitable we shall have to be better than our word. In a tight settlement I do not think it would be prudent to reserve less than £m10 a year for such contingencies.

13. I conclude that if all our creditors were to stick out for payment in full without any downward adjustment, the best we could manage would be repayment of capital at 1 per cent per annum without interest—which would cost £m30 a year. This might constitute one of our alternative offers. If it were more convenient to allow interest at Treasury Bill rates, say $\frac{1}{2}$ per cent, it would not, actuarially calculated, cost us very much more (it might cost us less—I can't do it in my head) to make this offer $\frac{1}{2}$ per cent per annum interest on the outstanding balances and $\frac{1}{2}$ per cent per annum capital repayment.

450

14. At the other extreme, it would look much better and cost us a little less to adjust the corpus of £3,500 million by (say) 40 per cent, which would bring down the outstanding balances from £3,000 million to £1,600 million, repayable over 50 years by 2 per cent annual instalments of capital with interest at $\frac{1}{2}$ per cent on the outstanding balance, which would cost £39·5 million in the first year gradually falling to about £32 million in the fiftieth year. Or we could reduce the *corpus* of the debt by a third, which would reduce the balances to about £1,800 million repayable over sixty-six years by $1\frac{1}{2}$ per cent annual instalments of capital and $\frac{1}{2}$ per cent interest, which would cost £36 million in the first year.

15. It seems to me that these figures set the range of our field of manoeuvre. It will be seen that it is somewhat narrow, and that there is more difference between the alternative solutions in their political and psychological flavour than in their net financial consequences.

16. It deserves consideration whether we should not start out with an absolutely *uniform* formula applicable to all our S.A. creditors alike. We should then proceed to further special adjustments, either upward or downward to suit individual circumstances and taking account of varying factors. In short, do the cooking at the second stage.

17. To start the discussion, I suggest that the initial general formula applicable to all alike should be as follows:

(i) One third of the *corpus*, ascertained on the lines of Section I above, (say) £m1,200, to be carried to suspense (the question whether what is carried to suspense is *cancelled* either at once or at some future date being reserved for treatment as will be explained below),

(ii) Of the two-thirds, not in suspense, $7\frac{1}{2}$ per cent to be made available forthwith,

(iii) The balance of the two-thirds to be released at the rate of $1\frac{1}{2}$ per cent per annum,

(iv) Interest at $\frac{1}{2}$ per cent per annum on the portion of the two-thirds which is not yet available,

(v) The service under (iii) and (iv) to be reduced in American waiver years in accordance with the American formula,

(vi) Subsequent instalments to be anticipated, if desired, in non-waiver years under discount at 3 per cent per annum compound, subject to our agreement in any year as to the amount which can be thus anticipated,

(vii) It would offer an appropriate symmetry and an important safeguard for us to provide that we on our side would be free to postpone any instalment of availability at 3 per cent. In this case it would not be necessary for us to make special mention of the American waiver,

(viii) Adjustments, e.g. in respect of Indian pensions, would come off the initial amount of the two-thirds, and all the subsequent percentages would relate to the sum thus reduced; though any substantial dollar payments for lend lease settlement (unless borrowed by the countries in question under $3c$)[3] might have to come, in whole or part, out of the initial release under (ii) above.

18. The reader will have perceived by now that, through the operation of compound interest, deferments of payment, especially if no interest is allowed, can be so arranged as to provide the equivalent of cancellation without that ill-sounding word having been actually mentioned. Mr Rowe-Dutton has suggested, precisely for this reason, that the part which it is proposed to 'suspend' under 17 (i) above should not be cancelled, but merely deferred without interest to a sufficiently distant date. There is, however, also another destination for the 'suspended' portion, to which I shall return below. Meanwhile it may be worth while to put forward an alternative general formula, which altogether avoids cancellation or suspension as such, and entirely depends for effective cancellation on the operation, not merely of compound interest, but of compound discounting.

19. Let the *corpus* be repayable in its entirety without interest

[3] See *JMK*, vol. XXIV, p. 419.

by instalments spread over a long period beginning (say) 10 years hence without any immediate release as in 17 (ii) above (though, as we shall see, the countries concerned will be able to get available sterling at once if they want). The instalments of availability might be as follows

5 per cent falling due in 1956;

1 per cent falling due in each year from 1956 to 1971

$1\frac{1}{2}$ per cent falling due in each year from 1972 to 1991

2 per cent falling due in each year from 1992 to 2016.

In non-waiver years, however, future instalments could be anticipated if desired at 3 per cent discount (compound) subject to our agreement as to the maximum to be so treated.

20. This system has two important advantages. In the first place, policing of the statistical amount to be held unavailable is facilitated, for we can if necessary deduct deficiency under discount from the next maturing instalments. In the second place, subject to *our* capacity (which under any system must be the ultimate limitation), there is no set limit to the available sterling of any of the countries involved within their total holdings, if difficult circumstances arise in which they need it. It should be mentioned that, of course, the same advantages exist under 17 (vi) above. The system of §19 primarily differs from that of §17 in that it cuts out both interest and cancellation.

21. It will be observed that the essence of the plan is to substitute, in respect of any instalments over and above a modest figure, a *negative* rate of interest of 3 per cent instead of a positive rate of $\frac{1}{2}$ per cent.

22. A compromise between the two, rather less favourable to ourselves, would be to postpone (instead of cancel) the suspended portion under 17 (i) without interest until all the other instalments have been met. This, I think, was what Mr Rowe-Dutton had in mind when he set me thinking along these lines.

23. There is, however, a further use for the suspended portion of fundamental importance, which we did not overlook

at an earlier stage of these discussions but have not mentioned lately. To this I now turn.

24. The above schedules should be regarded by the reader at this stage as purely schematic. There is, of course, an endless variety of formulae which could be devised along these lines. The conclusion I reach is that there is *no* solution offering outside these general lines. Does anyone dispute that?

III. *Exchange adjustments*

25. What follows relates primarily to India and the Middle East countries which have largely over-valued foreign exchanges. The method might, if we wished, be used to the *advantage* of Australia and New Zealand, which have under-valued exchanges.

26. The combination of our heavy internal expenditure in these countries with physical obstacles to imports has made it possible for the Eastern countries to get through the war without the least embarrassment *with their sterling exchange rates unaltered*, yet with a domestic price level at least 50 per cent above its appropriate parity with the outside world. The inevitable result is that they will soon find themselves in an intolerable position. If Egypt allows her cotton prices to rise to a proper parity with her cost of living, her cotton will be right above world prices. As the world shakes down to normal, this is just one example of what will become characteristic of the export economies of all these countries.

27. On the other hand, importation into these countries becomes wildly attractive. Every import, whether of motor cars or cotton piece goods, becomes absurdly cheap and yields a huge profiteering margin to the lucky holder of an import licence (and, equally, to the lucky holder of an export licence from this country).

28. The exchange controls of these countries, on the efficacy of which the Bank of England formula essentially depends, will

find the task far beyond their capacities in peace-time conditions.

29. There cannot be much doubt, in my opinion, that the position is untenable. The only alternative to devaluation is a drastic deflation of a character which these countries are incapable, politically and administratively, of carrying through. Besides *cui bono*? What is the object of forcing them through this painful process?

30. The following table illustrates the dimensions of the problem:—

(June–August 1939 = 100)

	Wholesale index	Cost of living index	Volume of note issue
Egypt	330	298	678
Palestine	358	258	807
Iraq	487	377	978
India			

(The dates are the latest available, Sept.–Dec. 1945)

31. The volume of the note issue indicates the enormously greater potential inflation which has been kept at bay to a considerable extent by wartime price controls, subsidies, etc.; broadly the note issue increase is double the price increase up to date. It also indicates the large potential profits of devaluation, in that a very large part of the note reserves is held in sterling.

32. *Any* sterling balances settlement is bound to bring this latent crisis to a head. At present they regard themselves as having virtually unlimited sterling. As soon as their available sterling is limited on the scale which is inevitable, it will only be a matter of months before they are completely bust.

33. I conclude, therefore, that to grapple with the devaluation problem of these countries is a necessary and inescapable part of the sterling balances settlement. Politically this is likely on balance to aggravate our difficulties. For whilst devaluation

455

always cuts both ways politically and many important influences gain by it, it will always make a good popular cry against us if it appears to be done at our instance and under our pressure. I propose below a possible means of mitigating these difficulties. But anyway the issue cannot be shirked. The problem has to be settled and the principles and motives of political appeasement, however powerful on their own *terrain*, are materially as incapable of implementation as when war has begun.

34. The problem would have to be faced even if it aggravated, instead of assisting, the rest of our problem. In fact it offers a heaven-sent means of liquidating the position by the most painless means conceivable. A devaluation would provide resources precisely on the scale necessary to take care of the suspended or cancelled portion. If these countries were to devalue by 33 per cent (and not less is necessary for their equilibrium), it would provide their governments with precisely the necessary surplus to discharge the appropriate proportion of their sterling balances.

35. It is, moreover, what is just and fair to us. We incurred these debts in local currency at inflated price levels. It would be monstrous if, on top of all the other reasons why these countries should contribute, we were expected to re-pay in a money worth 50 per cent more than the money we had expended.

36. How can this means of solution be put forward most tactfully and in a measure which lays itself least open to the charge that the change is being made under pressure from us?

37. Why should we not measure the amount of sterling to be repaid in terms of its value in the local money we had expended? But we need not finalise such a settlement here and now. Here comes the virtue of 'suspending' the one-third. It could be provided that, if and when sterling profits accrued from a devaluation, the corresponding amount would be written off the suspense account. Failing this, *per impossibile*, the suspense account would gradually come alive again at long last after all

the other instalments of availability had fallen due. We could, at the same time, urge the governments concerned to take the bull by the horns forthwith, pointing out that their immediately available sterling would certainly be insufficient to enable them to hold the position for any length of time.

38. It would not be much of a risk to make the arrangement symmetrical and agree to add to the suspense any loss incurred by them through a devaluation of sterling relatively to their local currencies. This might be a means of reducing the burden to Australia and New Zealand without infringing the general principles of the settlement. For these countries have under-valued currencies and might do well to restore their exchanges to the former parity between pounds A. and N.Z. and pounds sterling.

39. Devaluations have to be discussed in conditions of top secrecy. Nevertheless, I am not sure that the discussions with the Eastern countries should not open up with a frank exchange of views about what they think they are going to do about their exchange rates when the amount of their immediately available sterling is, inevitably, greatly curtailed.

IV. *The ultimate sanction*

40. If a country will not play, obviously it must not come off better than those who will. Anyway its unwillingness to play does not increase our capacity to satisfy it. Therefore it is inescapable that, whilst cancellation must remain, in accordance with our pledges, a matter of voluntary agreement, the ultimate terms and rate of repayment must be in the last resort imposed,—which is, if you like, a distinction without a difference.

41. There appear to be two alternatives. Either in such a case we block the countries' balances entirely and wait for them to come to terms. In the case of a neutral such as the Argentine, I should favour this course. But with the S.A. countries a gentler

procedure would be preferable. Let us, in such an event, offer them the best in our power to accomplish, having regard to the claims of others and our own capacity. This, presumably, would be something on the lines of §13 above.

42. These are preliminary first thoughts put down, as will be seen, in some disorder. There is a great deal more to be said both in principle and in detail. But there may be enough here to start the discussion and to bring us to grips with the fundamentals to be settled.

KEYNES

To SIR EDWARD BRIDGES, *1 February 1946*

THE STERLING AREA SETTLEMENT

When the Chancellor sees the Australian and New Zealand Ministers, I suggest the following line of discourse. It would avoid possible misunderstanding if they were given a paper on these lines to take away with them.

1. The American loan will enable us, and is so intended, to make future current earnings of the sterling area fully convertible, optionally after the effective date of the loan (say 1 April 1946), and definitely a year later than that. This enables us to give very important facilities to the sterling area countries which we could not afford otherwise. It is, therefore, very much to the advantage of these countries to make the proposed lines of the general settlement practicable.

2. On the other hand, we are not free to use any part of the American loan to discharge obligations incurred prior to its effective date.

3. These liabilities, as is well known, are of the order of £9,000 million at least.

4. We do not expect, therefore, to be able to release *on balance* any of the sterling balances accumulated at zero hour during the period of availability of the loan or before the end of

the transitional period which we place, provisionally, at 31 December 1951. We expect, however, some further accumulation of sterling balances during 1946, and we have, therefore, to be able to release an approximately equal amount, or—at best—an amount not significantly greater, in 1947–51.

5. After 1951 it is our aim gradually to increase the portion of the accumulated sterling which is available and fully convertible for current transactions. But the maximum of our capacity, even on an optimistic hypothesis, cannot much exceed 1 per cent of the total accumulations, unless some means is found of reducing the aggregate amount. Obviously this will drag the ultimate settlement over an interminable period.

6. Sterling balances, which are *not* released as above, will not be available for expenditure *anywhere*. It is important that this should be understood.

7. We are not yet in a position to propose an exact formula. But the Dominions must be prepared for certain inescapable conclusions.

8. Since their sterling balances are relatively small, any sacrifice asked from them will be relatively light compared with what we must ask from others. But we hope it can be *in preparation* a significant amount.

9. Their willing co-operation would help us enormously with the other countries concerned. The advantages Australia and New Zealand will derive are—

(i) the strengthening of the sterling position with which their external finances are so much bound up;

(ii) a more rapid release of the balances remaining after adjustment;

(iii) full convertibility of their future sterling earnings for all current transactions, which will be an inestimable benefit for them, and restore the pre-war position so far as future earnings are concerned.

10. To sum up:—

(i) We hope that they will co-operate in a general scheme on

459

a substantial scale to render the amount of the accumulated sterling balances more manageable.

(ii) After (say) 1 April 1947, any sterling they earn will be fully convertible for current transactions.

(iii) If a satisfactory general scheme can be agreed, we shall hope to relax before that date in respect of current earnings and anticipate subsequent arrangements to a considerable degree.

(iv) Pre-zero hour sterling balances will be made available as and when we can, but inevitably at a very slow rate; the provisions about these releases, both before 1951 and after that date, cannot be made definite until a general scheme has been agreed by all these concerned.

11. They must appreciate that we have assumed sole liability for the American loan whereas something between a third and a half of it will be used to make the future sterling earnings of the rest of the sterling area convertible. This deserves the greatest possible emphasis.

12. It would be very helpful to us if they could provide us, as soon as possible, with an analysed statement of their own balance of payments forecasts for 1946 and 1947.

KEYNES

STERLING AREA NEGOTIATIONS

Brief notes arising out of our first discussion:

1. Is there general agreement on the following?—

(a) Our contractual commitments after 1951 cannot safely exceed a figure of the order of £40 million a year (inclusive of interest), this figure being on the high, rather than the low, side for a commitment to be taken now.

(b) We cannot afford to repay any significant net amount of the accumulated sterling as of 31 December 1945, during the years 1946–51 inclusive; though we can hope for some further accumulation of sterling during 1946 (including military expenditure). The best, therefore, we can undertake is to release an

equal, or slightly greater, sum in 1947–1951. (We might, of course, find ourselves later on able to improve on this, if all goes well meanwhile and we are not drawing on the American credit too fast.)

(*c*) We cannot, therefore, allow *any* country an unrestricted claim (even when we think they are not very likely in practice to exercise it in full) on its uncancelled sterling.

2. The idea of making no promises whatever about what we do after 1951, though it has its attractions, would seem to mean giving up the idea of cancellations now (and perhaps permanently) and would involve a wide departure from what we have announced as our intentions.

3. Is it agreed that the existing rates of exchange cannot be sustained in India and the Middle East in conditions when they have little more than their current earnings wherewith to support these rates? If so, is it agreed that a re-ordering of exchange rates must inevitably become part of the negotiations?

4. I am attracted by Mr Rowe-Dutton's scheme of deferred cancellations. But I would point out:

(*a*) that, if the answer to (2) above is in the affirmative, his idea should be married to my 'suspense account' in relation to exchange devaluations as in §37 of my memorandum of 23 January.

(*b*) The proposal in §19 of my memorandum is, in substance, an alternative version of his idea. I do not know which looks better,—perhaps his does.

(*c*) We might offer rather better terms of subsequent release in return for immediate cancellation compared with releases promised against deferred cancellation.

5. Whilst the ultimate settlements will, after cooking, work out very differently in some respects, I still feel, after further reflection, that, unless we *start out* with some general formula, we shall be all at sea and will not be able to offer even the semblance of a justification of being fair. Is there any good

461

reason why the rate of subsequent annual release should vary from case to case?

6. If the Bank are right, as they well may be in ordinary circumstances, that a substantial proportion of the sterling balances is likely to stop here anyhow, that limits the inconvenience to the other party of turning a *de facto* into a *de jure* situation. But it is *not*, as I have already pointed out, a reason for our accepting *de jure* obligations which we shall be unable to fulfil, if the abnormal conditions arise (as, heaven knows, they are likely to in the world ahead of us), when we are called upon to do so. The bankers' 'ramp' of 1931 consisted not in what happened at the last moment, which was inevitable and indeed desirable, but in the reckless accumulation of liabilities in the immediately preceding years which we could not hope to meet when the tide turned. I think that we must ration ourselves this time in the extent to which we use the banker's bluff as a means of supporting (temporarily) the prestige of sterling.

7. It might be fruitful to put in some careful statistical work as to the extent to which currency reserves can furnish the wherewithal for cancellation (*a*) by substituting domestic for sterling Treasury bills; (*b*) through the profit arising from an appropriate devaluation.

8. What about the following target for immediate cancellation?—

	£ million
India	500
Egypt, Palestine and Iraq	250
Colonies	175
Australia, N.Z., S. Africa	75
	1,000

Even this, which looks stiff when set out in detail, falls appreciably short of the aggregates put forward in §14 of my previous memorandum. I believe, however, that it could be attained without insuperable difficulty by the methods of the

preceding paragraph (which are not, of course, applicable to the case of the Southern Dominions).

If we released in 1946–51 any excess over £3,000 million, we should, if the above target of cancellation is attained, be left with £2,000 million to discharge thereafter, which at 2 per cent annual service, including interest, would cost the £40 million a year.

This re-emphasises the narrowness of our field of manoeuvre.

9. I plead that this is not a case where we can muddle through without a drastic solution, grasping no nettles and just hoping it will be all right on the day.

KEYNES

5 February 1946

By the end of January, his pessimistic assessment of the domestic situation suggested by his comments to Lord Halifax at the turn of the year (*JMK*, vol. XXIV, p. 628) had deepened somewhat. By 29 January he could write R. H. Brand

From a letter to R. H. BRAND, *29 January 1946*

Here the Loan and associated matters have dropped almost entirely out of public sight. A mass of domestic legislation, most of it not in the least urgent and with no significant relevance to pressing current affairs, provides an alibi to all alike. This country is *not* in good order just now.

Meanwhile the mixed chauvinism and universal benevolence of the F.O. and other departments and the weakness of the Chancellor in these matters are slopping away on everything and everybody in the world except the poor Englishman the fruits of our American loan. Since I came back, though the germs of a good deal of this had been implanted earlier, I find the following overseas commitments, altogether apart from our adverse balance on current trade account (£ million):- for France, 140; Greece, 25; Burma, 87; Malaya, 10; Germany, 65;

UNRRA, 80; overseas military expenditure in 1946, 300, total, 707. Against this we are hoping (though not to my mind with absolute certainty) to get £40 to £50 million in gold from France, and a good part of the French loan relates to 1945. On the other hand, there are a good many other oddments, with China, Czechoslovakia and everyone else, not included in the above. So that the above total may appreciably overstate the prospective burden on our balance of trade. Nevertheless this relates only to 1946 and to things which have already happened before the end of January 1946. Compare with the total size of the American loan, namely £925 million! In one direction, however, there will be in the long run, I hope, a material improvement on the above. Largely owing to Bridges, there has recently, I understand, been a considerable victory over the Service Departments, by which the Cabinet have decided for a large reduction in the entirely preposterous proposed size of the Forces. I am afraid this will have only a delayed effect on the overseas military expenditure, but if this new move really materialises, the above figure of £300 million might come down quite a bit.

All the above, as you will have appreciated, is pretty irresponsible. It is not done on purpose. No one knows what is happening. I am proposing shortly to do my best to kick up a shindy. But it is only gradually after one's return that one discovers the facts. The Ministers, I am told, are reluctant to read their official papers and reach half the ramshackle decisions, particularly on overseas affairs, in the absence of anybody who really knows what it is all about. The Treasury, in the shape of Wilfrid, Sigi and the rest, work hard in the right direction, but with a singular lack of success (apart from Bridges' very important victory mentioned above).

Back of all this, England is sticky with self-pity and not prepared to accept peacefully and wisely the fact that her position and her resources are *not* what they once were. Psycho-analysis would, I think, show that that was the real

background of the reception of the American loan and the associated proposals.

Obviously, the above is to be kept to yourself, but will you show it to Edward Halifax?

One result of his pessimism was a long memorandum for the Treasury. The first draft of this has not survived. The second appears below.

POLITICAL AND MILITARY EXPENDITURE OVERSEAS

1. This is in response to your request that a summary statement of the position be prepared.

I. *Introductory*

2. The Treasury has the general import programme of the country well in hand. There is adequate machinery to prevent the civilian from consuming, or the domestic manufacturer from investing in, supplies from abroad, more than we can afford. In short, you can take comfort, in view of what follows, from the fact that administrative methods for imposing austerity at home are in good working order.

3. The most impressive fact which emerges from a study of the import programme is the high proportion of it which consists of products which are truly essential to our economy. Of the proposed total of £1,075 million no less than £1,030 million is classified as essential and only £45 million as supplementary easements. If a further £40 million could be devoted to easements or taken off exports, it would make a very susceptible difference to the standard of life. Please note that in this context an amount such as £20 million or £30 million is a significant figure and far from negligible.

4. On the other hand, the current and prospective demands upon us for political and military expenditure overseas have already gone beyond the figure which can, on any hypothesis,

be sustained. The figures given below are extremely shocking, and show that the position is rapidly getting out of hand. Ministers should not remain unwarned that they are going down the drain at a great pace, unless they can consider before it is too late whether a drastic and early change of policy may not be preferable. It is *not* yet too late, since, as will be shown below, many of the demands are not yet commitments.

5. It is not easy to estimate either the net ultimate burdens on the exchanges or the precise date at which they are likely to fall due. The clearest way of presenting the picture will be to start off with the full figure of the gross commitments and of the demands which are in sight. This will lead to a cumulative result which is certainly too high. How much too high it is difficult to say. But the various grounds for qualification and abatement can then be mentioned. And, in the light of these, a general impression can be formed of what we are in for.

6. It will be observed that the gross political commitments abroad already accepted and the similar demands already in sight, together with the prospective military expenditure overseas on the present basis, considerably exceed the *whole* of the projected American credit which is expected to cover us for the six years 1946–51 (namely £937 million).

7. It would not be a source of comfort to the hard-pressed British public if they were to become aware that (reckoning our overseas statistics globally) not a single bean of sustenance for themselves or of capital equipment for British manufacturers is likely to be left over from the American credit; and that we shall require, on balance, the whole of it, and, unless we change our ways, much more, to feed and sustain Allies, liberated territories and ex-enemies, to maintain our military prestige overseas, and, generally speaking, to cut a dash in the world considerably above our means.

8. In short, current developments abroad need to be reconsidered without delay; especially those which are being undertaken before the American credit is actually in the bag.

9. Our resources are strictly limited. Any one use of them is, therefore, *alternative* and not *additional* to some other use. We have reached the point when no commitment should be undertaken without our at the same time deciding what to forgo. If the maintenance of an army of 100,000 Poles in Italy involves the same burden on our overseas finances as the Ministry of Food's annual programme of additional desired easements, Ministers, if they prefer the former, should do so consciously and deliberately. This example is taken at random and may not be a good one. But it is a principle which applies to *all* the objects of overseas expenditure which are to be reviewed in what follows. Another example is the suggestion that the reduction in our forces overseas should be postponed until after the Peace Conference. The good reasons for this are obvious. But the cost should be worked out in terms of the cost of the bacon ration. If the Foreign Office argument prevails, then the bacon ration should be appropriately cut. We cannot have both without running into a hopeless position later on. Each item of expenditure, before it is accepted, should be regarded as a *choice* which is deliberately preferred to a clearly envisaged alternative. This is obvious; but it is seldom acted upon.

II. *Political expenditure overseas*

10. *UNRRA*

	£ million
Gross commitment: 1st instalment	80
2nd instalment	75

Of the first instalment £20 million had been exported or provided outside this country before the end of 1945. Thus the outstanding commitment as at the beginning of 1946 is £135 million.

Our contribution to UNRRA takes the form of (*a*) exports from this country, (*b*) the provision of freights, and (*c*) expenditure outside U.K. Expenditure under (*c*) in 1946 is estimated

at £13 million. But the burden on the balance of payments is the full amount of $(a)+(b)+(c)$, only reduced by the inclusion in (a) of surplus stores which could not be disposed of elsewhere. Unless, therefore, UNRRA fails to drawn on her U.K. credits in full, we must reckon our liability at not much less than £135 million, of which the whole or the greater part will fall within 1946.

Post-UNRRA Relief in Europe

The relief and rehabilitation needs of Italy, Austria, Greece, and perhaps Poland during 1947 have been provisionally estimated in the F.O. at £187½ million. It is hoped that this is considerably too high. In any case there has been as yet no decision that the U.K. should participate or what its share should be if it does. Nevertheless we are already under pressure from our representatives in Washington to prepare for the demands of the post-UNRRA period, and it is evident that we shall be pressed to provide something considerable for Italy and Austria in 1947 and perhaps in 1948, as well as for Greece.

France

For the year ending February 1946 we have advanced £150 million, of which £149 million had been drawn before the end of 1945. We are entitled to recover £40 million of this in gold. We are expecting (we hope not too optimistically) that the balance will be provided out of privately owned French assets in U.K. Except in so far as we receive securities which are marketable abroad (e.g. in South Africa), the fact that our long-term capital position is maintained does not, however, help our balance of payments during the relevant period.

Nothing is yet settled for the balance of 1946. But it is certain that we shall be strongly pressed to provide at least £50 million net (£75 million gross less £25 million in gold). Nor is this the

end. Those in touch with the French position believe that a further £60 million will be required in 1947/8. France also owes us £35 million for civil affairs supplies, the means of payment for which is at present undetermined. We are, however, hoping for $158 million for military and surplus supplies in respect of the 1945 agreement, of which $21 million has been already paid on account.

Holland

Nothing is yet agreed. But the Treasury believe that we shall be under strong pressure to find £50 million for Holland and £10 million for the Dutch Indies in 1946, and a further £30 million in 1947. Holland owes us £15 million for civil affairs supplies but will argue that she can only pay by borrowing the equivalent from us.

Belgium

		£ million
Cost of BAOR	in 1946	10
	in 1947/8	10
		£20

which is included subsequently in this paper in military expenditure. Belgium owes us £15 million for civil affairs supplies which she can pay.

Denmark

A modest short-term credit which is likely to be repaid within the relevant period and can, therefore, be ignored.

Czechoslovakia

Balance of credit to be drawn, say, £3 million.

Poland

1946

	£ million
Refugees (mostly sterling area countries)	4
Emigration costs	2

Polish Armed Forces
220,000
three services
$\left\{\begin{array}{l} \text{70,000 U.K.} \\ \text{45,000 Germany} \\ \text{90,000 Italy} \\ \text{15,000 Middle East} \end{array}\right.$

Total cost excluding mark and lire expenditure = £2½ millions a month, which enters into the balance of payments, either indirectly or as already included in military expenditure.

No one has any idea where they will all be in six months' time, with the result that they are of no use to us as a means of saving our own manpower.

1947–8

Refugees and Emigration costs	?£5 million

Greece

1946

(*a*) Stabilisation Loan	£10 million

There is no prospect of the Greeks spending the whole of this loan in 1946 but it is not unlikely that their present acute shortage of food, consumer goods and general raw materials will force them to draw on their resources if they can find no other means of payment.

(*b*) Cost of initial equipment to Greek armed forces of which a part, say £5m. has been spent in 1945 £11m.

(*c*) Maintenance of Greek armed forces £12m.

(*d*) Cost of British Missions (General Clark, police, elections) ?£1m.

The amounts which may be actually required in 1946 under the above headings are as follows:- (*a*) £5 million; (*b*) £6 million (*c*) £12 million; (*d*) £1 million, total: £24 million.

1947–8

The fog is even more obscure. If UNRRA disappears early in 1947 we may find ourselves burdened with the duty of keeping order in Greece:- (*a*) by taking a leading part in the supply of essential goods, and (*b*) continuing to assist the Greeks to maintain an army.

If our participation in the proposed civil air lines in Athens is arranged, we shall have to supply planes during this period amounting to £375,000 and if the Automatic Telephone and Electric Company of Liverpool obtain their contract we might have to provide equipment on credit terms to the value of £325,000.

On the present showing an estimate of £20 million for 1947 looks optimistic.

Turkey

1946

(*a*) It is to be hoped that the proposed arms credit, which might cost us £10 millions if the arms have to be manufactured specially, will not be agreed. If it is, we might be able to supply a portion from surplus stocks.

Very hypothetical expenditure in 1946 may be put at £5 million.

(*b*) Equipment likely to be supplied to Turkey in 1946 under the 1938 Guarantee Agreement   £1 million

(*c*) Naval equipment still to be supplied under the 1939 Armaments Agreement   (?) £1½ million

1947–8

During this period it is to be assumed that the whole of the unused balance of the 1938 Guarantee Agreement, i.e. £4,500,000, will be shipped. Anything else is a guess.

Russia

1946

Goods still to be shipped under the Civil Supplies Agreement amount to something like £14,500,000 of which £13 millions might be delivered this year if the Russians resume payment for past deliveries. The Agreement provides for 40 per cent cash so that the burden on our balance of payments will be £7,800,000. (The total credit which is now to be offered is £26 millions. The balance in excess of £7·8 million relates to goods already shipped before 1946.) There are at present no serious export credits commitments.

1947–8

Unable to venture a guess.

Yugoslavia

So far—nil.

Albania

Nil.

Germany

(*a*) 1946. Imports into the British zone in Germany from all sources, £88 million.

In principle £47 million of this should be recoverable from proceeds of exports from Germany to all destinations. The import total includes £38 million for wheat, of which slightly less than half will have to be from dollar sources; for the balance it may be possible to obtain Argentine or an easier currency wheat. It also includes £12½ million for wool, which will come ex stocks. The export total includes £2½ millions deliveries to the U.K.

(*b*) 1947–8. It is impossible to make any accurate calculations of imports into Germany or of the proceeds of exports after 1946. Provided always that there is a market for Germany's goods and the recipient countries pay for what they get, increased production should narrow the difference.

Hong Kong

We may have to lend (give?) them £10 million in 1946 for purchase of relief goods.

Borneo

Expenditure on relief goods for Borneo may be estimated at £2 million in 1946 and £2 million in 1947. The real effect of this on the balance of payments is very difficult to determine at this stage because of the complications arising from the constitutional changes.

Siam

The only issue here is whether we pay Siam for rice or not. If we do pay them it will cost us £3·6 million in 1946 and the possible amounts involved over a period may be of the order of £20 million.

China

China was given a loan of £50 million for *war* expenditure. In order to fulfil commitments already authorised China has purchasing power outstanding of some £5 million, some of which may be used in 1946. The Board of Trade will advocate further credits for post-war trade.

Burma

Required financial assistance from U.K. to the end of the first year of civil government was estimated, before VJ Day, as follows:

	Equipment to be ordered (£m)	Expenditure in Burma (£m)
(*a*) Key industries	11·8	12·1
(*b*) Public utilities	8·1	2·5
(*c*) Supplies for civil consumption	19·5	4·5
(*d*) Government services	3·9	7·5*
(*e*) Pre-evacuation liabilities	—	8.0
	43·3	34·6

The expenditure under (*a*) and (*c*) and expenditure of 2·6 under (*b*) will ultimately be recovered from industrialists, purchasers, etc. These recoveries total £32·8 million on equipment and £17·7 million on expenditure in Burma. But this will not relieve our balance of payments.

In the following year, the requirement would be £7·5 millions (Budget deficit only) all in Burmese currency.

The relevant figure for financial assistance is clearly nothing approaching this figure. Supplies are most unlikely to be needed to this extent, and if they were, they would not be available in 1946.

Probably the right figure to take is Burma's adverse trade balance with the whole of the world (plus the increase in Burma's balances in India resulting from our military expenditure on Indian troops). There is great difficulty in avoiding double counting, because the expenditure of our armed forces

* Budget deficit

is already included in overseas military expenditure. But it seems rather unlikely that the amount involved in 1946 will exceed, say, £20 million, tapering off rapidly in 1947–48.

Nevertheless, unless we revise our present (in my opinion preposterous) proposal to put up sterling cover against local Burmese expenditure covered by an expansion in the note issue, the whole of the above is an ultimate liability, especially when Burma receives a large measure of self-government.

Malaya

The Malayan position is very complex. Last April, the Malayan Planning Unit estimated the Government expenditure required in the first two years as:

	£m
Public utilities	17·9
Relief supplies	22·8
Rehabilitation of industry	2·7
	43·4

They estimated the net expenditure at £42 million in this period (outstanding commitments e.g. to civil servants £18 million, general administration £6 million, public utilities £17·9 million, rehabilitation of industry £0·2 million). Against this, they had free sterling balances of £32 million (excluding currency fund, etc.), so that they reckoned upon a deficit of only £10 million in the Government's accounts. On the same basis, damage having been much less than expected, they would probably in fact need no subsidy at all. However, there is a project to spend about £8¾ million on tin rehabilitation, which was not included above, some of which would be spent in Malaya.

Malaya may have a small adverse trade balance in 1946— financed by drawing down her sterling balances—but it cannot be very large. Sales of tin and rubber should be not far short

of £25 million, and imports are severely restricted by supply considerations. In 1947 and 1948 Malaya is bound to have an export surplus.

Colonial Development Fund

Estimated expenditure £9 million in 1946, and, say, £10 million in 1947 and £11 million in 1948.

Sudan

We have promised a grant of £2 million spread over 1946–9.

Estimate of Government overseas expenditure (excluding military) (£ million)

	1946			Total 1946–8	
Liabilities	Firm*	Contin-gent	1947–8	Firm	Contin-gent
Europe					
Holland and N.E.I.	—	60	30	—	90
France	—	60	40	—	100
Czechoslovakia	3	—	—	3	—
Poland (excl. Army)	6	—	5	11	—
Poland (Army)	15?	6?	—	15	6
Greece	24	—	20?	24	20
Turkey	1	5	9	4	11
Russia	8	—	—	8	—
Germany (imports)	88	—	150?	88	238
UNRRA	135	—	—	135	—
Post-UNRRA (including Italy and Austria)	—	—	25?	—	25?
Far East					
Hong Kong	10	—	—	10	—
Borneo	2	—	2	4	—
China	2	—	3	5	—
Japan	—	—	—	—	—
Burma	20?	—	15?	35?	—
Malaya	5?	—	—	5?	—
Other					
Colonies	9	—	21	30	—
Sudan	1	—	1	2	—

* In some cases the general commitment is firm but not the precise figure.

The order of magnitude may be something like this—

	£ million
Firm commitments 1946	320 (including 88 Germany)
Probable further demands 1946	130 (almost all France and Holland)
Probable demands 1947–8 (Excluding Germany)	150
Germany	150
Total commitments and demands	750

Against this we have certain paper assets for civil affairs supplies recorded above, £40 million in gold to come from France in respect of the 1945 credit, a hope of $137 million from France. The net cost of German exports will depend on what cash contribution we can collect out of her exports.

III. *Military expenditure overseas*

11. Last autumn provisional figures were adopted, with no detailed estimating behind them, of £300 millions in 1946 and £100 millions in each of the next two years. More recent calculations indicate that these figures were considerably too low on the basis of the forces outside Europe programmed before the recent decision of Ministers, for expenditure in the fourth quarter of 1945 was running well above £600 million a year. The crucial figure for the Treasury is the number 'outside Europe' rather than the number 'overseas'. The plan which was in force until recently provided for very small reductions outside Europe compared with VJ Day. Will the revised plan result in a reduction below 500,000 outside Europe by the end of 1946 (which, on the revised basis of a grand total of 1,200,000 in the forces, would be compatible with 300,000 in Europe and 400,000

in and around U.K.)? If not, this would give a year's average of (say) 650,000 outside Europe in 1946 compared with 725,000 on the unrevised plans and 820,000 at VJ Day. This would suggest a total cost of anything from £300 to £400 million in 1946, even assuming the proposed reductions. Moreover, at the beginning of 1947 the annual rate of cost would still be running at well above £200 million!

A figure of £300 million could be built up like this:—

India*	£125 m.	(end-1945 about £300 m, but estimated at less than £100 m in financial year 1946–7)
Middle East	£75 m.	(end-1945 about £100 m, but related to smaller force than *present* plan).
Food	£30 m.	(from North America, Australia, South Africa).
Oil	£20 m.	(say, for all U.K. Forces overseas (excl. BAOR)).
Other (net)	£50 m.	(Burma, Malaya, East and West Africa, etc., but certain credit items on the other side).
	£300 m.	

This, however, is not even the revised plan, which, unless still further revised, might cost anything from £600 million to £750 millions in the three years 1946–8.

IV. *Summary*

12. Altogether, without a drastic change of policy, political and military expenditure in the three years 1946–8 might run us into anything up to £1,500 million gross; whilst £1,000 million net would seem to be the minimum figure in sight on present lines.

* Includes *Indian* troops in SEAC, Greece or Middle East.

478

13. We have, of course, no margin of overseas resources approaching £1,500 million. Nor should we have, even if the figure was brought down to £1,000 million. The utmost provision allowed for in the calculations we made during the Washington negotiations was £600 million for the three years 1946–8.

14. What can be done about it? It is obvious that any proposals sufficiently drastic must encroach on the political sphere. But it is not easy to see that there can be any solution which does not involve the following:-

(*a*) A virtual cessation of further political loans. We must try to face the fact that we cannot lend money we have not got. Both France and Holland, which are the large claimants, have a substantial amount of gold and dollar securities in hand, and their *net* overseas resources are, proportionately, not less than ours.

We certainly do not want these countries to collapse, and it is difficult to refuse to let them use their sterling balances, though we really cannot afford to do so. But this is about the limit. Perhaps the most helpful line is to see how far the Dominions would be prepared to give credits to these countries independently.

(*b*) A reconsideration of our economic policy towards Germany. It seems monstrous that we should first de-industrialise and thus bankrupt the Ruhr to please Russia and then hand over the territory, or at any rate the industries, to an international body to please France, but that we alone should remain responsible for feeding the place. This responsibility ought to be shared by the countries which share in the international control of the Ruhr industries. Our present policy towards Germany, by which we have become involved in paying her large reparations, might rank as the craziest ever—if one did not remember last time.

(*c*) A reduction in our military forces *outside Europe* to 250,000 at the earliest possible date.

We simply cannot afford to make our plans on the basis of being half and half-heartedly ready for war with Russia. Yet, what else does a great deal of our military expenditure mean? We are spending twice too much for solvency, and twice (or four times) too little for safety in conditions of hostility and a war of nerves dispersed over two continents; thus making sure of the worst of both worlds.

Take the case of Egypt. How do we propose to reply to the Egyptian demand that we should take our troops out of Egypt? Is it appreciated that we are paying the cost of keeping them there by *borrowing it from Egypt*? What is the answer if Egypt tells us (as, of course, she will) that she is no longer prepared to provide us with the necessary funds? Has this hard fact been faced and answered?

From Greece we should take out our troops as soon as possible and reduce the Greek army from 100,000 to 50,000. Neither we nor the Greeks can afford £15 million a year to provide British equipment, including food, for an army which is, in any case, bound to be useless against Yugoslavia or Russia. When UNRRA stops feeding Greece, the Greeks will have to use up their foreign exchange reserves to some extent and, for the rest, we should try to get the Americans to do as much as we can.

And so on.

(*d*) In the *Far East* Burma obviously needs looking at again on a realistic basis, and we must try to see whether we can get some free rice from Siam in the future, though the Cabinet decided recently that, for the time being at any rate, we cannot get free rice now.

15. Some of our present activities will be futile unless they can be followed up and persevered in for an appreciable time. Nothing but waste and humiliation can result from not looking ahead and keeping within our long-run capacity.

16. The above summary, being limited to political and military expenditure overseas, takes no account of such claims on our overseas resources as:

(*a*) Subscriptions to the Bretton Woods Fund and Bank.

(*b*) Withdrawals of existing sterling balances by liberated countries etc. e.g.

	(£m)	(Balances held at 30 September 1945)
Norway	75	
Greece	57	
China	23	
Siam	13	

(*c*) Any net cost of releasing sterling area balances in the period 1946–5. We can expect to accumulate some further balances during the early part of 1946, and that is why the *momentary* position in respect of overseas finance is not acute in spite of the delay in the American credit. But we are likely to have to make at least corresponding, and perhaps greater, releases in 1947–51. In this connection it should be emphasised that our political and military expenditure overseas reduces correspondingly our ability to sustain the sterling area countries, both currently and later on. Thus the result of not curtailing this expenditure must be to make inevitable still harsher treatment of the sterling area balances than the severe treatment which will be unavoidable in any case.

KEYNES

11 February 1946

After his return from Savannah (*JMK*, vol. XXVI) and a conversation with the Chancellor, he met the Chancellor's request to put his views on paper. The reflections received limited circulation amongst ministers, going to the Prime Minister, Lord President, Lord Privy Seal, Foreign Secretary, Dominions Secretary and Colonial Secretary.

RANDOM REFLECTIONS FROM A VISIT TO USA
I

I judge the American Loan to be quite safe unless some quite unexpected factor develops. This view was held without exception by all the members and officials of the American Administration with whom I was in contact, including Mr Vinson and Mr Clayton. Certainly as regards the Senate, the latter have assurances behind the scenes that certain important Senators, who have either not declared their opinion in public or have appeared to be in opposition, will in fact support the Loan if it comes to a show down.

I have never myself much doubted that the proposals would go through. But the improvement in the situation is probably to be attributed primarily to the following factors:-

(i) The economic argument was already decisive with the, so to speak, converted. But it cut no ice with the unconverted. With the unconverted, on the other hand, the changed situation in relation to Russia has been fairly decisive. Almost no-one in America wishes to weaken Great Britain in present circumstances. Mr Dean Acheson in particular was emphatic that the political arguments had weighed with those with whom the economic argument failed. Moreover, even on purely economic grounds, some people are more willing to lend us money when this is less likely to involve a similar transaction on a large scale with Russia.

(ii) There is evidence that, after the Conclave of Cardinals at Rome, the Catholic authorities were at pains to call off opposition to the Loan from the Irish Catholic faction. Since they were much the most capable and formidable critics, this makes a significant difference. In particular, Mr Joe Kennedy, who was in opposition, has completely eaten his words. And, after the new orders went out, Mr Leo Crowley, who is reputed to be the most influential Catholic layman in the United States, announced that he was no longer prepared, as he had been

intending, to give evidence before the Congressional Committees against the Loan.

(iii) When I arrived I was informed on good authority that there had been considerable canvassing against the Loan in certain British quarters, both with members of the American Delegation when they were in London, and by British visitors to U.S. This was having quite a serious effect. It was, however, largely overcome by the firmness with which Mr Winston Churchill at every opportunity, public and private, took up the opposite line. He told all his friends that he was in favour of the Loan, that we needed it and that the argument against lending to a Socialist Government was a wrong and invalid argument, with which he would have nothing to do. I am sure this had a great effect in many quarters. In particular he persuaded Mr Baruch, who was one of the most dangerous critics we had to fear and had the intention of appearing before Congress to denounce the Loan, to agree to abstain almost as a personal favour to himself as an old friend. I believe that Mr Churchill told Mr Baruch that, if the latter were to denounce the Loan, people would not easily believe, in view of the close relations between them, that he, Mr Churchill, was not behind this, a misconception which he would regard as exceedingly unfortunate.

(iv) There has been admirable stage management by the Administration before the Senate Committee. For ten days members of the Administration and officials gave very full and careful official evidence in favour of the Loan, well documented with facts. For the next ten days they deployed representatives of various sections of organised opinion, both sections of the Labour movement, representatives of the associations of manu-facturers, retailers, bankers and so forth, all of whom spoke up firmly to the effect that the Loan was in American interests. Finally, on the last day they deployed the opposition which, in the absence of Mr Baruch, Mr Crowley and others, consisted of three hand-picked lunatics with straw in their hair. After these

three had raved for two or three hours, the Chairman of the Committee suggested that any further evidence they might wish to give should be in writing, and the proceedings were brought to an end. Thus there has been no responsible opposition whatever.

The above relates primarily to the Senate Committee. Unfortunately, the opening proceedings in the House Committee are still greatly delayed by other business. For weeks past the contest between the Administration and Congress over the continuation of price control through OPA has dragged a lengthy course and is still not completed. Since this is handled with the same Committee as would handle the Loan, no progress can be made with the latter. Nevertheless, when I left, it was still believed in Administration circles that the thing would be through by the end of May and perhaps sooner.

II

Judging both by the progress of the British Loan and also American intentions, as they appeared during the Savannah Conference, one can say that for the time being at least America is safely set on the course of trying to make a good job of international co-operation, on the economic as well as on the political side. There are critics, of course, and many of those who would like to criticise judge it prudent to be temporarily silent. But never in my experience of the country has there been less responsible support for any brand of isolationism. It would, therefore, be fatal for us to stand aside or be too sceptical or critical. Their methods will constantly irritate us. We shall have plenty of good reason for complaint. But, behind all this, their good-will and genuine intentions are real and reliable.

III

I came away this time more convinced than ever that the United States is well on the way to being a very high cost country. They seem to think it improper or undesirable to give an increase of wages until after a strike of varying duration has occurred. But, whatever the procedure, it always ends up the same way, namely by an increase of $18\frac{1}{2}$ cents per hour or about 15 per cent. Since the normal working week, apart from overtime, has now fallen to 40 hours, as compared with 46 to 48 hours during the war, this means that, in spite of the shorter working week, the worker will take home a pay packet which is nearly, though not quite, as large as before.

The result is that over a wide range of mass production industries, such as automobiles, steel, electrical industries, etc., the standard wage is now in the neighbourhood of 135 ¢ an hour, that is to say, very nearly 7s. I cannot believe that we are so inefficient as not to be able to compete on a basis of so wide a wage disparity.

The effect of the wage increases on prices is so far still very moderate. That is because the Office of Price Administration is still holding firm and is allowing price increases which are far short of the increase in wage cost. It is most unlikely, however, that this régime can continue for more than another six or nine months at the outside, probably giving ground all the time. There are already important cases where production cannot continue at the present price ceiling. Other cases where output is being hoarded with the expectation that the ceiling will be raised. Generally speaking, industry is able to produce at the OPA ceiling only as a consequence of full capacity output. What would normally be the extra profit of full capacity output is now being passed on to the wage earner. This means, however, that a very small recession in business activity would make output unprofitable at present costs and prices. Thus, unless OPA has

485

given way in the meanwhile, even an incipient contraction would rapidly put producers in an uneconomic position.

Apart from the above, one's impression is that money is worth increasingly less in the United States in spite of the remarkable relative success of the price control. The cost of house room and of any kind of services is prohibitive.

Furthermore, American producers are clearly giving as high priority to home consumption as we are giving to exports. It looks to me as though we should have a clear run for all the exports we can produce for two years at least.

There are no present signs whatever of the possibility of recession in U.S. Looking further ahead, there are wide differences of expert opinion. Some responsible economists say the position is quite safe for five years; others would indicate a briefer respite; my own view, for what it is worth, would be intermediate. What I do firmly believe, however, is that when the slump comes it will take on a quite different shape from the historic pattern, and the external repercussions will be quite different from what we have been accustomed to expect in the past. Certainly the most intense and vigorous measures will be taken to off-set recession. And I should judge that the date at which these measures begin to lose their original efficacy is still a good way off.

IV

I form the conclusion, after contact and conversation with the representatives of India and Egypt and other sterling area countries, that the sterling area countries are in no way inclined to force the pace in winding up the existing sterling area arrangements. The business is a hot potato for them just as it is for us. We cannot put off too long, since, on the assumption that the Loan goes through in May, the new arrangements have to be in force by May 1947. But I believe that we can safely drift, and that it would be advisable to do so, for another six months. This does not mean that we should not be preparing

486

our plans and ideas behind the scenes. But there now seems to be much less chance than I thought before of India and Egypt, in particular, pressing us into negotiations by, say, June or July.

There is a great deal to be said, if we can manage it, for going slow on the sterling area negotiations until the political issues have made further progress.

In fact it may suit both parties to drift for a few months. On a short view the sterling area countries have no reason to complain about the current position. They are most of them, including probably India, dollar deficit countries at the present moment, and we are supplying them with more dollars than they could find for themselves. In fact, there is no practical obstacle at the moment on their using their sterling balances in any quarter where goods and supplies are actually available.

On our side there is no reason to be in a hurry, since, in spite of the above, the sterling area balances are probably still increasing in the aggregate. We have to keep a close watch on this so that we know promptly when the tide turns. But currently the quantum to be ultimately handled is probably still increasing. I would, however, emphasise that the above relates to a period of, say, six months, not to a long period, of delay.

KEYNES

4 April 1946

Appendix

ALTERATIONS IN THE SIXTH DRAFT OF THE INTERNATIONAL REGULATION OF PRIMARY PRODUCTS

Changes from the Sixth Draft of 28 May 1942 in the draft printed at the close of the discussions of the Committee on Post-War External Economic Problems.

page	line	Change
136	6–17	The sentences 'Commodity Controls... technical progress generally' did not appear in the earlier draft.
136	25	The words 'and so on' which followed the word 'artificial', disappeared.
136	26	The word 'resist' replaced the words 'fight against'.
136	30	Paragraph 4 replaced the following passage.
137	11	'Buffer stocks, as their name implies, are intended to absorb shocks. They also have the purpose of steadying prices. To achieve the whole object, however, more than this is necessary. There must be a close interdependence between one Commodity Control and another, with probably some superimposed coordinating authority. There must also be an adequate measure of conformity to a common pattern as between the various controls. Only in this way can some semblance of order be introduced if

the primary producer of one commodity loses his market and some alternative form of economic acitivity has to be found for him.

4. Commodity Controls must be recognised as being instituted not from some profit motive, but to ensure that the necessary changes in the scale and distribution of output should take place steadily and slowly in response to the steady and slow evolution of the underlying trends. It must be made clear that the object of the Controls is not profit but service. The world as a whole wishes to get away from the old ideas of monopoly and restrictive cartels, —at least where Government-sponsored activities are concerned. World opinion to-day desires above all to evolve a state of society in which definite essential tasks are allotted and necessary services rewarded on a regular and equitable scale.

5. The Controls should be conceived of largely as correctives. Their intervention should not be at a constant level of pressure: they should only exert maximum pressure when this is needed to correct a balance, or when simultaneous action by two or more Controls is necessary. They should only intervene actively when they feel it necessary that

some check should be imposed on
the unregulated development of
new sources of supply. The Controls should however regard themselves as continuously responsible
for the maintenance of order and
the inculcation of a sense of
mutual interdependence. It will
be fatal if their activities come to
be regarded as synonymous with
the permanent strangulation of
local economic initiative. There
must be no suggestion that the
Controls are aimed at the permanent exclusion of the low-cost
producer, still less to deprive
efficiency of its due rewards. The
object of the Controls should be
to regulate the rate at which new
sources of supply should be
drawn on in such a way as to
promote the expansion of full employment and consumption and
to minimise the shocks to efficient
producers who may be losing
their markets. Rules for the Controls' constitution must therefore
be highly flexible, as indeed also
the provisions determining their
membership at any given time.

6. The problem of regulation
has two aspects—Stabilisation
and Restriction. In its first aspect
it aims at limiting and smoothing
out the short-term fluctuations of
price which in the past have been
disastrous to the operations of
producers and consumers alike.
In its second aspect it aims at
securing an economic price and a

page	line	Change
		gradual transference of trade in cases where it would appear likely that otherwise over-production would inevitably involve producers generally in prolonged distress. The treatment of the two aspects must be closely associated in practice. But for the purposes of exposition paragraph 14 of Section III below is primarily concerned with the first and paragraph 15 with the second; whilst in paragraph 16 an attempt is made to marry the ideas of buffer stock regulation and quota regulation.'
137	22	The word 'miserable' which preceded the word 'decade' disappeared.
137 138	34 to 26	The sentences 'We do not disguise...fruitful union' replaced the following passage: 'Provision is made, therefore, for organised restriction of output subject to certain safeguards, if and when there are convincing reasons that it is necessary. Indeed some provision on such lines is required, apart from the risk of chronic gluts, in order to deal with difficulties in changing the main sources of supply which, although they are not permanent, cannot be dealt with satisfactorily merely by short-term methods.'
138	28	The words 'to provide buffer stocks and steady prices' which followed the word 'Granary' disappeared.
138	30	The words 'wide and rapid' re-

page	line	*Change*
		placed the words 'constant and wide'.
138	31	The words 'i.e. raw foodstuffs and industrial raw materials' which followed the word 'products' disappeared.
138	31	The word 'frequent' replaced the word 'constant'.
138	32–3	The words 'supply of these commodities and the short-term apparent demand' replaced the words 'short-term apparent demand and supply of these commodities'.
139	1	The word 'absolutely' which preceded the word 'constant' disappeared.
139	2	The words 'carried forward from year to year' which followed the word 'years' disappeared.
139	3	The words 'steady level' replaced the words 'fairly constant figure'.
139	5	The word 'and' did not appear in the earlier draft as the word 'with' started a new sentence.
139	5–6	The words '(but not the supply)' did not appear in the earlier draft.
139	6	The words 'but with industrial raw materials the fluctuations are greater owing to changes in the rate of industrial activity' which followed the word 'periods' disappeared.
139	13	The words 'to make' replaced the words 'for making'.
139	13	The words 'It must be' did not appear in the earlier draft.
139	14	The word 'is' which followed the word 'control' disappeared.
139	15	The words '—not, of course, by

page	line	Change
		fixing prices' replaced the words 'This does not mean that all prices of primary products shall be fixed'.
139	16	The words 'but by providing' replaced the words 'but it does mean that such conditions shall be established'.
139	17	The words 'made gradually in accordance with the ' replaced the words 'gradual and determined by'.
139	19	Paragraphs 8–10 and the first two sentences of paragraph 11 followed the rest of the present paragraph 11 in the earlier version.
139	32	The words 'We are' replaced the words 'The whole world is'.
139	34	The word 'violent' replaced the words 'truly frightful'.
140	10–14	The sentence 'The damage... primary markets' did not appear in the earlier draft.
141	2	The word '*price*' did not appear in the earlier draft.
141	2	The word 'by' replaced the words 'That is'.
141	6–7	The words 'the seasonal fluctuations of agriculture' replaced the words 'unusual bounty or niggardliness of nature'.
141	10–11	The words '*output regulation* by fluctuating quotas' replaced the words 'regulation of supply by fluctuating quotas of output'.
141	12	The word 'is' replaced the words 'may be'.
141	15	The word 'very' preceded the word 'imperfect' in the earlier draft.

APPENDIX

III

'(i) An international body would be set up called the Commod Control on which the governments of the leading producing and consuming countries would be represented. The management would be independent and expert, and the interests of consumers equally represented with those of producers. Its object would be to stabilise the price of that part of world output which enters into international trade, and to maintain stocks adequate to cover short-term fluctuations of supply and demand in the world market. It would not be directly concerned with the domestic price and production policy of commodities produced and consumed within the same country. Exporting countries would have votes proportionate amongst themselves to their net exports in the three years previous, and importing countries similarly in proportion to their net imports. In questions affecting the basic price exporting and importing

494

page	line	Change
		countries might be given equal aggregate votes, and in all other questions the exporting countries might have aggregate votes (say) 50 per cent in excess of the aggregate votes of the importing countries. (The number of members on a Control would, of course, be much smaller than the number of importers and exporters who would have to be grouped for the purpose of representation.)'
142	20	The words 'one or more of' did not appear in the earlier draft.
142	22	The words 'for commod' preceded the word 'would' in the earlier draft.
142	34	The words 'in the management of future markets' followed the word 'practice' in the earlier draft.
143	25–6	The words 'and there...that method' replaced the words 'though state trading would remain open to any country which preferred that method'.
143	28	The words 'or state trading corporations' did not appear in the earlier draft.
143	31	The word 'traders' replaced the word 'merchants'.
144	4	The word 'agreement' replaced the words 'general agreement of all consumers'.
144	8–12	The word 'But' did not appear in the earlier draft and the sentence following appeared there as a footnote.
144	12	The words 'in each' did not appear in the earlier draft.
144	28–31	The sentence 'It has...should

page	line	Change
		facilitate' did not appear in the earlier draft.
145	8	The words 'so that it would have to maintain a favourable level of prices until it had acquired a sufficient mass of manoeuvre' followed the word 'adequate' in the earlier draft.
145	32	The word 'Commodity' preceded the word 'Control' in the earlier draft.
145	34	The words 'consumers' replaced the words 'the industry'.
146	14–17	The words 'save that...in one year' did not appear in the earlier draft.
146	31	The words 'if it comes into existence' did not appear in the earlier draft.
146	33	The words 'or possibly, failing this by an arrangement between central banks' followed the word 'accounts' in the earlier draft.
147	5–31	The sentences 'The question... paragraph 14' did not appear in the earlier draft.
148	29	The word 'well' preceded the word 'before' in the earlier draft.
148	31	The words 'little more than study groups' preceded the word 'accumulating' in the earlier draft.
148	31–2	The words 'as much...as possible' surrounded the words 'information and statistics' in the earlier draft.
148	32	The word 'and' replaced the word 'but'.
148	32	The word 'should' replaced the word 'would'.
149	2–3	The words 'these...through'

page	line	Change
		replaced the words 'this were done'.
149	27–8	The words 'be taken...if abused' replace the words 'safeguard the abuse of methods'.
149	30	The words 'In any event' replaced the word 'Moreover'.
149	31	The words 'in principle acceptable' replaced the words 'wholly admirable'.
150	1–18	The passage 'It may be ...The...are' replaced the words 'The object of...is'.
150 151	35 to 2	The words 'due to...temporary' replaced the words 'intended to be a continuing one or whether it is temporary'.
151	7–8	The words 'due to causes regarded as likely to be continuing' replaced the words 'a continuing one'.
151	28–9	The words 'required for reasons regarded as likely to continue' replaced the words 'of a quasi-permanent character'.
152	14–15	The words 'pay attention, amongst other considerations' replaced the words 'have regard'.
152	16–18	The words 'Whether...General Council' replaced the word 'but'.
152	29–30	The words 'aggregate as distinct from the individual' replaced the words 'absolute as distinct from proportionate'.
152	31	The word 'aggregate' replaced the word 'absolute'.
152 153	32 to 2	The sentence 'So long...otherwise' did not appear in the earlier draft.

page	line	Change
153	3–11	Paragraph 13 (vii) did not appear in the earlier draft.
153	13–14	The words 'including, for example...enforce it' did not appear in the earlier draft.
154	7–9	The words 'and in this...proportionate quota' did not appear in the earlier draft.
154	15–16	The words 'endeavour to...approve' replaced the words 'would ask the General Council for their approval of'.
154	26–32	The paragraph 'Nevertheless... this qualification' did not appear in the earlier draft.
156	31	Following paragraph 18, the following additional paragraph appeared in the earlier draft.

'22. Our criterion for justifying a quota regulation scheme is the likelihood otherwise of a price which falls below 'a reasonable international economic price'. What, more precisely, does this mean? In a sense the essential principle of the present proposal is that the long-term economic price, which will bring demand and supply into equilibrium without restriction, is the price that should be aimed at. But this must not be interpreted in such a way that a minority of producers with low standards of life or with no alternative output might depress prices to a level inadequate to all. For in conditions of a large excess of productive capacity, actual or potential, over that required to meet the effective demand, prices

page	line	Change
		might be lowered continuously until they were insufficient to provide a reasonable standard of life for the majority of the producers concerned. 'A reasonable international economic price' should be regarded as the price which would yield to the majority of producers a standard of living which is in reasonable relation to the general standards of the countries in which they live. It is in the interest of all producers alike that the price of a commodity should not be depressed below this level, and consumers are not entitled to expect that it should. The desire to maintain more adequate standards of living for primary producers has been the mainspring of the movement towards commodity regulation schemes in recent years, and they may still remain necessary for this purpose'.
157	8	The word 'serious' replaced the word 'real'.
157	35	The following additional sentence preceded the word 'Otherwise' in the earlier draft: 'Serious dangers would arise if a plan were to be adopted which bore a general resemblance to the foregoing, but which did not contain provisions to prevent the accumulation of stocks beyond a certain level.'
157	35	The words 'an attempt might be made' replaced the words 'it might well happen that the attempt would be made'.

APPENDIX

page	line	Change
158	17–31	The sentences 'It has already... may approve' did not appear in the earlier draft.
159	16	The words 'They are' replaced the words 'These again, it may be pointed out, are'.
159	19	The word 'practical' preceded the word 'importance' in the earlier draft.
159 160	30 to 19	Paragraph 24 did not appear in the earlier draft.
161	21	The word 'so' preceded the word 'greatly' in the earlier drafts.
161	21	The material in parentheses did not appear in the earlier draft.
161	24	The words 'that some might hold this project to be, in effect, conditional on the adoption of the former. This might, nevertheless, be an overstatement, if we remember that the scope of the proposed Commodity Controls could, if necessary, be linked to those cases where the Governments and central banks of the countries chiefly concerned felt strongly enough to arrange the necessary finance by agreement amongst themselves' followed the word 'granary' in the earlier draft.
162	11–28	Paragraph 27 replaced the following paragraph in the earlier draft:

'31. It might well be, if the scheme came eventually to cover a wide range of commodities, that there would be created an excess liquidity for the world as a whole, if the finance were to be provided entirely by Clearing Union credit.

page	line	Change
		In this case an appropriate part should be funded by a long-term international loan issued under the auspices of the Clearing Union and secured on the stocks of all the Controls, sufficient to cover an appropriate proportion of the stable, as distinct from the fluctuating, proportion of the pooled financial requirements of the Commodity Controls as a whole.'
162 163	31 to 20	The paragraph 'While the sufferings...policy generally' did not appear in the earlier draft.

DOCUMENTS REPRODUCED

IN THIS VOLUME

Where documents come from the Public Record Office, their call numbers appear before the date.

DOCUMENTS REPRODUCED IN THIS VOLUME

SPEECHES AND BROADCASTS

MINUTES OF MEETINGS

UNPUBLISHED LETTERS

ACKNOWLEDGEMENTS

We should like to thank the Humanities and Social Sciences Research Council of Canada for financial assistance, and Dr José Harris for advice.

Crown copyright material appears with the permission of Her Majesty's Stationery Office.

INDEX

Abundance, 261; plenty 'round the corner', 385

Abyssinia, 425

Acceleration, principle of, 378

Accounting, 111; Budget accounting, 225, 277, 376–7; 'above and below' the line, 406–7, 414, 448

Accumulation, 22
of pension funds, 205, 225
of sterling balances, 458–9, 462
of stocks, 5–6, 21, 24, 125, 145, 149, 154, 158, 161, 169, 177, 183, 186, 499; of buffer stocks, 184
of surpluses, 126, 159, 176

Acheson, Dean, Assistant Under-Secretary of State, U.S.A.: conversations on surplus policy, 22–6; draft letter to Leith-Ross, 27, 29–31; and UNRRA, 95
list of letters, 505

Addison, Viscount (Christopher), Dominions Secretary, 1946, 481

Africa
sisal prices, 13
surplus problem, 23
West and East Africa, British military expenditure in, 478
see also Egypt; South Africa

Agricultural crops (products)
and Commodity Control, 109–10, 113–14, 133, 145; prices, 116, 142–3, 177–8, fluctuations, 140; seasonal fluctuations in crop yields, 141, 178; storable stocks, 181
current and surplus, 13, 21
lend for lease agricultural products, 19, 64–5
seeds for relief, 83
uneconomic production, 163–6; Ferguson on planning, 195; subsidies, 163, 275
see also Maize; Rice; Wheat

Agricultural insurance, 220; unemployment scheme, 230

Agriculture, 315; agricultural land, 214; revolution in, 282, 342
see also under United Kingdom; United States of America

Aircraft, 300–1, 471

Albania, 472

Alcoholic drinks, 212; taxes on, 319, 417

Allied countries
effective, and non-effective, 74, 107

and relief plans, 59, 76; cost of post-war relief for, 466–76; paying Allies, 97–8
in World War I, 54

Allied (exiled) Governments in London: gold and dollar resources, 49–50; post-war relief, meetings on, 27 n 7, 31, 42, 71; relief requirements, 21, 22, 25, 30, 44, 48, 74–6, Dalton's ideas, 66 n 1; representation on Joint Boards, 77

Allocation: of relief supplies, 68, 72, 75, 78, 80, 82; of scarce commodities, 103, 181, 288

American
cotton prices, 12
domestic consumption, 91
industrial efficiency, 336–9; machine-tool design, 282
politics, 95
silver interests, 425
tourists, 438

American Red Cross, 55

Anderson, Sir John, 317
Lord President of the Council (1940–43), 37, 66, 257, 258, 333; Lord President's Committee, 37
Chancellor of the Exchequer (September 1943–July 1945), 99, 367, 391, 404, 413; notes for speech on employment policy, 374, 375–9

Anglo-American cooperation, 27, 28, 136; on surpluses, 5, 20, 21, 23, 27; on UNRRA, 96–7; on commodity control, 106

Anglo-American Joint Boards, for war supplies, 77
see also Combined Boards

Anglo-American Joint Committee (proposed), on post-war surpluses, 25, 27 n 7, 29–30

Anglo-American Loan (Washington Agreement)
need for post-war loan, 77; negotiations (JMK at, 1945), 423, 426, 479; Congress and, 425, 427, 483; Senate hearings, 436, 483–4; House Committee on, 484; support for, in U.S., 482–4
effective date of loan, 458, 486; proposed sum, 439, 440, 464, 466, 479; cost to Britain, 450, interest, 440–1; loan 'slopped away', 463, 466

509